Dr Denis Alexander is the Director  Science and Religion, St Edm (www.faraday-institute.org), where is also a Senior Affiliated Scientist Cambridge, where for many years he was Chairman of the Molecular Immunology Programme and Head of the Laboratory of Lymphocyte Signalling and Development. Dr Alexander was previously at the Imperial Cancer Research Laboratories in London (now Cancer Research UK), and prior to that spent 15 years developing university departments and laboratories overseas, latterly as Associate Professor of Biochemistry in the Medical Faculty of the American University of Beirut, Lebanon. Dr Alexander was initially an Open Scholar at Oxford reading Biochemistry, before obtaining a PhD in Neurochemistry at the Institute of Psychiatry in London.

Dr Alexander writes, lectures and broadcasts widely in the field of science and religion. Since 1992 he has been Editor of the journal *Science & Christian Belief*, and currently serves on the National Committee of Christians in Science and as a Fellow of the International Society for Science and Religion.

* * *

'This is a very timely book, thoughtful, thorough and full of integrity. It speaks the languages of both science and faith in a remarkably clear and accessible way, and I hope it will be widely read.' – *Rt Revd John Pritchard, Bishop of Oxford, UK*

'Denis Alexander brings scientific acuity, lively faith, and not a little humour to this judicious and thorough explication of a fully Christian, fully reasoned understanding of creation and evolution. This book will go a long way toward encouraging both believers and sceptics that the much-vaunted "conflict" between science and religion is a mirage. One can only hope that it will inspire more Christians to pursue scientific careers, and inspire many scientists to take a closer look at the claims of Christian faith.' – *Andy Crouch, Editorial Director, The Christian Vision Project, Christianity Today International, USA*

'This is the book that I have been awaiting for a very long time. I suspect that it will rapidly become, and will long remain, the standard work on its subject... Despite the profundity of the subject matter, the author writes with a light touch, it abounds in meaningful analogies and, despite its length, is difficult to put down.' – *Harold Rowdon, formerly lecturer at London Bible College (now London School of Theology) and general editor of Partnership Publications*

'Denis Alexander is both an eminent scientist who finds the evidence for evolution overwhelming, and a Christian who believes that the Bible is God's authoritative word for all people. In this excellent book he takes us on a masterful and enlightening journey through both the relevant biblical text and the science underlying evolution. He explains with clarity and conviction how the book of God's works and the book of God's words can be held in harmony. In doing so he shows great respect for those who would disagree with him, and asks for the same in return, eager that disagreements in this area should not hinder the saving work of the gospel. This book fills a notable gap and will go to the top of my recommended reading list for those wanting an informed and balanced approach to this topic.' – *Andrew P. Halestrap, Professor of Biochemistry, University of Bristol, UK*

'A timely, challenging and necessary book... this is important reading for any thinking Christian seeking to engage with one of the great cultural issues of our time.' – *Revd Simon Downham, Vicar/Senior Pastor, St Paul's Hammersmith, London*

'A trenchant, carefully argued substantive treatment of a sadly divisive issue. If you want to understand the debate and the central concerns at its heart, this excellent book, written by an eminent biologist and committed Christian, will help all of us who want to be true to our Christian faith and to the realities of scientific understanding and practice.' – *E. David Cook, Holmes Professor of Faith and learning, Wheaton College, USA*

CREATION OR EVOLUTION

DO WE HAVE TO CHOOSE?

DENIS R. ALEXANDER

MONARCH
B O O K S

Oxford, UK & Grand Rapids, Michigan, USA

First published in the UK in 2008 by Monarch Books
(a publishing imprint of Lion Hudson plc),
Wilkinson House, Jordan Hill Road, Oxford OX2 8DR
Tel: +44 (0) 1865 302750   Fax: +44 (0) 1865 302757
Email: monarch@lionhudson.com
www.lionhudson.com

ISBN: 978-1-85424-746-9 (UK)
ISBN: 978-0-8254-6292-4 (USA)

Distributed by:
UK: Marston Book Services Ltd, PO Box 269, Abingdon, Oxon OX14 4YN;
USA: Kregel Publications, PO Box 2607, Grand Rapids, Michigan 49501.

British Library Cataloguing Data
A catalogue record for this book is available from the British Library.

Printed and bound in Malta by Gutenberg Press.

Dedication

This book is dedicated to the memory of my brother, the late David Alexander, co-founder of Lion Publishing, and the one who first stimulated my interest in writing books. My first book, *Beyond Science*, was also one of the first books that Lion published.

Contents

Preface   11

1   What Do We Mean By Creation?   15
2   The Biblical Doctrine of Creation   27
3   What Do We Mean By Evolution? Dating, DNA and
    Genes   47
4   What Do We Mean By Evolution? Natural Selection
    and Reproductive Success   73
5   What Do We Mean By Evolution? Speciation, Fossils
    and the Question of Information   93
6   Objections to Evolution   130
7   What about Genesis?   151
8   Evolutionary Creationism   169
9   Who were Adam and Eve? The Background   191
10 Who were Adam and Eve? Genesis and Science in
    Conversation   214
11 Evolution and the Biblical Understanding of Death   244
12 Evolution and the Fall   254
13 Evolution, Natural Evil and the Theodicy Question   277
14 Intelligent Design and Creation's Order   293
15 Evolution – Intelligent and Designed?   312
16 The Origin of Life   332

Postscript   351
Notes   355
Index   369

Figures

Fig 1.   The main recent geological eras   52

Fig 2.   How DNA divides to form two daughter
         DNA molecules.   56

Fig 3.   DNA is packaged with histone proteins to form
         chromatin   64

Fig 4.   The Hox genes of a fruit fly   71

Fig 5.   Evolution is a two-stage process   74

Fig 6.   History of main evolutionary events   89

Fig 7.   The generation of a new species of Tragopogon by
         chromosomal doubling.   95

Fig 8.   Peaks of mass extinction over the past 550 million
         years.   105

Fig 9.   Fossil intermediates between fish and tetrapods   128

Fig 10. Eyes in living molluscs.   145

Fig 11. Understanding our ancestry   208

Fig 12. The insertion site in the genomes of human, chimp,
         gorilla and orangutan   209

Fig 13. A pair of human chromosomes joined at the
         centromere.   211

Fig 14. Chromosome fusion   212

Fig 15. The evolutionary history of *Homo sapiens* over the
         past 7 million years.   216

Fig 16. The way in which our mitochondrial DNA
         is inherited from a single woman, the so-called
         'Mitochondrial Eve'   223

Fig 17   The estimated levels of intentionality that may relate
         to the hominid ancestors of *Homo sapiens*   229

Fig 18. The bacterial flagellum.   298

Fig 19   The ways in which an enzyme can evolve to achieve
         optimal fitness for a particular task   325

Fig 20. Evolutionary convergence in the sabre tooth   328

Fig 21. The world of Genomic 'Design Space'   329

Preface

I have written this book mainly for people who believe, as I do, that the Bible is the inspired Word of God from cover to cover. Of course I can understand that others might wish to read a book on such a controversial subject, including people of any faith or none. I hope those who happen to be in this latter category will find it interesting to see how one practising scientist, at least, addresses this issue, but I make no apologies for writing primarily for those who share my own Christian faith, for it often seems to be those within this community who have the greatest questions on the subject of creation and evolution. I therefore make no attempt in this book to defend the role of the Bible as the authoritative Word of God, but simply assume that this is the starting point for all Christians. If that is not your starting position, I hope at least that the book will help you to see how the Bible and science can live together very happily.

Unfortunately this topic has often been characterised by rather strongly held positions amongst Christians, sometimes diametrically opposed to each other. Occasionally this has led to the kind of exchanges that generate more heat than light. There are even Christians who think that to be a real Christian necessitates adopting the same position on these issues as they do. So it is good for Christians as they read this book to remember that we are saved by the finished work of Christ on the Cross for our sins, and nothing can be added to our salvation other than what Christ has accomplished for us, for 'The only thing that counts is faith expressing itself through love' (Galatians 5:6). The last thing I would want is for this topic to be a matter for dissension or disunity amongst believers. This book is written as a discussion and a dialogue. Of course it expresses a particular point of view, but where there are differences I hope these can be aired amicably in a spirit of Christian love. One thing that we as Christians are not always very good at is disagreeing in a loving way. This can happen when peripheral doctrines not essential to salvation begin to be viewed as of central importance.

Essential and central biblical doctrines are that God created and sustains the universe, that human beings are made in his image, and that sin separates men and women from God in a way that only God's atoning work through Christ can remove. On such doctrines Christians are united. But sometimes we disagree over peripheral doctrines, such as the *methods* God used and uses to create, or the precise limits of our divine image as humans, or the best way to make people aware of the gulf caused by sin and God's remedy for it. If such peripherals come to be regarded as of central importance, then Christians can forget that it is by the way that we love one another that people are to recognise that we are disciples of Jesus.

So hopefully no one will tackle this book thinking that finding the correct answer to the question posed by its title is essential for salvation! I am glad to belong to a church in Cambridge where different members represent a broad range of views on this topic, and where we worship and work together quite happily. I count amongst some of my closest Christian friends those who share my view of God as creator and redeemer, but who see the way in which this ties up with scientific issues in terms very different from the line suggested in this book. Although it is always a good thing for Christians to find the truth and agree on it, we recognise that all of us 'know in part' (1 Corinthians 13:9), and that whereas knowledge will one day be fulfilled, only love that is developed now will have its culmination in the coming kingdom. In the meantime, then, we can rejoice that we can continue in Christian love in spite of some differing beliefs.

For many years I have been giving lectures on science and faith in churches, universities, schools and other venues. If I am giving a general lecture on the topic, I normally avoid the subject of creation and evolution altogether (wanting nothing better than a quiet life). But then it comes to the question and answer period, and the first question is usually something like 'What do you think about Genesis 1?' or 'How does biblical teaching about Adam and Eve fit with science?' In seeking to answer such questions I have found surprisingly few books written by professional biologists who take the Bible seriously and tackle hot topics like the interpretation of Genesis, Adam and Eve, the question of death before the Fall and so forth. Of course there have been some great books written on the topic, and I have taken care to cite those here, but with the science advancing so rapidly there is a constant need to up-date the discussion.

I am grateful to Tim Bushell, then President of the Imperial College Christian Union in London, for the title of this book. I was invited to give a talk there some years ago as part of a Christian Union Mission, and this was the title I was given to address. I liked it so much that ever since I have had a book buzzing around in my head with the same title. Here it is.

I would like to thank also kind friends who have made helpful corrections and suggestions on earlier versions of the manuscript, some contributing particular items of information; in particular Ruth Bancewicz, John Bausor, Sam Berry, Peter Clarke, Keith Fox, Julian Hardyman, Rodney Holder, Ard Louis, Hilary Marlow, Paul Marston, Hans Meissner, Hugh Reynolds, Julian Rivers, Peter Williams and Bob White. The errors and ideas that remain are all my own, and mention of these names should not be taken to imply that they are necessarily in agreement with the answer that I give to the question in the title. I would also like to thank the publisher for their help and patience during the preparation of the manuscript, in particular Tony Collins and Simon Cox and their team.

This is a book written by someone who is passionate about both science and the Bible, and I hope reading it will encourage you to believe, as I do, that the 'Book of God's Word' and the 'Book of God's Works' can be held firmly together in harmony.

Chapter 1:

What Do We Mean By Creation?

All Christians are, by definition, creationists. The writer of the letter to the Hebrews in the New Testament expresses this very clearly when he writes:

> By faith we understand that the universe was formed at God's command, so that what is seen was not made out of what was visible. (Hebrews 11:2)[1]

We cannot come to know God personally by faith without also believing that he is Creator of all that exists. The Apostles' Creed affirms: 'I believe in God the Father, maker of heaven and earth', a declaration central to the beliefs of all mainstream denominations. So Christians are by definition those who believe in a creator God; they are creationists.

Now of course there is the slight problem that in common usage the term 'creationist' is attached to a particular set of beliefs held by some Christians, as well as by some Muslims and Jews, and these beliefs relate to the particular way in which it is thought that God has created. For example, some creationists believe that the earth is 10,000 years old or less. Other creationists believe that the earth is very old, but that God has intervened in a miraculous way at various stages of creation, for example to bring about new species. Since words are defined by their usage, we have to accept that this is the kind of belief to which the word 'creationist' refers. But this should not mask the fact that in reality all Christians are creationists in a more basic sense – it is just that they vary in their views as to *how* God created.

Sooner or later (generally sooner) discussions about creation and evolution come down to how Christians interpret the Bible. Were Adam and Eve real historical people? Was the fruit on the tree in the Garden of Eden symbolic, or like fruit on the trees in the nearest orchard? Was there any physical death before the Fall? Can one believe in both the Genesis account and evolution at the same time?

The only way we can answer such questions is by reviewing what the Bible says about creation and considering whether it tells us anything about how God created living things. But before even embarking on that important task, we first have to think about how we interpret the Bible.

Interpreting the Bible

Have you ever met a fellow believer who tried telling you, 'Well I don't interpret the Bible – I just read it the way it is'? I have. I've also read such comments in print, not just in casual conversation. But of course most Christians are well aware that we are all involved in interpretation when we come to the biblical text.

The challenge of translation

For a start most of us do not read the Bible in its Hebrew or Greek original form, so we are dependent on translators to render the translation as faithful to the original text as they can. This is not always easy. For example, Hebrew has four words for *you*, distinguishing between masculine and feminine, as well as singular and plural, whereas English has only the one. Comparison of different English translations will quickly reveal that interpretation is involved in the precise rendering of many different verses, although in no case does this affect any basic Christian doctrine.

It is often quite difficult to bring out during translation the nuances of the original text in the way that the author clearly intended. The NIV version of Genesis 2:25 – 3:1 reads:

> The man and his wife were both naked, and they felt no shame. Now the serpent was more crafty than any of the wild animals the Lord God had made.

But the English loses the fact that the Hebrew words translated 'naked' (*arom*) and 'crafty' (*arum*) are almost identical in
spelling and pronunciation and serve to connect the two
verses. One attempt at a translation closer to the text makes
the key words rhyme:

> And the man and his wife were nude... Now the serpent was
> more shrewd...

but I suspect that this would get the kids giggling on the back row
in church if tried when reading the lesson, so perhaps best not.

Light is constantly being shed on the meaning of Hebrew
words by newly discovered texts in languages other than
Hebrew. The corpus of ancient Hebrew literature still only
consists of the Old Testament, the Dead Sea Scrolls (far shorter
than the Old Testament), a few parts of the apocrypha and
some short inscriptions. The King James translation was carried out in the early seventeenth century before archaeology
was known and without any modern sense of comparative lin-
guistics (the rules that govern the relationships between one
language and another). Furthermore, languages like Akkadian
(Babylonian and Assyrian) were completely undeciphered at
that time and these have sometimes helped us understand the
meaning of Hebrew words.

We might be surprised to read the injunction in the King
James Bible to 'Give strong drink unto him that is ready to perish' (Proverbs 31:6) and in fact 'strong drink' is mentioned 21
times in the King James Old Testament text, translating the
word *sekar*. But in more recent translations like the NIV we
read: 'Give beer to those who are perishing', and *sekar* is now
generally translated as 'beer' in place of 'strong drink' in the
NIV. How come? Did more recent translators get cold feet
about having so much 'strong drink' in the Bible? Not so – the
Bible comes down hard on drunkenness in any translation.
The actual reason is more prosaic. Akkadian texts were discovered in which *sikaru*, a word sounding very like the
Hebrew, clearly means beer because it is described as a 'sweet
beer made from grain'[2], and this was sufficient to swing the
translations in favour of beer.

As a Turkish speaker, and someone who has been for many years a supportive associate of those working to translate the Bible into modern Turkish, I have a special interest in that fascinating language. As with all translations, the team faced big challenges as they came to tackle certain passages. For example, how were they going to render Romans 12:20? In the English translation it reads: 'If your enemy is hungry, feed him; if your enemy is thirsty, give him something to drink. In this way you will heap burning coals on his head'. Now imagine a Turkish reader encountering the New Testament for the very first time without any Bible commentaries available. What might the reader make of this particular verse? Wisely the translators rendered in Turkish the final phrase of this verse to read 'In this way you will make that person ashamed'[3].

There are hundreds of examples like this that keep Bible translators intellectually and spiritually challenged all the way round the globe. We should pray for them. It is a tough task, but a task that reminds us that whether we like it or not we are already beginning to engage in the interpretative task of others as soon as we start reading our Bibles in any language other than the original.

Some key principles in interpreting the Bible

The next stage of interpretation involves our own grappling with the text, using this kind of checklist[4]:

- What kind of language is being used?
- What kind of literature is it?
- What is the expected audience?
- What is the purpose of the text?
- What relevant extra-textual knowledge is there?

The first two points in the list are particularly important when we start investigating what the Bible teaches about creation. The biblical authors use a very wide range of literary styles to convey God's message to us. 'All Scripture is God-breathed and is useful for teaching, rebuking, correcting and training in righteousness' (2 Tim. 3:16), but this does not mean that the Holy Spirit suppresses the author's personality, culture, language and idiosyncratic style. This is where the biblical view of inspiration is so different from that of the Qur'an. Muslims believe that the Qur'an has existed for all eternity in heaven in the Arabic language and was communicated to Mohammed in a series of visions in a particular cave. Mohammed is therefore viewed by Muslims as the mouthpiece of God's revelation without himself contributing to the text. In contrast Christians believe God inspired the authors of the 66 books of the Bible to write texts over a period of up to 1500 years bearing the indelible stamp of their own particular interests, context and culture. Bible-believing Christians have no doubt that what Scripture says, God says[5], but it is God speaking through real flesh and blood people, not through robots. As the writer to the Hebrews starts his letter (Hebrews 1:1):

> In the past God spoke to our forefathers through the prophets at many times and in various ways...

The range of literary and linguistic styles used in Scripture is indeed extremely wide. When we use our own mother tongue in a given culture, then we automatically fill in the correct meanings of texts and of speech almost without thinking about it. When we're driving and see a sign saying 'Warning, Heavy Plant Crossing', we don't look out for incursions into the road ahead from passing rhododendrons. When we hear someone described as having a 'chip on their shoulder', we do not look for bits of wood sticking out of their anatomy next time we meet them. If someone 'got out of bed on the wrong side' this morning, we know to keep well clear, not to interrogate them on the lay-out of their bedroom. Our daily language is saturated with idioms, metaphors, hyperbole, irony, slang and subtle humour, imbued with the flavour and character of the national culture in which it originates.

As we read different materials in our own language our minds effortlessly adapt to the context, even though in the course of a day we may be faced with understanding dozens of different literary styles. One moment we are reading our daily newspaper, the next moment cooking recipes, then a historical novel, or maybe Harry Potter, then a legal document relating to a house purchase, then some cartoons on the back of the newspaper, then a scientific paper (for some) or a business report (for others). We would not dream of understanding one type of literature as if it were another, but automatically interpret statements according to their literary context. When I read in an estate agent's description of a house for sale that 'it requires some attention', then I interpret accordingly (e.g. the house has been derelict for more than a year and needs major refurbishment); but if a kind friend has read a draft of my latest book and says, in a classic piece of British understatement, that 'Chapter Nine needs some attention', then I will take a second look at that chapter very carefully. When Slughorn says 'I must give you warning that Felix Felicis is a banned substance in organised competitions...'[6], then I read the literature accordingly, not as if I were an athlete reading the warning in a sporting manual prepared for the next Olympics.

Context makes a huge difference to nuance. If I say 'I am broken hearted that the technician has broken his promise to mend the broken equipment', this uses the same word in three different ways and only the context determines how literal the meaning is. My recent favourite on this point is the mother quoted as saying: 'You cannot expect your kids not to go out. You don't want them staying at home, fixed to the computer'[7] – the sort of remark any sensible parent might say, we think, and move on. But it makes a lot of difference to know that this was the particular mother whose 14-year-old son had just sailed a boat single-handed across the Atlantic, a unique achievement. Knowing the context changes the nuance entirely – some 'going out'!

Those who have been reading the Bible for a long time will also tend to interpret texts almost automatically according to the type of literature being read. Others just starting out might need more help (of course commentaries can be useful): but all of us need to be on our guard against reading one type of biblical literature as if it were another. This point becomes clearer when we consider that the types of literature used in the Bible include prose, historical narrative, poetry (in many different styles), prophetic writing, parables, apocalyptic writings, correspondence, theological essays, biography, genealogy, legal discourse, census data, hymns, descriptions of dreams and visions, and much else besides. We can be seriously misled if we treat one kind of narrative as if it were another, missing the main point of the passage altogether.

When Nathan the prophet told King David a parable in 2 Samuel 12, the king became very involved in the story. It was a real tear-jerker about injustice in which the rich man kills the poor man's only ewe for dinner, when actually the rich man had plenty of his own. To which story King David cries, 'As surely as the Lord lives, the man who did this deserves to die! He must pay for that lamb four times over, because he did such a thing and had no pity.' Then Nathan said to David, 'You are the man!' David had become so emotionally involved with the actual parable, not to say blind to his own sin, he had missed the point entirely that Nathan meant him and his adultery with Bathsheba, with its subsequent cover-up and arranged death of her husband Uriah the Hittite.

At other times the biblical writers give us both a straightforward narrative and a figurative account of the same events, in order to drive home the key theological message. For example, Ezekiel 16 says figuratively what Ezekiel 22 says by way of a more straightforward narrative account, and Ezekiel 23 does the same for the more historical account provided in Ezekiel 20[8].

Jesus himself often spent time trying to persuade his listeners away from a literalistic interpretation of his words, because if they took that route they would equally miss the point. When Jesus told Nicodemus that he needed to be born again, Nicodemus' immediate response was whether he had to 'enter again into his mother's womb', and Jesus had to explain to him that he was speaking of a spiritual rebirth. When Jesus spoke of the temple being raised in three days, his disciples protested that it had taken 46 years to build the Temple (John 2:20), so how could he possibly do it in three days? But John goes on to explain that Jesus was actually speaking of his resurrection. So what is the true interpretation of Jesus' words: that the Temple could be physically rebuilt in three days, or that he would rise from the dead on the third day?

A few chapters later in John's Gospel (6:51) Jesus declares: 'I am the living bread that came down from heaven. If anyone eats of this bread, he will live forever. This bread is my flesh, which I will give for the life of the world.' Not surprisingly we then read that 'the Jews began to argue sharply among themselves, "How can this man give us his flesh to eat?"' At which point we might expect Jesus to give a really clear explanation of what he means, but instead Jesus says, 'I tell you the truth, unless you eat the flesh of the Son of Man and drink his blood, you have no life in you. Whoever eats my flesh and drinks my blood has eternal life, and I will raise him up at the last day.' We might feel some sympathy with the listeners on this occasion if they were a bit shocked by such words. Indeed we read that 'many of his disciples said, "This is a hard teaching. Who can accept it?"' (verse 60). Getting the real point of Jesus' words took some tough thinking and effort. The Word of God is not simply handed to us on a plate as if it were a list of doctrinal points that we could tick off without personal thought and engagement.

Western readers, in particular, are not very practised at reading ancient literature and have a tendency to interpret with a wooden literalism. This is because scientific literature has become so dominant in our culture, influencing the way in which we instinctively read even those texts that come from a pre-scientific age. This can be a significant problem when we come to the biblical text, not only because of its antiquity, but also because it is set in cultures with which we may not be familiar. For example some Western readers are puzzled by the way in which Jesus rarely seems to give a straight answer to a straight question (although he did sometimes). Why doesn't he just say 'yes' or 'no' in answer to a direct question? (e.g. John 8:5; 8:25; 10:24). Of course Jesus' main purpose was often to get people thinking about the deeper issues by throwing questions back to them, but generally in Middle Eastern cultures it is not customary to give very straight answers, indeed not deemed very polite. Just listen to a discussion between diplomats from Western and Middle Eastern countries for a while and you will see what I mean!

Understanding other cultures can also help us with otherwise difficult passages like Luke 9:61 where a potential disciple says to Jesus, 'I will follow you, Lord; but first let me go back and say good-bye to my family', to which Jesus replies 'No one who puts his hand to the plough and looks back is fit for service in the kingdom of God.' At first that sounds a bit harsh, but certainly Jesus is not saying here that we shouldn't be concerned about our families. When we realise that 'saying goodbye' in the culture of the time was not a question of a brief 'Cheerio, mum and dad' but could involve a prolonged period of meals, visiting relatives in nearby villages etc, then it helps to put the challenge in perspective. If we come to the biblical text with our twenty-first century Western mindsets firmly in place, without any willingness to educate ourselves in the culture and world of the biblical writers, then we are likely to miss much of what the inspired Word of God has to say to us.

Such reflections should also make us cautious when referring to the 'literal meaning of the text'. The real literal meaning of the text is the one that the author intends us to understand. So when Luke records the words of Jesus (Luke 14:26) that 'If anyone comes to me and does not hate his father and mother, his wife and children, his brothers and sisters – yes, even his own life – he cannot be my disciple', what is the literal meaning of the text? If we were reading that text in isolation on a manuscript fragment recovered from some desert in Palestine, then we might have a problem in finding the correct interpretation. But of course by placing that text in the context of the rest of the New Testament, we know that Jesus is not actually encouraging us to literally hate our families. Instead our commitment to serve and follow him makes any other claims upon our allegiance look like hatred by contrast: this is a typical example of linguistic hyperbole, of which the Bible is full. Understanding the true meaning of a biblical text can take some time and effort.

The biblical language of creation

The words create, created, creates, creating and creation occur 84 times in the NIV translation of the Bible. But there are many other words also that refer to God's creative work. There is a temptation in studies of this kind to do an extensive investigation of all the various words used in Hebrew and Greek for the idea of 'creation' or 'creating' and then arrange them into a system of carefully defined (and sometimes overly dogmatic!) meanings attached to each word. The problem with this approach is that language is defined by its usage and context, and the biblical writers, inspired by the Holy Spirit, certainly chose their words carefully, but not necessarily for the benefit of twenty-first century systematic theologians. So certainly it is useful to study the different words and understand their different nuances, but at the end of the day it is context that will be most important in helping us to understand the meanings of the Hebrew and Greek 'creation language' of the Bible, just as it is in English.

There are three main words used for create in Hebrew: *bara'* ('create', Greek equivalent *ktizein*), *'asah* ('make', Greek equivalent *poiein*) and *yatsar* ('form', Greek equivalent *plasso*). The word *bara'* is generally used to refer to the action of God in bringing about his creative work. A classic example would be: 'In the beginning God *bara'* the heavens and the earth'. But in Hebrew thought the *bara'* works of God are by no means restricted to origins, often referring to any new beginning in the normal everyday processes of life and death. 'Remember how fleeting is my life. For what futility you have created (*bara'*) all men!' cries the Psalmist (Psalm 89:47), and 'Create (*bara'*) in me a pure heart, O God' (Psalm 51:10).

In Isaiah 54:16 we have a fascinating example of the way in which God's *bara'* expresses his sovereignty in bringing into being human existence, identity and judgement: 'See, it is I who created (*bara'*) the blacksmith who fans the coals into flame and forges a weapon fit for its work. And it is I who have created (*bara'*) the destroyer to work havoc...'. And then in Psalm 104 we have the remarkable observation that God's creative work is involved in the very processes of animal life and death that would have been so familiar to the rural communities of that time: 'When you hide your face, they [the animals] are terrified; when you take away their breath, they die and return to the dust. When you send your Spirit, they are created (*bara'*), and you renew the face of the earth' (verses 29–30). Note here that it is by *bara'* that the created order is renewed. Job reflects these realities perfectly when he says of God that

'In his hand is the life of every creature and the breath of all mankind' (Job 12:10).

God's *bara'* is not only involved in the life, death and being of both humans and animals, but also in other on-going processes of the world that are by no means limited to 'origins'. In Isaiah 45:7 God declares – in the present tense: 'I form the light and create (*bara'*) darkness, I bring prosperity and create (*bara'*) disaster; I, the Lord, do all these things.' And similarly in Amos 4:13 we read that 'He who forms the mountains, creates (*bara'*) the wind, and reveals his thoughts to man, he who turns dawn to darkness, and treads the high places of the earth – the Lord God Almighty is his name'.

When God wishes to remind his people of their limited knowledge, he tells them that his work of *bara'* is ongoing, so there is no way they can second-guess his plans and purposes: 'From now on I will tell you of new things, of hidden things unknown to you. They are created (*bara'*) now, and not long ago; you have not heard of them before today. So you cannot say, "Yes, I knew of them."' (Isaiah 48:6–7). God's *bara'* is also involved in the generation and blessing of nations: 'But now, this is what the Lord says – he who created (*bara'*) you, O Jacob, he who formed (*yatsar*) you, O Israel: "Fear not, for I have redeemed you; I have summoned you by name; you are mine."' (Isaiah 43:1 and compare v.7). The rest of Isaiah 43 then explains the many and varied ways in which God's faithful *bara'* and *yatsar* are being worked out in the lives of his people, God revealing himself as 'Israel's Creator' (*bara'*, v.15).

This passage from Isaiah also reminds us that there is a considerable degree of overlap among the various Hebrew words used for 'create', 'make' and 'form'. Of course we do not interpret Isaiah 43:1 as meaning that God's creative work in the formation of Jacob and of Israel is somehow different! It is very common in Hebrew literature for essentially the same point to be made twice in the same passage, albeit using slightly different language, acting like a refrain through the text – Psalm 145 provides a good example amongst many others. In this and other ways the different Hebrew creation words are often used interchangeably for the same event. 'It is I who made (*'asah*) the earth and created (*bara'*) mankind upon it' says God in

Isaiah 45:12. 'My own hands stretched out the heavens; I marshalled their starry hosts.' The people whom God is calling to himself from every part of the earth are those 'whom I created (*bara'*) for my glory, whom I formed and made (*'asah*)' (Isaiah 43:7).

Sometimes all three main 'creative' words in Hebrew occur in the same sentence: 'For this is what the Lord says – he who created (*bara'*) the heavens, he is God; he who fashioned (*yatsar*) and made (*'asah*) the earth' (Isaiah 45:18). From those types of example alone we might deduce that the words are completely interchangeable, but it is in fact the case that *bara'* always has God as the subject, whereas the other words like *'asah* are used also for human creativity, in addition to their frequent use in reference to God's creative work. For example, the designers who helped construct the Tabernacle and its accessories 'fashioned (*'asah*) the breastpiece – the work of a skilled craftsman'. We don't hear of a human craftsman *bara'* things in the biblical text – it is God's job to *bara'*. But it is quite different for *'asah*. From Genesis chapters 1 to 7 there are 15 examples of *'asah* where God is the direct subject of the making, whereas when we reach Genesis 8 we find Noah opening the window that 'he had made (*'asah*) in the ark' (verse 6).

Such word studies should be viewed as providing a useful tool-kit when reading biblical passages about creation, but no more. There is certainly no room for holding dogmatically to a particular interpretation of a passage based on word studies alone. But knowing a bit about the linguistic background can certainly be helpful as we begin to paint the broad brush-strokes that give us an overall picture of the biblical understanding of the doctrine of creation. The more detailed discussion of the Genesis text will come in later chapters; for the moment we are interested in the 'big picture'.

Chapter 2:
The Biblical Doctrine of Creation

Many people think that when Christians talk about 'creation' they are referring mainly to 'origins'. Of course the biblical teaching on creation includes origins, but if we become too focused on origins then we can forget that the biblical understanding of creation is not primarily concerned with how things began, but why they exist. Also the preponderance of biblical teaching on creation is not located within the first few chapters of the book of Genesis, important as they are, but is scattered throughout the rest of the Bible.

If we take Scripture as a whole, then there are four key points that emerge about God in relation to his creation[9]:

God is transcendent in relation to his creation

Christians do not generally go around hugging trees, because they worship a transcendent Creator who is not to be found in trees but who has certainly brought them into being and who sustains their being. The transcendence of God refers to his otherness, his eternal nature, the fact that he's nothing like us. As the psalmist prays in Psalm 90:2:

> Before the mountains were born
> or you brought forth the earth and the world,
> from everlasting to everlasting you are God.

The God of the Bible is not a local or tribal god who can be pinned down to some neat time-bound or culture-bound formula. 'My thoughts are not your thoughts, neither are your ways my ways, declares the Lord. As the heavens are higher than the earth, so are my ways higher than your ways and my thoughts than your thoughts' (Isaiah 55:8–9). We cannot second-guess God. We cannot tell him how he should have done creation – those of us who are scientists can only describe what he actually has done, to the best of our ability. The properties of the created order are contingent upon God's will, meaning that they are dependent upon his ultimate say-so. Many historians of science believe that this Christian conviction was important in stimulating empirical thinking during the emergence of modern science. If we cannot work out how God's creation operates by pure reason – especially fallen reason! – then we'd better do some experiments to find out how it works[10].

God's transcendence also means that all the metaphors we use to describe God are highly inadequate. He is not a kind of heavenly engineer tinkering around with bits of the created order. He is not restricted to the notion of the Divine Architect as promoted by the Freemasons. And he's certainly not any kind of super-human as Richard Dawkins mistakenly understands theists to believe, very complex because made of lots of parts 'like a Boeing 747'[11]. The transcendence of God is a reminder that we can never put God in a box. We are made in his image, but he is certainly not made in ours.

Implicit in God's transcendence is the concept that he creates out of his free and unfettered will. There was no necessity in God creating the universe. He did not have to create it. His transcendent being is all-sufficient. 'The Lord does whatever pleases him' writes the Psalmist, 'in the heavens and on the earth, in the seas and all their depths' (Psalm 135:6). The God whom Paul proclaimed to the Epicurean and Stoic philosophers at Athens was quite different from anything they had heard of before, a God who 'is not served by human hands, as if he needed anything, because he himself gives all men life and breath and everything else' (Acts 17:25).

God is immanent in his creation

An understanding of God which depended only on the notion of transcendence could easily degenerate into the deistic idea of a distant and remote God who winds up the universe at the

beginning and then occasionally returns to intervene or med-
dle around with it. Such a scenario is disallowed by the biblical insistence that God is also *immanent* in his creation,
meaning that God is intimately involved in continued creative
activity in relation to his universe. All that exists only continues to do so because of his continued say-so. The properties of
matter continue to be what they are because God wills that
they should continue to have such properties. God's faithfulness is constantly displayed by that continuity and consistency
in the properties of matter. It is what makes science possible.

Page after page of the books of Psalms, Isaiah and Job
remind us that God creates and sustains the smallest details of
biology, including making grass grow for cattle (Psalm 104:14),
supplying food for lions who 'roar for their prey and seek their
food from God' (Psalm 104:21) and 'for the raven when its
young cry out to God' (Job 38:41). We have already noted
above when discussing the *bara'* terminology that the word is
used to refer to God's complete involvement in the common
daily processes of animal life and death (Psalm 104:29–30).

Obviously this psalm is providing us with a theological and
not a biological interpretation of the natural world. As a rural
and agricultural people the Israelites were perfectly aware of
the natural processes of animal birth and death. The poetic
description that is being provided is not a theological description rivalling what everyone knew by simple observation took
place in the natural world, but a fuller interpretation of a deeper
creative reality that underlies all events without exception.

When reading such psalms – and many others like them –
one is forcibly struck by the biblical insistence that our creator
God is no distant potentate, but one who is actively creating
and sustaining the amazing universe that he has brought into
being, complete with all the richness of its biological diversity;
an aspect of God's creative actions sometimes referred to by
theologians as his 'providence'. God is the one who 'gives life
to everything' (Nehemiah 9:6) in the present tense. In the book
of Job God is the one, in the present tense, who generates
earthquakes (chapter 9, verses 5–6), brings about eclipses
(chapter 9, verse 7), wraps up water in the clouds (chapter 26,
verse 8), spreads his clouds over the moon (chapter 26, verse

9), brings down hail and snow from his storehouses (chapter 38, verse 22) and moulds Job himself like clay (chapter 10, verse 9). 'The Lord reigns, let the earth be glad; let the distant shores rejoice... His lightning lights up the world; the earth sees and trembles' (Psalm 97:1 and 4, and see Jeremiah 51:15).

The New Testament likewise underlines the fact that all things exist by the creative and sustaining power of the Lord Jesus, the Word of God. 'Through him all things were made; without him *nothing* was made that has been made' (John 1:3, my italic). In Colossians 1, in one of the most amazing passages in the whole of the New Testament, Paul speaks of the Son as being 'the image of the invisible God, the firstborn over all creation' (verse 15), and then immediately goes on to say: 'For by him all things were created: things in heaven and on earth, visible and invisible, whether thrones or powers or rulers or authorities; all things were created by him and for him. He is before all things, *and in him all things hold together*' (verses 16–17, my italics).

In other words, the complete created order, in all its breadth and diversity, goes on consisting by the same divine Word, the Lord Jesus, who brought everything into being in the first place. The point is further underlined by the writer to the Hebrews when he writes that 'The Son is the radiance of God's glory and the exact representation of his being, *sustaining all things by his powerful word*' (Hebrews 1:3, my italics). God is the one 'for whom and through whom everything exists' (Hebrews 2:10). If God did not keep on willing the created order to exist by his powerful Word, then it would stop existing. As Jesus said of his heavenly Father: 'He causes his sun to rise on the evil and the good, and sends rain on the righteous and the unrighteous' (Matthew 5:45). The impression here is not of a God who has set up the laws of the universe and then retreated into the shadows, occasionally returning to intervene in his creation, but rather of a God who *causes* things to happen as they do happen, who actively sends rain and is completely immanent in his created order. There are echoes of Psalm 104 in Matthew 6 where we read of our heavenly Father feeding the birds (verse 26) and clothing the grass of the field (verse 30).

It is this generosity of God in his daily provision of the bounty of his creation that Paul and Barnabas used so powerfully in their preaching in first century Lystra (now in modern Turkey): 'Yet he has not left himself without testimony: He has shown kindness by giving you rain from heaven and crops in their seasons; he provides you with plenty of food and fills your hearts with joy.' (Acts 14:17). No wonder that the twenty four elders of John's vision in the book of Revelation worship before the throne, saying 'You are worthy, our Lord and God, to receive glory and honour and power, for you created all things, and by your will they were created and *have their being*' (Revelation 4:11, my italics).

The present tense of creation is strikingly apparent throughout Scripture.

All analogies are limited, but God's continuing creative activity has been likened to the continual flow of digital signals without which there would be no picture on our TV screen. Your favourite TV soap is a self-contained drama, and talk of digitally encoded signals will add nothing to it, yet without the continuous signals the drama would cease to be conveyed to your living-room. God is the continuing author of creation.

To use a different analogy, he is both the musical composer and conductor in relation to the symphony of creation, the one who is immanent in the whole creative process as the beautiful harmony emerges from the coordinated output of the many different musical components.

Once we grasp the biblical teaching on the immanence of God in his creation, we can then understand why the Bible has no concept of 'nature' in its contemporary sense of referring to the 'natural world', for the simple reason that the term is redundant: instead it speaks of 'creation' to refer to the complete panoply of God's activities that we as scientists struggle to describe so inadequately[12].

The notion of 'nature' as a quasi-independent entity was an idea inherited from Greek pagan philosophy and promoted by the eighteenth century deists. They saw God as the distant lawgiver who bestowed 'nature' with a suite of fixed properties, but who then retired from the scene without further active involvement. But biblical theology renders the very concept of 'nature' as a semi-independent entity unnecessary because God as the author of creation is so thoroughly involved in his created order, meaning all that exists.

The early natural philosophers (as scientists were called prior to the second half of the nineteenth century), who did so much to lay the foundations of modern science, recognised better than most the incompatibility of the biblical account with the idea of 'nature'. Robert Boyle (1627–91), in particular, an early member of the Royal Society and one of the founders of modern chemistry, was also a committed Christian who learnt Hebrew, Greek, Chaldean and Syriac in order that he might understand the Bible more effectively. Boyle refuted the whole idea of the deity of nature in his *Free Inquiry into the Vulgarly Received Notion of Nature* (1682). For Boyle, the 'vulgar notion' was the idea that 'nature' had any kind of autonomous existence, or that it acted as a mediator between God and his works. He attacked the expression, popular at the time, that 'God and nature do nothing in vain', since this implied the old Greek idea of divine nature, rather than the relationship of 'creator and creature'.

Since, said Boyle, God made the world by divine *fiat*, and sustained his creation at every moment in time, there was no need to invoke any necessity in the workings of nature, as if the created world had its own mind, or could operate as a separate agent. Boyle saw biblical theology as completely subversive of the idea derived from Greek philosophy of an autonomous entity known as 'nature' that was in any sense independent of God's creation.

Christians today should take a tip from Boyle and likewise refuse to think of 'nature' as any kind of quasi-independent entity. Once we grasp the Bible's powerful teaching about the immanence of God in his created order, then we will become suspicious of terminology such as 'Mother Nature'. In truth 'nature' does nothing, but the whole material world has been brought into being by the Word of God, and continues to be sustained moment by moment by his powerful Word. The notion of 'nature' itself, for us as for Boyle, has been demythologised by biblical creation theology.

The biblical insistence on the immanence of God in his creation also highlights the mistake of thinking that creation is mainly to do with origins. Of course beginnings are important, but so are continuations (otherwise we wouldn't be here to tell the tale!), and the biblical notion of creation encompasses not only both of those, but also the future tense of creation as we shall consider further below.

The immanence of God in his created order has enormous implications for the science–faith debate. It means that the central role of scientists, whether or not they acknowledge the fact, is to describe the activities of God in creation. There is nothing that we can describe that was not brought into being and sustained by God's providential power. As Augustine put the point succinctly back in the early fifth century: 'Nature is what God does'[13]. Galileo was reflecting this Augustinian tradition when he wrote that nature is the 'executrix of God's will' (meaning that nature was simply the outworking of God's will, no more, no less). This does not at all mean that every particular event in 'nature' is micro-managed or specifically determined by God – far from it – a theme to which we shall return several times in later chapters.

God is personal and Trinitarian in his creation

The transcendent–immanent character of God's creative relationship to the universe could, in principle, be claimed as referring to a God who was an abstract designer, or some kind of heavenly supercomputer. The biblical claim, however, is quite distinctive in its insistence that this creator-God is a Trinitarian, personal God, and that the creation of other personalities is therefore what one expects in a universe which exists because of his creative activity. We live in a relational universe.

We have already highlighted the work of God the Father and God the Son in the work of creation. We encounter God the Holy Spirit in the second verse of the Bible as 'the Spirit of God was hovering over the waters', preparing to bring form and beauty to an earth that was 'formless and empty' (Genesis 1:2). One of Job's comforters, Elihu, was reminding Job of mainstream Hebrew understanding and thinking when he said that 'The Spirit of God has made me; the breath of the Almighty gives me life' (Job 33:4). We have already noted that animals are created when God sends his Spirit (Psalm 104:30).

Clearly in the New Testament the greatest emphasis is on the work of God the Father and God the Son in creation, the work of God the Spirit receiving particular attention in the context of his ministry in the lives of individuals and of churches. In Luke 10:21 we receive a wonderful insight into the inner workings of the Trinity as 'At that time Jesus, full of joy through the Holy Spirit, said, "I praise you, Father, Lord of heaven and earth, because you have hidden these things from the wise and learned, and revealed them to little children. Yes, Father, for this was your good pleasure."' Jesus in his incarnation receives joy from the Holy Spirit as he praises his heavenly Father as 'Lord of heaven and earth': a remarkable picture of unity in diversity expressed through personal love and communication.

This glimpse into the very life of the Godhead also gives us a clue about how the Trinitarian God interacts with his creation. There has been much recent discussion about how exactly God does interact with the world. The main answer that the Bible gives is that he does so by that most personal of activities – speaking: 'And God said' is repeated again and again in Genesis 1 to describe God's creative actions. 'The Mighty One, God, the Lord, *speaks* and summons the earth from the rising of the sun to the place where it sets' (Psalm 50:1), not meaning a literal voice with sound-waves, but communicating power, authority and information so that the created order operates harmoniously.

The supreme biblical example of God's communication is of course Jesus himself, the Word of God. Christians worship not the written word, but the incarnate Word of God: 'In the beginning was the Word, and the Word was with God, and the Word was God' (John 1:1) and we have already noted that it was through Jesus, the divine Word, that 'all things were made; without him nothing was made that has been made' (John 1:3). Jesus speaks to the waves and they obey him (Mark 4:39–41). We are living in a universe created, shaped and sustained by the personal God who speaks, Father, Son and Holy Spirit.

The three tenses of creation

There is no doubt that the creation of the world is often viewed in the past tense in Scripture. 'In the beginning', said the Psalmist, 'you laid the foundations of the earth' (Psalm 102:25). In Jesus' parable of the sheep and the goats, the sheep's inheritance was 'the kingdom prepared for you since the creation of the world' (Matthew 25:34). Paul writes that 'since the creation of the world God's invisible qualities – his eternal power and divine nature – have been clearly seen...' (Romans 1:20). The great creative events described in Genesis in which order was brought out of emptiness at God's command provide the essential backcloth for the whole of the rest of the biblical narrative. The arrow of time is implicit throughout the biblical text.

We have also seen how creation in scriptural thought is very much an on-going activity with God involved in *bara'* in dynamic processes such as life and death: but there is a third vital aspect of creation in biblical thought, and that is the future creation. Creation, like salvation, has three tenses: past, present and future. By that I do not mean that ancient Hebrew itself has these three tenses, which it does not, but rather that these three aspects of creation are implicit in the text and are rightly translated as such.

So we find the Old Testament already looking forward to the future *bara'* of God. God tells us through Isaiah the prophet: 'Behold, I will create (*bara'*) new heavens and a new earth. The former things will not be remembered, nor will they come to mind. But be glad and rejoice forever in what I will create (*bara'*), for I will create (*bara'*) Jerusalem to be a delight and its people a joy' (Isaiah 65:17–18)[14].

The same theme is picked up in the New Testament where the writer to the Hebrews reminds his readers, based on Psalm 102:25–27, that the present created order is only a temporary state of affairs in contrast with the eternal nature and plan of God: 'In the beginning, O Lord, you laid the foundations of the earth, and the heavens are the work of your hands. They will perish, but you remain; they will all wear out like a garment. You will roll them up like a robe; like a garment they will be changed. But you remain the same, and your years will never end' (Hebrews 1:10–12). Peter also explains that '…in keeping with his promise we are looking forward to a new heaven and a new earth, the home of righteousness' (2 Peter 3:13). This great programme of creation is finally brought to completion with John's vision of 'a new heaven and a new earth, for the first heaven and the first earth had passed away, and there was no longer any sea' (Revelation 21:1).

So the biblical doctrine of creation tells us about a dynamic process in which God is the author of the narrative, and Jesus is 'the Alpha and the Omega, the First and the Last, the Beginning and the End' (Revelation 22:13). God's creation encompasses past, present and future.

Creation and miracles

Some Christians look upon all or most of the creative actions of God as being equivalent to miracles. Other Christians invoke miracles to explain the existence of those aspects of the created order which they believe can never be understood or explained by science. It is therefore quite interesting to investigate how the Bible sees the miraculous in relation to creation.

There are three main Greek words used in the Bible that can be translated as 'miracle' or 'wonder'. The Greek word *terata* and its Hebrew equivalent *mopheth*, translated as 'wonders', are frequently used to draw attention to events which are so remarkable that they are remembered[15]. The term focuses more on the amazement produced in the witnesses of the event rather than on the specific purpose of the event.

The Greek word *dunameis*, from which we derive our word 'dynamite', is translated as 'acts of power' or 'mighty works' and emphasises the biblical conception of miracles as the result of the operation of the power (*dunamis*) of God, who is perceived to be the source of all power. Whereas the word *terata* points to the impact the miracle made on the observer, *dunameis* points to its cause.

The third word is the Greek word *semeion*, or 'sign', particularly used in John's Gospel when describing the miracles of Jesus. The intention of a *semeion* is to reveal aspects of God's character – especially his power and love. As Monden comments: 'Miracles are set apart from natural happenings not by the fact that they demonstrate a manifestation of power, but rather because their unusual nature makes them better fitted to be signs'[16].

The words *terata*, *dunameis* and *semeia* (plural, 'signs') are not the only words used by the New Testament to refer to the miraculous, but they are the most commonly used, and are frequently mentioned together in the same sentence[17]. Remarkably the word *terata* ('wonders') is always combined with one or the other, or both together, emphasising the reluctance of the biblical text to dwell on the merely marvellous character of the miracles. In the Hebrew text of the Old Testament, equivalent words are brought together to express the same sets of meanings, so that as Moses looks back to the exodus of the Israelites from Egypt, he reminds his people that 'With your own eyes you saw those great trials, those miraculous signs and great wonders' (Deuteronomy 29:3).

By far the most frequent references to miraculous events in the Old Testament are in the context of the deliverance of the people of Israel from Egypt, including those many times when the Jewish leaders and prophets look back later to remind the people of their remarkable deliverance (which they had a bad tendency to forget). This emphasis comes right through into the New Testament as Stephen, for example, also reminds his Jewish listeners of the God who 'led them out of Egypt and did wonders and miraculous signs in Egypt, at the Red Sea and for forty years in the desert' (Acts 7:36).

So it is striking in this context, in which miraculous language was used quite frequently, that the writers of neither the Old nor the New Testament generally view God's creative work as 'miraculous'. Instead God's normal work in creation provides the backcloth against which his unusual workings, as in the plagues in Egypt and the crossing of the Red (or Reed) Sea, can more readily be appreciated as miracles. True, in Job we find Job recounting the works of God in creation and using the language of miracle: 'He is the Maker of the Bear and Orion, the Pleiades and the constellations of the south. He performs wonders that cannot be fathomed, miracles that cannot be counted' (Job 9:9–10). However it is clear from the context that in these passages Job is making no distinction between creation in the past tense and the wonders of creation in the present tense as God sustains the created order: 'He performs wonders that cannot be fathomed, miracles that cannot be counted. He bestows rain on the earth; he sends water upon the countryside' (Job 5:9–10).

More common is the prayer of the Levites recorded in the book of Nehemiah where the people praise God for his wonderful creation: 'You alone are the Lord. You made the heavens, even the highest heavens, and all their starry host, the earth and all that is on it, the seas and all that is in them. You give life to everything, and the multitudes of heaven worship you' (Nehemiah 9:6). No mention of miracles here: but as soon as they start praising God for what he has accomplished specifically through their own history, then they pray: 'You sent miraculous signs and wonders (*mopheth*) against Pharaoh, against all his officials and all the people of his land' (Nehemiah 9:10).

The point here is not that the people were any the less in awe of God as Creator than they were of God as the worker of wonders and miracles. It is just that in biblical thought the language of miracles seems to be generally reserved for those special and unusual workings of God in his created order and in the lives of his people. This does not exclude the possibility that God performs particular miracles during his work of creation, but if that is the case then Scripture is silent about that aspect of his creative work. When Jesus intervenes to turn water into wine, or calm a rough sea, or raise Lazarus from the dead, these miraculous signs stand out as such because they are so different from God's normal way of working in creation.

Science is based on observed regularities and logical induction to unobserved regularity. The secular scientist assumes that everything works in a regular, reproducible kind of way because that is what science has always found to be the case so far. The scientist who is a Christian agrees, but in addition believes in a logical basis for that order, the creator God who faithfully endows the universe with its regularities. There is something paradoxical about the suggestion that miracles can be regular or even predictable events in God's general work of creation. The whole point about miracles is that they are unexpected, irregular events, particular signs of God's grace, so my suggestion is that Christians use the language of miracle with this biblical understanding in mind.

Does the Bible teach science?

A question that is often raised when thinking about the biblical doctrine of creation is whether the Bible itself presents its teachings on the subject as if they represented some form of modern science.

Answering this question is a lot trickier than it might at first seem. One of the reasons for that is the various uses that people make of the word 'science', a situation not made easier by the fact that the word tends to change its meaning also when translated between different languages (the word in German and French, for example, has a broader meaning than in English).

The term 'science' in the Middle Ages was used to refer to virtually any body of accurate constructed knowledge. Theology was famously known then as the 'queen of the sciences' because it was deemed to encompass all other forms of knowledge. In past centuries what we now know as 'science' was more commonly called 'natural philosophy' and those who pursued it were known as 'natural philosophers'. The word 'scientist' is of relatively recent origin and was invented in 1834 by a cleric called William Whewell who was Master of Trinity College and one of the great polymaths of nineteenth century Cambridge, although the word was not in common usage until much later in the century.

Modern science is a highly specialised activity using highly specialised techniques and terminology. It may be defined as 'an organised endeavour to explain the properties of the physical world by means of empirically testable theories constructed by a research community trained in specialised techniques'.

Scientific output is published in thousands of journals using language and concepts that are completely opaque to all but the initiates who have been trained in that particular field. Scientists across the road working in a different department will very often be no more able to understand their scientific colleagues working in a different discipline than the informed layperson. Physicists and biologists frequently stare at each other in mutual incomprehension, not only unable to understand each other's language, but equally unable to appreciate the very different ways of doing research and thinking about scientific problems that characterise each others' disciplines.

The specialisation of scientific language and concepts has been developing steadily since the founding of the first scientific societies, such as the Royal Society, in the mid-seventeenth century. In fact the early Royal Society made a concerted effort soon after its founding to introduce a more rigorous and well-defined language to express scientific ideas. Early members of the Royal Society were for a large part nonspecialists of enquiring mind who dabbled in a wide range of interests, and the early proceedings of the Royal Society could be appreciated by virtually any educated person. Reports of 'ye double-headed calf from Tewksbury' and 'ye monstrous birth of a dog from Bristol' were accessible to anyone then, as now. Contrast that with today where the *Journal of Immunology* may be bedtime reading for specialists in the field, but is too abstruse for the non-scientist. Instead popular science magazines like *New Scientist* and *Scientific American* undertake the valiant task of explaining science to the general reading public.

Scientific literature today is characterised by highly specialised language, by technical descriptions of methods in the 'Materials and Methods' sections of papers, by quantification and statistical methods, by scientific theory building and testing, and by numerous citations referring the reader back to related key points in the scientific literature. Papers are only published following a process of rigorous peer review that is exceptionally tough for the more prestigious journals.

It is a tribute to the continuing power and influence of modernism that many people today still take you to mean something is untrue if you describe it as 'not scientific'. Modernism is that stream of ideas suggesting that science and technology have all the reliable answers, or at least all the answers that really matter, and these answers are all that societies round the world need to function properly. Modernism has supposedly given way to post-modern ways of thinking in the Western world[18], but often one would not know it. So pervasive is the cultural influence of modernism that both theologically conservative and liberal Christians can interpret the biblical text in the light of modernist assumptions, albeit with different conclusions.

Quite common today are those conservative Christians who rightly wish to remain faithful to Scripture, but in the process unwittingly bring modernist, secular assumptions to the interpretative process. Of course they would not (like some theological liberals) deny miracles in the name of science. But they assume that scientific knowledge possesses a higher kind of truth, and that therefore they honour Scripture by treating it as 'modern science' in some way. Or, worse, they delve around in biblical texts, taking them out of context to 'prove' that many modern scientific discoveries were already known in Bible times. Such an approach is very common also in the Muslim world where many Muslims assure us that virtually all modern science is found somewhere in the Qur'an.

It is very important that we understand that there are many different ways of knowing things, and many different types of well-justified knowledge, besides scientific knowing and in addition to scientific knowledge. Think about the way in which universities are structured with their various departments and disciplines. Each different discipline has its own valid ways of justifying its beliefs: legal beliefs require legal justifications; historical beliefs require historical justifications; poetic beliefs require poetic justifications and so forth.

The same can equally be true of personal beliefs. If someone has been happily married for forty years to a partner who has shown consistent love and faithfulness over those years, demonstrated by repeated acts of kindness (including lots of washing-up), then that person is well justified in the conviction that their partner loves them. That is not science, but nothing in this week's scientific journal will be better justified than such a belief. So well-justified beliefs are definitely not just found within the realm of science.

There are plenty of things that are true without being scientific truths, inappropriate for publication in the scientific literature. The following piece of poetry gives a profoundly true description, with a far greater depth to it than any merely 'scientific' description of the same scene is likely to achieve:

> The barge she sat in, like a burnished throne
> Burnt on the water. The poop was beaten gold,
> Purple the sails, and so perfumed that
> The winds were love-sick with them...[19]

Shakespeare's evocative language is able to recreate an aspect of reality that analysis of the bare facts will always leave unexpressed.

There is a certain irony in the reflection that the keen atheist Prof. Richard Dawkins shares with some Christians their idea that religious and scientific truths belong to the same domain. Dawkins writes: 'I pay religions the compliment of regarding them as scientific theories and ... I see God as a competing explanation for facts about the universe and life.' This is not really a compliment, as Dawkins well knows, but simply a muddle in which the rhetoric is being driven by a modernist agenda. By suggesting that science is superior in the types of explanation that it generates, Dawkins hopes to show that religious explanations are thereby redundant. Yet religious explanations are in no sense rival to scientific explanations.

Without God's will there would be no science: since God is the ultimate source of all that exists, scientific journals can only be full of attempts to describe his works, for there is nothing else to describe. So the best way to understand theological descriptions of things (Why are they there? What is their purpose? What does God intend for them?) is to see such descriptions as complementary to scientific levels of understanding. We need both scientific and religious levels of understanding to do justice to our understanding of God's world.

So does the Bible contain science? Hopefully by now we can see that this is a non-trivial question! If someone asking that question is simply saying 'Is it true?' then the Christian may reply, of course the Word of God is true in all that it claims, for 'All Scripture is God-breathed and is useful for teaching, rebuking, correcting and training in righteousness...' (2 Timothy 3:16). But if the question 'does the Bible contain science?' is suggesting that a non-scientific statement cannot be true, or asking whether the Bible contains scientific narratives representing the same kind of literature as contemporary scientific papers, then clearly that is not the case. As we have noted, scientific literature of the kind with which we are familiar today was not established until a few centuries ago, and even then it was very different from current scientific prose, so clearly the Bible could not have been written as scientific narrative in that sense, for the simple reason that such a specialised literature had not yet been invented.

The dangers of extracting non-scientific narrative passages from the Scriptures and using them as if they were science is well illustrated by the Galileo affair. Everyone knows the famous story of how in seventeenth century Italy Galileo defended the Copernican theory that the earth moves in orbit round the sun, rather than being stationary as had previously been thought. The various reasons for the opposition to Galileo by the Catholic Church are quite complex and have been described many times[20].

The most pertinent aspect of the conflict for our present purposes is the way in which some of the Jesuit priests of the time who were opposed to Galileo (who was himself a Catholic) tried to use passages from the Psalms and elsewhere to criticise Copernicanism. Amongst these passages were Psalm 93:1: 'The world is firmly established; it cannot be moved' and similarly Psalm 96:10: 'Say among the nations, "The Lord reigns." The world is firmly established, it cannot be moved; he will judge the peoples with equity.' Now we today, as Galileo did in his day, would understand these psalms as poetic hymns of the kind we now sing as worship hymns in our churches. A few verses on from Psalm 96:10 we read of the fields being jubilant and of the forest singing for joy (verse 12). In verse 5 of Psalm 93 we read that 'holiness adorns your house for endless days, O Lord'. No one thinks that forests go around singing or that God actually lives in a house. The Psalms in question are poetry.

All this might seem trivial if it were not for the fact that it contributed to a serious rift between Galileo and the medieval Catholic Church, compounded by Galileo's own lack of diplomatic skills. Although Galileo was never tortured or imprisoned by the Inquisition (despite continuing popular mythologies to the contrary), he was subjected to house arrest for the remainder of his days and later in the nineteenth century the Galileo affair became an icon for the warfare model that emerged in the second half of that century as a way of describing the relationship between science and faith. Even today the Galileo affair is still cited as an example of the conflict between science and faith, although it would be more accurate to call it an internal dissension within the Catholic Church, since Galileo himself remained a loyal Catholic to his dying day.

The moral of the tale is that we should be resistant to the idea that biblical passages can be removed from their original contexts to score scientific points. Although Galileo is unlikely himself to have read widely in Augustine and the other early Church Fathers, he did draw on the knowledge of clerical friends who had, and produced a paper which came to be known as his 'Letter to the Grand Duchess Christina' (1615) in which he tackled the whole issue of how the Bible relates to science. This remains one of the earliest publications written by a natural philosopher making a serious attempt to relate the use of Scripture to the new 'mechanical philosophy' (meaning modern science as we know it). According to Augustine, wrote Galileo, the writers of the Old and New Testaments had been well aware of the truths of astronomy, and he quoted from Augustine to demonstrate the point:

> Hence let it be said briefly, touching the form of heaven, that our authors knew the truth but the Holy Spirit did not desire that men should learn things that are useful to no one for salvation[21].

In Augustinian thought, the purpose of the Bible was not to propound astronomical theories, since in any case these would not have been understood by the great mass of people, but rather to explain to people the way of salvation. In Galileo's time this principle of 'accommodation' as it came to be called, in which God 'accommodated' himself to the level of the readers of the biblical text, became very widespread. On such grounds Galileo maintained that it was therefore quite inappropriate to use passages from the Psalms to teach astronomy: they were written for the purposes of salvation, not for astronomy, to 'tell how to go to heaven, not how the heavens go'.

This principle of accommodation was also dominant in Calvin's writings and in those of the Protestant natural philosophers. As Calvin put it, Moses 'adapted his writing to common usage'. The Bible was 'a book for laymen' and 'he who would learn astronomy and other recondite arts, let him go elsewhere'[22]:

> The Holy Spirit had no intention to teach astronomy; and, in proposing instruction meant to be common to the simplest and most uneducated persons, he made use by Moses and the other prophets of popular language...the Holy Spirit would rather speak childishly than unintelligibly to the humble and unlearned[23].

Edward Wright echoes this theme when he wrote the preface to William Gilbert's 'De Magnete' (1600), the first major original contribution to modern science published in England. In defending in his preface the idea of the motion of the earth that Gilbert was presenting, Wright explained that Moses had never intended to expound mathematical and physical theories, but rather 'accommodated himself to the understanding and the way of speech of the common people.'

John Wilkins, an early founder of the Royal Society in England, who repeatedly referred to Calvin's commentaries in his writings, maintained that:

> It were happy for us, if we could exempt Scripture from Philosophical controversies: If we could be content to let it be perfect for that end unto which it was intended, for a Rule of our Faith and Obedience, and not to stretch it also to be a Judge of such Natural Truths as are to be found out by our own Industry and Experience[24].

Wilkins was totally opposed to those who 'look for any Secrets of Nature from the Words of Scripture, or will examine all its

Expressions by the exact Rules of Philosophy', telling us that he found neither Aristotelianism nor Copernicanism in the Bible, which does not express things as they 'are in themselves, but according to their appearances, and as they are conceived in common opinion'. When Kepler, a devout Lutheran, wrote his 'New Astronomy' (1609) he argued that the biblical writers had accommodated their stories to the human sense of sight. So when Ecclesiastes (1.5) says that 'the sun rises and the sun sets, and hurries back to where it rises', Kepler comments that 'The fable of life is ever the same; there is nothing new under the sun. You receive no instruction on physical matters [from the Bible]. The message is a moral one...'[25]

This historical excursion is important for us. The church has been here before. The seventeenth century natural philosophers and biblical scholars were united in their desire to maintain the authority of Scripture in a positive relationship with the new science. To a large degree they were successful in this endeavour and their writings come down to us as an example of how the task might be done. We may not today have quite the same idea of 'accommodation', in which the biblical writers like Moses knew all that there was to be known about the natural world, but chose under the guidance of the Holy Spirit to 'dumb down' the message for the common reader. Still it is certainly the case that the Word of God is written for the understanding and salvation of all humankind in all epochs, written in timeless narratives which are not tied to the latest scientific advance or insight. It is important in what follows that we seek to remain faithful to authorial intent, understanding Scripture within its culture and context, and not trying to force upon it a modernist secular agenda in which scientific knowledge is given a privileged status.

A thorough immersion in the overall biblical understanding of creation, together with a general grasp of how that theological perspective relates to scientific knowledge, provides us with the key conceptual tools that we need as we now go on to explore the science in more detail, and then later return to the Bible once again to see how the worlds of science and faith relate to each other.

Chapter Three:
What Do We Mean By Evolution? Dating, DNA and Genes

It is quite possible to have a long discussion about evolution in a group context, and then at the end find that everyone round the table has a very different idea in their head about what the term actually means. This makes for a rather fruitless exchange of ideas, because it means that in reality the participants are merely talking past each other, rather than actually engaging with the topic in hand.

For some people the term 'evolution' means a Godless philosophy that is more or less equated with atheism. They may have been brought up during the communist era in a country in which the full propaganda and educational apparatus of the state was used to identify the term 'evolution' with atheism. That ideological identification remains even today in some communist countries. Others may have listened to Richard Dawkins, professor of the public understanding of science from Oxford, or read his books, and heard his clear message that belief in evolution and belief in God are incompatible.

Others may have encountered the term 'evolution' in rather different contexts, for example the idea of society in general, or humankind in particular, evolving towards some better condition than the present one. In everyday conversation the term 'evolution' or 'evolved' is often used as a substitute for the word 'development' with its implicit understanding of 'progress'.

We will leave to a future chapter the task of investigating whether these particular ideological associations of 'evolution' are justified, in particular whether it is appropriate to identify evolution with atheism. The purpose of this chapter, and of the two that follow, is quite different: to summarise for the nonspecialist the current scientific understanding of biological evolution. Our purpose here is neither to defend nor to critique the theory, a task reserved for Chapter Six, but to explain what biologists mean when they talk about evolution. Even those who happen not to believe the theory of evolution do well to have a clear understanding of what they disagree with! These chapters explore some material with which not everyone may be familiar, but if we are to understand what evolution is about, then it is important to gain some relevant background knowledge about biology in general and genetics in particular. Christians often criticise atheist scientists for their poor grasp of theology, with some justification, but sometimes the boot is on the other foot, and Christians make embarrassing declarations in public that reveal their inadequate grasp of biology and geology. As a bonus, much of what we will survey, particularly the genetics, is relevant to our own medical health and that of our families and friends.

The first point to emphasise is that the biological understanding of evolution is far more restricted than the broader philosophical meanings mentioned above. The purpose of Darwinian theory is to explain the biological diversity that we see all around us on our planet. As we look out of the window, if we're fortunate enough to have a garden, or at least a few trees nearby, then we're looking at a world of immense diversity in which we are accustomed to encountering hundreds of different biological species in the normal course of everyday life. If our home or work keeps us far from visible living things, then we can always think about (though fortunately not see) the hundreds of species of bacteria and other organisms that inhabit our own bodies. Most people do not realise that they have about 10^{14} bacteria living in their bodies (that's a 10 followed by 13 more noughts), about 10 bacteria for every one of the roughly 10^{13} cells that make up our own bodily tissues. We are all walking zoos!

The purpose of biological evolutionary theory is to explain where this teeming mass of life comes from and to work out how different living things are connected with each other. Our planet contains an estimated 10–20 million living species. Where do they all come from and how? Solving a scientific challenge like this is a bit like a 'whodunit': how? where? when? The aim of science is to find the best explanation for these kinds of question. Answering such scientific questions as well as we can is in no sense a rival enterprise to the Christian's attempt to understand the biblical doctrine of creation as summarised in the last chapter. Far from it: describing God's world for the Christian is a holy enterprise and we will be concerned to understand all of God's works as accurately as we can.

Our purpose here is not to review the way in which Darwin's theory was originally put forward and then developed over the years into the theory that we have today[26], but instead to jump straight to the present. What do we understand by evolution today? In this chapter we will look at two of the key components that we need to understand as background information: dating methods plus genetics. These go well together because they are both rooted in the science of the present, based on experiments done in the laboratory today, but then extend back into the past in ways that will become clearer as we proceed. In Chapter Four we will explain the core concepts of evolutionary theory, then in Chapter Five consider the particular issue of speciation and how that relates to the fossil record.

Evolution is a long process

Biological evolution is a slow process taking place over many millions, in fact billions, of years. A brief overview of why scientists believe that the world is very old might therefore be useful by way of introduction[27].

The best current estimate for the age of the material which forms the earth is 4,566 million years. The universe is three times older, at 13,700 million years. Many people wonder how scientists can arrive at such dates, given the huge time-spans involved. Fortunately there are now many different methods that can be used to arrive at essentially the same result. It's a bit like drawing many different lines across a page – if they all intersect at exactly the same point, then we can be pretty sure that the intersection point has some particular significance.

Radioisotopes

The decay of radioisotopes provides one of the most important methods for dating the age of the earth as well as the dates of rocks and events since the earth began. The method relies on the fact that many atoms have unstable nuclei (the 'parent' nuclides) decaying spontaneously to a lower energy state (the 'daughter' nuclides). For example potassium-40 (the 'parent' nuclide) decays to argon-40 (the 'daughter' nuclide) at a fixed rate so that 50% of the parent is lost every 1,260 million years. This is known as the 'half-life' of the isotope, meaning the time it takes to lose half of the parent nuclide. This rate of decay is independent of physical and chemical conditions such as pressure, temperature and chemical binding forces, so radioisotopes make excellent 'clocks'.

The method works by measuring the ratio of the daughter to parent nuclide in a sample of rock or other material. This involves two main assumptions: first that no atoms of the daughter nuclide were present when the rock was formed, or at least that the initial ratio is known; and secondly that no parent or daughter atoms have been lost preferentially from the rock since its formation. In fact daughter atoms tend to escape preferentially when the rock is heated or otherwise disturbed, so if dates are inaccurate they tend to err in a 'young' direction because some of the daughter atoms have escaped. Fortunately it is often possible to use two or even three different parent–daughter isotope systems in the same sample, so providing an important crosscheck for consistency. For example, the most accurate methods in current use for dating geological rocks are uranium–lead and argon-40/argon-39 methods. These both rely on different decay systems, which enables internal consistency checks to be made that no isotopes have been gained or lost.

There are now more than forty different radioisotopes in regular use for dating methods, stretching all the way back across the earth's history. Half-lives of commonly used isotopic systems include 106,000 million years for samarium-147 to neodymium-143; 18,800 million years for rubidium-87 to strontium-87; 1,260 million years for potassium-40 to argon-40; and 700 million years for uranium-235 to lead-207. Shorter time periods are best investigated using isotopes generated in the atmosphere, such as 1.52 million years for beryllium-10; 300,000 years for chlorine-36; and 5,715 years for the well-known carbon-14. In most cases decay rates are known to within 2%, and uncertainties in the dates derived from radiometric decay are only a few per cent.

To understand how radioisotopes are used for dating the origins of our own planet, it is important to remember that the solar system was formed from a massive collision of material derived from meteorites which collected into discrete planetary bodies, including our own planet earth. So the date of the earth is more or less the same as the date of the formation of the solar system. How can we possibly measure an event that took place so long ago? The age of the earth has been determined as 4,566 ± 2 million years using the uranium–lead decay system on samples taken from lead ores in the crust of the earth, uranium being ideal for such measurements because of its long half-life (700 million years). On its own, knowledge of the present lead–uranium ratios only tells us the age since they separated from the parent mantle of the earth. The trick in using them to date the earth itself is to measure the uranium–lead ratios found in meteoritic material which has recently fallen to earth and to compare those ratios with the ratios found in the lead ores. Because such meteorites have remained isolated as they travelled through space since the formation of the solar system, they record the original isotopic ratios of the material which initially came together to form the earth.

At the beginning of the earth's history it was a molten fiery ball, but gradually cooled sufficiently for rocks to form. The oldest rocks with well-established dates occur in western Greenland, dating from 3,806 ± 2 million years ago and showing signs of submersion in water, suggesting that oceans already existed at this early stage of the earth's history. In comparison the ages of most fossils of animals and plants seem quite young, since they date from only the last 10% of the earth's history. Because we will need to keep referring later to the great geological eras that cover this last slice of the earth's history, the terminology in common usage is illustrated in Figure 1.

Era	Period	Epoch	Myr BP (approx)
Cenozoic	Quaternary	Recent	
			0.01
		Pleistocene	
			1.8
	Neogene { Tertiary	Pliocene	
			5.3
		Miocene	
			24
		Oligocene	
			34
	Palaeogene {	Eocene	
			55
		Palaeocene	
			65
Mesozoic	Cretaceous		
			144
	Jurassic		
			206
	Triassic		
			251
Palaeozoic	Permian		
			290
	Carboniferous	Pennsylvanian	
			323
		Mississippian	
			354
	Devonian		
			417
	Silurian		
			443
	Ordovician		
			490
	Cambrian		
			543

Figure 1. The main recent geological era. Myr BP means 'Millions of years before present'.

Measuring cycles

If the fixed decay rates of radioisotopes were the only means that we had of measuring the ages of rocks and the fossils found in them, then we might worry that we were becoming too dependent on a single dating method. But, as already mentioned, there are several other methods for measurement that depend on quite different principles.

One of these methods depends on Milankovitch cycles, named after the Serbian civil engineer and mathematician Milutin Milankovitch. These refer to long-term cycles in climate patterns that are caused by three different well-understood changes in the earth's orbit round the sun, which is in the shape of an ellipse. The eccentricity is a measure of the departure of this ellipse from circularity and this produces 100,000- and 413,000-year cycles. The second type of cycle comes from the fact that the earth's tilt on its axis changes gradually, generating cycles of 40,000 years. The third type of cycle arises from what is known in astronomy as 'precession' – the change in the direction of the earth's axis of rotation relative to the fixed stars, which happens with a period of roughly 26,000 years.

The importance of these various cycles for our present discussion is that their impact can be measured on earth. For example, they have rhythmic climatic effects on ancient sediments, allowing precision dating back to 30 million years[28]. These dates can then be matched with those obtained from radioactive decay methods.

A second type of irregular cyclic changes, which in this case is useful for dating rocks, depends on their magnetic polarity. Fluid motions in the earth's liquid outer core create a dynamo which generates a global dipole magnetic field roughly aligned with the earth's axis of rotation. The magnetic field reverses its polarity on average 2–3 times per million years. Magnetic North becomes South and Magnetic South becomes North. Since rocks bearing magnetised minerals record the direction of the magnetic field at the time they were deposited, the polarity reversals can be recognised and used to date the volcanic basement of the sea floor back 170 million years. This was the key to the recognition that the sea floor is spreading, leading to the plate tectonics theory, which in the 1960s revolutionised geological interpretation of the earth's history.

Counting rings and core layers

Everyone knows that counting the rings in a tree trunk allows us to estimate the age of the tree, some trees being as much as 4,000 or more years old. What is less well known is that individual tree ring widths vary according to local climate changes. If all the trees in one region exhibit the same climate-controlled patterns, tree rings can be counted back beyond the lifespan of individual trees by finding older timber with sufficient overlap to correlate the distinctive tree-ring pattern from the younger to the older. A unique tree-ring chronology has been built from trees in central Germany extending back beyond 8400 BC and similar chronologies have been developed elsewhere.

Counting the annual layers from ice cores drilled out of the Antarctic ice-cap can take us much further back in time than this. One 3,190 metre (10,500 feet) core has now reached ice 740,000 years old[29]. Counting annual layers in the uppermost ice is unambiguous, but at greater depths, as layers become compacted, it is possible that some annual layers may be overlooked, or that near the base of the ice sheet re-melting or folding has distorted the annual layering. Conservative estimates of the errors in counting annual layers increase from about 2% at 11,000 years to 10% at 150,000 years ago. Huge amounts of data can be obtained from the analysis of these core layers, including the composition and temperature of the atmosphere at a given time, as well as the existence of dust and other pollutants. Volcanic ash and chemicals are washed out of the atmosphere by rain and snow-falls to end up as tell-tale signatures in particular layers, pointing to high volcanic activity in certain years.

Whether it is radioactive decay, cyclical changes in the earth's orbit, flipping of the magnetic field, or the more prosaic counting of ice layers or tree rings, all of these various dating methods combine to form a powerful set of tools for establishing the extremely long periods of time required for evolution to occur. As we shall see later on, changes that occur in genetic material also provide a useful 'internal clock' for estimating age.

What are genes?

To understand evolution it is first necessary to understand a little bit about genes. Genes are encoded by a chemical called DNA[30]. All the information for our inheritance, from our blue eyes to our knobbly knees, is encoded in our DNA. This consists of two strands of chemical 'letters' of the genetic alphabet, called nucleotides, which are wound round each other like intertwined coiled springs – the famous double helix. Each nucleotide on one strand pairs exactly with its opposite number on the other strand (known as 'base-pairs'), so that when a cell divides each DNA molecule makes copies of itself by 'unzipping' the two strands, each of which then replicates itself to make two 'daughter' DNA molecules (as Figure 2 illustrates).

There are four different nucleotides which comprise the genetic 'alphabet' and it is their precise sequence, like beads with four different colours on a string, that provides the genetic information needed to build living organisms. Defining a 'gene' has become much more complex over the past decade due to our increased understanding of the various ways in which genes encode information[31]. In general we can define a 'gene' as any DNA segment that provides information needed for the development and functioning of the organism. Three main types of genetic information are involved: first there are the 'traditional' genes that encode proteins, the molecules that make up living things and that enable them to function as they do. Proteins consist of strings of 20 different amino acids and their properties are entirely dependent on the precise amino acid sequence, defined by the sequence of the nucleotides in the DNA[32]. Genes which encode proteins are the best known of the genes, so sometimes the term 'gene' is used just with these types of nucleotide sequence in mind, but over the past decade it has become increasingly obvious that other DNA segments besides these 'traditional genes' carry vital genetic information.

Most of the DNA is found in the nucleus (not all cells have a nucleus), a membrane-enclosed sac-like structure in the

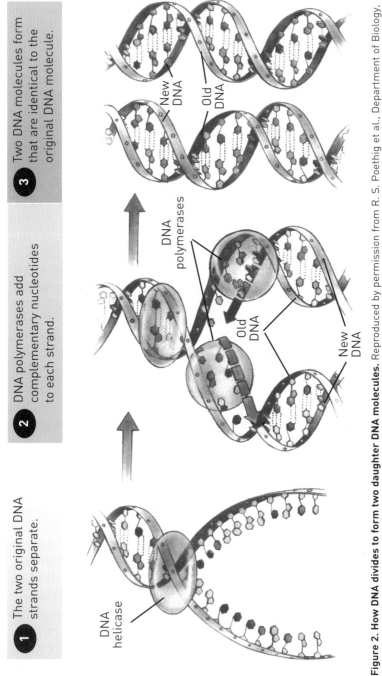

1 The two original DNA strands separate.

2 DNA polymerases add complementary nucleotides to each strand.

3 Two DNA molecules form that are identical to the original DNA molecule.

DNA helicase

DNA polymerases

Old DNA

New DNA

New DNA

Old DNA

Figure 2. How DNA divides to form two daughter DNA molecules. Reproduced by permission from R. S. Poethig et al., Department of Biology, University of Pennsylvania, USA (adapted from George Johnson and Peter Raven, *Biology*, Holt Rinehart and Winston, 2004).

middle of each cell which acts as the command centre for cellular operations. But protein synthesis occurs in the cell's cytoplasm, the part between the nucleus and the outer cell membrane (wall). So there has to be a way of getting the information from the genes out of the nucleus and into the cytoplasm. This job is carried out by a chemical very similar to DNA called, suitably enough, messenger RNA (or mRNA for short)[33]. The DNA translates its code into the RNA which then dutifully shuttles off to the cytoplasm where it 'downloads' its information into the amino-acid sequence of proteins by a complex process, the details of which needn't concern us here.

The second type of information encoded by DNA is to do with regulation – the timing of switching protein-encoding genes on and off, and the control of how much protein is made from each of these genes. The third type of 'gene' are those that don't encode proteins at all, but instead encode various types of RNA which, unlike the mRNA mentioned above, are not involved in protein synthesis, but have independent regulatory roles in their own right which are being increasingly understood. Some of this newly discovered class of RNAs are involved in regulating how much of any given protein is made from one particular protein-coding gene. They do this by chopping up mRNA once it has been made, or in other ways suppressing the role of mRNA. Conversely, they may even be involved in boosting the expression of genes in some cases[34].

The sum total of the DNA nucleotide sequence in a given organism is known as its 'genome', so the term 'genomics' refers to the sequencing and ensuing comparisons of the genomes from various organisms. The complete genome sequences (sequences of all the nucleotide 'letters' in the DNA) from hundreds of organisms have now been determined, leading to fascinating new insights into the ways in which all living organisms are connected. Our own DNA contains about 3 billion nucleotides and the draft sequence was announced with great fanfare in 2001 with a much fuller and more accurate version following along in 2004 which has an error rate of less than 1 in every 100,000 nucleotide base-pairs. We now know that we have only about 20,000–25,000 protein-coding genes. The uncertainty of the exact number of genes arises from a small percentage of the DNA which is really difficult to sequence for technical reasons, and also the possibility that some genes have been missed, or mis-identified as functional genes.

The completion of the sequencing of the human genome has already led to important discoveries about the links between genes and diseases such as diabetes, rheumatoid arthritis and cancer. In the future lies the rapid sequencing of individual human genomes that will no doubt one day be routinely stored on the computers of our doctors' surgeries. The cost of sequencing is rapidly coming down: the '$20,000 genome sequence' is on the way, and there is a funding programme to generate a $1000 human genome sequence by 2014[35]. The complete sequence of the entrepreneurial Craig Venter's genome was published in 2007 at a cost of considerably more than $1000[36]. In fact this was the first sequence obtained from the two copies of each DNA molecule that all human cells contain, analysed separately, which is why it was heralded as the first 'full' genome sequence. Comparison of the two copies revealed more than 4 million variations between them, and no less than 44% of Venter's protein-coding genes contained a genetic difference between the two copies. So it appears that we may be containing more genetic variation within our DNA than we had first imagined[37].

In this context it is also worth highlighting the fact that the completion of the great project to sequence the whole human genome has been coordinated by a committed Christian, Francis Collins, who recounts his conversion from atheism to personal faith in Christ in his bestselling book *The Language of God*[38]. All those who have the privilege, as I do, of carrying out research on the functions of genes, will be able to share in Francis Collins' own sense of wonder at the complexity of the genome when he writes that:

> The work of a scientist involved in this project, particularly a scientist who has the joy of also being a Christian, is a work of discovery which can also be a form of worship. As a scientist, one of the most exhilarating experiences is to learn something...that no human has understood before. To have a

chance to see the glory of creation, the intricacy of it, the beauty of it, is really an experience not to be matched. Scientists who do not have a personal faith in God also undoubtedly experience the exhilaration of discovery. But to have that joy of discovery, mixed together with the joy of worship, is truly a powerful moment for a Christian who is also a scientist.

Understanding genetics in general, and genomes in particular, is a great way to appreciate more fully the wonder of God's creative works, but appreciation takes understanding, and that requires some work on our part!

As we might guess from the fact that we have 25,000 protein-coding genes or less, such genes are quite sparse in our own DNA. In fact less than 2% of our DNA encodes proteins and about 3% is thought to be involved in encoding the other kinds of regulatory information mentioned above. But that 5% of 'useful DNA' might yet go up much further. It is an unfortunate fact that very early on in DNA research, the DNA not used for encoding proteins was written off rather dismissively by some scientists as 'junk DNA'. Big mistake. It is now becoming clear that much more than 5% of our DNA might have important functions, though the jury is still out as to how high that percentage might be[39]. A big surprise is the finding that mRNA comes not only from protein-coding genes, but also from many other parts of the DNA that have, as yet, no known functions. A major project called ENCODE ('The Encyclopaedia of DNA Elements') is currently under way and its aim is to identify all the parts of DNA that are functional[40]. The field of genomics is rapidly turning upside down many previously held ideas in genetics, and there will almost certainly be many more surprises to come.

One of those surprises is already with us: the great variety in the size of genomes, which seems to bear no relationship to the complexity of the organism involved. Common sense predictions might dictate that the more complex a living organism becomes, the bigger and more complex become its genome and the number of genes required to encode all that complexity. But common sense in this case is quite wrong. Onions, for example, have 17 billion nucleotide base-pairs in their DNA compared to our measly 3 billion, and I have yet to meet the person prepared to argue that this means that onions are biologically more complex than we are! The pufferfish's genome is the smallest of all the vertebrates sequenced so far at 350 million nucleotide base-pairs, but another fish, the marbled lungfish, is the largest at 130 billion base-pairs, nearly 400 times as many[41]. One really tiny bacterium, which rejoices in the name of *Carsonella ruddii* and lives inside insects, has a mere 159,622 base-pairs in its DNA, and can only get away with having such a small genome because it is so dependent on its host.

Instead of being related to the complexity of the organism, the size of genomes seems to depend more on the amount of 'parasitic DNA' that they contain. This includes a large amount of so-called transposon DNA that is found in genomes, including our own, where transposons make up nearly half our genomes. Transposons are the so-called 'jumping genes' and comprise multiple copies of easily identifiable repeated sequences that are incorporated into genomes during the course of evolution. They have a restless lifestyle, often jumping from one chromosome to another, and it is increasingly being realised that far from being mere 'junk', some of them contribute diversity to genomes that turns out to be functionally useful. In addition, genomes contain plenty of retroviral DNA sequences; 8% of the human genome comes from retroviruses. Despite the rare exceptions just mentioned, overall this 'parasitic DNA' has no known function and is simply replicated along with the rest of our genomes, in the process providing a valuable record of our evolutionary past, as we shall consider further below.

The number of protein-encoding genes also varies considerably among organisms. It takes only a few thousand genes to build a bacterium, 5,000 to build a yeast cell, and about 15,000 genes to build a worm or a fruit fly. But as with the variation in the total size of genomes, there are plenty of anomalies as well in the varied numbers of protein-encoding genes required to build different organisms. The extreme example of the bacterium *Carsonella ruddii* mentioned above has only 182 genes, understandable when we realise that it's a freeloader, getting lots of goodies by living inside insects. But why do plants need so many genes? *Arabidopsis*, a small plant of the mustard family, has an estimated 26,500 genes, whereas rice has as many as 41,000 genes. It turns out that much of this expansion in gene number is explained by the duplication of genes that has occurred during the course of evolution. This is not the same as the duplication of the DNA which occurs as a normal part of cell division, but refers to the permanent retention of duplicate genes in the genome over many generations, an event that can be advantageous for the organism[42].

The relative paucity of protein-encoding genes in a large sea of 'other' DNA in most genomes means that reading the genetic story is a bit like coming to a large encyclopaedia of many volumes and finding that the first few hundred pages are blank. For the sake of the analogy, if we colour the pages red to indicate protein encoding regions, and yellow for DNA that encodes regulatory information, then after the few hundred blank pages we come across a few red pages, then some yellow pages, followed by more flipping through another hundred blank pages before you get to the next interesting bit.

Could there be any good reasons for scattering key genes around the genome in what appears at first glance to be a rather random kind of way? One reason could be similar to the strategy that the British RAF adopted during the Second World War when they scattered their fighter bases around the country in an attempt to minimise enemy bombing damage. Our genomes continue to be bombarded with retroviruses and the 'copy-and-paste' transposons which every now and again incorporate parasitic DNA right in the middle of a functional gene, disabling it and causing disease. In fact it has been estimated that two of the major classes of transposable elements are added to human DNA once every 10 live births[43]. By 'padding' the key 'command-control' DNA regions with lots of interspersed DNA regions that don't really matter, parasitic DNA has much less chance of landing up smack in the middle of a key information-containing gene. But even so, human diseases caused by such hits on 'key targets' still occasionally happen[44].

As for the variable size of genomes, there may be some good

reasons for this, though the explanations remain somewhat speculative. Larger genomes need larger nuclei to house them, which in turn means the cells must be larger too. This can be a disadvantage for getting oxygen into muscle cells, for example, because the bigger the cells, the slower the uptake of oxygen. This might explain why flying creatures that have high rates of metabolism, like bats and birds, tend to have smaller genomes. Conversely it's useful to have a big genome if you want to slow down your rate of cell replication, which in turn slows down development. Salamanders, for example, have big genomes, and they do not undergo metamorphosis, so there is no particular hurry in their development. Contrast this with desert frogs that have to undergo metamorphosis to adults in a very short space of time before the desert pool dries out. Such frogs have some of the smallest genomes yet known amongst the amphibians.

Chromosomes and DNA packaging

The tight packaging of DNA into cells is one of the most remarkable feats of biological engineering in the living world. I was reminded of this fact recently in a rather unusual way. At the church I attend in Cambridge we baptised an undergraduate in the natural sciences who had come to a personal, saving faith in Christ from a completely atheistic background. As is usual in our church, just before being baptised she explained publicly to the whole congregation how she had become a Christian, telling us she had become convinced there must be a God while sitting through a standard university biochemistry lecture, hearing the amazing story of how two metres (about six feet) of DNA are packaged into a single cell. Of course the lecturer was not talking in religious terms at all, but she described to us how the beauty of that engineering feat overwhelmed her as she listened, giving her the deep intuition there must be a God, so leading her onward in her personal pilgrimage to put her trust in this creator God through Christ. Truly natural theology at work!

How does that DNA packaging work? Our bodies have two types of cells: germ cells and somatic cells. The germ cells refer to the eggs and sperm used to pass our DNA inheritance on to the next generation. The somatic cells refer to all the rest, the cells that actually make up our bodies, specialised into more than 200 different types of tissue (like hearts, brains, kidneys etc). Each of the approximately 10^{13} cells in our bodies contains an astonishing six foot length of DNA packaged with proteins to form 23 pairs of chromosomes. Now that is definitely counter-intuitive because cells are very small: typically human cells are only about 10 microns in diameter[45]. In fact if all the tightly-packed DNA in all the cells in a single human being were stretched out, it would reach to the moon and back 8,000 times![46] As millions of our cells divide every second, each individual cell produces thousands of miles of newly copied DNA every minute. We are all walking photocopying machines, but fortunately we don't have to think about it – DNA replication is on automatic.

Different animals and plants have different numbers of chromosomes, humans possessing 22 pairs of identical chromosomes, whereas the 23rd pair is either XX for females or XY for males, thereby defining our sex differences. The germ cells contain only single chromosomes, and sperm contain an X or a Y chromosome in roughly 50:50 proportions. Since all eggs contain a single X chromosome, if the sperm with an X wins the race first up the Fallopian tubules to fertilise the egg then you will be female, but if it's a Y chromosome sperm, then you will end up male. Fortunately the swimming abilities of X and Y sperm are pretty similar, which helps to keep the population reasonably balanced between male and female.

Each chromosome consists of a single molecule of double-helical DNA wound round with lots of proteins to form a mixture called chromatin, as Figure 3 illustrates. These interactions between protein and DNA are crucial in regulating which genes are switched on and off[47]. So we can never think of DNA in isolation, but as part of a dynamic system, constantly active: the chromatin can either be in a closed conformation in which the flow of information to the mRNA is low, or in an open active conformation in which lots of mRNA is being produced. Imagine a busy DNA dockside with ships constantly moving in and out, loading and unloading their cargoes. The closed chromatin itself is packaged even further into

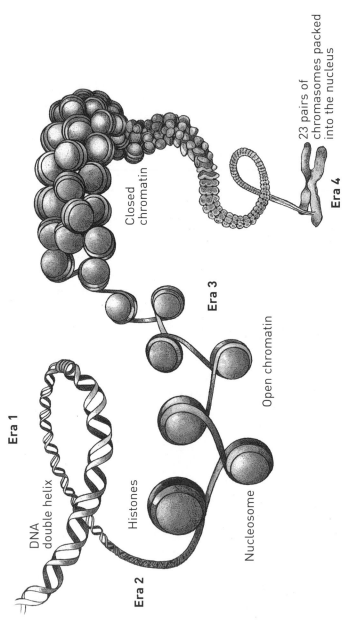

Figure 3. DNA is packaged with histone proteins to form chromatin, the central units of which are the nucleosomes, which then pack up even further to make chromosomes. The 'eras' refer to the eras of biological research during which the various stages of this amazing packing process and its functional consequences began to be understood. [Reprinted by permission from Macmillan Publishers Ltd: *Nature 448*, 548–549, 2007.]

tight bundles which make up the chromosomal structures that can be seen by staining cells to reveal the karyotype, meaning the pattern of paired chromosomes 1–23 plus the sex chromosomes XX or XY (at least in mammals like us).

The total genome of an organism is spread right across all its chromosomes, so one of the tasks in sequencing genomes is to construct a map of each chromosome describing the precise position on the chromosome of each gene. Fortunately we have pairs of identical chromosomes, in other words two complete copies of our genomes in each cell, because that means we have a back-up information system in case one fails. In practice we are probably all carrying many deleterious or even lethally defective genes, but we will usually never know what they are because our back-up gene on the other chromosome of the pair does the same job just as well. The exceptions to this general rule are fortunately quite rare, occurring when even a single defective gene is sufficient to cause disease.

How do genes build living organisms?

If we extract some DNA from cells and look at it in a test-tube, then all we can see is little strands of white, pasty kind of material. It is truly remarkable that the information contained in this DNA – in genomes – can be translated into complex living entities like whales, kangaroos and human beings. Anyone who has had the privilege of having children will know the sense of awe that comes from seeing a baby born after all those months of cell growth, tissue shaping and brain development.

Genomes are like symphony orchestras which have to play together in a coordinated way to generate the needed outputs. For the sake of argument, let's say we have 20,000 genes, so imagine a vast orchestra with 20,000 different instruments, conducted not by a single maestro, but via a complex interactive network of messages. And great banks of instruments of a certain type are dedicated to certain kinds of gene product. First we have the violins, the structural proteins that make up the bulk of our bodily tissues. Then over here we have the trumpets, genes encoding the enzymes that catalyse all the bodily processes and make them run at the correct rate. The flutes are the receptors embedded in the cell walls that enable messages to be passed from the outside of the cell to the inside. The drums are the genes that make regulatory proteins that control the switching on and off of other genes. And there are many other instruments besides, but the key point is that all the 20,000 genes have to cooperate in harmony to produce a healthy living organism. One single discordant note may be sufficient to spoil the whole symphony.

This is why the term 'selfish gene' is not a very helpful metaphor for describing the role genes play in living organisms. In reality each gene is dependent on the actions of many other genes. Genomes are systems for building organisms in a cooperative, interactive way; there is nothing 'selfish' about that. And the functioning of one gene may change considerably depending on the presence or absence of variants of other genes. In a real orchestra a musician playing a particular instrument may flourish if the environment provided by the rest of the orchestra generates the best interactions to play a great symphony, but equally the sound of even a very gifted player will quickly be spoilt if the rest of the performers are off-key. So it is with genes: the very same gene can exert a rather different effect in building and running the organism depending on the company that it keeps.

By this time you might be wondering how as few as 20,000 genes can encode sufficient proteins to run all the complex organs and systems of the body like brains, livers and kidneys. There are some wonderful tricks in place to make this possible.

The first is that many genes can generate different versions of themselves by a process known as 'alternative splicing'. When the mRNA is made from the DNA it undergoes a slimming-down exercise in which only the sections of information actually needed to encode the protein are included in the final product. But the trimming can happen in different ways to make a range of final variant mRNA molecules, each of which encodes slightly different proteins, which may all have different functions. For example I have spent the last 17 years working on a molecule known as CD45 (immunologists have a nasty habit of labelling different proteins with boring numbers). The CD45 gene undergoes alternative splicing to generate eight different versions of the CD45 protein which are important in regulating the body's defence against attack by viruses and bacteria.

The second method for generating diversity from a limited number of genes is by chemically modifying the functions of the proteins once they are made, for example by adding phosphate groups to particular amino acids in a process known as phosphorylation. The addition of even one phosphate group can profoundly change the properties of the protein, for example by switching an enzyme (a protein with catalytic function) on or off. These protein modifications are often reversible, so are used to control the dynamic processes responsible for cell growth and division. There are at least ten different ways of chemically modifying proteins and more are still being discovered[48]. We do not yet have a complete catalogue of all the slightly different chemically modified versions of all the proteins that comprise our own bodies, but once that catalogue is complete, putting this number together with the number of gene products generated by alternative splicing, it would not surprise me at all if the final total of different versions of our proteins generated by our 20,000 genes surpasses one million. Combinatorial systems of this kind are hugely powerful in generating a vast array of diversity, as every combinatorial chemist knows who is involved in making hundreds of slightly different versions of a drug for pharmaceutical purposes.

Understanding the way that genomes work is really important for understanding evolution, as we shall see in a moment, and appreciating the kinds of differences that exist among genomes is also vital. Firstly there are the slight differences that exist between different individuals of the same species. For example, every human individual differs from every other in the world by about one in every thousand of the nucleotides in their DNA, as well as other quite significant differences in sections of their DNA that have only recently been identified[49]. In addition, a further recent surprising discovery is that human individuals, as well as members of other species, differ in the actual number of copies that we have of various genes[50]. This is work in progress, but it may turn out that many hundreds of our genes can exist in our genomes in copies ranging from three upwards instead of our normal two copies (one on each chromosome). Most of the time the variation in copy number seems to make no difference, despite the extra protein that is made from the extra copies. But other times it can make a huge difference and be the cause of disease, as in Parkinson's disease where people born with a third copy of the gene encoding the brain protein alpha synuclein are predisposed to the disease. On the more positive side, it has been speculated that the multiple copies that our genomes contain of a gene called aquaporin 7, encoding a protein that transports water and sugary compounds into cells, may give us endurance during long-distance running, something to meditate on when you next try running the London marathon!

For medical reasons the International HapMap project aims to map the diversity that exists among individuals all round the world[51]. To take DNA samples, all that's necessary is to swill your mouth around and spit into a clean receptacle – it is that simple, as every reader of crime novels knows by now! The initial goal is to focus on those one in a thousand nucleotides that vary among individuals. Approximately 90% of this variation can be explained by about 10 million differences. That might sound like a lot but it represents only one relatively common difference for every 300 nucleotides in our DNA. Why are these differences restricted to a relatively few DNA sites? One reason is that some differences are lethal. In order to be alive we absolutely must have the sequence exactly right, so not surprisingly we don't find any variation in those nucleotides. Another reason is that we are all descended (of course) from other humans, and so once a variant comes into a population, it will spread gradually round the world as the descendants travel and have children. The particular set of nucleotide variants on a particular chromosome is known as the 'haplotype', hence the abbreviation 'Hap' in 'HapMap'. Taken altogether, the average genetic differences distinguishing individuals may represent as much as 0.5% of our genomes, more than the 0.1% difference that we thought just a few years ago.

Overall we should be happy (to interpret 'Hap'Map in a different way) about this genetic diversity, because if we were all genetically identical then we would look like one giant cloning exercise! In other words we would all look identical and life would be very boring. I say 'look identical' not 'be identical' advisedly, because of course our choices and our environment make a huge difference to who we are – there is no room here for genetic determinism – but having made that important proviso, it is also the case that our genes are very important in providing us with the basic parameters of our lives as far as our physical existence is concerned. Identical twins (whose genomes are identical) are no more and no less unique and distinctive individuals made in the image of God than anyone else, but if the whole of humanity were genetically identical we would certainly have a harder time recognising our value as unique individuals loved by God. At the same time, medically the HapMap project and other similar investigations of human genomes are revealing fascinating connections between our genetic haplotypes and our chances of developing certain diseases along life's way. We will be considering the theological implications of genetic diversity later on in Chapter Thirteen.

A different kind of genetic diversity is that which exists among different species and here the sequencing of the entire genomes of many different species has provided some fascinating new insights. Look at a mouse, a 12-year-old boxer dog called Tasha and a typical human and they all appear quite different, but all are mammals (animals which suckle their young) and it turns out that their genomes have some remarkable similarities. Tasha is not any old dog because she had her whole genome sequenced and published in 2005. In fact it now looks as if all mammals probably have a basic 'kit' of around 20,000 or so protein-coding genes necessary for generating mammalian types of being. Virtually all (99%) of the protein-coding genes in both the mouse and the dog can be found in the human, with minor changes in their sequences, although it is reassuring to discover that humans have some extra genes as well. This explains why mice, in particular, provide such brilliant models for studying genetics and human disease; at the genetic and cellular level they display striking similarities – and they breed a lot faster than dogs.

Given this level of similarity, one might wonder how we can end up looking (and being) so different from mice. There are certainly differences in protein-coding genes that make a real difference; but the real answer to that question brings us back to the main theme of this section: how do genes build bodies? The answer is, by means of regulatory genes. Imagine that the basic building materials used to build an ancient city like Cambridge (where I'm writing this) represent the mammalian repertoire of protein-coding genes. The huge diversity of buildings in Cambridge and other medieval cities depend on the decisions of the architects who put the building blocks into their diverse different shapes. In this analogy it is the architects that represent the key regulatory genes. They make the big decisions about how the building blocks are assembled. And a change of architect could change everything.

One of the most famous collections of regulatory genetic 'architects' are known as the Homeobox genes (or Hox genes for short) which regulate the segmental pattern so characteristic of vertebrate animal bodies. Reach down and feel your ribs (hopefully you can feel them) – the segmental pattern indicated by your ribs is generated by your Hox genes. The role of these genes was initially worked out in fruit flies (*Drosophila*) that have only four chromosomes and 13,676 genes, and also multiply rather quickly, making them a favourite tool of the geneticist. There are eight Hox genes located in a specific region (the 'homeobox') of the fly's third chromosome and each gene is responsible for shaping the development of body regions at different positions along the body axis of the fly. The genes are arranged neatly in order along the chromosome in the same sequence as the eight body segments of the fly (see Figure 4). The Hox genes encode 'transcription factors', proteins that in turn regulate a whole array of other genes responsible for building body segments during development, ensuring that wings, legs and other appendages are formed in the correct place[52]. In fact just a few hundred genes are involved in the complex construction and patterning of the fruit fly. Geneticists can manipulate single key control genes and legs will grow out of the fly's head or wings will grow where legs should be. Bodies are built up in modules during development. Remove the tinman gene and Drosophila will be born without a heart; ablate another gene called Pax-6 (actu-

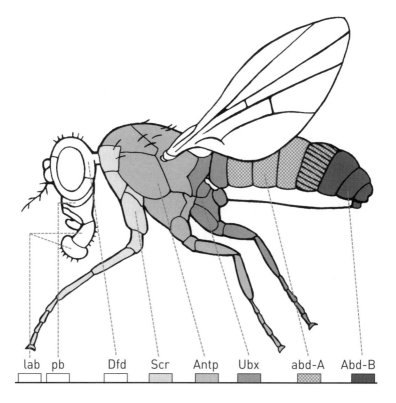

lab   pb   Dfd   Scr   Antp   Ubx   abd-A   Abd-B

Figure 4. The Hox genes of a fruit fly. The eight genes are given names like lab, pb etc. and are arranged along a fly chromosome in the same order as the body region that each one regulates, as shown. The development of each body region, indicated by different shading, is regulated by one Hox gene. [Reproduced by permission of Orion Publishing from S.B. Carroll, *Endless Forms Most Beautiful*, London: Weidenfeld & Nicolson, 2005. Figure 3.4, p. 62.]

ally Pax-6 is the name of this gene in mammals, where it does the same job) and the flies will have no eyes. Suppress the actions of a single control gene (called Cnox-2) in a jellyfish and it grows multiple heads[53].

Old-fashioned railway signal boxes are furnished with a long row of big levers. Imagine that you have before you a row of just ten big master control levers all coloured differently. Behind the row of ten, there is another row of 100 levers, arranged in batches of ten, each batch attached to one of the ten master control levers and coloured the same. Then behind the 100 levers there is yet another array of 1,000 smaller levers, arranged in batches of 100, each batch of 100 regulated by a batch of ten levers in the second row and coloured the same. Now try out the system. Get hold of the red master control lever and pull it gently and watch as a wave of red levers also begin to move, first in the batch of ten, then in the batch of 100. Pull the master green lever and you see ripples of smaller green levers moving into action. This gives some idea as to how the key regulatory genes like Hox genes exert their effects, acting like big master control levers in sending a wave of instructions down the line to build wings, eyes and legs during development. In practice it is the precise timing of the activation of each genetic lever that is so crucial.

These kinds of combinatorial systems occur frequently in biology, helping to explain how a relatively small number of genes can be used to build complex systems during the development of the organism. They also help to explain why mammals as different as mice, dogs, elephants and humans develop to become such different beings despite the huge similarities in their genomes[54]. Tiny differences in the principal genetic 'control levers', and in the way that they are organised, can exert effects out of all proportion to their size. Tweak a tiny rudder and even very large ships have to obey and change course. That insight is very important for understanding how evolution works, a topic to which we shall now turn.

Chapter 4:

What Do We Mean By Evolution? Natural Selection and Reproductive Success

Evolution – the big idea

With some basic information about dating, genetics and genomes now in place, we are better positioned to explain how evolution works. The theory of evolution consists of two 'big ideas' joined together and we need to understand both to make sense of the overall process (see Figure 5). First, there is the generation of diversity in the genome, for example by mutations of various kinds which occasionally make a difference to the ability of the resulting organism to survive and reproduce. Second, there is the ensuing process of natural selection, whereby genomes generating organisms with slightly better survival and more offspring tend to be the ones passed on to succeeding generations. The reverse is also true: genomes generating organisms with slightly or significantly worse survival and fewer offspring are less likely to be passed on. Therefore evolution is a two-step process: a device to generate diversity followed by a method for testing that diversity by natural selection. We shall now consider each of these steps in greater detail.

Generating genetic diversity

We have already introduced the idea of diversity among genomes. All the humans in the world differ by an average of one nucleotide per thousand, plus some other differences already mentioned. All the mammals in the world, that have

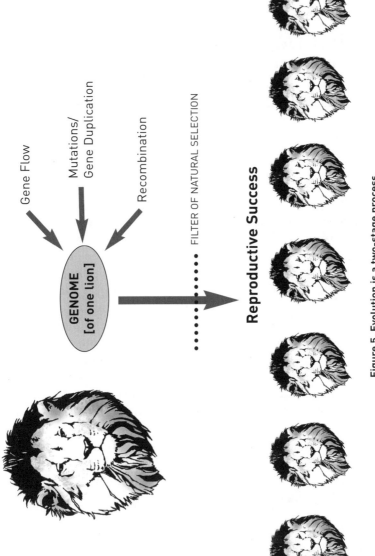

Figure 5. Evolution is a two-stage process.

been studied so far, differ by much more than that but their genomes are still remarkably similar. The genomes of monkeys, ferns and bacteria differ by even more. How do all these differences accumulate in the different genomes? There are three main mechanisms: mutations, sexual reproduction and gene flow, and we will explain them in turn.

'Mutations' refer to any heritable changes in genes occurring as a result of physical alterations to the DNA itself. For example, mutations can occur when DNA is exposed to irradiation or to certain chemicals – hence the stringent health and safety regulations that surround the use of radioisotopes or mutagenic chemicals in the laboratory. Mutations can also occur when DNA divides. Normally one strand in the DNA double helix is copied very faithfully into the daughter strand, and the fidelity of replication is checked by proof-reading enzymes (catalytic proteins) that shuttle up and down checking that the replication was carried out properly. But very occasionally a change gets through the checking system without being detected, just as happens when even several proof-readers can miss an error in the text. In one sense we can call these types of mutations 'errors', but error is a loaded word in this context. For example, the changes that occur most often make no difference to the organism (they are said to be 'neutral'), whereas sometimes they are bad for the organism in terms of its ability to survive and reproduce, and very occasionally they represent changes that are beneficial by those criteria.

Many different types of mutation can occur in DNA. 'Point mutations' refer to changes in a single letter of the genetic alphabet, a switch from one nucleotide to another. Sometimes this makes no difference at all to the protein encoded by the gene for the simple reason that the genetic code is redundant: three nucleotides in a row (a triplet codon) encode a single amino acid in a protein, but often more than one triplet encodes the same amino acid. For example the nucleotides GCA and GCG both encode the amino acid alanine, so if a mutation in a gene changes the A to a G it will make no difference to the protein that is made.

Yet many times nucleotide bases are changed that do make

a difference to the amino acid encoded, and these kinds of differences, analysed in many different human populations, are the focus of much interest in the HapMap project mentioned above, because the subtle changes in protein function ensuing from such changes can be really important for our health and well being.

Other mutations completely disrupt the gene and stop it making a protein altogether. This can happen because a nucleotide base is deleted and so the meaning of the whole of the rest of the gene is lost. If we imagine the same principle of triplet codons applied to the English language, we then have no difficulty in picking out the sentence: thecatatetherat, but if we are only able to read letters in triplets from the beginning, then with a mutation deleting the third letter we would completely lose the meaning of: thc ata tet her at.

Just as we have capital letters and full stops to indicate the beginning and end of sentences, so genes have 'start codons' and 'stop codons' that tell the molecular machinery transcribing the message into mRNA where to start and stop. Sometimes a mutation will introduce an aberrant stop codon right into the middle of the gene so that a truncated mRNA is made, leading to the synthesis of a truncated protein that is unlikely to be useful for its normal function, but which might on occasion acquire a new function because of its novel structure.

Other mutations involve deletions of whole sections of DNA, either involving genes or not, or insertions of sections of DNA that were not there before. Such 'insertion/deletion' types of mutation comprise many of the differences that are seen between the genomes of related species.

Gene duplication is another type of mutation that has played a vital role in the evolutionary process. Normally during DNA replication and cell division the same number of genes are passed on to the daughter cells. But occasionally a segment of DNA is duplicated twice and passed on in the germ line cells, and occasionally this segment may contain one or more genes. There are now sophisticated methods for detecting these gene duplication events. For example a comparison of human, bonobo, chimp, gorilla and orangutan DNA revealed more than 1,000 genes that had been duplicated and that were specific to one of these species[55]. Copy number expansions were particularly pronounced in human (134 genes specifically duplicated in humans) and include a number of genes thought to be involved in the structure and function of the brain. Taking the human genome as a whole, more than 20% of genes are thought to be the product of the duplication and evolutionary emergence of ancestral genes, and in plants the proportions are much higher. Gene duplication provides an important way of generating novelty during the course of evolution because with time the duplicated gene can accumulate other types of mutation that provide it with new functions, different from those of its original parental gene. In other cases there is a 'division of labour' in which the two duplicated genes evolve to carry out different aspects of the single job carried out by the original gene[56].

Some mutations are so large that they take place at the chromosomal level involving segments of chromosomes or even the whole chromosome itself. Remember that when we talk about mutations occurring at the 'chromosomal level' we are still talking about DNA because each chromosome contains one large double-helical molecule of DNA. But these larger types of diversity within the genome are best analysed using a distinct set of techniques that detect such big changes, so this type of mutation tends to be treated separately. The most common changes at the chromosomal level occur by inversions and translocations. Inversions occur when a segment of DNA is flipped around through 180° on the same chromosome. Translocations occur when a segment of DNA from one chromosome is swapped over with a segment from a different chromosome, either of the same length or a different length. This means that genes might now come under quite different types of regulatory control in their new environment. At other times a completely new gene is formed by this method as the translocation cuts one gene in half and joins it to the other half of a gene from the other chromosome. Individual chromosomes can fuse head-to-head and form one much larger chromosome that is then passed on in the germ cells, permanently changing the number of chromosomes in that species. In plants it is relatively common for the complete set of chromosomes to double in number, so forming a new species of plant – and gardeners manipulate that ability to their advantage as we will consider further in the section below on speciation.

It should be apparent from this brief survey that diversity in genomes is generated by a huge array of different types of mutation. But it should not be thought that the largest physical changes are necessarily the ones with the biggest effects on the organism's ability to survive and reproduce. For example, ordinary house mice have 40 pairs of chromosomes, but there is a population of mice in the Central Apennines in Italy that have only 22 chromosome pairs, apparently due to the fusion of different chromosomes, yet they seem to be remarkably similar in all other respects[57]. Perhaps this is not particularly surprising because if all the same genetic information is still present on 22 somewhat larger chromosomes (on average) compared to 40 smaller ones, then the mouse will still end up looking the same. But contrast this with the mutation of a single nucleotide in a gene encoding important regulatory information – the 'red master lever' in the analogy used above – and the effects on the organism can be far more profound. Size is not all that matters in the world of mutations.

How often do mutations happen? It depends on the organism and there are various ways of measuring mutation rates: this can be confusing because there are different ways of expressing the result. Mutation rates are easier to measure in bacteria as they have only one chromosome and divide very fast (every 20 minutes for some bugs under optimal conditions, which is why you need to watch out for wedding buffet food kept in a marquee for a while on a warm summer's day!). The rate of mutation, per nucleotide base, per replication, is about one in a billion; so mutations don't happen very often[58]: but the chances of cellular mutation in an organism obviously becomes higher in proportion to the number of cells the organism contains. That mutation might be significant for the health of the individual, but only mutations that occur in the germ cells will be passed on to succeeding generations.

In humans and other multicellular organisms the mutation

rate is around one for every one million germ-line (sex) cells and it has been estimated that the human mutation rate is roughly one mutation per 10,000 genes per generation (of people not cells). If we have 20,000 genes, then this means that each individual harbours on average two new genetic mutations, but this estimate should be taken as very approximate for the time being. Only when we get to the point that sequencing of human genomes is carried out routinely as part of normal medical practice will we be able to calculate the precise mutation rate for humans.

Mutations are not the only way in which variations enter the genome. In asexual reproduction, as occurs in bacteria, cells simply divide into two by a process known as mitosis. But in sexual reproduction life gets a bit more complicated because nearly all our cells have pairs of chromosomes. If the sperm and eggs also had pairs of chromosomes then fertilisation would result in cells with twice as much DNA as we need, and this would double in the next generation again ad infinitum, which is of course not possible. So, to avoid this, the sperm and eggs have only a single copy of each chromosome, and when fertilisation takes place the chromosomes from the mum and dad then combine to make chromosome pairs once again in the cells of the growing embryo. So this in itself will ensure that children will look different from their parents because they have one chromosome each per pair from each parent. It is those slight variations inherited from either mum's side or dad's side that make all the difference in creating a unique individual.

But there's also another fascinating event that helps to make us the unique beings that we are, and that is the swapping of sections of DNA that takes place between paired chromosomes during the formation of the gametes (sperm or eggs). During the development of these cells in the father or mother, segments of DNA are swapped between the paired chromosomes by a process called 'recombination'. Typically only one or two swaps occur on average for each human chromosomal pair. Once this stage of germ cell development is completed, then the cells divide further to generate the gametes that have only a single chromosome, and the newly modified chromosomes are shuffled randomly into different gametes. Remember that the genes on each of the paired chromosomes are not necessarily identical – there may be small differences in their nucleotide sequence that in some cases make a difference to their function. So recombination has the effect of 'gene shuffling', of generating a new chromosome in which the variant genes have new opportunities for expressing their outputs. The function of genes is defined by the company they keep, just as the costly transfer of players between different football teams can have very different outcomes depending on the quality of the rest of the team. Genomes are team efforts par excellence.

The third and very important mechanism for generating variation in the genomes of populations is called gene flow. If a small interbreeding animal population becomes isolated from other populations of the same species, then genes will gradually begin to vary less between individuals of that population because interbreeding means that the total gene pool becomes more homogeneous. The same outcome happens when pedigree cats or prize bulls are inbred to keep the pedigree going. The inbreeding might be good for winning prizes at shows, but it's often not so good for the immune systems (responsible for defence against viruses and bacteria) of these animals that benefit more from genetic diversity. 'Gene flow' is the term used when breeding from the isolated population takes place with incoming animals from some other location. The visitors bring with them new genetic variants and start spreading them in the previously isolated population. The resulting new genomes in the next generation might now generate animals better able to cope with their environment. This certainly happens if a pedigree cat escapes and outbreeds with an alley cat. The gene flow occurring from the alley cat is likely to give you much healthier kittens even if they win no prizes.

We have spent time on these three main ways of introducing variation into genomes because it is often erroneously thought that evolution involves just the slow, plodding change arising from 'point mutations' in single nucleotide base-pairs. As we have seen, that is far from the truth: the generation of novelty in the evolutionary process is driven by an impressive array of different mechanisms. Genomes are designed to change. If that were not the case, we wouldn't be here to discuss the matter.

Natural selection

Once the variant genome is generated, the next big step is to test out the organism it generates in the workshop of life; the process known as natural selection. We have already given an introductory description of the main idea of natural selection, but a slightly more detailed definition might now be useful: 'Natural selection is the differential reproduction of alternative genetic variations, determined by the fact that some variations are beneficial because they increase the probability that the organisms having them will live longer or be more fertile than organisms having alternative variations. Over the generations beneficial variations will be preserved and multiplied; injurious or less beneficial variations will be eliminated'[59].

In practice much variation in genomes is selectively neutral, giving rise to 'genetic drift'. In other words, this is the kind of variation that really makes no difference to the organism in question. If we have one amino acid rather than another at the 816th position in the string of amino acids that make up a particular protein, it really makes no difference either way. So the variant amino acids at that particular position will drift around quite happily in a population (through breeding) without any effects, beneficial or otherwise, on the carrier. But it is quite feasible that a mutation 'next door', changing the 817th amino acid in the same protein, might be really crucial, leading to a very ineffective immune system[60].

When genetic variation does make a difference to the organism, for good or for ill, natural selection begins to operate and the organism will tend to leave, over many generations, greater or fewer numbers of offspring, a process known as 'reproductive success'. The term 'survival of the fittest' has sometimes been used to describe natural selection, but is not very accurate because survival is not really the main point in this process. Of course if an animal does not survive then it won't reproduce, but the key point about natural selection is the successful reproduction that ensures that an individual's genes are passed on to the next generation.

Natural selection therefore acts as a rigorous filter to reduce the amount of genetic variation in a population. The reason for this is that the great majority of genetic changes, if not neutral, are likely to be deleterious for the organism, and it is these that will be removed from the population after some generations – or even immediately if lethal – since they lower reproductive success. On the other hand, the few beneficial changes that will readily pass through the filter of natural selection will quickly spread throughout an interbreeding population as they bestow reproductive benefits on their recipients.

What might those benefits be? In general they are adaptations that allow the organism to flourish in a particular ecological niche. A geneticist called Michael Majerus in Cambridge (UK) recently demonstrated this clearly by releasing dark-coloured and light-coloured peppered moths in his garden every night for seven years from May to August under controlled conditions (yes, scientists are quite obsessive!), and measuring which ones were more likely to get eaten by birds[61]. Over the seven years the darker moths were eaten more frequently than the lighter ones, because they are easier to see against the lighter background of bark and foliage. In this way Majerus confirmed some earlier findings by Bernard Kettlewell from Oxford suggesting that the incidence of dark peppered moths increased in industrial areas where they were better disguised from predators when sitting on sooty branches. Some methodological concerns cast doubt on Kettlewell's original experiments, but those by Majerus suggest that the peppered moth continues to provide a valid example of natural selection in progress. The decline in the percentage of dark peppered moths in the UK from 12% in 2001 to 2% in 2007 has been attributed to the decrease in air pollution over this period (a happy thought).

Another example of adaptation is provided by the anteater which needs a long snout to delve down into big ant-hills and narrow crevices to fish out those delicious little ants, finding his snout getting longer and longer over succeeding generations only so long as its advantages outweigh its disadvantages. Crevices are only so deep and at a certain point the snout will get so long that it slows down escape from predators. So a kind of equilibrium is reached in which genomes build snouts of just the right length to do the job that needs to be done without being a handicap: anteaters with that optimally useful length of snout will eat lots of ants, flourish and have loads of offspring, passing on their useful genomes to succeeding generations. Notice that this natural selection process is very different from the idea that the anteater tries hard to get ants just out of reach, thereby lengthening her snout, so passing her long snout on to her offspring. That is not how it happens!

Note the key phrase above: 'in a particular ecological niche'. If the supply of ants suddenly dries up for some reason, an anteater with a long snout may be in trouble. A different selection pressure now begins to operate, in which other adaptations might develop enabling the anteaters to be successful in using alternative food sources. It really is the ecological niche that defines what kind of adaptations will develop – an anteater's long snout is not going to be of much help to polar bears.

Some fascinating examples in human populations demonstrate how local adaptations work in practice: this is evolution in action. Each year about 400 million people contract malaria, 2 to 3 million of whom die from their illness. Most malaria victims are children. In parts of the world where malaria is endemic there is a high level of certain mutant genes in the population helping to protect carriers of these variants against infection with the malarial parasite following mosquito bites. These mutant genes are generally present only as single copies, in other words the variant gene occurs on only one of the paired chromosomes. Despite being present only as a single copy, the gene product can give some protection. A good example is provided by certain mutant genes encoding the protein haemoglobin, which is responsible for transporting oxygen in our red blood cells. One of the mutant forms of the gene encodes haemoglobin S. When present in double dose (where the variant gene is present on both chromosomes), the mutant haemoglobin S results in sickle cell anaemia in which red blood cells change their shape (become 'sickle shaped') and block the capillaries that take oxygen into the bodily tissues. About 80% of patients with sickle cell anaemia die before reproducing. So why doesn't natural selection weed out this deleterious gene from the population? The answer is because in a single dose the mutant gene helps to protect against malaria, which is why it is frequent in African populations where malaria is common, much less so where malaria is rare. Only when two people who both carry the mutant gene have children will there be a one in four chance of any one child having a double dose of the gene, and so destined to develop sickle cell anaemia. Such an event does not happen often enough for the mutant gene to be weeded out of the population.

Another example of evolution in action with which many people will be sadly familiar is the 'superbug' Methicillin-resistant *Staphylococcus aureus* (MRSA) bacteria that have acquired genes encoding antibiotic resistance to all penicillins, including methicillin and other related antibiotics. MRSA was discovered for the first time in 1961 in the UK, but is now widespread in the hospital setting and causes hundreds of deaths in hospitalised patients. This is just one example of many bacteria that have acquired antibiotic resistance of various kinds. Resistance can be spread between bacteria by means of plasmids, circular DNA molecules, separate from the main chromosome, that can pass from one bacterium to another, carrying the resistance genes with them. As an anti biotic is widely used to kill a certain strain of bacteria, so eventually one bacterium out of billions will acquire the mutant gene that provides resistance. Not surprisingly this bacterium and its progeny will triumph in the reproduction stakes (remembering that reproduction for most bacteria just involves asexual cell division), and at the same time as it multiplies will pass round its newly acquired resistant genes by means of plasmid transfer. This is natural selection in action – and in this case it can happen fast – too fast for comfort!

So when modern biologists say they have observed evolution, they mean that they have detected a change in the frequency of genes in a population. If we put the generation of genetic diversity together with natural selection, then the overall process of evolution can be succinctly summarised in three short phrases:

- Genes mutate
- Individuals are selected
- Populations evolve

This is what evolution means. Some people find it hard to see how such a basically simple two-step process (the first two phrases above) could lead to all the creativity and complexity that we see all around us in the living world. Later on we will give some further examples to show how this happens: but for the moment it is worth noting that this basic biological principle of 'make lots of something and then select the best for the job to be done' applies to all living things, not least our own bodies. Think of those millions of sperm swimming up the Fallopian tubes in a race to fertilise the single egg that eventually became you. Talk about wasted effort for all the millions that didn't make it to the finishing line! The Grand National has nothing on the process of human fertilisation. But of course it's a great system because it provides a way of checking the genomes of the swimming sperm. In some cases (not all), sperm with the less than optimal genomes won't swim so fast or will fall by the wayside, so natural selection is probably operating quite strongly on this process. Though it might appear too much of a lottery to human engineers, the winner-takes-all mechanism has been remarkably successful in helping humankind to fulfil the command given in Genesis 1:28[62].

As we look around at the way other organisms reproduce, we see the same principle of abundance and selection operating time and again. Watching a sycamore tree in a big storm with the winged seeds fluttering their way through the wood to the damp leafy ground, we know that only a very few of those will ever become a new sycamore tree, and it is the same as we watch the dandelion seeds wafting along like a white wispy cloud on a warm summer's day right over the lawn. Fortunately for those of us who like to keep our lawns free of weeds (unsuccessfully of course) not all dandelion seeds will become a new dandelion. Jesus himself used the same idea in his famous parable of the sower who needs to scatter far more seed than will ever germinate and lead to a good crop (Matthew 13:3ff).

The development of our brains also depends on abundant production followed by selection. Amazingly our brains contain around 10^{11} neurons with a total of more than 10^{14} connections with each other. During the early stages of embryonic development the neurons have to connect up correctly in order to form our brains, and this process continues apace during the early years of childhood. Neurons do this by sending out exploratory feelers, as it were, to other neurons. If the connection is an appropriate and successful one then the receiving neuron sends a survival message to the sending neuron, basically saying 'all is well, keep up the good work'. But if the connection is not a fruitful one then the sending neuron will shrivel up and die. In fact, believe it or not, more neurons die in the developing brain than make it through to become part of our adult brains. Only one neuron survives to tell the tale for every two that are formed. A huge amount of 'natural selection' has been involved in the shaping of our own brains. Without it I would not be writing these sentences.

Evolution – the wider picture

Many people somehow have the impression that evolution began billions of years ago with single-celled organisms like bacteria, and then since that time there has been a steady increase in the complexity and diversity of living organisms, until finally we arrive at the level of diversity we see all around us today. Although the first part of that assumption is correct, the rest is quite wrong. In reality the evolutionary story is not a smooth trajectory at all, but a narrative with long periods when not much new seemed to be happening, interspersed with times of high drama when creative novelty burst upon the scene. Just as human history in a particular country is rarely a smooth progression, but is marked by long periods of peace followed by various kinds of social upheaval, so evolutionary history, under the sovereignty of God, is marked by a similar type of pattern.

One useful way to envisage history as viewed through the lens of evolution is to imagine the whole 4.6 billion year history of the earth as being crammed into a single day.

If we had a bird's-eye view of the whole day, what would we see the Creator do, starting our 24-hour clock at zero and imagining that midnight is the present moment in time? Simple forms of life would already be appearing by 2.40 a.m. with single-celled organisms (prokaryotes) flourishing by around 5.20 a.m. The great oceans of the world start to change colour as cyanobacteria (blue-green algae) spread across the planet. At the same time the genetic code becomes established that will dominate the generation of biological diversity for the remainder of the day.

After this early-morning start, there would then be quite a long wait until single-celled organisms containing nuclei (eukaryotes) become visible around lunch-time. A further seven hours pass before multicellular organisms (living things with more than one cell) start appearing in the sea by 8.15 in the evening. About half-an-hour later the planet changes colour as cyanobacteria and green algae invade the land.

From then on the biological pace picks up and there is a busy evening of observation ahead. The Cambrian explosion starts at 9.10 p.m. and in an amazing three minutes an immense diversity of phyla appear, each with a distinctive body-plan, with many of the anatomical features introduced continuing in many of the phyla right up to midnight. Twenty minutes later plants start appearing on land for the first time, followed very soon afterwards by the earliest land animals. At 9.58 p.m. this is followed by the mass extinctions of the Devonian period.

At 10.11 reptiles start roaming the land, followed half an hour later by the mass extinctions which mark the end of the Palaeozoic period.

By 10.50 p.m. the earliest mammals and dinosaurs are appearing, but five minutes later there is further mass extinction at the start of the Jurassic period.

By 11.15 archaeopteryx are flapping around and within minutes the sky begins to fill with birds. Another mass extinction occurs at 11.39 in which the dinosaurs are wiped out.

Just two minutes before midnight hominids start to appear and a mere three seconds before midnight anatomically modern humans make their entry onto the scene, the whole of recorded human history until now being compressed into less than one fifth of the second before midnight, the mere blink of a human eyelid. This late flourishing of biological diversity is illustrated in a rather less dramatic way in Figure 6.

One striking aspect of this account is the way in which cellular life got going on planet earth within a relatively short time (in geological terms) after the earth began. There is strong evidence for the existence of cells 3.5 billion years ago and fairly good evidence for life having already started 3.8 billion years ago. That is 'only' 200–500 million years after our planet first became habitable, indeed a long period of time, but cells are highly complex entities. There is nothing 'simple' about the organisation of any cell, and we will consider in the final chapter the ways in which the first life forms may have come into being, with the establishment of the very same genetic code that we use in our own bodies today.

Another striking aspect of the 24-hour thought experiment is the very long wait before the first multicellular organisms start appearing around 8.15 p.m. Living things on earth were really small for a very long time: being big is a recent phenomenon. Biologists would get very excited if they could travel back in a time machine to our evolutionary past, but for the ordinary observer it might look extremely boring, because during the first 2.5 billion years of life on earth (approximately), things rarely grew bigger than 1 millimetre across, about the size of a pinhead[63]. No birds, no flowers, no animals wandering around, no fish in the sea, but at the genetic level lots going on, with the generation of most of the genes that were later used to such effect to build the bigger, more interesting (to us) living things that we see all around us today.

Not until the advent of multicellular life did living organisms start to get bigger, although even then they were generally on a scale of millimetres rather than centimetres. With the flourishing of the late Ediacaran fauna (named after the Australian hills where their fossils were first found) during the period 575–543 million years ago, we move into the centimetre scale.

Only in the so-called 'Cambrian explosion' during the period 525–505 million years ago did sponges and algae grow up to

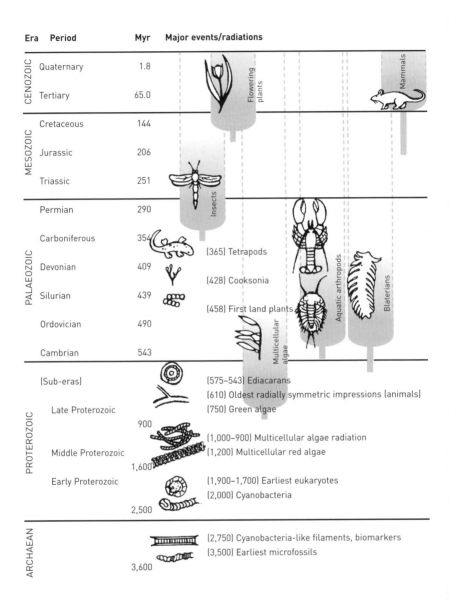

Figure 6. History of main evolutionary events. The earliest record of particular groups of animals is shown with the expansion ('radiation') of particular taxa. Myr means millions of years before present. [Reprinted by permission from Macmillan Publishers Ltd: *Nature* 409, 1102–1109, 2001.]

5–10 cm across, and the size of animals began to increase dramatically from that time onwards. The Cambrian explosion has drawn particular attention because it refers to that 'explosion' of new animal life forms and body plans that began to appear from about 525 million years ago onwards, and it is from these that virtually all the animals were derived with which we are familiar today.

The Cambrian explosion provides just one of several examples during evolution, known as 'adaptive radiation', when the emergence of new life-forms has been followed, often after some delay, by the filling up of different ecological niches by a great array of new living things. This happens when these new forms of life become adapted to capitalising on the food and other resources provided by a particular environment. For example the emergence of insects during the Devonian and Carboniferous periods (during the period about 400–350 million years ago) was followed by a huge proliferation in types of insects, and the radiation of the flowering plants that took place in the late Cretaceous period (after 144 million years ago), and of mammals in the early Tertiary period (after 60 million years ago), followed a similar pattern. The generation of novelty leads to adaptive radiation because novelty opens the way to new opportunities for organisms to flourish in particular ecological niches.

If we focus on the big picture of evolutionary history, increased complexity has also been a striking feature. 'Complexity' in biology (as elsewhere) is a bit of a slippery term, but can be taken to include the number of different physical parts as well as the number of different interactions between those parts. We have already noted that there is a general increase in the number of protein-coding genes required to encode multicellular compared to unicellular organisms: unicellular bacteria generally make do with fewer than 5,000 genes, whereas multicellular life forms like mammals need around 20,000 genes, although as already noted there is clearly no simple linear relationship between gene number and bodily complexity. There has also been an increase in the number of different cell types used to make up different organisms, from only one in bacteria, to seven in mushrooms (an evolutionarily ancient fungus), to about 50 in fruitflies, to the 200 or more present in humans.

The consequences of adaptive radiation can readily be seen by travelling around the continents and islands of the world and studying their animals and plants. Each continent has its own distinctive collection of living things[64]. In Africa we find rhinoceroses, hippopotamuses, lions, hyenas, giraffes, zebras, lemurs, monkeys with narrow noses and nonprehensile tails (tails not adapted to grasping objects), chimpanzees, and gorillas. South America, which has a very similar latitude to Africa and plenty of similar habitats, has none of these animals, but instead has pumas, jaguars, tapirs, llamas, raccoons, opossums, armadillos and monkeys with broad noses and large prehensile tails. Africa and South America were once all part of the same supercontinent known as Gondwana, but the tectonic plate on which they are located began to break apart around 150 million years ago. Cutting out Africa with scissors from an old geography book and doing the same for South America, we find that the west coast of Africa and the east coast of South America fit quite well like two pieces of a jig-saw, for the simple reason that they were once joined. But once they went their separate ways, their animals evolved separately, giving rise to the very different animals that we see today.

Australia is likewise characterised by a different set of animals. Instead of the placental mammals that typify other continents – mammals that feed their developing young using the placenta[65] – Australia is dominated by marsupials in which early development takes place in an external pouch, as in kangaroos, moles, anteaters and Tasmanian wolves.

Small islands have even more dramatically different flora and fauna, especially if isolated from other land, because the first few species to arrive there have a huge advantage if they face no competition in filling up the different ecological niches. As they do so they diversify further to take full advantage of all the resources provided. For example, the Hawaiian Islands are more than 2,000 miles away from North America and have a completely different collection of flora and fauna, including many species endemic to those islands, found nowhere else in the world. Of all the 1,500 known species of *Drosophila* fruit flies in the world, nearly one third of them live in Hawaii and nowhere else[66], whereas there are no mosquitoes or cockroaches (oh bliss!). Of the 3,750 species of insects that live on the island, all are endemic, and 94% of the flowering plants and more than 1,000 species of land snail have likewise evolved uniquely on these islands. By contrast there are no local mammals at all on the Hawaiian islands – it was presumably just too far for any mammals to swim, float or paddle to Hawaii...

Like all scientific theories, evolution is a theory that seeks the best explanation for what is observed. Evolution makes perfectly good sense of the biological diversity that exists around the world. But is it only relevant as an explanation for minor changes within a species? What about bigger changes? Can one animal or plant gradually change into something quite different with the passage of time?

Chapter 5:

What Do We Mean By Evolution? Speciation, Fossils and the Question of Information

Speciation

Many people think that evolutionary processes are sufficient to explain the kind of variation that exists within a species of the kind already discussed, but do not think that these same processes are involved in the development of one species into another. This discussion is tied up with the terms 'microevolution' and 'macroevolution'. The term 'microevolution' is traditionally used to refer to variation within a species, whereas 'macroevolution' refers to changes above the species level.

It is important to clarify first of all what biologists understand by the term 'species'. A species refers to a population of organisms which interbreed with each other but not with other organisms, and are therefore said to be 'reproductively isolated'. Clearly this is only a useful definition for living species. Extinct species have to be defined based on the fossil record by looking at differences in morphology (body shape, plan, size etc), so classification of dead species runs the risk of being less reliable.

Many mechanisms of speciation are quite well understood, but there are likely to be other mechanisms yet to be discovered as our knowledge of genomes increases and we understand more of the varied ways in which they translate their information into living organisms. But although different mechanisms of speciation remain an active topic of research and discussion amongst biologists, there is no doubt at all about the following three facts. First, speciation definitely happens. Second, in some cases it can be observed occurring in the wild during the lifetime of a single biological investigator. Third, there are different mechanisms that account for speciation, not just one mechanism.

Speciation is thought to occur either by allopatric mechanisms, which happen when a population is split into two (or more) geographically divided subdivisions that organisms cannot bridge (such as the formation of a new ocean separating two landmasses as a result of continental drift), or by sympatric mechanisms occurring when two subpopulations become reproductively isolated without first becoming geographically isolated.

In plants speciation can happen rapidly by the process of chromosomal doubling (known as 'polyploidy') and this results in sympatric speciation because reproductive isolation occurs even when the species is living in the same habitat as the parental species. Polyploidy happens in the following way. Occasionally one species of plant can fertilise another to form a hybrid. Normally hybrids are sterile, just as a female domestic horse and a male domestic ass can mate to generate a mule (a hybrid), which is also sterile. However, unlike mules, hybridisation in certain plants can be followed by doubling of the chromosome number, giving rise to a new species. A much studied example of this kind comes from the genus *Tragopogon* in North America, otherwise known as salsify, a root that can be eaten as a vegetable. Three new species of *Tragopogon* were introduced to North America during the first few decades of the twentieth century and flourished in regions of east Washington State and Idaho[67] (see Figure 7). Two of these are known as *T. dubius* and *T. porrifolius* (where T is short for *Tragopogon*) and they both have six chromosome pairs. By 1950 a biologist called Ownbey had discovered two new species of Tragopogon, one of which was called *T. mirus*. Further analysis since that time has established that *T. mirus* has 12 pairs of chromosomes, one set derived from *T. dubius* and one set from *T. porrifolius* and can no longer interbreed with either of its parents, thereby representing a new colony of plants that can fertilise each

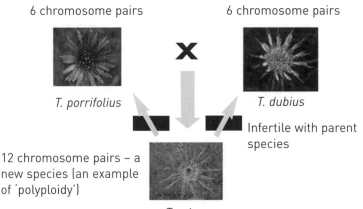

6 chromosome pairs

6 chromosome pairs

T. porrifolius

X

T. dubius

Infertile with parent species

12 chromosome pairs – a new species (an example of 'polyploidy')

T. mirus

Figure 7. The generation of a new species of Tragopogon by chromosomal doubling. The two parent species *Tragopogon porrifolius* and *Tragopogon dubius* were introduced to the USA in the early part of the twentieth century. The new species *Tragopogon mirus* was discovered by 1950 and the chromosomal analysis was carried out recently showing that the new species contains the chromosomes from both parents. *Tragopogon mirus* is infertile with both parents, so fulfilling the key criterion of a new species.

other – the definition of a new species. Several other examples of *Tragopogon* speciation have been described from North America and there is also evidence that identical *Tragopogon* speciation events involving chromosomal doubling have occurred multiple times on separate occasions within North America over a period of a few decades.

Nearly 50% of existing flowering plant species are thought to have arisen by polyploidy, so rapid speciation of this kind is very common in the plant kingdom[68]. In addition, plant breeders have utilised polyploidy for years to create new and often commercially valuable plant species artificially. The pollen of one plant is painted on the stigma of another from a different species, and the resulting hybrid plant is then treated with a chemical called colchicine to cause polyploidy, leading to the formation of a new species. The first artificially created hybrid species was a primrose called *Primula kewensis* which has 36 chromosomes and which was derived from two different parental *Primula* species both having 18 chromosomes. In fact in this case colchicine wasn't used as the chromosomal doubling happened spontaneously[69]. To see the fruit of recent speciation events we need only look out of the window, for it is very likely that about a third or more of the plants in the garden have been created recently by artificial hybridisation.

For rapid speciation in the wild, lupins (one of my favourite flowers as it happens) currently hold the record. When the Andes mountains in South America were pushed up to near their final height between 2 and 4 million years ago, they created a new habitat for plants and animals. Such geological events provide similar opportunities for radiation and speciation as we have noted occurring in islands such as Hawaii. As the mountains rose (caused by the movement of the Nazca tectonic plate beneath the South American plate), so many of the plants adapted to living at low altitudes could no longer flourish, leaving the way open for new and hardier species, adapted to living in alpine conditions, to fill up the ecological spaces so generated. The Andes contain around 45,000 plant species and as many as 60% of those found in the high north Andean plateau are endemic. Studies have shown that the first lupins arrived in the Andes about 1.5 million years ago, and since that time no less than 81 different species of lupin have evolved from these original founders as demonstrated by botanic fieldwork in conjunction with lupin DNA sequencing[70]. This gives an average of one new speciation event occurring about once every 19,000 years, which is one of the most rapid speciation rates yet described, rivalling that of the cichlid fishes of the African lakes that we will describe below.

Polyploidy is much less common in animals than in plants, but is not uncommon as an explanation for the origin of species with parthenogenetic females in which the growth and development of an embryo occurs without fertilisation by males. Such species include some shrimps and moths, as well as some beetles, fish and salamanders.

Chromosomal changes have also been responsible for the emergence of seven different species of the mosquito *Anopheles gambiae* within the last 5,000 years[71]. These are the deadly mosquitoes in Africa which carry the malarial parasite, so continue to be an active focus for research. These new *A. gambiae* species are of particular interest since they can breed only in environments modified by human agriculture, and so their history is very much intertwined with the human history of Africa. Extensive agriculture in Africa began only about 3,000 years ago and this correlates with the emergence of more virulent strains of the malarial parasite and with the rapid speciation of its carrier A. *gambiae*. The seven different species of A. *gambiae* that evolved over this period are distinguished genetically not by polyploidy but by various inversions on their chromosomes which have promoted reproductive isolation. Once inversions occur affecting genes that in turn influence reproduction, then mosquitoes will tend to breed only with other individuals that share the same chromosomal inversion, until a separate breeding colony is established which eventually splits off to form its own species.

Perhaps it is because speciation can occur quite suddenly in plants, and to a lesser extent in some (rather special) animals, that I sometimes get asked at lectures as to how speciation can occur in sexually reproducing animals when, the questioner presumes, a male and female animal give birth to an individual that represents a new species. Who can this new individual breed with, given that it is (presumably!) the only one in the world? As it happens the assumption behind this question is quite wrong.

By far the most common type of speciation amongst animals that practise sexual reproduction is thought to occur by gradual reproductive isolation, mainly allopatric, in which populations of animals become separated by barriers of some kind, and then each interbreeding population gradually accumulates its own unique set of genetic variations until finally, if brought back together, the populations are either unwilling or unable to reproduce together. In other words, two new species have emerged by a lengthy process. We might need to wait for hundreds of generations before we could detect any particular differences between the two species, and even then we might need the trained eye of the zoologist. Also the term 'barrier' is clearly going to mean very different things depending on size, agility, and so forth. A barrier for a snail is not the same as a barrier for a tiger. For a fish living at one end of a big lake, all that water between the home end and the further end might represent a very significant barrier. For a land animal living on a continent that breaks up to generate Africa and South America, the intervening ocean represents a very significant barrier to reproduction whatever the animal's size or shape.

But the important point to note in this discussion is that there is no question of parental animals giving birth to off-spring that suddenly represent a new species. Remember the 'three phrase' summary of evolution above – the third phrase highlights the fact that it is populations that evolve. In an interbreeding population, as various kinds of genetic variation accumulate, some giving rise to beneficial adaptations – longer legs, thicker fur, bigger tails, whatever it might be – so that population will gradually become more and more different from the parental population until a new species emerges.

Yet even though speciation in sexually breeding animals is never instantaneous, animal speciation can still be surprisingly fast. A good example of rapid speciation is provided by the cichlid fish that live in the great lakes of Africa, such as Lakes Victoria and Malawi[72]. Amazingly, the cichlids in these lakes account for more than 10% of the world's freshwater fish species, and the cichlid species in one lake are quite distinct from those in another. More than 1,000 species of cichlid have arisen during the past 1 million years in these lakes. Until very recently there were still more than 170 species of cichlid fish living in Lake Victoria in Africa and initially it was thought that these all evolved from a single species of fish since the lake's origin about 750,000 years ago in the mid-Pleistocene era. However, recent genetic and geological studies have revealed a more complex picture[73]. Geological evidence suggests that the lake dried out completely about 14,700 years ago and that it was then 'seeded' by two distinct lineages of cichlid fish from the more ancient and much smaller Lake Kivu. Irrespective of the precise sequence of events, the large number of cichlid species found until recently in Lake Victoria provides a striking example of rapid speciation in action. The different species show differences in morphology (body structure and appearance) linked to their feeding habits. Virtually every major food source in the lake is exploited by one species or another. Some cichlids eat insects, others crustaceans, others eat plants, and yet others molluscs. Each new species has found its particular ecological niche. In fact one species, *H. welcommei*, has the odd habit of feeding on fish scales which it scrapes off the tails of other fish! Just 4,000 years ago a small new lake called Lake Nabugabo became isolated from Lake Victoria by a narrow sandbar and this lake already has seven different cichlid species, of which five are not found in Lake Victoria and therefore most likely evolved during these past 4,000 years. The Lake Nabugabo species vary most from the Lake Victoria species in male colour. So the cichlid species of these two lakes provide a vivid example of the way in which speciation can be rapid (in terms of geological time) and abundant, given the right environment.

Other striking examples of speciation, which we can observe right before our eyes in field studies, are provided by the so-called 'ring species'. Birdwatchers in Europe will find both herring gulls – which have white heads and grey backs – and the much darker lesser black-backed gulls. These are distinct species and they don't interbreed. Meanwhile in North America you will find only herring gulls, whereas travelling west from North America towards Siberia the coloration of the herring gull changes until somewhere around central Siberia it becomes so dark that we can classify it as the black-backed gull. So gulls form a classic 'ring species' round the northern hemisphere in which the species merge to form an interbreeding population in the middle of the spectrum of difference, whereas at either end they have evolved into distinct species.

One way of envisaging this process is to imagine a straight line across a continent going from east to west with an interbreeding population in the east which gradually varies as we trace the line westwards. Now imagine the straight line bent round into a circle. If the population at the west end can no longer breed with those at the east end, even though they have now met – then we have a ring speciation event. In the gull example it is northern Europe which provides the meeting of the two ends, for it is here that the two separate species (the herring gull and the lesser black-backed gull) mingle without interbreeding. This is speciation that we can watch happening.

There are many other examples of ring speciation of this

kind, though in practice they are not always arranged as neatly in a circle as the gull example given above. Birds provide useful examples of ring speciation events because of their mobility over long distances. Even the evolution of different bird songs can generate a reproductively isolated population – putting it bluntly, wrong tune, no sex. In central Asia there is a small, greenish, insect-eating warbler that delights in the name of *P. trochiloides* which is distributed in a ring round the treeless Tibetan plateau. The species migrated up from the south, probably India, and then migrated round the east and west sides of the plateau. Finally the populations met up again in central Siberia but by this time had evolved songs so different that the birds of the eastern population no longer interbreed with those from the western population[74], giving a new twist to Rudyard Kipling's famous line that 'East is East and West is West and ne'er the twain shall meet'[75].

Animals speciate in rings as well, and the salamander *Ensatina* found in California provides a well studied example. In Southern California, there are two species of salamander, the strongly blotched *E. klauberi*, and *E. eschscholtzii* which is more uniform and brighter, with bright yellow eyes, apparently in mimicry of a deadly poisonous newt. These two populations coexist in some areas but do not interbreed; they are separate species. In this case the 'middle' of the ring is at the northern end of the San Joaquin valley where the single ancestral salamander species is located. As the salamanders moved south they divided along each side of the valley, forming two different groups, the ones in the Sierra Nevada evolving a blotchy coloration, whereas along the coast they gradually became brighter and brighter. The division between the two groups is not absolute, some interbreeding still takes place to form hybrids in this region, but the hybrids don't do well with predators and have difficulty in finding mates, so do not reproduce successfully. These two factors keep the two forms from merging, even though they can interbreed.

By the time the salamanders reached the southernmost part of California, the separation caused the two populations to evolve enough differences to become reproductively isolated. In some areas the two populations coexist, closing the 'ring', but do not interbreed. They have evolved into two distinct species[76]. As the biologist David Wake, who has studied the salamanders for more than two decades, remarks: 'All of the intermediate steps, normally missing, have been preserved, and that is what makes it so fascinating'.

It should be clear by now that there is nothing particularly special about speciation from a scientific point of view and as our understanding of genomics increases, so the distinction between micro- and macroevolution begins to look less useful. For the fact of the matter is that there is often greater morphological variation within a species than there is between species. For example, because of controlled breeding there is a huge range of domestic dogs in existence, of all kinds of weird and wonderful sizes, yet they can all interbreed in theory, if not much in practice (when it comes to an Alsatian and a chihuahua, for example). There are estimated to be between 350 and 1,000 breeds of dog, with a world population of 400 million dogs, mostly pets, of whom 65 million live in the USA[77]. Dogs evolved from wolves and their domestication can be traced back 14,000 years based on archaeological evidence. Comparison of gene sequences from a wide range of dog breeds shows that their genomes differ at about one nucleotide base in a thousand, which is comparable with the variation between individual humans. Yet the ranges of dog size, shape and behaviour are far wider than in the human population. Irish wolfhounds can grow up to 50 times larger than chihuahuas. The differences in size can be largely attributed to a single variant gene known as 'insulin-like growth factor 1'. Therefore organisms varying greatly in appearance can all belong to the same species and have very similar genomes.

Now contrast this with two species of worm called *C. elegans* and *C. briggsae*, not something one might do every day, but *C. elegans* has the honour of being the very first animal to have its genome sequenced (in 1998), so should be treated with respect. Even trained worm people have a hard time telling these worms apart. In fact the two not only look almost identical but have a very similar biology and developmental process. Imagine the surprise, then, of the gene jockeys when they found that the genome of *C. briggsae* is significantly different from that of *C. elegans*, with 800 genes unique to each species out of approximately 20,000 protein-coding genes per genome[78]. Indeed it appears that the two species of worm last shared a common ancestor around 80–110 million years ago, compared to a mere 14,000 years for the various domesticated dog breeds. So should we use the word 'macroevolution' to refer to the genomes of the worms, despite the fact that their appearance and behaviour are virtually identical and they are in fact two separate species – or would it be more appropriate to use the term to describe the huge differences between different dog breeds, even though they are all of the same species and have much more similar genomes than do the two species of worm?

Answering that question becomes even more difficult when we realise that there are far more 'cryptic species' on the planet than previously realised. Cryptic species refer to animals that appear identical but are genetically quite distinct, and it has been suggested that as many as 30% of all animal species may turn out to be of this cryptic variety[79]. Cryptic species include the African elephant, which in 2001 was shown to consist of two separate non-interbreeding species, the African bush elephant and the African elephant. The skipper butterfly, previously thought to be a single species, has now been shown to consist of ten cryptic species. Modern genetics is changing the species landscape.

So there is nothing about becoming a separate species which is biologically that distinctive when compared with other types of variation. Of course the various mechanisms of speciation continue to be an active and fascinating area of biological research, and the species concept itself is important for biology. But if singing the 'wrong' song is enough to put a bird on the pathway to becoming a new species, whereas having even 800 unique genes is not necessarily enough to make a worm look very different from its neighbour down the road (hole?), then probably the traditional distinction between micro- and macroevolution is not a very useful one.

The amazing diversity of species

Because most of us can see only a limited number of animals and plants around us, and even the TV natural history programmes have time to introduce us to only a few hundred more, we can easily end up thinking that the number of species on the planet isn't that great, maybe tens or hundreds of thousands, but certainly not millions. In fact the number of living species on the earth is definitely in the millions.

No one actually knows the exact number of species on earth. The number already classified is around 2 million. There are 4,629 mammalian species, about 10,000 species of birds, 15,300 fish species, 250,000 flowering plants, 69,000 species of fungi and 50,000 species or groups of species of tree. Yet all of these numbers fade into insignificance compared to the 850,000 insect species named so far, of which 300,000 are beetles, and it has been estimated that 80–95% of insect species have yet to be named and classified[80]. So the final tally of species in the world could be nearer 20 million than 2 million, especially if the proportion of cryptic species turns out to be as high as some people think. Adam was brought by God in Genesis 2:19–20 to name all the animals, but we have a long way to go in finally fulfilling that command!

Despite the slow progress in proportion to the total yet to be classified, the number of species being newly characterised each year is still about 10,000, and the whole process of discovery and classification is being speeded up by new genomic approaches. One current project is to genetically 'barcode' all species. The Consortium for the Barcode of Life is an international initiative devoted to developing DNA barcoding as a global standard for the identification of biological species[81]. DNA barcoding is a new technique that uses a short DNA sequence from a standardised and agreed position in the genome as a molecular diagnostic for species-level identification. DNA barcode sequences are very short relative to the entire genome and they can be obtained reasonably quickly and cheaply. In a different initiative, the Census of Marine Life is an international £590 million project involving more than 300 scientists from 53 countries which aims to discover and analyse all life in the sea by 2010. More than 99% of the oceans of the world have yet to be sampled for marine life – so the project is ambitious! These and other projects are likely to greatly increase the rate of species identification in the years ahead.

We are living in a dynamic world in which new species are constantly emerging but where, sadly, the extinction rate now far outweighs the birth rate. Until humans came on the scene, the background extinction rate was in the range of 0.1 to 1 species extinction per million species per year, but today species are disappearing at a rate 100–1,000 times faster than that, largely through removal of natural habitats.

Species extinctions

We have already highlighted the fact that evolutionary history has been an uneven affair as far as key developments in the diversity of life forms are concerned. The mass extinctions that have occurred relatively frequently (in geological time) during the earth's history have played an import role in triggering off new waves of species diversification. Figure 8 illustrates the peaks of mass extinction that have occurred in marine animals during the extinctions of the past 500 million years. More than 99% of all the species that have ever lived on this planet are now extinct. We know this from the fossil record that we will consider further below. This means that if there are 10 million species (for the sake of argument) currently alive on earth, then at least one billion different species have been alive on the planet at one time or another.

Going back in time from the present, the first major extinction that we encounter is the famous event that is thought to have led to the extinction of the dinosaurs, the mass extinction that occurred at the border between the Cretaceous and Tertiary eras 65 million years ago, the so-called K/T boundary[82], when about 60–75% of all species went extinct. Although the cause of the extinction is not known with certainty, the most likely explanation is the huge asteroid that is thought to have struck the earth at that time, estimated to be up to nine miles in diameter, which left a massive crater (called the Chicxulub crater) about 112 miles in diameter and 30 miles deep buried beneath the sediments off the Yucatan coast in the Gulf of Mexico[83]. The collision is estimated to have released as much energy as exploding 108 megatons of TNT, equivalent to 1,000 eruptions of the Krakatoa volcano. A key finding that pointed to an asteroid collision even before this crater was dis-

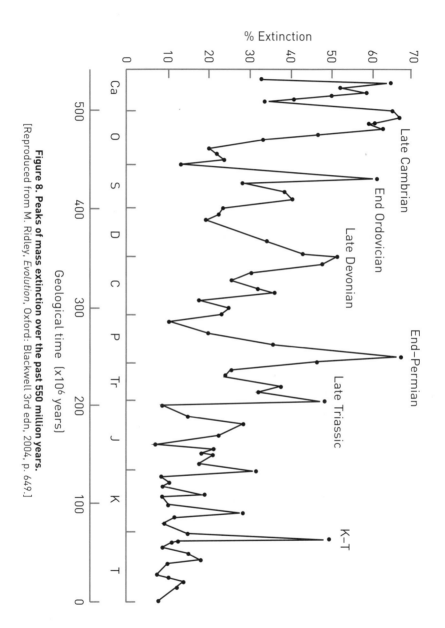

Figure 8. Peaks of mass extinction over the past 550 million years.
[Reproduced from M. Ridley, *Evolution*, Oxford: Blackwell 3rd edn, 2004, p. 649.]

covered was the high levels of rare earth elements such as irid-
ium that were found at more than 100 sites round the world in
the layer of clay that is characteristic of the K/T boundary.
Such elements are found concentrated in extraterrestrial
objects but not on earth, so the tell-tale 'signatures' dating from
rocks of that period are certainly consistent with the asteroid
impact model. Other geological specimens characteristic of
rocks exposed to high impact, such as shocked quartz, have
also been collected from the Chicxulub crater and other places.

When Krakatoa erupted in 1883 it blasted 18 cubic kilometres of dust and ash into the atmosphere. Winds carried the
dust round the planet, hiding the sun. But this appears trivial
compared to the effects of the huge asteroid hitting the Gulf of
Mexico, the darkening of the sun leading to polar winters that
would have caused extinction by starvation of many species
surviving the initial catastrophe.

Dinosaurs flourished during the Cretaceous period 145 to
65 million years ago, but went extinct at the K/T boundary
along with thousands of other species. As the earth recovered
from the shock and climates were restored, so new opportunities were created for adaptive radiation. The situation after a
mass extinction is comparable with that found in the Andes
following its elevation to new heights, or in Hawaii when it
was first colonised by founder species. Ecological niches are
empty or sparsely occupied, so competition for food resources
is not as fierce as in more normal times. Previous predators
have now been eliminated.

It has been suggested that the extinction of the dinosaurs,
that previously ruled the land before the end of the Cretaceous
period, played a critical role in mammalian evolution. Until
the K/T boundary, so this account goes, there were small
shrew-like mammals around, but they never had an opportunity to flourish or diversify much further because they were
prey to the dinosaurs – life was just too competitive. But they
survived the asteroid catastrophe and, once the dinosaurs died
off, evolved rapidly into the profusion of mammalian species
that we know today.

Such an account has some support, but the jury is still out
when it comes to the question of the origins of mammalian

diversity and the question is hotly debated amongst biologists[84]. More mammal fossils from the Cretaceous period are being discovered, including a well-preserved mammal in Mongolia dating from 71 to 75 million years ago[85]. But however the matter is finally resolved, it is clear that the K/T boundary mass extinction did generate new opportunities not only for mammals, but for the adaptive radiation of many other species around the world.

Even bigger than the K/T boundary extinction was the Permian mass extinction that took place about 251 million years ago, which was a real whopper, with as many as 80–96% of species going extinct. The extinction was abrupt by geological standards, taking place in a few tens of thousands of years, leading to some fascinating speculations about the cause(s) of the extinction, ranging from volcanoes and asteroids to global warming and changes in the amount of oxygen in the earth's atmosphere[86]. Robert Berner of Yale University first put forward the theory, now widely accepted, that the present oxygen level of 21% was as high as 30% or more during the Carboniferous period 300 million years ago, but then reduced to a mere 13% in the late Permian period just prior to the mass extinction. The drop in oxygen might well have caused the dramatic extinction as animals, plants and aquatic life adapted to the higher oxygen levels were unable to cope as it declined. Whatever the precise cause, the trilobites were wiped out at this time plus several other major groups of animals, and lots of plants. The insects took a severe battering, the only time that an extinction has really made a dent in the number of insect species (I have always thought that if we ever have a nuclear war, cockroaches, which have a fossil record extending back 300 million years, might well be the last survivors on earth).

The Permian mass extinction is thought to have had a major creative influence on the diversity of the life forms that we see today. A mammal-like reptile called Lystrosaurus was one of the few animals to survive the catastrophe on land and, clearly an opportunist, soon managed to fill up many of the vacated ecological niches, becoming exceptionally abundant all round the world. Other species underwent adaptive radiation to increase the diversity of living things once again.

Catastrophes represent a big stirring of the evolutionary pot. New opportunities for the proliferation of novel life forms are opened up in their wake. And although the loss of 90% of all species might appear to be a cataclysmic event indeed, yet eventually an even greater diversity emerges from the ruins. Catastrophes are all part of the rich tapestry of the evolutionary history of speciation.

Genetic fossils

Calling something a fossil might imply that it is dead, buried and of no further use. But I am using the term 'genetic fossil' here to refer to the fact that evolution is incredibly 'Scottish' (I can say that because, with a name like Alexander, the ancestry of a good number of my own genes is Scottish). In other words, if we discover something useful, it should be preserved carefully for future generations. The 'canny Scot' will see how to use things to good advantage without undue waste. Today we live in a throwaway culture, but I well remember my mother repeatedly darning the same pair of my socks at different times until they bore their own vestiges of their unique evolutionary history.

Genomes are like canny Scots. If they find a gene that works well, they try not to lose it. And even if they cannot use it immediately, they store it away for use later. Or we can liken genomes to our garages where, instead of putting the car, we store (ok, males store, let's be honest here) all kinds of bits and pieces, 'just in case they might come in useful one day'; as sure enough they do!

The whole point about evolution from the biologist's perspective is that it explains so well all those many things that other theories can't explain: and it is the garage-like composition of the genomes of living organisms that is explained so well by an evolutionary process involving common descent. All genomes of organisms that have evolved recently are littered with ancient genes, still in use, that we can identify as going deep back into evolutionary time. But in addition they are replete with the relics of genes no longer in use, and additionally with stretches of non-functional DNA, such as those derived from retroviruses, which are simply replicated in the DNA every time a cell divides, providing indelible signatures of evolutionary histories.

If we imagine all the species that ever lived as comprising branches and twigs on one enormous bush, with mammals and flowering flowers on the branches near the top, and single-celled organisms like bacteria and yeast near the bottom, then we immediately notice three things. The first is that the species living today are not evenly representative of all the species that ever lived for the simple reason that many of them have gone extinct. But despite that, there are still enough living species to take us back quite close to the origin of life, enabling us to sequence their genomes and construct a 'bush' based on genomics[87]. The second point we notice is that the roots of the bush represent living things that must have existed during the emergence of life and the first cells. Of these we have no trace and we will consider this question and the wider question of the origin of life in the final chapter. Third, we note that the genomes of all these living organisms are connected. If the bush model is correct, then we should see many genes from simple unicellular organisms at the base of the tree being found in the mammalian and plant twigs at the top, albeit darned like socks because of their great age. That is exactly what we do see. At the same time we should see new genes appearing at the top that we don't see at the bottom – and that is observed also. Besides all that, if stretches of retroviral and other parasitic, non-functional types of DNA start appearing at different heights of the bush, then we should see these 'flowing upwards' to the higher branches, but not appearing in the lower branches, and that is indeed the case. In fact that latter point is so important that we are going to consider it separately when we come to consider the question of our own evolutionary history.

We also note that the whole bush is united in having the same genetic code. The triplet nucleotide codon system for encoding amino acids is universal throughout all living organisms, with some very minor variants. All independently-living organisms use DNA to encode themselves. The whole bush is united by sharing the same encryption system. By genetic engineering we can take a human gene and put it into bacteria and the bacteria will happily 'read' the human gene and make the human protein. It is like taking a file from a PC and running it on a Mac. Likewise we can take a human gene and genetically engineer a mouse to express that gene and in most cases it will do the same job as the mouse gene.

There are very good reasons why we would not want to try changing an encryption system once it's established, since any changes are likely to be lethal. So the genetic code may be displaying the QWERTY phenomenon characteristic of the laptop keyboard on which I'm typing this. Early typists used a different keyboard, but they were too fast on the old-fashioned typewriters and certain sets of keys kept getting stuck. In the process of solving the problem they put the QWERTY letters in a row, and there they have remained until this day, fixed by the evolutionary history of the typewriter – and don't you dare change it!

All cells need to do certain 'housekeeping' jobs like divide, repair damaged DNA, break down food and use it to supply energy, grow, defend themselves from outside attack, and so forth. Once genes evolved to do this, then many of them stayed more or less the same throughout billions of years of evolutionary history. If genes are doing a good job, why change them? There are many examples of such genes. For example the coral *Acropora* (the material called coral is made by these small anemone-like animals) flourished in the Precambrian mud before 540 million years ago. A sampling of 1,300 gene sequences from this ancient life form revealed that no less than 90% were present in the human genome, suggesting that many genes thought to be specific to vertebrates in fact have much older origins[88].

Anyone who likes baking bread at home will be familiar with using yeast. Yeasts are single-celled organisms from the fungi kingdom possessing a nucleus (so are neither plants nor animals) and are really small: one gram of yeast contains 20,000,000,000 (20 billion) living cells. Yeast emerged as a distinct species along with lots of other fungi in the pre-Cambrian era. Because yeasts have a nucleus in which to locate their DNA (unlike bacteria), they divide in a very similar way to cells found in multicellular organisms like us. This was how Paul Nurse won his Nobel Prize. Cancers are caused by cells that can't stop dividing. Nurse took the risky career step of deciding to investigate how normal cells divide using yeast as his model system. Many people at the time (1980s) thought that yeast cells would turn out to be very different from animal cells and would tell us little about what goes wrong in cancer. In fact exactly the opposite is the case. Nurse, along with others, discovered how a key class of enzymes called kinases regulate every stage of cell division, a vital insight for those trying to understand cancer. It now turns out that this basic 'toolkit' of gene-encoding proteins is found in virtually every nucleated cell in the world, including our own, regulating how cells divide. Nurse both won his Nobel Prize and became for some years Director of the Imperial Cancer Research Fund in London (now Cancer Research UK). Choosing the right questions to ask is often the biggest challenge for the scientist.

Even older than yeast in evolutionary time are the single-celled chaonoflagellates that emerged as a separate species very approximately 900 million years ago. There are about 150 species of chaonoflagellate and some are free-swimming, propelling themselves along with whip-like flagella with which they swim and draw in food. Chaonoflagellates are thought to represent living examples of what the ancestors of multicellular organisms looked like. Imagine, therefore, the excitement of researchers when they identified a gene from a chaonoflagellate species called MBRTK1 which encodes another type of kinase from the ones mentioned above, a kinase with 'first cousins' broadly distributed within the genomes of multicellular organisms, including ourselves[89]. Those millions of years of early evolutionary history, when the planet would have looked rather boring from our present perspective, were in fact hives of genome production activity in which the basic toolkit genes evolved that are needed to run the basic cellular machinery of all today's living organisms.

Storing bits and pieces in the garage has the disadvantage that if they're not used, then eventually 'moths and rust do corrupt' until finally the pressure will be on to do a little throwing away. But genomes are loathe to throw away old genes, even when they're no longer in use. For example our own genomes are loaded with 'pseudogenes', stretches of DNA that are so similar to functional genes that there is no doubt where they came from, yet so full of mutations that they are functionally incapable of making protein, as can be shown experimentally in the laboratory. Just taking chromosome 7 alone as an example, this stretch of DNA contains 1,150 protein-coding genes, but also has 941 pseudogenes, sitting there like genetic fossils of our evolutionary past. We shall consider some further fascinating examples of this genre in the next section and in Chapter Nine.

Where does new genetic information come from?

Non-biologists who look at how evolution works are often puzzled as to where the information comes from, especially if they are mathematicians, engineers or computer scientists who are used to studying information storage and handling devices that are very different from those found in biological systems. 'Information' can mean many different things depending on the context. The mistake comes in trying to force its meaning in one context on to another.

Clearly there is useful information contained in the genes found in DNA, but this rather begs the question as to where the DNA came from in the first place. We will return to that question later. But for the moment let's just note that new information in biological terms is coming in (and out) of the genome all the time, not just in evolutionary history, but during the course of our own lives as well.

Genetic mutations that cause changes in the sequence of the amino acids in a protein can clearly be said to be the cause of new information. The genome and its products are not the same as before. The organism that it generates may be subtly or dramatically different. The same can be true of mutations in regulatory genes if they are the cause of a change in the way the gene functions, and the same applies to the more than 500 sequences in the human genome that encode the newly discovered class of small RNA molecules that themselves encode important information in their own right. Gene flow likewise introduces new information from one interbreeding population into another. In all these cases, remember that the information content of a gene is defined by the company that it keeps: it is the complete orchestra that counts. New information can arise from the same gene being placed in a new genomic environment. And genes are frequently co-opted to carry out new tasks as they are placed in different teams. Novelty often comes not by adding a new gene to the genome, but by using genes already there in new organisational combinations. All the genes necessary for building new and complex body plans during the Cambrian explosion predated this period of diversification by about 50 million years, as discovered by analysing the genomes of living species that predate this period[90]. In this case it appears to have been the co-opting of 'old genes' for new tasks that was critical. But when a new gene is added to a genomic repertoire, the potential informational repertoire increases enormously. It has been estimated that the effect of adding one new gene to a genome containing 30,000 genes can theoretically generate a staggering 10^{287} possible new functions![91]

Inherited gene duplication events can also be the source of new information. The 'extra' gene is now less likely to be under the pressure of natural selection, because its parental gene is already in the genome anyway doing a good job. So the newly duplicated gene may start to accumulate mutations in succeeding generations by the process of 'genetic drift', in this way acquiring a new function advantageous to the organism, thereby undergoing natural selection. An analogous situation can occur during chromosome doubling in which whole genomes duplicate themselves as discussed earlier in the context of plants. This generates huge scope for further novelty, because now not just one duplicated gene, but a whole genome, is free to wander off mutationally and do new and exciting things. In practice the big genome is often eventually trimmed down to a more manageable size, but is now quite different from what it was before. Indeed there is good evidence that whole genome doubling was involved more than

once in the evolution of the vertebrates. So all of these duplication events involve the production of new information.

To see how this works out in practice we can use an example from our old friends the Hox genes, in the process seeing
how a neat piece of reverse engineering can actually reconstruct past evolutionary events. Around the time of the
Cambrian explosion half a billion years ago, when new vertebrate evolution was in full swing, the genomes of the ancestors
of present living vertebrates appear to have quadrupled, as
mentioned above, by two successive doublings during the
course of evolution. By that time there were 13 Hox genes controlling the development of the body plan, which therefore
quadrupled in number to 52. The ones that didn't later mutate
to do useful things were subsequently lost from the genome,
and so mammals have ended up with 39 Hox genes today.

Two of the genes that were originally duplicates (as we can
tell by looking at their very similar DNA sequences) are called
Hoxa1 and Hoxb1, derived from an ancestral Hox1 gene, and
in today's mammals they both do different jobs. Hoxa1 con-
trols brain stem development in the early embryo whereas
Hoxb1 directs nerve growth in an area of the brain that con-
trols facial expression. The two genes make an identical protein but in different parts of the brain and at different times
during early embryonic development, showing that in this case
it is the regulatory region of the gene that differs between the
gene, not the protein-coding portion. Now here comes the
clever reverse engineering part of the story. Researchers were
interested in seeing whether they could turn back the evolutionary clock by reconstructing the ancient ancestral Hox1
gene in a line of genetically modified mice. So they took the
regulatory region of the Hoxb1 gene, the part responsible for
turning the gene on during fetal development, and attached it
to the Hoxa1 gene to reconstruct the original Hox1 gene. Then
they incorporated it into a line of mice in which both the
Hoxa1 and Hoxb1 genes had been removed by genetic engineering techniques (called a 'double knock-out' in daily lab
language). The resulting mice developed normally, showing
that the ancestral Hox1 gene could function perfectly well[92].

Now here is an interesting question: does this gene duplication event during evolution lead to a net increase of information in the genome or not? In one sense the answer is 'no': the single ancestral gene can do the task of both the evolved genes. But in another sense the answer is 'yes', because we now have a 'safer' control system in mammals than before. A single mutation in the Hox1 gene that previously would have wiped out all normal development is now safeguarded by the information being spread in two different locations. A deleterious mutation might now affect facial expression, certainly not to be welcomed, but without affecting the much more important brain stem development. The genome has now become a slightly different information-containing device from previously. If you are flying across the Atlantic then there is some comfort in the fact that your plane has two engines on either wing and if one fails then the plane can still land safely (or so they always tell you).

At other times during evolutionary history there have been rather special and even bigger influxes of information into the genome than that generated by the duplication of individual genes. The classic and perhaps most dramatic example of this arose when bacteria that had probably started living symbiotically inside cells, that is they had found a lifestyle that gave some advantage to both partners, then became permanent residents and developed into the mitochondria and chloroplasts that we see in cells today. Symbiosis is something that we all live with: there are about ten times more bacteria living in our own bodies than our own cell number (very roughly 10^{14} bacteria compared to 10^{13} cells). Bacteria could not live without us and we certainly need them to provide us with vitamins and other nutrients. The mitochondria we now have are little organelles found in the cytoplasm (region outside the nucleus) of all cells of multicellular animals, functioning as the 'power-plants' of the cell, generating the energy from food that cells need to keep going. Chloroplasts are organelles found in plant cells responsible for photosynthesis, also 'power plants', but with a different energy source (the sun).

Both mitochondria and chloroplasts contain their own DNA, separate from the main storehouse of DNA that is found in the nucleus. Our own mitochondrial DNA contains only 37 genes out of our total 20,000–25,000 genes. Mitochondrial DNA is inherited only from our mothers because it is the cytoplasm of the egg, with its contents, that is used to make more cells following fertilisation, the mitochondria from the sperm being lost during this process. This is quite useful for geneticists who want to track down ancestry, as we shall discuss later in the chapter about human evolution. But in the present context it is the influx of extra information that came with the incorporation of micro-organisms into cells, to later become permanent organelles, that is the key point. It is a bit like acquisitions and mergers. If a big pharmaceutical company has too few drugs in development, the normal strategy is to buy up a smaller biotech company that has some new technology and promising drug leads, both parties benefiting in the process.

How do we know that mitochondria and chloroplasts came into being through an acquisition and merger exercise during early evolution? What finally convinced scientists were the great similarities between these organelles and bacteria. As soon as mitochondria were discovered in the late nineteenth century it had been noticed that they looked very like bacteria, and now we have a range of evidence pointing to their bacterial origins. The composition of their membranes is characteristic of bacteria, but it is their own little genomes that are the real giveaway, with more similarities to their parental bacterial genomes than to their host genomes. In 1998 Siv Andersson in Sweden found that the mitochondrial genome sequence is particularly close to that of *Rickettsia prowazekii*, the nasty aerobic bacteria that cause typhus. This doesn't mean that our mitochondria originally came from this precise strain of bacteria, but it does mean that they came from something very like it. The word 'aerobic' is the key here, because it refers to those bacteria using oxygen for their metabolism ('anaerobes' live without oxygen). It was the incorporation of an aerobic bacteria into those early cells, to eventually become what we now call mitochondria, that is thought to have bestowed upon them the ability to use oxygen, an enormous influx of useful genetic information that had a huge impact on evolutionary history. In a similar *tour de force* it has been shown that chloroplast DNA is very similar to the DNA found in cyanobacteria, the light-harnessing bacteria that live in oceans and fresh water, turning the water green at about 6.00 a.m. in our 24-hour metaphor for evolutionary history. It should be noted that the DNA in both mitochondria and chloroplasts undergo natural selection just like the nuclear DNA. The influx of genetic variation that came into cellular genomes by this process was certainly out of the ordinary, but the variation that resulted still remained under the normal pressure of natural selection.

Sexual reproduction also involves producing new genetic information. The genome of every child in the world is unique, save identical twins. I was amused to get into conversation one day with a married couple, both computer scientists, who were expressing doubt concerning the ability of normal evolutionary processes to generate novelty in organisms, while their own children were running around looking distinctly different from each other! The process of recombination during gamete formation together with subsequent pairing of male and female chromosomes is just another way of introducing variation into the genome.

We normally associate viruses with contracting flu or other unwelcome diseases. But not all viruses are harmful to us and they represent a huge pool of genetic information. Viruses consist of some DNA or RNA with a few proteins packaged together to infect host cells where they live as parasites, using the host cells' own molecular production machinery to churn out more copies of themselves. We are increasingly beginning to understand the huge variety of viruses around the world. Viruses are everywhere – 2,000 metres down below the surface of the earth, in the sands of the Sahara Desert and in icy lakes. There are estimated to be 10^{31} viral particles on the planet[93], an astronomically huge number (especially considering that there are roughly 10^{22} stars in the universe). A kilogram of marine muck was found to contain up to a million genetically variant viruses. Our own guts may contain as many as 1,200 different viruses. As already mentioned, roughly 8% of our own genomes come from DNA copies of RNA-based viruses that have incorporated themselves as long-term fixtures. Some of these insertions have ended up having useful functions, such as a viral gene that is now essential for normal development of the placenta in both mice and humans. Bacteria have drawn even more useful genes from their infection by viruses, including toxins that they use to kill their competitors. An estimated 10^{24} new viruses are being created every second somewhere in the world. The vast majority of these die virtually immediately as they are completely unsuccessful in infecting host cells (bacteria in most cases). But the number being generated is so vast that fairly frequently their rapid mutation rate ensures that new genes are formed, which may eventually be incorporated into the genomes of other organisms. The huge number of viruses in the world may therefore be viewed as a giant gene production factory, generating a constant stream of new information, some of which is taken up and adapted for use by other genomes.

Genetic information can also be *lost* from the genome, pseudogenes providing a good example. Cars that are not serviced will eventually become dysfunctional. Genes that are in excess of requirements for an organism to flourish in a given ecological niche will no longer be under the pressure of natural selection to conform, so they will accumulate mutations and eventually stop making proteins. For example, no less than 63% of our own olfactory genes are permanently switched off. All mammalian genomes studied so far contain about 1,000 genes involved in smell. So the 63% of our olfactory genes no longer in use are derelict genes lying around in our genomes doing nothing, but still being faithfully replicated with every cell division. Since starting to read this chapter, you yourself have been making miles and miles of pseudogene DNA. It is just like going into a factory and seeing lots of derelict machines lying around, no longer being used. They might be obsolete, but they would still impart a great deal of information about the evolution of the factory.

Now if we look at the same olfactory or smell genes in New World monkeys, we discover that nearly all the 1,000 genes are in use – only about 5% are switched off, because smell plays such a crucial role in the survival and reproductive success of monkeys. In the mouse genome 20% of the genes are switched off. So in species for which a very fine sense of smell is crucial, most of the smell genes are active, whereas for species like ours – who just need to distinguish between a pizza and a curry for survival – most of our smell genes are inactive. What that means in practice is that mutations have occurred in the genes that have made them non-functional, but these non-functional genes have been passed on to us without any problem, because as a matter of fact they're not really important for our biological success as a species.

So genomes are not static entities with fixed levels of information, but dynamic systems in which the information content is always changing to some degree for different reasons. Personally I'm happy about that – who wants to be clonal? We shall have more to say later about the generation of new information and new biological systems when we come to the question of our very early evolutionary history, intelligent design and the origins of biologically complex systems.

Traditional fossils

Time was when any explanation of evolution would invariably start with fossils[94]. Certainly the study of the fossil record was critical in getting evolutionary theory off the ground in the first place. So my placing of it this late in the discussion is not at all meant to be a put down – fossils are crucially important – but it does reflect the way in which the advent of genomics has hugely changed the nature of the discussion about evolution. In fact if there were no fossils at all, we would still be able to construct much of evolutionary history just from genetics. Also, unlike the fossil record, there are no gaps in the genetic record. By that I do not mean that we have a complete record of all the genome sequences of every species that ever lived – of course we do not and never will have because 99% of them are no longer around to get DNA samples. Nevertheless, in the 1% that remains we have a DNA record, including disused genetic fossils, that take us back to the dawn of life.

But of course 'traditional fossils' are important as well[95]. A fossil is any trace of past life. Most fossils are hard body parts such as bones, teeth and shells, as well as the woody tissues of land plants and insect cuticles. Fossils can also include traces of an animal's activity, like burrows and footprints in the mud, and the chemicals formed by different organisms. When an organism dies, its body is usually eaten by various scavengers, including bacteria. Therefore organisms that consist mainly of soft parts, like worms and plants, are less likely to leave fossils than those possessing hard parts. Some fossils of soft parts do exist, but they tend to be deposited in exceptional circumstances or preserve exceptionally abundant life forms.

The original mineral components of the hard parts, such as the calcium carbonate in most shells and the calcium hydroxy apatite in bone, are sometimes preserved. At other times water percolates through the surrounding porous rock and dissolves the skeletal material away, filling up the space with crystalline minerals to form a cast of the original fossil. These casts often reproduce very precisely the original living material. In the Painted Desert of Arizona there is a petrified forest consisting of trees with tissues slowly replaced by silica and other minerals until now, 200 million years later, the trees are made of stone, but still displaying many of their original cellular details. In the hills round the village of Rhynie in Scotland an entire ecosystem has been preserved by being engulfed in the silica-rich waters from a volcanic spring dating from 410 million years ago. The fossil plants are still standing upright with their cells visible. Insects are preserved in incredible detail, some still clinging to the stems of plants on which they lived and died[96].

Which fossils in which rocks?

There are three main types of rock recognised by geologists. Igneous rocks begin as molten lava, which in turn is molten rock. Metamorphic rocks are those found deep in the earth's crust and are formed by the metamorphosis of other rock types. Sedimentary rocks such as limestone and sandstone are formed from tiny fragments that are ground gradually from other larger rocks or from other hard materials such as shells. Carried in a suspension of sand, silt or dust, these tiny particles are then carried elsewhere to be deposited as sedimentary layers. As the sediments compact, so they are gradually turned into rock. It is in these sedimentary rocks that most fossils are to be found.

Fossilisation is rare and the further a species lives from a sedimentary layer the less likely the members of the species are to be fossilised. Species that live just above a sediment, such as marine creatures near the sea bed, are more likely to be fossilised than fish with habitats nearer the surface. Least likely of all to be fossilised are terrestrial animals.

Sometimes so much organic material becomes compacted into one sediment that it forms a material homogeneous enough to make up a large part of the sedimentary layer itself. For example coal, formed during the Carboniferous period (hence the name), originates largely from ferns and related plants that flourished during that era (290–354 million years ago), gradually converted into this precious fossil fuel under the immense pressures exerted by the rock layers that accumulated above.

Chalk is a type of limestone made up of the compacted bodies of billions upon billions of very small single-celled marine creatures called plankton. It is therefore composed of micro-fossils. For example the great chalk bed visible as the white cliffs of Dover is 1,329 feet thick. The accumulation rate of sedimentary limestone made of chalk is in the range 1–10 centimetres per 1000 years. So even at the very (unlikely) fastest rate, the Dover chalk bed would take 4 million years to form, and the actual time period for the deposition of the chalk beds that characterise much of the southern UK is 35 million years. These things do not happen overnight. Most chalk beds were laid down during the Cretaceous period, between 100 and 60 million years ago. Cretaceous chalk is much whiter than other forms of limestone because it is freer from impurities. Sea levels were very high during the Cretaceous period, so there was little nearby land exposed to supply other sediments that would darken the texture (one of the many reasons, by the way, that we know that chalk was not deposited by a universal flood).

The very earliest fossils date from the period 3 to 3.5 billion years ago and consist of fossilised mats of bacteria known as stromatolites, ranging in size from a few millimetres to more than 10 metres. Stromatolites are layered structures that are formed when bacteria grow in giant colonies on the cell surface and sediments are deposited above or among the cells, building up many mineralised layers. Stromatolites are still being formed in the world today from photosynthetic cyanobacteria, but more rarely than at that ancient time, presumably because there are now predators in the seas that happily graze on this rich food source, whereas such predators did not of course exist in those far off days. The characteristic cone shapes of many samples of stromatolite formed during the period 2.5–3.5 billion years ago is also reproduced in contemporary stromatolites. Although there has been some controversy as to whether stromatolites do indeed represent ancient fossilised bacteria, the most recent data support such an interpretation[97].

We have fossil data for cells with a nucleus (remember that bacteria do not have nuclei) from as early as the period 1.8–2.2 billion years ago, and such cells can be recognised mainly by their much larger size than bacteria (ten times bigger or more). The earliest fossil evidence for multicellular life forms, in this case algae, is from 1.2 billion years ago. By 1 billion years ago microbial fossils are found on land – until this time all life of any kind was in the sea and the land was barren.

By the time we reach the period 550–670 million years ago, the fossil record really starts to take off, with the Ediacaran fossils found in Australia and other similar fossils found in other parts of the world. These are mainly of soft-bodied aquatic animals such as jellyfish and worms. Many of the fossils from new animals emerging during this period were first discovered in the Burgess Shale, a black shale fossil bed named after nearby Burgess Pass high up in the Canadian Rockies in British Columbia. The Burgess Shale alone contains about 140 species of animals representing more than ten phyla[98]. Similar shale fossil beds from China, such as Chengjiang in Yunnan Province, have provided further wonderful fossils, even older (by 15 million years) than those found in the Burgess Shale. The Ediacaran animals continued on into the early Cambrian period, but then went extinct, making biological classification more problematic.

At the same time, or even earlier, the bilateral symmetry of body plan – the mirror image of arms and legs that is so characteristic of animals ever since – starts appearing. The first 'bilaterians', as all such creatures are called, were discovered in rocks dating from 580 to 600 million years ago from Guizhou Province in China[99]. There tiny fossil bilaterians were identified (named *Vernanimalcula* meaning 'small spring animal'), only the width of a few hairs across, but with the classic mirror-image body structure of a bilaterian. These little creatures probably zoomed around on the seafloor feeding on microbes which at that time covered the floor in great mats.

It is from the Cambrian period onwards that we obtain our most complete fossil records of the evolution of species. As skeletons and other hard parts evolved, so the numbers left behind to be fossilised increased sharply, greatly improving the quality of the record. The various sedimentary layers provide an invaluable record of the history of life on this planet, with the oldest rocks at the bottom and the youngest at the top. This so-called 'geological column' became well established during the nineteenth century as a result of observations made during mining and by the great Victorian naturalists who established the modern science of geology. One of the main figures in establishing the geological column was an evangelical cleric, the Revd Adam Sedgwick (1785–1873), appointed as first professor of geology at Cambridge at the age of 33. The historical roots of geology are deeply embedded in theistic soil.

So characteristic are the fossils found in certain rocks that from early days in geology fossils were used as markers for identifying sedimentary layers. That might sound like a circular argument: 'date the rocks by the fossils and the fossils by the rocks'. However, the initial correlation of fossils and strata was developed by the engineer William Smith (1769–1839), who made no theoretical assumptions at all but had simply noted the consistency of the association as he saw strata uncovered by engineering works. Sedgwick, who first established far more strata than anyone else in history, used a three-dimensional geometric approach working from a 'base line' to map out the strata, backed up by and sometimes amended in the light of palaeontological study. The basic structure of the geological column was completed several years before Darwin published *The Origin of Species* in 1859, and was in no way dependent upon evolutionary assumptions (Sedgwick himself was never convinced by evolution). The development in the twentieth century of radioisotopic dating simply offered an independent confirmation that the original stratification was in fact correct. Moreover, after a long flirtation with Lyellian 'uniformitarianism' in geology (the arbitrary assumption of uniform rates of geological change), the geological world has now reverted to a form of 'catastrophism' very similar to that advocated by Sedgwick and his colleagues, and this is what is assumed in the present book.

Today, therefore, the same types of strata with the same type of fossils crop up all over the world. Devonian rocks can readily be recognised by any geologist wherever they are found, such as the 'Old Red Sandstone' of the British county of Devon, which even amateur geologists can identify without difficulty. Just as scholars can readily identify the book of Isaiah embedded in the Dead Sea Scrolls by comparison with previously known texts, so geologists can identify rocks by the fossils found within them[100]. Sometimes a large geological convulsion, such as a volcanic eruption, can turn the column upside down, but it is always fairly obvious what has happened and these are the exceptions rather than the rule.

Fossils and the history of life from the Cambrian period

In the rocks of 505–525 million years ago we have a sudden profusion of complex animals with limbs, antennae, eyes and tails, in fact the 'complete kit' so familiar to us in today's life forms. This is the Cambrian explosion, the Big Bang of animal evolution. The fossils from this period include representatives from all the modern groups, including arthropods (such as crabs), chordates (organisms with backbones like us) and molluscs.

At 500 million years we find fossils of fish, but very different kinds of fish from the ones we have today, with a bony armour protecting the body and no jawbones in the skull. Rocks dating from 350 to 500 million years old now have fish with jaws, but there are no fossils of amphibians such as frogs or reptiles to be found. Only in rocks from 350 million years ago do we begin to discover fossilised land animals, amphibians and insects, followed at 300 million years ago by reptiles. From 230–65 million years ago dinosaurs ruled the world and are major features of the terrestrial fossil record. It is not until we come to rocks 150 million years old that we begin to find fossilised birds and, as highlighted earlier, mammalian diversity is not written into the fossil record until after the extinction of the dinosaurs.

The evolution of plants is likewise extensively written into the fossil record. Fossil spores already begin to appear clearly in rocks dating from 475 million years ago, with possible dates much earlier than this. The earliest fossils of complete plants, rather than just spores, date from 430 million years ago. The earliest land plants lacked roots and leaves, and just had branching stems, where all their photosynthesis took place. Fossilised plants with leaves begin to appear during the period 390–350 million years ago, coinciding with a dramatic fall of about 90% in the atmospheric carbon dioxide concentration, events that might well be connected[101]. Fossilised flowering plants began to appear from about 125 million years ago.

Imagine a filing cabinet with lots of drawers. Each drawer is full of fossils. The bottom drawer contains only very small, simple organisms, many of them representing species no longer alive today. Working up the drawers to the top, the complexity and variety of the fossils begins to increase, until finally in the last few upper drawers fossilised species are to be found which look very familiar, typical of what we see all around us today. The drawers in the metaphorical cabinet are like the different sedimentary rocks. Such a record is consistent with an evolutionary history involving common descent in which every twig and branch on the great bush of life can be traced back in time to the trunk and the roots from which the whole bush originates.

From sea to land

Let us now imagine that we take one of the drawers from our cabinet and subdivide all the fossils in that single drawer into a more detailed and orderly sequence, representing transitional forms all the way from one species to another, with intermediates linking the species. This is a bit like zooming in on Google Earth to look at our own town or city and the way that the roads are all specifically connected up in our neighbourhood.

Many people think that there are still missing links in the map of life, but that depends on what they mean. To the question: 'Do we have a complete map of the whole "city" of evolution, showing in detail how every single road (= species in this analogy) came into being and is connected with every other road?', then the answer is 'No. We don't even have a complete catalogue of all the road names, let alone know how they all interconnect to form the complete city'. But if the question is the more manageable one: 'Do we have some detailed maps of quite a few areas of the "city" with a good idea as to how the main areas join up?' then the answer is definitely 'yes'. Of course in a sense every time we find an intermediary fossil illustrating transitional forms between two species, then we have generated two more gaps to fill! But with some very recent fossil discoveries on board, we do now have some clear and detailed step-by-step transitional fossil records illustrating the evolution of one life form into something quite different.

Space does not permit descriptions of all these various well-established fossil sequences, so here we will illustrate the idea with just one example, the transition that took fish out of water to become terrestrial creatures. Other equally well-attested examples include the evolution of mammals, evolution of the whale (a mammal that returned to the sea from land via *Pakicetus*, *Ambulocetus* and the fossil whale *Basilosaurus* which retains a complete mammalian hind limb), the evolution of elephants and horses, the evolution of turtles and many other examples besides[102].

The evolution of fish into tetrapods, animals that live on land, has become well established over the past few decades, with some spectacular recent discoveries helping to fill in previous gaps in the story (see Figure 9). Modern bony fish can be divided into two main groups: the abundant ray-finned fish and the much less abundant lobe-finned fish. It is from the lobe-finned fish that the tetrapods evolved. Living lobe-finned fish include the lungfishes which are found in Africa and South America. These are freshwater fish that can breathe air if their lakes dry up or if the oxygen level in the water becomes too low. It can readily be seen how natural selection would favour the reproductive success of such fish living in aquatic environments liable to dry up in the hot season. Lobe-fins have a body plan that has a number of similarities with tetrapods, including muscular fins with the same basic body arrangement as forelimbs and hind legs, connecting to a pair of long bones, in turn connecting to a pair of smaller bones. 370 million years ago lobe-finned fish were more diverse than now; and extinct, fossil specimens have been discovered looking even more like tetrapods than the lungfish.

Panderichthys, for example, is a species found in Latvia and dating from the mid-Devonian period 385 million years ago, which is still definitely fish-like, but also somewhat resembles a crocodile, with a pectoral fin skeleton and shoulder girdle intermediate in shape between those of a lobe-finned fish and a tetrapod. It was therefore able to waddle along through shallow water but probably not to walk on dry land.

Like the builders drilling the Channel Tunnel between Britain and France, we can start from both ends in the fossil record and see how the two ends meet up in the middle. *Ichthyostega* and *Acanthostega* are clearly tetrapods with the flat-topped skulls that are characteristic of later tetrapods, and possessing front limbs and hind limbs with digits on, but they also have unmistakably fishy tails[103]. Found in Greenland, they date from 365 million years ago. The gap in the tetrapod evolutionary fossil record between around 385 and 365 million years ago was one of the spurs that led a Canadian research group to make repeated research trips back to northern Canada to look for further fossils, where they were ferried by helicopter to a spot on Ellesmere Island just 887 miles from the North Pole. Conditions were challenging on their fourth and final dig in the area – frozen fingers and the need to carry shotguns to fend off polar bears[104]: but their persistence was rewarded by some stunning findings published in 2006, in which they described the discovery of several late-Devonian

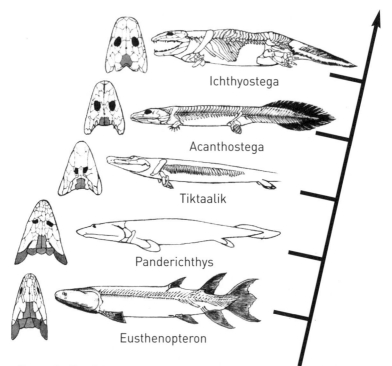

Figure 9. Fossil intermediates between fish and tetrapods (land living animals). [Adapted by Ayala, F. from *Nature* 440: 747–749, 2006. Reproduced with permission from Macmillan Publishers Ltd and from the National Academy of Sciences, Courtesy of the National Academies Press, Washington, D.C.]

fossil specimens of a new species, named *Tiktaalik* (after the Inuit for 'big freshwater fish'), precisely fitting as intermediates in the tetrapod evolutionary sequence (see Figure 9)[105]. *Tiktaalik* was about the size of a crocodile, with scales like a fish but also fins like limbs and an elbow joint that could push the animal off the ground – as one of the team who made the discovery remarked, 'it's like a fish that can do push-ups'!

The present understanding is that these early fish took advantage of the lush coastal wetlands that developed on earth for the first time during the Devonian period, as trees began to grow along coasts and rivers. Although the *Tiktaalik* fossils were found in northern Canada, 400 million years of continental drift means that they were originally living near the equator in an environment similar to the present Mississippi delta region. Living happily in those far-off shallow waters as well as on the slimy, wet land nearby, *Tiktaalik* was a trendsetter, and certainly the land has been getting more crowded ever since.

So despite the gaps in the fossil record, the well-attested evolutionary sequences that we do have are impressive, and from time to time further discoveries of new fossils are helping to make the story more complete. If we translate the bush of life into the metaphor of a giant jigsaw puzzle, laid out across the nearest football pitch (for example), then what we see are huge swathes of puzzle well joined together, but we also see other areas (like the pieces representing the Ediacaran fauna) still lying separated, without enough data to join the pieces up properly. But of course evolutionary biologists are delighted by the bits not yet resolved. Not only do they represent a fascinating challenge, but they also keep them happily employed with a job yet to do!

Chapter 6:
Objections to Evolution

One of the very enjoyable aspects of being in the scientific community is the robust debate about research results and their meaning. Science thrives in open societies where dissent and discussion are encouraged, but tends to shrivel or perhaps never gets going properly in the first place where the opposite is the case. Evolutionary theory is not immune from such debates and sometimes these can be long and drawn out, and even acrimonious, occasionally spilling over into the popular press who love nothing better than reporting a whiff of cordite in the corridors of academia. But such debates are not about whether evolution happened or not, which virtually no biologist in the research community actually doubts, but about mechanisms, interpretations, classification disputes and indeed, to tell the truth, sometimes quarrels about matters that would make discussions about how many angels can dance on a pinhead look quite sane by comparison.

I have sometimes been told by critics outside the scientific community that there would never be any hope of publishing data that looked likely to subvert evolutionary theory, because evolution for biologists is a 'holy cow' that must be protected at all costs. In fact exactly the opposite is the case. It is every biologist's dream to make discoveries that would upset some cherished theory. If you do that then your career is made for life. If you found rabbit fossils in the pre-Cambrian era, or indubitable evidence for human and dinosaur fossils in the same sedimentary layer, or evidence for new forms of life from the bottom of some deep ocean that displayed a different genetic code, or solid evidence for the inheritance of acquired characteristics, then your first author paper in *Nature* or *Science* is assured and you can live happily ever after.

One of the deep mysteries of life, far more mysterious than the origins of the Ediacaran fauna, is why people spend their time going round churches telling people that they don't believe evolutionary theory. If people wish to challenge a theory then that is an excellent and honourable path to follow in the best of scientific traditions. But there are well-established ways of carrying out a scientific critique and these involve the tough course of becoming a member of the scientific research community, and then finding and publishing results in peer-reviewed journals that may challenge a particular theory. That is how theory testing is done and it is the only way that will win the respect of the scientific community. Public votes, popular articles, political pressures, campaigns or even sermons by famous preachers will have no effect on scientific opinion because that is not how science is done. So really serious objections to evolution, if there are any, have to be presented the tough but proper way, by publication of solid results in reputable scientific journals.

Of course that does not mean that Christians cannot have serious questions and objections about evolution, and it is perfectly valid to exchange views on these in a friendly spirit, which is the purpose of this chapter; but in carrying out such an exercise it is important to be reminded how the scientific enterprise itself is carried out.

I have posed the objections below not as theoretical questions, but as points that I have had addressed to me personally following lectures on science and faith, or else read in books critical of evolution. The main purpose of this chapter is to air the scientific objections, posed as a series of questions. I have included some theological concerns as well, although sometimes getting the science right dissolves the theological worry at the same time. The biggest theological concerns expressed are usually to do with Adam and Eve, death and the Fall, so I have dedicated separate chapters to those hot topics.

'Evolution is a chance process and this is incompatible with the God of the Bible bringing about his purposeful plan of creation.'

It is intriguing that this question comes up so often because, taken as a whole, evolution is in no sense a chance process. Atheistic biologists like Richard Dawkins, and Christian evolutionary biologists like Simon Conway Morris, equally conclude that the evolutionary process is not a matter of chance. The point is sometimes missed that one of Dawkins' aims in writing his book *The Blind Watchmaker*, as he states in the preface, is 'to destroy this eagerly believed myth that Darwinism is a theory of "chance"'.

The key phrase is 'evolution taken as a whole'. To think about this a bit more we need to consider our own lives and the various meanings of that slippery little word 'chance' that might be relevant in that context. Consider the course of your life until now. If you are a Christian, then you believe that God in his providential care has been sovereign over all the details of your life, even from the time before you were born. This includes the fact that one particular sperm fertilised one particular egg at a particular moment in time to generate that genetically unique individual that you became. Millions of sperm were involved in that race to get to the egg first – you could so easily have been of the opposite sex to what you are now, and you could easily have looked physically quite different. Fertilisation is truly a chance process. Yet you still believe (I hope!) that God was sovereign in all these contingent events that brought you into existence.

Why stop at biology? Think about all the myriad events that have been woven together in an immensely complex tapestry to bring about God's will in our lives. Some of those events may have been painful – perhaps things that happened quite out of our control. Other events were quite mundane, yet made a profound difference to outcomes and events.

In the film *Sliding Doors*, one life unfolds in two very different ways, cleverly woven together through the film, depending on whether someone did or did not catch a particular train on the London Underground as the sliding doors slammed shut. The film was right – seemingly trivial differences in life can have enormous effects. At one level they represent chance events – there is no way that we or anyone else can predict them – but Christians also believe that God is ultimately in control of everything that happens.

The Bible is consistent in its teaching that events many people would ascribe to chance are within the boundaries of God's sovereignty and plan. When the prophet Micaiah predicted that King Ahab would be killed in battle at Ramoth Gilead (1 Kings 22:15–28), this indeed came to pass, but it happened by someone who 'drew his bow *at random* and hit the king of Israel between the sections of his armour' (I Kings 22:34, my italics). As Proverbs 16:33 so vividly puts the point: 'The lot is cast into the lap, but its every decision is from the Lord'. The Bible sees God's works occurring equally in all the various manifestations of his activity, whether in the more 'law-like' workings of the natural world (Psalm 33:6–11), in chance events (Proverbs 16:33), or in his control of the weather (Psalm 148:8), which today we describe using chaos theory. There is never a hint in the Bible that certain types of event in the natural world are any more or any less the activity of God than other events.

But what do we mean by chance and how does that understanding relate to evolution? Unfortunately the word 'chance' can be used with at least three quite distinct meanings and people are not always clear in discussion which meaning they have in mind. First, there is the kind of chance events that are predictable in principle but not in practice. For example, if we had enough information about each of the millions of sperm racing to fertilise an egg, then providing we had a complete description also of the environment, we could theoretically predict which one would win the race. But in the second kind of chance, that which typifies events at the quantum level, our ignorance about the future is complete. When a radioactive atom decays we have no way of knowing when the next high-energy particle will be emitted, and this reflects our inability to predict in principle and not just in practice. Some people call that kind of chance 'pure chance'. Then there is a third type of chance, which we can label 'metaphysical chance'. This is something very different from the other two types of chance and refers to the philosophy that in some ultimate sense the universe came into being 'by chance' and has no real rhyme, reason or intentionality.

It is only the first two types of chance that are relevant to evolution. The reason for this is that mutations in DNA can, as we have considered already, be due to failures in the actions of DNA repair enzymes that occasionally miss errors during the 'proof-reading' process. This is an example of the first type of chance – it might be predictable in principle if we knew enough about the details of the system, but not in practice. But mutations in DNA can also happen by exposure to radiation – this is an example of the second type of chance, non-predictable in theory as well as in practice. But so far as evolutionary mechanisms are concerned, it really doesn't matter whether the mutation arose by the first or second kind of chance. Either way a change has come into being in the gene sequence, and if that change occurs in the germ cells (sperm and eggs) so that it is passed on to the next generation, then the change will in any case be tested out by the 'filter' of reproductive success. As already noted, in many ways evolution is a very conservative process: natural selection preserves some genes so carefully during millions of rounds of replication and millions of years of evolution, that some encoded proteins in human and rabbit even have identical amino acid sequences.

So if we look at the overall process of evolution, it is very far indeed from any notion of 'metaphysical chance'. It is a stringently regulated series of events in which food chains are built up in precisely defined ecological niches. The process has occurred in particular environments characterised by parameters such as cold and heat, light and darkness, wetness and dryness, with the constraints of gravity playing a key role in defining animal and plant sizes and shapes. There are good reasons why elephants don't fly. And there are good reasons why the eye has evolved not once but many times during the process of evolution. Later we will consider the phenomenon of 'convergence' in more detail, whereby the same organs or biochemical pathways have evolved multiple times in independent lineages during evolutionary history.

Therefore evolutionary mechanisms are nothing like the processes that we normally think of as 'random' in any ultimate sense. When the TV breaks down and a horrible meaningless fuzz replaces the programme on the screen, we might rightly think of that as 'random noise' without ultimate meaning. But the biological diversity generated by the evolutionary process is very far from that type of random fuzz, being the outcome of a highly organised collection of mechanisms that are possible only in a carbonaceous world with a particular set of elements and physical laws. The physical properties of the universe were defined in the very first few femtoseconds after the Big Bang, and the process of evolution depends utterly on that particular set of properties. Without them we would not be here.

So as Christians we can perceive the evolutionary process simply as the way that God has chosen to bring biological diversity into being, including us. That is the way things are and our task as scientists is to describe the way things are – what God has done in bringing this vast array of biological diversity into being. Of one thing we can be sure: the evolutionary process provides no grounds for thinking that the universe is a chance process in any ultimate metaphysical sense. In fact, quite the reverse, as we shall consider later. As biologists we marvel at the complexity and diversity of this planet's life forms, and at the fact that we as humans are indissolubly linked by our evolutionary history with every life form on earth.

It should also be obvious from these reflections that chance *does* nothing. 'Chance' is simply a handy description that we humans use for our beliefs about the properties of matter. There is no such agent as 'metaphysical chance', but there *is* the human belief held by some people that the universe has no ultimate meaning. However, those who try propping up that particular belief-system using the prestige of scientific theories will find not a shred of comfort in evolutionary theory.

'The theory of evolution is not truly scientific because it does not involve repeatable experiments in the laboratory.'

The idea behind this question is that 'real science' is carried out by scientists with white coats doing experiments in the laboratory, whereas anything else is not real science. As it happens, I belong to the white-coated brigade of biochemists, but it is clear to every scientist, in whichever discipline, that there are many different ways of doing valid science. Many branches of science, such as cosmology, geology and anthropology, involve painstakingly piecing together a great array of historical data to render a particular finding or phenomenon coherent. The big difference between the 'historical sciences' and history as practised in the humanities is that the former is about what happened to things in the past, whereas the latter is about what happened to people and what they did. Even for that definition the demarcation line is somewhat fuzzy because anthropology studies human origins and behaviour within the sciences, but that is not the same as the history studied in the humanities, and the key difference here is that the former is about the nature of humans as a species whereas the latter is about the actions of humans as individuals and as nations, especially when written records are available.

The ways in which scientists work have many similarities to the legal profession. The aim of the rules of evidence in the legal process is to establish beyond reasonable doubt that an event has or has not occurred. The legal profession has developed over the centuries a set of meticulous criteria for distinguishing truth from error. Of course they can be wrong. But their task is a quasi-historical exercise: to establish from the available data that an event did or did not happen and was brought about by whom, and how did they do it. A convincing case is built up step by step until judge and jury are finally persuaded.

Biologists are in a very similar position with respect to the theory of evolution. They were not there to observe the millions of years of gradual evolution, nor all those incremental steps leading to speciation, but they can make an 'inference to the best explanation' whereby firm conclusions can be drawn based on the wealth of evidence available. The reason that evolutionary theory is so powerful is that it explains so much so well, and the preceding chapters represent just the tip of the iceberg in terms of describing the types of evidence that are routinely assessed. The geographical distribution of species, the existence of ongoing speciation events, the fossil record, comparative anatomy and, above all, genomics, all provide an immense array of persuasive data in support of common descent with variation. The fact that there is much yet to be discovered and to be clarified does not really affect the core of evolutionary theory.

A powerful, big scientific theory that explains a huge disparate array of data, as in the case of evolution, will inevitably take many years of work to develop. Gaps in knowledge are seen as challenges for further research, not as a challenge to the theory itself. The theory itself is only challenged if *refuting* data are uncovered, as already discussed (rabbit fossils in the pre-Cambrian, variant genetic codes in different species, that kind of thing).

In passing it is also worth pointing out that when biologists speak of the 'theory of evolution' they do not thereby mean that they doubt its veracity, as in the phrase used in common speech: 'it's only a theory'. The term 'theory' in science is used in rather a technical sense to refer to that overarching scheme of ideas making sense of a certain set of data. For example, physicists are not expressing doubt about Einstein's great discoveries when they speak of 'the theory of relativity', but again using the term 'theory' to refer to a whole set of understandings (including some difficult maths) which help us to understand the physical behaviour of things when they are either very big or very small. A scientific theory connects up a disparate set of facts and observations and weaves them into a coherent story. Scientific theories are like maps that help us to find our way around a complex landscape by linking up its various features and making sense of them.

As it happens there is a lot of experimental work that has been, and continues to be, carried out to generate data clarifying and/or supporting evolutionary theory. Field studies are performed on animal and plant populations in the wild; reproductive success can be measured by counting viable off-spring over many generations and relating success to genetic variation between individuals; controlled experiments are set up to introduce well-defined populations of species into defined environments in order to track the consequences; new fossils are discovered; new species are identified, classified and placed within the context of their evolutionary lineages; and above all the science of genomics forges ahead at great speed, providing some stunning new insights into the fossil record written into the genomes of all organisms, and offering exciting new understanding of the ways in which genes encode organisms in particular environments. Genomics includes the kind of experiments already described, whereby 'reverse engineering' in a mouse line can reconstitute the function of an ancestral gene. And just as astronomers can stare with their telescopes at light that left stars on the other side of the universe millions of light years away, so biologists can stare into our own genomes and there read the ancient language of the genes stretching back billions of years into our evolutionary past.

'Evolution runs counter to the second law of thermodynamics.'

The second law of thermodynamics states that the entropy of a system, taken overall, always increases. Entropy is a measure of the uniformity of the distribution of energy. So an increase in entropy involves an increase in the level of disorganisation of a system. The melting of ice provides a classic example in which, within a complete thermodynamic system that includes the sun, the room heated by the sun and the melting ice within it, there is a net increase in entropy. Indeed one of the predictions for the final state of the universe is a 'heat death' in which the second law of thermodynamics will have the final word and all matter will become further and further apart and dis-organised until entropy has increased to a maximum extent.

The concern behind the question is therefore that evolution appears to be a story about going 'uphill' in terms of the increased complexity and organisation of systems, which is contrary to the second law. But of course one has to consider the system taken as a whole, which includes the energy derived from both the sun and the earth, without which life would be impossible. Photosynthesis provides a classic example, in which energy from the sun is translated into cellular energy using the chemical chlorophyll inside plant cells. In a further example, the molten interior of our planet is constantly releasing heat through the earth's crust, but also from vents at the bottom of oceans where complete ecosystems thrive on the energy so provided. So the important point to grasp here is that indeed the entropy of the system taken as a whole is increasing, including the sun in this equation, but as one system (the sun) 'runs down' so another system (life) 'runs up'. There is therefore no violation of the second law of thermodynamics.

'Perhaps God makes things look old, although in reality they are much younger, in order to test our faith?'

This and similar queries often come with the best of intentions. All Christians believe in God as the all-powerful Creator. So why couldn't God just bring everything into being quite suddenly, for example over a period of six days around ten thousand years ago, but give everything the appearance of great age? I say this question comes with the best of intentions, because its purpose is entirely laudable, to highlight God's power and majesty in his great creation.

Those who have this question in mind are in good company. Philip Henry Gosse FRS (1810–88), inventor of the word 'aquarium', was one of the most widely read naturalists of the Victorian era. He was also Darwin's correspondent, responding to his queries on the minutiae of the behaviour of rock pigeons as Darwin was writing *The Origin of Species*. Gosse was also a committed Christian. In his book *The Aquarium: an Unveiling of the Wonders of the Deep Sea* (1854), Gosse reminded his readers that whereas (in his biographer's summary) 'natural science can teach us many useful lessons and brings us, in a sense, into the presence of God...there is no way it can help us to salvation. That is only through the blood of Christ and through the written word of God'.[106] Gosse once wrote that 'I cannot look at the Bible with one eye, and at Nature with the other, I must take them together', exemplary advice for any Christian active in the sciences. Stephen Jay Gould, not known for his enthusiasm for the Christian faith, once wrote a sympathetic essay about Gosse, describing him as the 'David Attenborough of his day'.

Whilst Darwin was preparing his *Origin of Species* for publication, Gosse was working on a very different kind of book, the only book he wrote that proved to be a complete failure, although it is the one now for which he is chiefly remembered and the reason why Gosse is mentioned in this particular context. Philip, a firm believer in the fixity of species, was very optimistic that he had found a theory reconciling 'Scriptural statements and Geological deductions'. It was called *Omphalos*, the Greek word for 'navel', for central to the book's theme was the question: 'Did Adam have a navel?' Gosse did not believe (despite his son's later claim) that creation took place in six literal days, preferring instead an interpretation of Genesis that allowed for long periods of time. Nevertheless he did believe that each species, including humankind, had been created separately by God, a view still shared at this point by most of his fellow scientists (remember that Gosse's book was written before 1859 when Darwin's *Origin of Species* appeared).

Gosse's own rendering of his belief in the fixity of species and a literalistic reading of the early chapters of Genesis was nothing if not imaginative. Ironically his position led him to adopt a non-linear view of time, in contrast to the widely accepted view that biblical teaching has nurtured understanding of a universe with a beginning and an end, with a 'timeline' of God's actions in between. Instead Gosse tried to argue that all the processes of nature move in circles: '...when the Omnipotent God proposed to create a given organism, the course of that organism was present to his idea, as an ever-evolving circle, without beginning and without end'. Therefore the whole of creation, complete with its biological diversity, exists in the mind of God who, by divine *fiat*, wills that his creation is actualised at a particular moment in history. At the dramatic moment of creation, wrote Gosse, 'the world presented, instantly, the structural appearance of a planet on which life had long existed'. The merry-go-round of creation is invisible until the whistle blows, when it appears complete with tree rings, tortoises with laminae on their plates and human navels. It was surely his reading of Gosse that led Bertrand Russell to comment at a later date that 'God could have created us all two minutes ago complete with our memories and the holes in our socks' (a point he made more formally in the ninth chapter of *The Analysis of Mind*).

The most charitable word that contemporary reviewers could find in describing *Omphalos* was 'ingenious'. More typical was the comment by the *Westminster Review* that Gosse's theory was 'too monstrous for belief'. The reactions of his Christian friends were also robust. Gosse's good friend the Anglican cleric Charles Kingsley made the rather obvious point that the whole fantastic theory made God into a deceiver on a grand scale ('You make God tell a lie' wrote Kingsley). Worried for his own children's faith if they read such material, Kingsley also commented: 'I would not for a thousand pounds put your book into my children's hands'; presumably not quite the response that Philip had been hoping for, given that the intention of his book had been to defend biblical faith against the sceptics!

Gosse's book never sold well and much of the printing was pulped. After this debacle Gosse returned to writing scientific papers and *Omphalos* never really harmed his career at the time. But its memory stands as a warning to think carefully about the implications of making rash claims that come from the best of motives but are both scientifically and theologically ill-conceived. For Kingsley was surely correct in his objection to Gosse that if God has made everything with the appearance of great age, complete with tree rings, ice cores, fossils in ordered layers of sedimentary rocks, and genetic fossils in our genomes, but in reality everything is only a few thousand years old, then this surely makes God into a deceiver on a grand scale. It's as if God created Adam instantaneously with a birth certificate, family photo album and first tooth in his back pocket. Yet from Scripture we as Christians believe in a God who is 'the Rock, his works are perfect, and all his ways are just. A faithful God who does no wrong, upright and just is he' (Deuteronomy 32:4), and 'God is not a man, that he should lie' (Numbers 23:19).

The idea that God deceives people by creating things that look as if they are very old when in reality they are not, is potentially damaging for our biblical understanding of the nature of God's faithfulness, and subversive to the whole scientific enterprise. For if God can deceive in one area, then might he not deceive in any area of the created order? And if that is the case, then how can we do science? The scientific enterprise depends completely upon God's faithfulness in creating, upholding and sustaining the properties of matter and energy so that we can expect to find general principles describing these properties which we call 'laws'. Because of God's faithfulness in creation we expect the properties of matter to be reproducible so that we can keep repeating experiments and (hopefully) get the same result. Without that assurance science itself would be impossible: but our findings are in fact reliable – the principles of the natural world are consistent; God does not deceive us.

So although the question with which we started this section sounds innocent enough at first look, once we start thinking about it, the implications are potentially grave for both science and faith.

'What use is half an eye?'

An important aspect of evolutionary theory, as we have noted above, is that it involves the emergence of new properties by gradual incremental steps, each one of which is so favoured by natural selection that the genes involved become more frequent in a population. How does this apply to complex multicomponent organs like the eye, which have to pass through many intermediate stages until they reach their present structural elegance in our own bodies? What use is half an eye? We might also add to that list the many other complex organs and systems in the body: but since the eye is such a classic example, which also worried Darwin, let's consider the eye.

The first point to make is that to the question 'What use is half an eye?' the answer is 'a lot'. In a world of light and darkness, all detection systems that increase awareness of the environment automatically have a big impact on survival and reproductive success. To be able to see a predator coming only dimly has to be better than not seeing the predator at all. People with defective vision are certainly grateful for the limited vision that they retain in comparison with people who are blind – it is an enormous advantage to them.

Furthermore, we now have quite a good understanding as to how the eye evolved based, to a large degree, on living organisms with eyes representing the various stages of the evolutionary process.

Many single-celled organisms have patches of photosensitive cells on their surface known as eye-spots. For example, the stigma of the *Euglena*, a single-celled photosynthetic flagellate (coloured green like a plant because it contains chlorophyll), represents part of its light detection system. This allows the *Euglena* to move towards light sources in order to promote photosynthesis.

A disadvantage of having clusters of photosensitive cells on the cell surface is that while the presence of light can be thus determined, the direction of light is less easily discerned. The next evolutionary development addresses this problem by the formation of small depressions in the skin to accommodate the patches of photosensitive cells. The formation of such 'cups', lined inside with photosensitive cells, allows the light to fall on some cells more than others, depending on the direction of light. Such 'pit eyes' had already evolved by the Cambrian era and are seen in some ancient snails and also in freshwater flatworms such as planaria. Planaria do not contain chlorophyll and in fact use their eye-pits to move themselves away from light, having no need to photosynthesise. Their eye-pits contain heavily-pigmented retina cells, which shield the light-sensitive cells from exposure in all directions except for the single opening for the light.

We are fortunate in having clear examples of all the main

stages of eye evolution in living molluscs, permitting us to study these stages in some detail (see Figure 10). Limpets have simple pit-shaped eyes of the kind described above and are very slow moving molluscs, grazing on rocks. But a shadow falling on its primitive 'eyes' has a powerful effect, causing the limpet to hold on to the rock with incredible force.

An increase in the 'pigment cup' is seen in the slit-shell mollusc *Pleurotomaria*, then even more in the classic 'pinhole' camera design appearing in *Nautilus*, with its floating coiled shell a living example of the ancient ammonites which once thronged the sea but are now largely extinct. Pinhole eyes can also be found among sea snails such as the abalone (*Haliotis*). There is no cornea or lens in these pinhole type eyes and they provide poor resolution and dim imaging, but are still a major improvement over the early eye-spots.

Transparent cells could now begin to grow over the aperture to provide protection from infection, and to provide nutrition, in the ongoing evolutionary history of the eye. With time these cells divided into two layers, with liquid in between. The liquid originally served as a circulatory fluid for oxygen, nutrients and wastes, but multiple interfaces between solids and liquids also increase optical power, allowing wider viewing angles and greater imaging resolution. The epithelial cell layers then eventually developed into the crystalline lens by co-opting crystallin proteins (described below), as seen in *Murex*, a marine snail. The introduction of a crystalline lens greatly increased the refractive power, and being an inert material, crystallin reduced the 'upkeep' that was necessary to keep the eye in good shape.

With time two further specialised cell layers known as the cornea and the iris split away from the crystalline lens, the cornea providing an outer protective covering as the aperture once again grew in size to allow the entrance of more light, now that the older pinhole design was left behind. This is the eye of the octopus and is basically the same plan that we have for our own eyes, complete with cornea, iris, refractive lens, retina, optic nerve and an aqueous humour (alkaline liquid similar to blood plasma) which fills the space between the lens and the retinal photosensitive cells, thereby increasing refractive power.

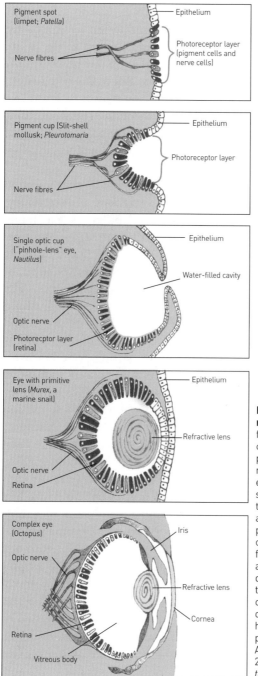

Figure 10. Eyes in living molluscs. The simplest eye is found in limpets (top), consisting of only a few pigmented cells, slightly modified from typical epithelial (skin cells). Slit-shell molluscs (second from top) have a slightly more advanced organ, consisting of pigmented cells shaped as a cup. Increasing complexity is found in the eyes of *Nautilus* and *Murex*, the next two down, with the octopus eye at the bottom still more complex and containing most of the components of the human eye. [Reprinted with permission from the National Academies Press, Copyright 2007 F.J. Ayala, *Darwin's Gift to Science and Religion*].

The eye of an octopus, unlike our own eyes, has no 'blind spot'. In our eyes the nerve fibres are collected inside the eye cavity, so the optic nerve has to cross the retina to get to the brain. This creates a small gap, although in practice our brains simply fill in the missing piece of information. But in the octopus eye the nerve fibres and optic nerve are collected outside the eye cavity, so go to the brain without crossing the retina, a neater arrangement. This provides a good illustration of the various ways in which our organs reflect their own sometimes idiosyncratic evolutionary histories.

The eyes illustrated in Figure 10 refer only to the evolution of the camera-like eyes that are characteristic of vertebrates, whereas the compound eyes employed by crabs and many other animals follow a somewhat different series of evolutionary stages. Also the sequence in Figure 10 does not imply a direct sequence from one species to another as some of these species lie on parallel evolutionary pathways. The importance of the series of mollusc examples is to illustrate the way that 'half an eye', and indeed a 'quarter of an eye' and '10% of an eye' can have marked advantages for the animals that possess them, all evolving under strong selection pressure. In fact eyes are thought to have bestowed such huge advantages that they first evolved rather quickly (as far as evolutionary time is concerned), a matter of a mere few million years. Mathematical modelling suggests that the complete evolution of an eye such as the octopus eye could have been accomplished in 2,000 steps that could occur in about 400,000 generations. Assuming a gestation time of one year, the evolution of an eye from a rudimentary beginning could take less than half a million years[107].

Eye evolution also provides some excellent examples of the 'bits and pieces in the garage' phenomenon, more formally known as co-option, which is conceptually the same as pre-adaptation. The term 'co-option' is normally used for molecules, and 'pre-adaptation' for morphology (body shape and plan), but both terms refer to the take-up during evolution of pre-existing entities to carry out new functions. The crystalline proteins that make up the eye lens provide a remarkable example of co-option. Many different proteins can function as lens proteins as it is the gradient in protein concentration in the lens rather than the molecules themselves which appear to be the key factor, so this means that co-option during evolutionary history has involved all kinds of proteins, some of them quite bizarre. The lens of the human eye, like eye lenses in most vertebrates, contains α-crystallin which is very similar to a heat shock protein, one of a very abundant family of proteins that protect cells from stress. The gene encoding α-crystallin almost certainly arose by gene duplication. A few birds, as well as crocodiles, use ε-crystallin, just another name for the enzyme lactate dehydrogenase which plays an important role in metabollising the lactic acid produced in muscles during exercise. The usual crystallin for birds and reptiles is arginosuccinate lyase, another important metabolic enzyme. There are many other examples of this kind. It is easy to get a bit lost in the terminology, but the important point to remember is that bodily systems often evolve by using the bits and pieces that are already around in the 'genome garage'. There is no need to evolve a new gene when one is already on board to do the job quite well. Also don't forget that Pax-6 is a key 'master-gene' for the regulation of eye development in animals with all kinds of eyes from the flatworms to the vertebrates. Once this and other key regulatory genes were in place, they didn't need to keep evolving again but were available to pull the key levers and switches needed to build eyes.

Later on we shall also see how eyes evolved multiple times in independent lineages, underlining the fact that evolution is a highly organised and constrained process, channelled along a relatively limited number of feasible pathways.

'Surely if evolution were true, God would have simply told us so in his Word so that we don't need to have all this discussion?'

It is indeed a tempting thought, that everything we really need to know is included in the pages of the Bible, and of course that is certainly the case for our salvation and growth in

Christ. Many is the time that I have chatted with Muslims met on trains while travelling in Turkey and they have assured me that effectively all of science is included within the pages of the Qur'an, including general relativity, big bang cosmology, genetics and many other things besides. I have to say that when we have looked up the relevant Qur'anic verses together, their purported connection with those aspects of science has been less than persuasive.

The Bible, however, has other purposes than telling us everything that we might want to know about any particular topic. It is just as the seventeenth century puritan Bishop Wilkins said, (quoted in Chapter Two) that it is better 'if we could be content to let it [Scripture] be perfect for that end unto which it was intended', and 'not to stretch it also to be a Judge of such Natural Truths as are to be found out by our own Industry and Experience'. God has given us minds and abilities to use our God-given gifts to explore and understand his creation for ourselves. No loving parent will give their child all the knowledge they need to know on a plate, but will expect them to continue their education as they explore and discover the world for themselves.

There is of course the practical point that if God had chosen to give a scientific, rather than theological, account of his creation, then no one would have understood it anyway, and our Bibles would have ended up about ten times their present size! Remember that the growth in our scientific understanding is very recent and science is going out of date all the time as new data come along, contrasting with God's revelation regarding salvation, which is for all time. At the same time God's key salvation message to humanity would have been completely lost in the detail had the Bible attempted to convey a scientific understanding of creation to us. By expressing his creative purposes for the earth and humankind in such compressed and elegant theological language, God has ensured that we should focus first of all on what is necessary for our salvation and, as Bishop Wilkins so rightly says, leave the rest for humans to find out for themselves.

'Perhaps God made the original kinds by special acts of creation which then underwent rapid evolution to generate the species diversity that we see today.'

Those who believe in a young earth that was created around 10,000 years ago, followed by the separate creation of a number of different 'kinds' of animals, have to explain both their present diversity and also their obviously predatory structures which in an idyllic non-violent pre-Fall world, as young earth creationists imagine it to have been, would have been unnecessary.

Ironically the founder of modern young-earth creationism, Henry Morris, was forced to believe in a form of evolution by natural selection that was far more rapid than anything ever described by mainstream evolutionary biologists, in order to explain such structures. This led to real confusion, because having argued that evolution by natural selection could not produce complex organs over millions of years, he had to believe that complex mechanisms of attack and defence could evolve over a mere few thousand. Having argued that, for example, the bombardier beetle could never have evolved an elaborate chemical mechanism to explosively squirt out a noxious defence liquid, young earth creationists have to explain why the beetle needed it in an idyllic Eden – unless, of course, it evolved after the Fall by natural selection.

There are some very significant problems with such scenarios, to put it mildly. For a start, the rejection of current dating methods means rejecting virtually the whole of current physics and chemistry, since dating methods are based on the same physical laws and principles that govern these disciplines. Radioisotopic dating methods and the use of radioisotopes in cancer therapy both depend on the same physics; one cannot arbitrarily reject science as it applies to dating, yet retain the same science when useful for one's own well-being.

Turning to the biology involved, there simply are no mechanisms that will generate that amount of biological diversity in that small space of time. Remember that there are currently as many as 10–20 million different species on planet earth. So however many 'kinds' we would like to create, we cannot have 850,000 species of insect (for example) evolving in 10,000 years. The examples of 'very rapid speciation' given above, as described in mainstream science, suggest time spans of 14,000 years for the speciation of different cichlid fishes, or half a million years for the evolution of an eye. We also have plenty of ancient DNA samples going back much further than 10,000 years from known species, including humans, and there is no evidence in this genetic record of the kind of rapid sequential changes envisaged that would be necessary to generate huge amounts of new diversity if the young-earth idea were correct.

So holding fast to such a scenario basically involves throwing out the whole of current science. If Christians do find themselves in such an impasse, then maybe it is time to go back to the beginning and start again, a good moment to turn to the opening chapters of the book of Genesis.

Chapter 7:
What about Genesis?

Some people believe that the early chapters of Genesis are incompatible with the kind of evolutionary scenario that we have been painting in the course of the past few chapters. This chapter will consider whether that belief is well justified, using the general principles of scriptural interpretation already introduced in the first part of the book.

Two points are worth underlining by way of preamble. The first is the primacy of the authority of the Word of God. I personally take Scripture as my final authority in all matters of faith and conduct. I have always done that ever since becoming a Christian at the age of 13. For me the Word of God has the final say on the matter. It is not to be subjected to any other authority from whatever direction that might come, although of course our interpretation of Scripture is influenced by our own particular church tradition. Throughout my forty years within the biological research community I have never seen the slightest reason to doubt such a stance.

Secondly, modern science may shed light on a biblical passage, but I don't think it should be used as a tool for interpreting the passage – there is a subtle difference. Indeed, I have already been critical (in Chapter Two) of those who read ancient texts through modernist eyes, treating them as if they were scientific texts, in the mistaken supposition that scientific literature offers a truth superior to that found in the literature of other disciplines exploring different aspects of reality.

So the purpose of our discussion of the Genesis text is not at all to see how the text responds to 'enquiries' from the direction of evolutionary theory, but rather to see how we should understand the book of Genesis in the context of the rest of Scripture and of the ancient Near East culture in which it was written. For that reason biblical commentators who wrote about Genesis many centuries before Darwin will also be cited, because in this way we can be sure that we are looking at an interpretative stance taken by Christians down the ages, not new interpretations imposed upon the text as evolutionary theory became widely accepted by (many but not all) conservative biblical scholars, and more broadly by the churches, during the later part of the nineteenth century.

Genesis 1–2 in its broader context[108]

Before homing in on any particular biblical passage, it is always a good idea to place it first within its context. Genesis is a book about families: about God's very first family, comprising those who knew and worshipped him as a personal God; and about other families called to follow and obey him within the same covenant relationship.

The structure of the Genesis text can be understood in various ways, all valuable in pointing to the overall purpose of the book. One striking type of structure is characterised by the elevenfold repeated Hebrew phrase 'elleh toledot (abbreviated to 'toledoth' here) which can be translated as 'these are the generations', 'this is the family history' or 'this is the account'. The phrase is typically followed by a key representative name from the family or generation about to be described. An exception is Genesis 2:4 which says: 'This is the account of the heavens and the earth when they were created'. For this reason some commentators have suggested that this toledoth is pointing 'backwards' to the preceding creation account. However, the formula is clearly used as an introduction in the rest of Genesis, so it seems safest to take it that way in Genesis 2:4 also, where it 'must describe that which is generated by the heavens and the earth, not the process by which they themselves are generated'[109]. The remaining ten toledoth formulae are as follows, with the introductory family names given in brackets: 5:1 (Adam); 6:9 (Noah); 10:1 (Noah's sons); 11:10 (Shem); 11:27 (Terah); 25:12 (Ishmael); 25:19 (Isaac); 36:1 and

36:9 (the formula is given twice for Esau); 37:2 (Jacob). We may therefore perceive the structure of Genesis as a prologue (Genesis 1:1 – 2:3) followed by ten episodes of varying length, each introduced by the toledoth formula. It is very likely that these toledoth sections were originally stored as separate family histories and then brought together into the single book of Genesis. This is suggested by the words of Genesis 5:1: 'This is the book (*sefer*) of the *toledot* of Adam'.

Genesis introduces the reader to the God who is going to call Abraham, and initiates the great patriarchal narratives leading on to the accounts of the history of Israel in the rest of the Old Testament. The primeval history of Genesis 1–11 is the essential background to an understanding of the covenant purposes of God for his people recounted in greater detail from Genesis 12 onwards. God's faithful covenant promises provide a key to understanding the great themes of the book.

What kind of literature is Genesis 1:1 – 2:3?

How we interpret Genesis 1 will clearly be highly influenced by the kind of literature that we think that we're reading, and also by the way that the text is treated in other parts of Scripture. Over the centuries much ink has flowed in the attempt to find the precisely correct designation. But since this chapter is clearly unique and distinctive from any other passage in the Bible, trying to force it into a generalised literary genre is perhaps not that helpful. It is clearly not scientific literature in the way that we currently understand that term, any more than any other passage of the Bible is scientific literature, for reasons that have already been explained in Chapter Two. It is entirely inappropriate to force a modern, scientific understanding of language on to any ancient text written in an era before such literature was even in existence.

Neither is Genesis 1 Hebrew poetry, although it has some poetic resonances in places, and may have been used as a hymn in communal worship. It is describing creative events that occurred before anyone was around to describe them, so it cannot be history in any normal use of that term. There are many internal considerations within the text, to be considered further below, indicating that the language should be taken figuratively. 'Elevated prose' is a term that has been used for Genesis 1; 'theological essay' is another; 'theological manifesto' is yet another, for this is the key text that lays down the distinctive creative character of the one true God who stands in stark contrast to the polytheistic deities so dominant in the Near East religious culture of that era. Genesis 1 is indeed foundational to the whole of the rest of Scripture, and we cannot grasp the rest of the biblical message unless we understand who it is being revealed to us in these verses.

The chapter tells us that God, by speaking his divine Word, brought order out of emptiness. In Genesis 1:2 we start with an earth that was *tohu vebohu*, a powerful Hebrew way of expressing 'formless and empty' or 'waste and void'. When these words occur elsewhere in the Old Testament they are often likewise coupled together to describe the desolation that occurs when the land is under judgement as in Isaiah 34:11: 'God will stretch out over Edom the measuring line of chaos (*tohu*) and the plumb line of desolation (*bohu*)' and in Jeremiah 4:23: 'I looked at the earth, and it was formless (*tohu*) and empty (*bohu*); and at the heavens, and their light was gone'. In Genesis 1 *tohu vebohu* acts like a 'base-line' from which God's creative acts are then launched during six successive days of action. Everything about the rest of the chapter is very tightly ordered: a careful literary structure in which every word counts, with a text built completely around certain numbers in a way that is clear in the Hebrew, not so clear in English[110]. But for the Hebrew reader the very structure of the text was shouting 'Order! Order!' – coming out of the disordered background described by *tohu vebohu*.

The days themselves are displayed using a literary structure which is familiar to anyone who has used a commentary on Genesis, but is worth repeating here for the sake of completeness. In this structure it is Days 1–3 that tackle the problem of *tohu*, providing the general form of the new created order, whereas Days 4–6 then address the problem of *bohu*, filling up the different created forms with a variety of wonderful plants and animals. This 'Form and Fullness' structure looks like this:

THE EARTH WAS

Tohu (formless)	and	**Bohu** (empty)
Form was created		Fulness was created

DAY ONE The separation of light and darkness	DAY FOUR The creation of lights to rule the day and the night
DAY TWO The separation of the waters to form the sky and the sea	DAY FIVE The creation of birds and fishes to fill the sky and the sea
DAY THREE The separation of the sea from the dry land. The creation of the plants	DAY SIX The creation of animals and humans to fill the land and eat the plants

DAY SEVEN
The heavens and the earth were finished and God rested

The figurative use of the term 'day' in Genesis 1 is made clear both from the immediate context formed by the narrative and from the way the passage is treated in other parts of Scripture. Early Jewish and Christian commentators writing many centuries before modern science also explained to their readers that the days should be interpreted figuratively. The Jewish philosopher and theologian Philo (c. 15 BC – c. AD 50) lived at the same time as both Jesus and Paul and certainly believed that Genesis was the inspired word of God written by Moses. But Philo taught that God had made all things instantaneously and the six days of creation therefore provided a way for Moses to explain the orderly way in which God had created. Early Christian commentators on Genesis such as Augustine (AD 354–430) and Origen (c. AD 185–254) also explained the figurative use of language in the early chapters of Genesis to their readers. As Origen robustly expressed the point:

> What man of intelligence, I ask, will consider that the first and second and the third day, in which there are said to be both

morning and evening, existed without sun and moon and stars, while the first day was even without a heaven? And who could be found so silly as to believe that God, after the manner of a farmer 'planted trees in a paradise eastward in Eden'... I do not think anyone will doubt that these are figurative expressions which indicate certain mysteries through a semblance of history[111].

Origen used here the principle that should be used by any biblical interpreter, which is to use the context to understand the meaning. Since the 'great lights', the sun and moon, are not created until Day 4, reasoned Origen, clearly the days cannot be referring to our normal days of 24 hours, and so the use of the term must be figurative.

In his commentary entitled 'The Literal Interpretation of Genesis', the final version of which was published in AD 405, Augustine also adopted a distinctively figurative interpretation of the days of Genesis. In fact the twenty-first century reader coming to this volume expecting to find the term 'literal' interpreted in terms of strict creation chronology and days of 24 hours, is in for a surprise. Far from it: Augustine saw God's creative activity as having two different aspects;

...Some works belonged to the invisible days in which he created all things simultaneously, and others belong to the days in which he daily fashions whatever evolves in the course of time from what I call the primordial wrappers. (6.6.9)

The 'invisible days' in Augustine's exposition were the days as described in Genesis 1, which he understood not chronologically but as a kind of inventory of all God's acts of creation which were performed simultaneously. This single act of creation then brought forth, in due course, all the rest of the diversity of the created order. Of course when Augustine uses the word translated as 'evolves' we should not read into that the modern scientific meaning, but Augustine did appear to believe that all of the potentiality of the created order was encompassed within those original 'primordial wrappers' created by God at one fell swoop.

A figurative understanding of Genesis 1 was the dominant approach to the text amongst both Jewish and Christian commentators until at least into the fourteenth century, and it is not until the twentieth century, with the rise of modernist interpretations of the text, that one finds a growing trend to interpret the passage as if it were written in the language of modern science.

Returning to the text of Genesis itself, it is interesting to note the varied ways in which the word 'day' is used in the context of these narratives. In 1:5 God called the light 'day', so clearly a 24 hour day is not in mind for this usage. Then in 2:4 we read that 'These are the generations of the heavens and the earth when they were created in the day that the Lord God made the earth and the heavens'. The word for day in Hebrew (*yom*) used in this verse is exactly the same as in Genesis 1, so 'day' in this case refers back to the whole panoply of God's creative actions described in that chapter.

It has also often been noted that whereas Days 1–6 are always completed by the phrase 'and there was evening and morning – the [1–6]th day', this phrase is lacking from the seventh day upon which God rested. Jesus himself gives us insight into what this means in John 5:17 when he was criticised for healing on the Sabbath day, defending himself by saying that 'My Father is always at his work to this very day, and I, too, am working.' In other words Jesus is interpreting the seventh day figuratively as referring to the whole extended work of God in creation. As Jesus says elsewhere 'The Sabbath was made for man, not man for the Sabbath' (Mark 2:27). The whole point about the seventh day in Genesis 1 is not that God himself actually stopped his work of upholding the universe, as Jesus points out, but that humans need to rest from their labour on a weekly basis if they are going to keep refreshed and renewed in body and mind. The Genesis pattern of six days of work followed by a day of rest is for our benefit, not for God's; it is to indicate that a Sabbath principle is inbuilt and necessary to our well-being, and introduces the concept of 'active rest' – a creative employment of our time. For creatures made in God's image, God himself sets the pattern that we are to follow. Unlike days, months and years, the pattern of the weekly cycle of work and rest is based on no particular physical cycles of sun or moon, but is specifically revealed by Scripture to be the pattern for our daily lives. It is one of the Bible's great gifts to the world, which up until that time had no system for established regular periods of rest.

Some cite Exodus 20:11 (and 31:17) as a kind of 'proof-text' in support of interpreting the days of Genesis as literal days of 24 hours: 'For in six days the Lord made the heavens and the earth, the sea, and all that is in them, but he rested on the seventh day. Therefore the Lord blessed the Sabbath day and made it holy'. But this prompts the question, how would the people of Israel have understood such teaching in its context? They certainly knew that it meant resting with all their household on the seventh day of each week, but we simply do not know precisely how they conceived the allied teaching about God as Creator. Our minds are shaped within cultures strongly influenced by science and technology, which means that we come to texts with a set of questions and assumptions that probably would not even have occurred to their original listeners.

This point may be seen rather clearly with the modern passion for timekeeping and chronology, both relatively recent interests within the Western world, and largely the fruit of the industrial revolution. Often the biblical writers organise their material in a topical fashion that bears little relation to chronology. The classic example is within the Genesis creation narratives themselves, where in 2:4 onwards we see a second creation narrative, only completely reversed in order compared to Genesis 1, with Adam being created at the beginning, for reasons that we will consider below. The history of King Jehoash recorded in 2 Kings 13–14 provides another interesting example. 2 Kings 13:10–13 provides a brief biography of the 'wicked king' Jehoash and already by verse 13 he is dead and buried. But then in the very next verse King Jehoash pops up again and makes a visit to the ailing Elisha. In fact we get eleven mentions of Jehoash and what he did between his recorded death in 13:13 and his recorded death repeated once more in 14:16. Does this mean that Jehoash was resurrected after 13:13 to continue his reign? No, it just means that

10:10–13 is what we would call now an abstract to prepare the reader for the main account which is to come (or the trailer for the main film to put it another way).

Another example of chronological surprises in the Bible is found in the temptation narratives of Luke 4 and Matthew 4. Although both accounts read to our Western ears as if they are straightforward chronological narratives, Matthew has the order of temptations as: bread–temple–high mountain, Luke's narrative has the order as bread–high mountain–temple. These differences are not mistakes, and they are not indicative of indifference to chronology or history. The Gospels are crafted with astonishingly concise precision, and the evangelists use literary structure as a teaching tool. Chronological anomalies, inversions and juxtapositions are there to serve the theological purpose which determines the nature of the work. We should not be worried by such discrepancies; following their lead will open theological teaching of richness and depth for us. It is not that the writers were primitive, careless or naïve; but though historical in their material, they are expounding *theological* history; this is not Hansard[112].

A further red herring that can lead to unnecessary distraction is the little Hebrew word *min* translated as 'kind' in Genesis 1, as in verse 12: 'The land produced vegetation: plants bearing seed according to their kinds (*min*) and trees bearing fruit with seed in it according to their kinds (*min*)'. All this is intended to highlight once again is the bringing into being of order out of *tohu vebohu*. Animals and plants are distinguished by the fact that they breed according to their kind, as any rural people could see by simple observation. Again it is a quite mistaken use of the text to read back into *min* the categories of modern biology, such as 'species', 'phyla' and the like[113]. As noted in previous chapters, there are currently millions of species on the earth, perhaps as many as 10–20 million, so the proposal that *min* means the same as the biological term 'species' is clearly a problem. Even if *min* refers to broader categories of living things, all created separately about 10,000 years ago, we have already noted the lack of evidence for the incredibly rapid evolution that would be required to generate the millions of species alive today. Suffice it to say that in any case this kind of interpretation involves a misuse of the Hebrew text.

Numbers and Genesis 1

The numerical structure of the Genesis 1 text also highlights its interpretation as a figurative and theological narrative. Even reading the chapter in English, we cannot fail to notice the way that the structure of the text is built round the number seven. Apart from the seven days, we have the seven-fold repeat 'and it was so' and that 'God saw that it was good' (or very good). But this is nothing compared to the detailed attention to a numerical structure for the text that is revealed once the original Hebrew is examined. For example, Wenham points out that the Hebrew verses comprise multiples of 7 words, with the first verse containing 7 words, the second verse 14 words, and the summary in 2:1–3 at the end of the passage containing 35 words. The word 'God' is mentioned 35 (5 x 7) times in the passage, whereas 'earth' and 'heaven/firmament' occur 21 (3 x 7) times each.

Why this fascination with the number 7? At one level, as we shall consider further below, Genesis 1:1–2.3 may be read as a polemical and sometimes satirical attack on the Babylonian and Sumerian creation stories that were widespread in the Near East during the period 500–2000 BC. According to one Babylonian tradition, the 7th, 14th, 19th, 21st and 28th days of each month were regarded as unlucky, whereas in Genesis 1 it is the seventh day that is set aside as being a special day characterised by God's blessing, a day of rest consecrated to him (2:2–3). It seems possible that the Israelite Sabbath was introduced as a deliberate replacement for this lunar-related cycle. Far from being a day of ill omen, the Sabbath was to be a day blessed and made especially holy by the creator. The way the narrative is structured around the number 7 provides a way of highlighting to the reader this critical point. When the psalmist promises that: 'The Lord watches over you – the Lord is your shade at your right hand; The sun will not harm you by day, nor the moon by night' (Psalm 121:5–6), it is not God's protection against sunburn that is in mind here, but rather the fear of the malevolent intentions of the heavenly bodies.

Genesis 1 as a critique of pagan creation stories

One of the striking features of Genesis 1 is its insistence that the one true God speaks the divine Word and everything comes into being day after day in obedience to his Word. This stands in stark contrast with the polytheism that was dominant in all other creation accounts that have come down to us in the ancient literature of the Near East. Instead of having a different god, or a collection of squabbling gods, in charge of the different creative activities on the different days, Genesis 1 is insistent that there is just the one God who does everything without exception. The sun, moon and stars that played such a central role as gods to be worshipped and feared in the pagan pantheon, do not even make an appearance in the Genesis account until the fourth day – talk about relegation to the second division! And here they are introduced simply as created objects made by God for functional reasons, to give appropriate levels of light in the day and the night and to 'serve as signs to mark seasons and days and years' (verse 14), quite lowly functions in comparison with their elevated status in most Mesopotamian literature of that era. The Hebrew word 'light, lamp' used to refer to the sun and moon in this passage is also used to refer to the sanctuary lamp in the Jewish tabernacle, and it is possible that the writer is pointing out by this usage that the order introduced by God into the days and seasons by such heavenly 'lamps' is parallel to the God-given order which characterised the running of the tabernacle. The almost throwaway line in verse 16, that God 'also made the stars', certainly gives no room for viewing them as having any role to play in human affairs, thereby subverting all forms of astrology. Again and again later in their history the people of Israel were tempted to worship sun, moon and stars, but again and again they were challenged to return to the pure monotheism of Genesis 1. God reminds his people as they head towards the Promised Land that 'when you look up to the sky and see the sun, the moon and the stars – all the heavenly array – do not be enticed into bowing down to them and worshipping things the Lord your God has apportioned to all the nations under heaven' (Deuteronomy 4:19).

Another example from Genesis 1 where a counter-pagan

critique seems to be particularly in mind crops up in the use of the word *bara'*, the word for create that we introduced in Chapter One, for which God is always the subject. The word is used in verse 1, an expected use for the creation of the 'heavens and the earth', and then three times in verse 27 to highlight the work of God in the creation of humans, again an unsurprising usage, but its appearance in verse 21 to describe the *bara'* of the sea monsters might at first seem more puzzling. Since the word *bara'* is used only in these three places in Genesis 1, why should one of those usages be reserved for sea monsters? Ernest Lucas points out that in the main Mesopotamian creation story the creator god has to battle with and subdue the forces of chaos, depicted as sea monsters in raging waters, before he can create the heavens and the earth. Genesis rejects this by stressing that the sea monsters are just part of the world created by the God of Israel. No struggle is involved here – God simply made them and that was that. Psalm 104:26 makes a similar point: 'There the ships go to and fro, and the leviathan, which you formed to frolic there'. The 'leviathan' here is the same kind of 'sea monster', representing the forces of chaos, that we meet in Genesis 1:21, made by God not to be out of control, or scary, but to 'frolic'. Pagan readers would have been deeply shocked by that description!

Looking more generally at the theology of the Genesis account of creation in contrast with the other competing Near Eastern creation stories, there are many striking contrasts. For example, whereas in Genesis 1 God does all the work of creation and provides for the physical and spiritual needs of humankind, in the pagan epics man is created to be a slave of the gods. According to the Babylonian Enuma Elish ('The Epic of Creation') one group of gods rebelled against another and was defeated. As a punishment they were imprisoned and forced to act as servants of the victors. But Marduk, one of the victorious gods, decided to relieve the vanquished gods of these duties and create man instead to be the servant of the victors. The ringleader of the rebels, Kingu, was therefore killed, his arteries were severed and mankind was created with his blood. A similar reason for the creation of man is found in the Atrahasis epic:

Belet-li the womb-goddess is present –
Let her create a mortal man
So that he may bear the yoke...
Let man bear the load of the gods!

In contrast men and women are created in Genesis not as slaves, but as free beings having major responsibilities over the created order which has been given to them for their well-being (1:29–30).

There is also a strong ethical and moral element in the early chapters of Genesis which is lacking from the Mesopotamian creation stories. Matter is not evil in Genesis but has divine approval. There is no hint here of the platonic concept that the spiritual is on a higher plane than the material. The creation of humankind is marked by a strikingly earthy materialism. There is no earthier name than Adam! Already by Genesis 2 Adam is being faced with choices of obedience or disobedience, good and evil. The way of evil is totally opposed to God's clear command. But in the Babylonian epics the gods are as corrupt as humankind. Marduk, the principal deity in the Enuma Elish epic, defeated the rebel goddess Tiamat, split her skull with his club, cut her arteries, and finally divided her enormous body into two parts to create the universe. With one half he formed the sky and with the other he made the earth. Not a very nice piece of work! This creation of the world out of a murder does not bode too well for what is to follow and, all-in-all, the gods continue to act like a murderous bunch of thugs in these accounts, sending vicious plagues onto mankind for trivial offences like making too much noise, and forcing them to be their slaves.

Since man was made from the blood of the gods in Babylonian mythology, how could he possibly shake off the nature of the gods? In Genesis humankind was created in communion with God, made in his image, but then fell by moral choice. In the Babylonian accounts there was no possibility of a Fall, for humankind was made morally flawed. We will pursue the question of Adam and Eve, and the Fall account, in a later chapter.

Genesis Chapter 2:4–25

As already mentioned, those who come to the second creation account in Genesis 2 with strict chronologies in their mind will invariably end up with a headache. In marked contrast to Genesis 1, the narrative places the creation of Adam first (verse 7), followed by the placing of Adam in a garden where God made trees grow (verses 8–9), then the creation of the animals in verse 19, followed by the creation of woman (verse 21).

In an attempt to reconcile this chronology with that of Genesis 1, the NIV translation has made liberal use of the pluperfect in its translation of these verses, for example in 2:5 and 2:8, where we read that 'no shrub of the field had yet appeared on the earth and no plant of the field had yet sprung up' (verse 5) and 'the Lord God had planted a garden in the east' (verse 8). The intention of the translators is to suggest that the vegetation and garden were created before man in an attempt to impose the chronology of Genesis 1 on to the text. A similar strategy can be seen in 2:19 where, following the creation of man from the 'dust of the ground' in verse 7, the NIV reads: 'the Lord God had formed out of the ground all the beasts of the field and all the birds of the air. He brought them to the man to see what he would name them...' Again the intention of the translators is clear. By using the pluperfect they wish to reconcile the chronology of Genesis 2 with that found in chapter 1, where the animals and birds are created before man.

There are, however, significant problems with the use of the pluperfect in these verses, and indeed it is not used in this context in other standard Bible translations such as the NKJV and NRSV. For a start, the Hebrew language does not have a distinct pluperfect tense and the verb tenses used for create and form in Genesis 2 are no different from Genesis 1. So a more natural translation of Genesis 2:8–9, for example, closer to the Hebrew text, is provided by the King James translation: 'And the Lord God planted a garden eastward in Eden; and there he put the man whom he had formed. And out of the ground made the Lord God to grow every tree that is pleasant to the sight, and good for food...' And then the same version renders 2:19: 'And out of the ground the Lord God formed every beast of the field, and every fowl of the air; and brought them unto Adam to see what he would call them: and whatsoever Adam called every living creature, that was the name thereof'. In other words Genesis 2 provides a straightforward narrative text, providing a different sequence of events from Genesis 1, and most translations are faithful in rendering the text according to the most likely Hebrew intention.

So what is the purpose of Genesis 2? The text has no interest in providing us with chronology but has quite different purposes. One can well imagine the naïve Westerner, with a mind shaped by timekeeping and a scientific use of language, being teleported back thousands of years ago to an early Jerusalem instruction class on Genesis 2, and being given a withering look by the teacher upon asking how the chronology of Genesis 2 might be fitted with that of Genesis 1. If the same Westerner could teleport a local from that same class back to London to watch a cricket match, then he might be surprised to be asked why public attempts at the (apparently unsuccessful) ritual killing of enemies were carried out using a hard ball. Assumptions really do make a lot of difference to understanding texts and events when moving between cultures and eras.

The first clue to the purpose of Genesis 2 is given in verse 4 during the toledoth introduction when God's covenant name of Yahweh is found for the first time in the Bible: 'When the Lord (Yahweh) God made the earth and the heavens...' Eleven times the term 'the Lord God' (*Yahweh Elohim*) is used in the chapter, highlighting God's creative actions in giving humankind responsibilities for the earth and everything in it, and establishing marriage as a crucial aspect of the created order. Whereas Genesis 1 established that humankind is uniquely made in God's image, Genesis 2 explains the responsibilities that arise from the fact of being made in God's image. So the man is made the focal point of the narrative by being created first, and then the rest of the living world is brought to the man to look after, highlighting the role of humankind in caring for the earth. The Hebrew text plays upon Adam as the one made from the earth (*adamah*) (2:7) who is then installed as God's earth-keeper. There is a perfectly good word for man used in Old Testament Hebrew ('*ish*), but it is not used in the Genesis text until 2:24 where we read that 'For this reason a man ('*ishû*) will leave his father and mother'. This refers generically to any man who leaves his father and mother to get married. Up until that moment it is always 'Adam' with the definite article that is used in the text for 'the man', 20 times in all in Genesis 1 and 2. So the earthy roots of Adam, and his earthly responsibilities to care for the Garden (2:15), are clearly being highlighted here in a way that no one can miss. And as Adam works (2:15), names the animals (2:19–20) and gets married (2:22–24), he demonstrates what it means to be made in God's image.

The purpose of Genesis 2, like Genesis 1, is to teach theology. The literal interpretation of these chapters is to lay the theological foundations for all that is to follow in the rest of Scripture. Unless we understand that there is only one God, who has brought a good creation into being by his divine Word, and who has created humankind in his image to care for the earth and walk in obedience to him, then we will be unable to understand the rest of the biblical message. These chapters represent the opening manifesto of the Bible, setting its parameters and its priorities, and the danger is that if we start interpreting the text as if it were scientific literature, or was intended to tell us how God created biological diversity, then we run the risk of missing the central theological messages.

All Christians interpret the early chapters of Genesis figuratively

I have never yet met a Christian, nor indeed read one in print, who does not take the language of the early chapters of Genesis figuratively. To illustrate this point, Paul Marston has provided a helpful analysis of the writings of Henry Morris, a key founder of the modern movement that has come to be known as young-earth creationism. Morris claims that 'the Scriptures, in fact, do not need to be "interpreted" at all, for God is well able to say exactly what he means'[114]. But as Marston points out, in reality Morris frequently does interpret passages from the early chapters of Genesis figuratively, illustrating his point by reference to Morris's book *The Genesis Record* (1976)[115].

For example, although Morris holds to a strict 24-hour interpretation of the 'days' of Genesis 1, nevertheless when it comes to Genesis 2:4, Morris then says that the words can 'refer to the whole period of creation'. When Genesis 1:7 speaks of the 'water above the sky', Morris interprets this as meaning 'steam', but there is no mention of steam in the text. When the serpent is cursed in 3:14 with the words 'You will crawl on your belly and you will eat dust all the days of your life', Morris comments 'It would not "eat dust" in a literal sense, of course, ...the expression is mainly a graphic figure of speech'. And Morris takes the curse of the snake 'as more than a reference to the physical enmity between men and snakes'.

One could go on, but the point here is not that Morris's interpretations are necessarily wrong, but rather that interpretations are being made at all, so indicating that the texts in question are being treated figuratively and theologically, as of course they should be. For myself I have never met a Christian who, upon reading Genesis 3:8 – 'the man and his wife heard the sound of the Lord God as he was walking in the garden in the cool of the day' – imagines that God was physically walking around in the garden with two legs. No Hebrew reading this would have imagined that the God of Israel, of whom no form was seen when he spoke out of the fire (Deuteronomy 4:15), was clattering round the garden in noisy footwear. In reality, this is a rather vivid and heartaching picture of the results of sin: where before there had been close fellowship with God, now Adam and Eve were hiding from God, ashamed of their nakedness and disobedience. This is the God of grace, who takes the initiative in salvation, calling out to the man 'Where are you?'. Later in Genesis we learn that 'Noah walked with God' (6:9), clearly referring to his spiritual fellowship with God.

If we read the early chapters of Genesis and end up discussing evolution, then we've definitely lost the plot! These key passages are nothing to do with evolution. But they do have much to say to us about God's plan and intentions for humankind, the way that God's plan has been rejected by humankind, leading to our alienation from God and from each other, and the good news that God is the God of grace calling out to us in the garden 'Where are you?', gently but insistently calling us back to fellowship with himself.

Those who do think that the early chapters of Genesis are connected in some way with evolution, often have a very different idea in their mind as to what the word 'evolution' really means when compared to the strictly biological sense with which we have been using the word so far. It is to the source of those different meanings that we now turn.

Chapter 8:
Evolutionary Creationism

One of the problems with the word 'evolution' is that it carries a lot of historical baggage along with it. As we look at the history of how evolution has been used and abused for various ideological and political reasons down the years since Darwin, then this is perhaps not surprising. But Darwin himself introduced his ideas in the *Origin of Species* (1859) as a strictly biological theory and went out of his way to allay any concerns that his theory had any religious implications.

Some people have seen in Darwin's writings a sinister plot to subvert belief in God, but there is no historical evidence for this. Darwin himself read divinity at Cambridge, following an abortive attempt to study medicine at Edinburgh, but was never ordained as his father had planned. Instead Darwin ended up undertaking his famous voyage on HMS *Beagle*. When he wrote the *Origin of Species*, Darwin was clearly still a deist, someone who believes that God establishes the laws of nature but otherwise remains distant from the process of creation. This is clear from the very last sentence of the *Origin*, quoted here from its sixth and last edition (1872):

> There is grandeur in this view of life, with its several powers, having been originally breathed by the Creator into a few forms or into one; and that, whilst this planet has gone cycling on according to the fixed law of gravity, from so simple a beginning endless forms most beautiful and most wonderful have been, and are being, evolved.

This passage is striking also because it is one of the few places in the *Origin* where the word 'evolved' appears. In fact if we look at the first edition of the *Origin of Species* it mentions the words 'creation', 'creator' or 'create' no less than 104 times, but the word evolution not at all! One reason for this is that the word 'evolution' already had an established meaning in the biology of Darwin's time, referring to the development of the embryo, and Darwin preferred to refer to his theory as 'descent with modification'. But it also reflects the way in which Darwin couched the *Origin* within the thought forms of Victorian natural theology; his habits of mind inclined him to ascribe to the work of the Creator the establishment of the laws of nature that generated all the biological diversity of the world. From Darwin's deistic perspective it was still the Creator who was responsible for life's origin, breathing life 'into a few forms or into one'.

Darwin was never an atheist and oscillated for much of the latter part of his life between a fear that there was really no design or purpose, and a hope that perhaps there might be, gratefully adopting the term 'agnostic' once the word had been invented by his contemporary and robust defender of evolution, Thomas Henry Huxley. As the Open University historian James Moore comments: 'Darwin's understanding of nature never departed from a theological point of view. Always, I believe, until his dying day, at least half of him believed in God'. But Darwin found Huxley's pugnacious use of evolution to attack the power and prestige of the church of his time somewhat distasteful, and much preferred to spend his time in seclusion at Down House, where he lived with his large Victorian household, collecting vast amounts of data from all over the world and writing papers on worms and barnacles. The image of anti-religious crusader fits rather well for Huxley, who was the Richard Dawkins of the late nineteenth century, but doesn't fit at all for the mild-mannered and gentlemanly Darwin. When Darwin in later life was replying to a letter asking whether theism and evolution were compatible, he replied saying that indeed it was possible to be 'an ardent Theist and an Evolutionist'.

How did Christians receive Darwin's theory?

Like any really novel theory, Darwinism generated a very wide range of reactions in the years immediately following 1859 and a truly balanced view is one that describes the variety in some detail, which we will not attempt here[116]. There were scientists, both religious and secular, who rapidly incorporated the theory into their scientific world-view with the minimum of fuss. There were other scientists who opposed the theory on scientific grounds. There were scientific popularisers and clerics who readily accepted Darwin's theory and quickly adapted it into the traditional framework of natural theology. There were some clerics, a minority as it happens, who opposed the theory strongly, thinking that it would undermine Christian morality and notions of human value and uniqueness.

One Cambridge academic cleric who warmly embraced Darwinism provides an interesting exemplar. The novelist and socialist Charles Kingsley, who in 1860 became professor of modern history in Cambridge, was delighted when Darwin sent him an advance copy of the *Origin of Species*. Kingsley wrote to Darwin: 'All I have seen of it awes me', going on to comment that it is 'just as noble a conception of Deity, to believe that He created primal forms capable of self-development…as to believe that He required a fresh act of intervention to supply the lacunas [gaps] which He Himself had made'. Darwin was so impressed with this response that he quoted these lines in the second edition of the *Origin*.

Another great Victorian clerical enthusiast for Darwinism was Aubrey Moore, a Fellow of St John's College, Oxford, and Curator of the Oxford Botanical Gardens. Moore maintained that Darwinism had done the church a great service in helping to get rid of the more extreme forms of natural theology and claimed that there was a special affinity between Darwinism and Christian theology, remarking that 'Darwinism appeared, and, under the guise of a foe, did the work of a friend'. The reason for this affinity, claimed Moore, was based on the intimate involvement of God in his creation as revealed in Christian theology, for

There are not, and cannot be, any Divine interpositions in nature, for God cannot interfere with Himself. His creative activity is present everywhere. There is no division of labour between God and nature, or God and law... For the Christian theologian the facts of nature are the acts of God.

Moore therefore welcomed evolution as restoring a proper Christian doctrine of creation in which a transcendent God is intimately involved both in its coming into being as well as its ongoing existence. The problem with too much emphasis on natural theology, claimed Moore, was that it tended to generate a concept of a distant God who sets the laws in motion and then retreated from creation, rather than the personal God of the Bible who is completely involved ('immanent') in all its aspects.

Some of Darwin's supporters amongst the theologians were almost embarrassing in their excesses. The Scottish evangelical Henry Drummond, who was much involved in the missions of Moody and Sankey, maintained that natural selection was 'a real and beautiful acquisition to natural theology' and that the *Origin* was 'perhaps the most important contribution to the literature of apologetics' to have appeared during the nineteenth century. Indeed, Drummond built Darwin's theory into his own apologetics for Christian faith in his highly popular writings.

Meanwhile in the United States Darwinism was rapidly accepted by many evangelicals within the academic community. For example, Asa Gray, professor of natural history at Harvard and a committed Christian, was Darwin's long-term correspondent and confidante who helped organise the publication of the *Origin of Species* in America. James McCosh, who was firmly in the Calvinist tradition, was president of the College of New Jersey (later to become Princeton University). McCosh held strongly to the concept of natural selection, but equally strongly believed that 'the natural origin of species is not inconsistent with intelligent design in nature or with the existence of a personal Creator of the world'. Upon looking back over 20 years as president of the College of New Jersey, McCosh remarked that 'I have been defending Evolution but, in so doing, have given the proper account of it as the method of God's procedure, and find that when so understood it is in no way inconsistent with Scripture'. It is intriguing to see the language of 'intelligent design' being used here in the nineteenth century to refer to Darwinian evolution, a discussion to which we shall return later.

This rapid baptism of evolution into the Christian doctrine of creation, so characteristic of many thinkers on both sides of the Atlantic, was facilitated by a strongly providentialist theology that emphasised the total sovereignty of God over the whole created order. The theologian and geologist George Wright (1838–1921), whose books on glacial geology were for years the standard texts on the subject, was not only a vigorous proponent of Darwinism, but held, as Moore points out, 'that Darwin's work actually allies itself with the Reformed faith in discouraging romantic, sentimental, and optimistic interpretations of nature'. Wright even wrote 'that Darwinism has not improperly been styled 'the Calvinistic interpretation of nature'. If this was the way that God had chosen to create things, went the argument, then who are we to tell God how he should have done things?

A leading spokesman amongst the Methodists, Alexander Winchell, professor of geology and palaeontology at the University of Michigan, came progressively closer to a Darwinian understanding of evolution during the course of his career. Winchell played a major role in organising geology as a science in the United States and was a founding member of the American Geological Society. By 1877 Winchell was assuring the readers of the *Methodist Quarterly Review*, in an article entitled 'Huxley and Evolution', that it was now preferable to accept the 'doctrine of derivative descent of animal and vegetal forms' than to reject it. James Dana, professor of natural history at Yale, and editor of *The American Journal of Science*, was another American geologist of orthodox Christian conviction who accepted Darwinian evolution after some initial doubts, initiating an influential series of lectures on evolution at Yale in 1883. Dana's concluding remarks of his opening lecture are informative, because they summarise what was clearly an influential opinion in Christian American academic circles of the late nineteenth century:

1. That it is not atheism to believe in a development theory, if it be admitted at the same time that Nature exists by the will and continued act of God.
2. That we cannot tell when we have ascertained the last limit of discovery with regard to secondary causes.
3. That God is ever near us, ever working in and through Nature...

The historian James Moore writes that 'with but few exceptions the leading Christian thinkers in Great Britain and America came to terms quite readily with Darwinism and evolution', and the American historian George Marsden reports that '...with the exception of Harvard's Louis Agassiz, virtually every American Protestant zoologist and botanist accepted some form of evolution by the early 1870s'.

What I find particularly fascinating is that amongst the writers of the *Fundamentals*, that mass-produced series of 12 booklets published in the period 1910–15 which later contributed to the emergence of the term 'fundamentalism', we find a number of evangelical writers firmly committed to Darwinism, such as Benjamin Warfield, who called himself a 'Darwinian of the purest water', James Orr and the geologist George Wright. But already by this period we find Wright commenting that the word evolution 'has come into much deserved disrepute by the injection into it of erroneous and harmful theological and philosophical implications'.

Wright highlights an important point; that already by his time, writing near the beginning of the twentieth century, the term 'evolution' was being hijacked to support various ideologies that have nothing to do with the biological theory of evolution itself.

The ideological transformations of biology

There is a very familiar process in the history of science whereby one of its big theories, like Big Bang cosmology or evolution, becomes highly successful, and then various interest groups move in to utilise the prestige of the scientific theory in support of their particular ideology. Unfortunately the end result is that in the public consciousness the actual meaning of the label given to the theory itself changes, and so 'Theory X' becomes socially transformed into 'Theory Y' with all kinds of philosophical barnacles attached to it. So we have to keep knocking off the barnacles and allow the scientific theory to do the job for which it was intended.

Evolution has suffered particularly badly from this kind of process and has been used in support of virtually every kind of 'ism' imaginable. During the time of Darwin, the philosopher Herbert Spencer (1820–1903) was already presenting evolution within a framework that Darwin himself viewed with distaste. From the 1840s onwards, well before Darwin published the *Origin of Species*, Spencer had begun to develop a grandiose sociological system, expanded in a verbose series of 10 volumes published from the 1860s onwards entitled *System of Synthetic Philosophy*. After the *Origin* was published, Spencer then proceeded to build evolution into his grand schema, maintaining that the entire universe was ascending towards ultimate perfection through the operation of inexorable physical laws. It was Spencer, not Darwin, who coined the phrase 'survival of the fittest', using the word 'fittest' with distinct moral overtones, even though this is a poor description for the overall process of evolution, which involves not just survival, but reproductive success. It is not surprising that Spencer's optimistic progress-oriented philosophy proved so popular, because it fitted well with the spirit of the age – particularly in the United States, where evolution was seen by the general reading public largely through the interpretative lens provided by Spencer. But Darwin wrote in his autobiography that Spencer's ideas 'have not been of any use to me'.

George Bernard Shaw once remarked that Darwin 'had the luck to please everybody who had an axe to grind'. The Tories liked natural selection because it seemed to underpin ideas of capitalist laissez-faire economics in which only the 'economically fit' survived. When Spencer visited America in 1882, the businessman Andrew Carnegie was there to hear him. Later Carnegie wrote 'The Gospel of Wealth' (1890) in which he argued that the wealth and improvements of modern civilisation had happened only because of the law of competition. We must 'accept and welcome...great inequality' wrote Carnegie, 'the concentration of business, industrial and commercial, in the hands of a few; and the law of competition between these, as being not only beneficial, but essential to the future progress of the race'. Why? Because capitalism alone 'ensures the survival of the fittest'. J.D. Rockefeller (1839–1937) later maintained that 'The growth of a large business is merely a survival of the fittest' and that capitalism was 'merely the working-out of a law of nature and a law of God'.

Not to be outdone, the socialists of the time were equally insistent that evolution supported theories of class conflict in which progress occurred in society as one class overthrew another. Karl Marx wrote to Lassalle (16 January 1861) that 'Darwin's book is very important and it suits me well that it supports the class struggle in history from the point of view of natural science. One has, of course, to put up with the crude English method of discourse'. When Engels was giving Marx's graveside eulogy at Highgate cemetery in 1883, he declared: 'Just as Darwin discovered the law of development of organic nature, so Marx discovered the law of development of human history'. Socialists in Britain agreed. The *Bradford Labour Echo* asked rhetorically in 1871: 'What is Socialism but the development of a new social organism, where each part works for all, and all for each? It is in the direct line of evolution'. The Fabian Annie Besant declared in a pamphlet of this era: 'I am a Socialist because I believe in evolution'.

Evolution was also enlisted on the side of colonialism. In his book *Sunshine and Storm in Rhodesia* (1896), F.C. Selous tried to defend the brutalities of colonial rule, arguing that the black should either accept the white man's rule, or die in trying to resist it, since this was 'a destiny which the broadest philanthropy cannot avert, while the British colonist is but the irresponsible atom employed in carrying out a preordained law – the law which has ruled upon this planet ever since... organic life was first evolved upon the earth – the inexorable law which Darwin has aptly termed the "Survival of the Fittest"'.

Being an 'irresponsible atom' in a 'preordained law' was a very convenient role for someone engaged in suppressing another nation. During the First World War, German expansionism was justified by the Kaiser's officers who extolled the virtues of German militarism according to the philosophy of 'might is right'. Vernon Kellogg, a professor at Stanford, was an entomologist and a leading evolutionary biologist of his time. During the earlier period of the War when America remained officially neutral, Kellogg was posted to the headquarters of the German General Staff in his capacity as a high official in the international effort for Belgian relief. His fascinating book *Headquarters Nights* is the account of his conversations with the Kaiser's military officers at the dinner table. Many of the officers had been university professors before the war and were therefore of a similar background to Kellogg, who recounts that:

> Professor von Flussen is Neo-Darwinian, as are most German biologists and natural philosophers. The creed of the Allmacht ['all might' or omnipotence] of a natural selection based on violent and competitive struggle is the gospel of the German intellectuals; all else is illusion and anathema... This struggle not only must go on, for that is the natural law, but it should go on so that this natural law may work out in its cruel, inevitable way the salvation of the human species...

Perhaps most notoriously of all, evolution was used in support of eugenics in an attempt to weed out the 'unfit', an official policy that led to legislation in several countries during the first half of the twentieth century, finally culminating in the horrors of Hitler's holocaust. Nineteenth century writers such as Spencer had set the scene. A central part of Spencer's thesis was that different races were going through different stages of 'cultural evolution' or development, and so one had to take such 'facts' into account when assessing the level of understanding of a given group of people.

In Britain it was Francis Galton, Darwin's cousin, who coined the term 'eugenic' (from the Greek meaning 'well born'), promoting the idea vigorously through his book *Hereditary Genius* (1869). In the final section of his autobiography Galton concluded that with the developed mind of modern man, 'I conceive it to fall well within his province to replace Natural Selection by other processes that are more merciful and not less effective. This is precisely the aim of Eugenics.' But by the early part of the twentieth century eugenics was anything but merciful, and during the period 1895–1945 the USA led the way in passing eugenic legislation. In 1907 the State of Indiana enacted America's first compulsory sterilisation statute which established the sterilisation of certain 'confirmed criminals, idiots, rapists and imbeciles' whose condition was pronounced incurable by a committee of three physicians. Indiana's example was followed by 15 other States over the next decade. By 1914, over half of the States had also imposed new restrictions on the marriage of those with mental defects. The geneticist Charles Davenport suggested that American society should:

> prevent the feebleminded, drunkards, paupers, sex offenders, and criminalistic from marrying their like or cousins or any person belonging to a neuropathic strain. Practically it might be well to segregate such persons for one generation. Then the crop of defectives will be reduced to practically nothing.

In general, leading American biologists supported the eugenics movement, or at least did not oppose it. American legislation became a pattern that many other countries were to follow, not least Nazi Germany where a law was enacted to enforce the sterilisation of those suffering from a wide range of genetic diseases, including schizophrenia, manic depression, hereditary blindness or deafness, and severe alcoholism. 'We must see to it that these inferior people do not procreate,' declared the famous German biologist Erwin Baur, 'No one approves of the new sterilisation laws more than I do, but I must repeat over and over that they *constitute only a beginning*.'[117] More than 300,000 people were sterilised under this law between 1933 and 1939, when it was replaced by a euthanasia programme designed to rid the Fatherland of its mentally handicapped. Hitler reminded his dinner guests that 'the law of selection justifies this incessant struggle by allowing the survival of the fittest'.

It would be an exaggeration to say that the theory of evolution provided the main inspiration for the eugenics movement, and even less so for Nazi policies. There were many strands involved, including the aspirations of nineteenth century educated Victorian gentlemen to create the world in their own image. But equally the various ideological transformations of evolution, including Spencer's notion of the survival of the fittest, provided what appeared to the eugenicists of the time to be scientific support for their programmes. Neither can one claim that such ideological transformations had nothing to do with Hitler's monstrous policies, although they were not their main inspiration, depending more in Hitler's mind on the nationalist mythology of blood purity.

The main point here is the way in which the prestige of the big theories of science, in this case evolution, can so readily be utilised and abused by interest groups to support ideologies that are not intrinsic to the theory itself. In the process the very meaning of the word 'evolution' changes, until it becomes inextricably linked in peoples' minds with the kind of horrors discussed above. If that is what evolution involves, then little wonder that people react against it – so would I, if I really thought that evolution were equivalent to racism, eugenics and naked capitalism!

The process of ideological transformation of Darwinian evolution is certainly not over yet, indeed is currently undergoing something of a renaissance in the hands of the 'new atheists' such as the biologist Richard Dawkins in the UK and the philosopher Daniel Dennett in the USA. Dennett asks whether the complexity of biological diversity can 'really be the outcome of nothing but a cascade of algorithmic processes feeding on chance? And if so, who designed that cascade?' Dennett answers his own rhetorical question by saying: 'Nobody. It is itself the product of a blind, algorithmic process'. 'Evolution is not a process that was designed to produce us'. In his book *Darwin's Dangerous Idea* Dennett pictures evolution as a 'universal acid' destroying in its path any basis for ultimate meaning and purpose in life.

Likewise Dawkins takes the position that science in general, and evolution in particular, provide rival explanations to those offered by religious believers. '...Although atheism might have been *logically* tenable before Darwin' claims Dawkins, 'Darwin made it possible to be an intellectually fulfilled atheist'.[118] Dawkins is not treating evolution here as 'merely' a biological theory, but is investing it with a particular ideological agenda. His rhetorical device is to place stark opposing alternatives before the reader, arguing that there are only three possible ways of seeing the world: Darwinism, Lamarckism, or God[119]. The last two fail to explain the world adequately; the only option is therefore Darwinism:

> I'm a Darwinist because I believe the only alternatives are Lamarckism or God, neither of which does the job as an explanatory principle. Life in the universe is either Darwinian or something else not yet thought of[120].

But if we investigate beyond the rhetoric, does evolutionary theory really stand the weight of such ideological investment?

Evolution, atheism and evolutionary creationism

Our earlier chapters dealing with the biology of evolution give a very different flavour to the subject compared to the 'isms' discussed in the present chapter. Instead of genes, diversity and the mechanisms of speciation, we have been speaking of topics such as racism, eugenics and atheism. The fact of the matter is that none of these ideologies can be rationally derived from the biological theory of evolution itself; all are parasitic upon the theory, attempting to extract plausibility by repeated association of each ideology with the biological theory itself. As Karl Marx once said, if you go on repeating things long enough, then people will believe anything. This seems to be Dawkins' propaganda style: if the 'evolution' word is linked with the 'atheism' idea long enough, then eventually people will think that one implies the other.

Ironically, young-earth creationists agree with Dawkins! The opposite extremes in a debate are often more similar than either pole is ready to admit. Those Christians who interpret the early chapters of Genesis as if they represent science are playing right into Dawkins' hands, because by confusing theology with science they are setting up a false antithesis that suits Dawkins' agenda perfectly. Yet as we noted in Chapter Two, in the section 'Does the Bible teach science?', it is more appropriate to see the biblical text as providing the theological narrative, answering questions about God's dealings with people and the world, rather than pressing scientific meanings upon a narrative never intended to bear such meaning.

A better route to follow is that adopted by those Bible-believing Christians of an earlier era, such as B.B. Warfield, Asa Gray and James McCosh, who saw themselves as evolutionary creationists, believers who fully accepted the authority of Scripture and the biblical doctrine of creation, but who traced God's providential purposes and handiwork throughout the long evolutionary process. For as already outlined in Chapter Two, Christians believe in a God who is intimately involved in every aspect of the created order. Scientists may have plenty of gaps in their understanding of what God has done and continues to do in his creation, but there are no gaps when it comes to God's interaction with the world. Think of creation like one great book. Running through the text is an evolutionary narrative thread which describes how God brought biological diversity into being and continues to sustain it all moment by moment. There are many other narratives running through the book also – the histories of the nations, the account of God's own people, and indeed our own biographies. Theologically these represent different aspects of God's sovereign creative actions in the world. Certainly God's great work in creation is distinct from his wonderful plan of redemption, but the point here is that the whole book is God's book. The various narratives running through the book all stem from the same author. The evolutionary creationist is one who has a very firm belief in God's sovereignty over the whole created order, worked out in his plan and purposes for both creation and redemption.

Once we have baptised evolution into our Christian world-view, just as countless Christians have been doing ever since the time of Darwin, then of course we will see no need to view evolutionary theory as the sinister intruder or 'universal acid' that the Dennetts and Dawkins of this world appear to imagine, but rather as the process that God has chosen, by his sovereign will, to bring into being all the amazing biological diversity that we see all around us. Indeed, such robust theism subverts the Dawkins delusion just as surely as Genesis 1 once subverted the Babylonian creation mythologies. For Dawkinism is a bit like the sea monsters of Genesis 1:27 that we were thinking about in the previous chapters. Ascribing the power and mystery of pagan deities to some aspects of creation makes them seem threatening and unsettling: but once evolution is perceived as simply the method that God has chosen to create living things, no more, no less, then it ceases to be a bogey-man and takes its place along with all the other wonders of God's creation.

I am not suggesting for a moment that adopting the position of evolutionary creationism resolves at a stroke all the problems, and we shall be considering some of those in the next few chapters, but I would suggest that it provides a well-justified framework for continuing to hold together the book of God's Word and the book of God's works in a way that does justice to both.

Once we adopt this position, the ruse of annexing 'evolution' in support of ideological agendas loses its power to persuade. For example, there is nothing that I can see in evolutionary theory that supports atheism. Of course, if we view evolution through an atheistic lens, we shall inevitably interpret it within an atheistic framework, as Dawkins does when he writes that in evolution he sees 'no design, no purpose, no evil and no good, nothing but blind pitiless indifference'. How could it be otherwise? – the conclusions are built into the starting presupposition. This is what the atheistic world-view delivers, it is not what evolution itself delivers.

Evolutionary creationists will obviously look not to the created order to derive their morality but instead to God's Word, the Bible. The basis for establishing principles fit to govern our life choices is in revelation, not in trying to extrapolate an ethical rationale from biological processes in the world around us. Of course to apply God's moral standards we often have to do some hard praying, thinking and seeking counsel on occasion from others, coupled with some serious work to understand the various issues involved, but ultimately our moral foundations are in Scripture, not in nature. This has always been the case either pre- or post-Darwin.

If we look out of the window and see the cat playing with a mouse, either in the first century or the twenty-first century, we would (hopefully) not base our own moral behaviour towards either animals or humans upon the behaviour of the cat. The fact that animals do or do not do certain things is irrelevant to the moral standards that God sets before us in Scripture. Equally the mechanisms and processes of evolution are not provided for us as examples to follow – thankfully!

Is evolution naturalistic?

Sometimes a particular use of language can muddy the waters in these kinds of discussion, and this is nowhere more true than in the usage of that rather malleable term 'naturalistic'. Anyone who reads articles or books about the creation/evolution question or, even more, the literature of intelligent design advocates that we will look at more closely in later chapters, will have come across terms such as 'naturalistic explanations' or 'methodological naturalism'. A red warning light should immediately start flashing somewhere amongst our many neurons when we encounter such terms, because they can import so many assumptions and a considerable quantity of unwanted baggage. In the immortal words of Humpty-Dumpty, 'When I use a word, it means just what I choose it to mean, neither more nor less.'[121]

The word 'naturalism' in philosophy has a very clear meaning. It is defined as the 'view of the world that excludes the supernatural or spiritual' (*Oxford Dictionary*). In art and architecture the word has a different meaning, but in philosophy that is what it means. Now there is a tradition in modern science not to use 'God' as an explanation in scientific discourse. This tradition was nurtured by the early founders of the Royal Society, partly in an attempt to let the natural philosophers (as scientists were then called) get on with their job without becoming embroiled in the religious disputes of the time, but also in recognition that the universe is in any case all the work of a wise Creator – so using God as an explanation for bits of it didn't really make much sense, given that God was in charge of all of it.

The earlier natural philosophers were not always equally consistent on this point. For Newton, God was certainly central to his creation theology, but in his science he famously maintained that God brought about an occasional 'reformation' in the movement of the planets to correct the irregularities that accrued from the supposed friction occurring as they passed through the 'ether' (an 'ether' which we now know does not exist). Even at the time the German Lutheran philosopher and mathematician Leibniz took Newton to task for invoking occasional miracles in order to remedy the deficiencies in his creation. In the words of Brooke, Leibniz insisted that 'miracles were to supply the needs of grace, not to remedy second-rate clockwork'[122]. Indeed, by the end of the eighteenth century the French mathematicians Laplace and Lagrange had shown that irregularities induced in planetary orbits could be self-correcting. Apparently there was no need for God's occasional corrections.

Such illustrations from the history of science demonstrate how easily the kind of argument used by Newton can become a hostage to fortune when we neglect to apply the type of robust theism of biblical creation theology. Once a 'god' is brought in to explain a particular gap in our current scientific knowledge, then what happens is that science eventually advances to fill the gap, and our so-called 'god' shrinks with the passage of time. This is the infamous 'god-of-the-gaps argument' that still crops up with such monotonous regularity in the literature of both Christians and atheists alike.

Biblical theism completely subverts such a position, for the God we believe in is the one who creates and providentially orders and sustains all that exists. So whether we have a current gap in our scientific knowledge or not is irrelevant to the question of God's creative actions, and least of all should that gap in our knowledge be utilised as an argument for God. Christians have no hidden theological investments in scientific ignorance!

Today's scientists who are believers do not bring God into their daily scientific discourse for three very good theological reasons. First, because to do so runs the 'Newtonian risk' of promoting a defective god-of-the-gaps argument. Second, because such a strategy demeans God in seeming to make him just one more explanatory device amongst a whole array of competing material explanations. But God is either author of the whole book of creation or he isn't, we can't have it both ways. It is worth reiterating here the point made previously: there is only one great 'dualism' in biblical thought – that which describes the relationship between God the creator and everything else that exists. Which highlights the third theological reason for not bringing God into scientific discourse: if we do, it immediately implies that God is some-how less involved in the other aspects of God's creation under scientific investigation.

Does that mean that Christians who are scientists provide 'naturalistic explanations' when they write their scientific papers? Of course not. Christians believe that all biological descriptions without exception are attempts to understand God's world. Scientists are engaged in a voyage of discovery through the universe that God has brought into being and continues to sustain. We can only discover what God has already created, for there is nothing else to discover.

Now we understand what some Christians wish to say when they refer to science as providing 'naturalistic explanations'. They simply wish to point out that we don't invoke God in our scientific explanations for the various reasons given above. But I would like to suggest that the use of the adjective 'naturalis-tic' in this context is quite inappropriate. When I walk into my laboratory I do not suddenly stop believing in God – far from it, I go in as the Christian explorer looking forward to uncov-ering more of the wonders of God's world. The more we dis-cover, the more we glorify God by revealing his thoughts in the created order.

We don't call Christian accountants 'naturalistic' because of the absence of theological terminology as they check the com-pany accounts, any more than we expect our doctor to use the-ological language when she tells us that we've got the flu, or the mechanic to refer to biblical texts when servicing our car. The absence of specific references to God does not render our lives suddenly 'naturalistic'. Quite the opposite: Christians walking with God in the power of the Spirit will be only too aware of God's presence and leading, permeating every aspect of their daily lives. Naturalism is the philosophy that there is no God in the first place, so only an atheist can provide truly naturalistic explanations for anything.

For the same reason I would not myself use the term 'methodological naturalism' to refer to what scientists do in their scientific research, irrespective of their own personal beliefs. The idea underlining the term is that the scientist does not invoke God as an explanation for things in the course of his or her daily scientific research, for all the good theological reasons already listed. The idea is fine, it is just the terminology which is quite unnecessary, for again the unstated implication is that the Christian will somehow leave their faith in God behind at the laboratory door, whereas precisely the opposite is the case. I would therefore suggest simply dropping the term 'methodological naturalism' as being misleading in this context. Why not just talk about 'scientific explanations' for things? – that does the job just as well and retains neutrality about the personal world-view of the scientist involved in providing the explanations.

How does God create the evolutionary process?

If one is going to call oneself an 'evolutionary creationist', then it is a perfectly reasonable question to ask how God interacts with the world in bringing this process into being. As part of the creative process we are trying to observe, we are not in a very good position to answer that question satisfactorily, because obviously we can perceive the situation only from the very limited perspective of time-bound creatures. Multivolume works and substantial conferences seek to address answers to this question, and we are not going to resolve the answers in a few brief paragraphs.

One thing is clear: the only proper answer to the question

'How does God interact with the world?' is 'At all times, in all places and in every way'. As Paul preached to the Epicurean and Stoic philosophers in Athens, God is the one who 'gives all men life and breath and everything else' (Acts 17:25) and 'is not far from each one of us. "For in him we live and move and have our being".' (Acts 17:27–28).

In Chapter Two we highlighted the way in which God creates by speaking in Scripture, Genesis 1 providing the prime example. When we speak as humans, the world changes – nothing is quite the same as it was before we opened our mouths to speak, a sobering thought. How much more is this the case when God speaks, bringing things into existence by top-down causation through his powerful Word. And just as we break no physical laws when we ask someone to pass the salt at table, our words acting in a top-down causal way to bring about the required response, so at an infinitely more exalted level God speaks to bring about his intentions and purposes.

So it is not particularly helpful to think of God as tweaking the occasional mutation here, or bringing about the extinction of a species there, because the unavoidable implication from such a suggestion is that then God is less involved in some other aspect of the process. If the immanence of God in the created order means anything, then it means God's working through all the processes of the evolutionary process without exception, in the billions of years when (to our minds) not much was happening on the earth and things were very small, just as much as in the Cambrian explosion when life became more diverse and interesting (again to our minds), and as much again as in the relatively rapid process of evolution that led eventually to our own appearance on the planet. In other words, God is the author of the whole story of creation, not just of bits of it.

This does not mean that all parts of the story are of equal value. Only humankind was made in God's image in the Genesis account, as we shall consider in more detail in the next chapter. When a human author writes a novel, there is backcloth material that provides a context for the main narrative, but it could be otherwise without changing the main plot.

If the hero drinks tea instead of coffee on page 78, it is probably not of great significance. But if the hero gets killed on page 144, then the whole novel would have worked out differently had that not happened. So it is with God's story of creation. Many details along the way might well have been different, and it is really not that important from a theological perspective (though it keeps scientists happily occupied, no bad thing), but other parts of the story are crucial and important. Precisely this point was raised by Darwin in his famous correspondence with the Harvard Christian botany professor Asa Gray. '...Do you believe', wrote Darwin to Gray, 'that when a swallow snaps up a gnat that God designed that that particular swallow should snap up that particular gnat at that particular instant?' Gray wisely replied that he didn't perceive God's interactions with the created order in those terms.

The language of primary and second causes is not perfect, but it can help us at this juncture. God is the primary cause who defines and energises all the properties of matter that comprise the universe. He is both transcendent and immanent in relation to this space-time continuum. He is completely faithful in upholding the properties of energy and matter, which is why they continue to have the properties they do. Were this not the case, we would be unable to speak of the 'laws of physics' and science would be impossible. God as the prime cause is the guarantor of the properties of the universe and the reason that we live in a coherent cosmos and not a random or magic universe, where what was going to happen next would always be a matter for conjecture.

Secondary causes are then what we as scientists investigate and describe in our research, referring to all the myriad interactions that occur between all the physical energy and matter of the universe. All we do, and all any scientist can do, is to describe the properties of matter that God has so graciously brought into being.

Imagine a visiting Martian seeing a car for the first time and immediately ascribing its creation to the work of humans. When the Martian is then told that it was actually built by robots in a factory, but that humans designed and built the robots, the visitor's admiration for humans as designers is lessened not one bit, rather increased, by the discovery that humans, in this analogy the primary cause, bring about their purposes through robots, the secondary causes.

This understanding of God's work in creation is not Deism. Deism is the idea of a distant God who winds up the universe at the beginning, sets up the physical laws, and then retreats, no longer to interact with his creation, except possibly to perform the occasional miracle. What we are describing here is theism, something very different, the biblical doctrine of the creator God who is intimately involved with every atom of the universe, initiating, writing and sustaining the text of the created order.

Some people find it disappointing that the Bible does not generally describe God's work of creation, either in its initiation or in its continuation, in terms of the 'miraculous', as we discussed in Chapter Two. They would like to interpose a miracle at each one of God's creative words, for example, as listed in Genesis 1. But the Bible doesn't use the language of miracles for this account, so neither should we. Miracles in Scripture are to a large extent brought about by God as particular signs of his grace in the lives of his people. And whether believers in evolution or not, we are all agreed that there were no humans around during the creation of all other living things, whether plant or animal. So there were no people to whom God could show his grace by the particular means of miracles during the origin of life, and the creation of the plants and animals.

This should lessen our appreciation and praise to God for his creation not one whit. For whether he chooses to work by the normal processes of creation, or by his dramatic intervention in the life of an individual, such as the raising of Lazarus from the dead, it is all God's work, and we should give him the glory accordingly. The medieval church encouraged an unhealthy over-interest in miracles and it was left to the reformers to bring Christians back to a more biblical balance in which God's providence was perceived more broadly in his working in the world, not at all to deny miracles, but to emphasise the fact that we walk by faith and not by sight (2 Corinthians 5:7). It does not honour God to call things miracles that God himself in his Word does not.

So evolutionary creationists today, like their Bible-believing forebears of the nineteenth century at the time of Darwin, have the great privilege of enjoying every aspect of God's creation, including an understanding of both God's patience and his power in bringing the present created order into being through the evolutionary process. At the same time they can flourish in the scientific community, or in their study of biology, or in their interactions with their scientifically minded friends, confident that whatever new things science may uncover, they can be received gladly and will bring yet further glory to God the Creator of all things.

Chapter 9:

Who were Adam and Eve?
The Background

To find out who Adam and Eve were, we need to start with the biblical text. We do not start with the evolutionary narrative and then try and impose it on the biblical text, but rather do the reverse – listen to what the Bible has to say and then see whether there are any interesting resonances with the evolutionary account. Once we have looked at the text, we will consider the evidence for human evolution, focusing on the genetics in this chapter, then on the fossil and anthropological evidence in the next chapter. Finally we will place the science and the biblical account in conversation with each other by the use of various models to see how the narratives might interact. So if the accounts look very different as we proceed, fear not, their integration will be carefully considered in the end. But as usual we cannot even begin to relate the two stories together, the theological and the scientific, unless we have a good grasp of both.

Adam and Eve in their biblical context

The Hebrew word *'adam'* is used in the early chapters of Genesis in three distinct ways. In unravelling the nuances of these uses we will adopt the same interpretative stance that was used in Chapter Seven, emphasising the theological and figurative aspects of the narratives.

Adam as humankind
The very first mention of 'Adam' in the Bible comes in Genesis 1:26–27 where the meaning is unambiguously 'humankind':

'Then God said, "Let us make *adam* in our image, in our likeness, and let them rule over the fish of the sea and the birds of
the air, over the livestock, over all the earth, and over all the
creatures that move along the ground." So God created *adam*
in his own image, in the image of God he created him; male
and female he created them'. Just to make sure that we get the
point that *adam* can refer to humankind, these verses are reit-
erated in the opening words of the second toledoth section of
Genesis in 5:1–2: 'When God created *adam*, he made him in the
likeness of God. He created them male and female and blessed
them. And when they were created, he called them *adam*.'

Placing Genesis 1:26–27 within the context of the 'theological manifesto' with which the Bible starts, we immediately
notice three key points. First, unlike the animals, it is only
humankind that is made in the image of God, and of all the
days of creation, only the creative work of this sixth day is
picked out as being 'very good' (verse 31), so the creation of
humankind is portrayed as the climax of the narrative. In addition the 'very good' may refer to the whole process of creation
described in all the days. Second, the text is at pains to emphasise that both males and females are made in God's image.
Third, the emphasis on humankind being made in the image
of God is given along with the command to rule over living
things, and the linkage is so close that it is difficult to avoid the
conclusion that there is a connection between the two. As soon
as the wild animals are made (1:25), humankind is created to
rule over them (1:26).

There has been much debate over the centuries as to the
precise content of the term 'made in the image of God'. The
terms 'image and likeness' together occur only here and in
Genesis 5:3 where Adam's son Seth is so described, the two
words being used interchangeably. For our present purposes,
two aspects of the 'image of God' concept can be highlighted.
First, the delegation of divine authority does seem to be a key
element of the term. In Near Eastern culture it was common
for kings to place their image at the boundary of their territory
as a representation of their power and authority. In 1979 a
statue of a king dating from the ninth century BC was dug up
in north-eastern Syria inscribed with his achievements, refer-

ring to the statue in both Assyrian and Aramaic equivalents as the 'image and likeness' of the king[123]. The notion of divinely delegated authority bestowed by God upon humankind is consistent with the use of the word 'rule' in verse 26 and 'subdue' in verse 28. Whereas in Babylonian and Assyrian texts it is only kings who are described as being in the image of the gods, here in Genesis the kingly responsibility of caring for the earth is given to all humans, both male and female alike. The psalmist David picks up the kingly language in Psalm 8:5–6: 'You made him ("man", "humankind") a little lower than the heavenly beings and crowned him with glory and honour. You made him ruler over the works of your hands; you put everything under his feet…'

A further important aspect of being 'made in God's image' is that it involves relationship with God. God didn't speak to any of the animals in Genesis 1, but in verse 28 he blessed humankind and spoke words to them. Here we are encountering a new type of being that had never existed on earth before, people who could hear God's voice. And in verse 29 God gives humankind gifts: 'I give you every seed-bearing plant on the face of the whole earth and every tree that has fruit with seed in it. They will be yours for food'. As the implications of what it means to be made in God's image are worked out in Genesis 2, through work, marriage and caring for the earth, so the relational language continues. The Lord God personally places man in the Garden of Eden (2:15), gives him commands (2:16), provides man with a marriage partner (2:22), and then after the Fall calls to the man 'Where are you?' (3:9). Whereas in the Babylonian creation myths humans are created in order to be the slaves of the gods, here God cares for humankind and provides for them. We are introduced to the personal God who seeks relationship with those made in his image.

Adam as 'the man' and as a personal name
The purpose of Genesis 2 is not, like chapter 1, to provide a broad overview 'creation manifesto', but rather to focus on the role of humans made in God's image in the context of creation. So the creation of *adam* is now placed at the beginning of creation, not at the end. As previously emphasised, if we come to

the first two chapters of Genesis with chronology in mind, rather than theology, then we can expect to end up with a headache. Here in Genesis 2 we have the curtain go up on the stage of life – enter a king, God's ambassador on earth! But this is a dusty king: 'the Lord God formed [Hebrew: *yatsar*] *adam* from the *adamah* [dust of the ground] and breathed into his nostrils the breath of life, and the adam became a living being' [Hebrew: *nepesh*, breath, soul] (2:7). The very material nature of the creation, including the man, is underlined by verse 9: after placing the man in 'a garden in the east, in Eden', God then 'made all kinds of trees grow out of the ground [*adamah*]'.

There are many important points packed into these verses. First, there is a perfectly good word for 'man' in Hebrew (*'ish*), the word most commonly used for man in the Old Testament (in fact 1,671 times), so the choice of *'adam'* here for man seems a deliberate teaching tool to explain to the reader that *adam* not only comes from the *adamah*, but is also given the important task by God of caring for the *adamah* – earthy Adam is to be God's earth-keeper.

Second we note the use of the definite article in front of *adam*, so that the correct translation in English is 'the man', and the definite article remains in place all the way though to Genesis 4:25 when Adam without a definite article appears and 'lay with his wife again'. Personal names in Hebrew do not carry the definite article, so there is a particular theological point being made: here is 'the man', not any old man but a very particular man, the representative man perhaps of all other men. However we are to understand the use of the definite article, there is no doubt that it is a very deliberate strategy in this tightly woven text, with no less than 20 mentions of 'the man' in Genesis 2 and 3.

But at the same time there is some ambiguity in the use of the word *adam*, perhaps an intentional ambiguity, which makes it quite difficult to know when 'Adam' is first used as a personal name[124]. For example in some verses, instead of the definite article in front of *adam*, there is what is called in Hebrew an 'inseparable preposition', translated as 'to' or 'for' in Genesis 2:20, 3:17 and 3:21. Different translations apply their own different interpretations of when *adam* starts being used as the personal name Adam, and these differing interpretations depend on the context. So it is best not to be too dogmatic about the precise moment in the text when 'the *adam*', the representative man, morphs with Adam bearing a personal name, a point to which we shall return.

The third important point highlighted in Genesis 2:7 is that '*adam* became a living being' or, as some translations have it, 'living soul'. The language of 'soul' has led some Christians to think that this verse is a description of an immortal soul that is implanted in 'the *adam*' during his creation, but whatever might be the teaching of Scripture elsewhere on this point, it is difficult to sustain such an idea from this Genesis passage. The Hebrew word used here is *nepesh*, which can mean, according to context: life, life force, soul, breath, the seat of emotion and desire, a creature or person as a whole, self, body, even in some cases a corpse. In Genesis 1:21, 24, 20 and 2:19 exactly the same phrase in Hebrew – 'living *nepesh*', translated as 'living creatures' – is used there for animals as is used here in Genesis 2 for 'the *adam*'. And we note also that *adam* became a *nepesh*, he was not given one as an extra, so the text is simply pointing out that the life and breath of *adam* was completely dependent upon God's creative work, just as it was for the 'living creatures' in Genesis 1. There is certainly no scope for understanding this particular passage as referring to the addition to *adam* of an immaterial immortal 'soul'.

I remember during an early stage of my Christian life becoming mighty confused by the many different ways in which the terms 'soul' and 'spirit' were employed by different preachers and Christian writers. So I did what I have always practised in such circumstances – carried out my own word study using the Bible alone, but with the help of commentaries to find out which Hebrew or Greek word was being used in what context. And as I steadily worked through the many hundreds of uses of these words in the biblical text, two points became very clear. The first is that the words 'soul' and 'spirit' are often used interchangeably in the Hebrew text, so there is a fair degree of fluidity in their usage. The second is that the Bible encourages us to think of human nature more as a body–soul–spirit unity than as a tripartite composition of body

+ soul + spirit. And when we come to the New Testament, immortality is linked not to the soul, but to the resurrection of the body. The earthy very material *adam* introduced to us here in Genesis 2, made from the dust of the ground, lays the foundation for the theological exposition of the nature of humankind that then follows in the rest of Scripture. A full discussion of that point would of course require a much longer consideration than space allows, but my recommendation is to carry out a personal exploration of the biblical text, for it can be surprising to find out how different may be our own assumptions about the matter from what the Bible actually teaches. The word *nepesh* is used 695 times in the Hebrew Old Testament (and most of those times is not translated as 'soul' in our English texts, because the context gives it a different meaning), so such a study can take quite a long time!

The creation of woman

Just as the creation of 'the man' in Genesis 2 is a special creative work of God that highlights his role as being made in the image of God, so the text portrays the creation of 'woman' as a special act of creation fulfilling God's relational plan and purposes for humankind. Central to the account is the creation ordinance of marriage. Genesis 2:18 tells us that marriage is God's idea – it is God who sees that 'the *adam*' is lonely, and in verses 19–20 'the *adam*' exerts his stewardly responsibility over living things, yet without finding a suitable partner. As is fitting with a traditional Middle Eastern culture, it is an arranged marriage. So God takes the initiative to put 'the *adam*' to sleep, remove one of his ribs (or side), and use that to form the woman, whom he then brings to 'the *adam*' (verse 22). Once again, we may lose some important nuances if we do not refer back to the Hebrew text, which now begins to mingle two different Hebrew words for 'man' in order to deliver the two punchlines in verses 23 and 24: 'The man (*adam*) said, "This is now bone of my bones and flesh of my flesh; she shall be called 'woman' (*issa*), for she was taken out of man (*'ish*)." For this reason a man (*'ish*) will leave his father and mother and be united to his woman (*issa*, wife in this context), and they will become one flesh.' Unlike 'the *adam*' and the animals who were made out of the ground, the woman is distinctive in being made directly from 'the *adam*'. Furthermore, the beasts that are paraded before 'the *adam*' in 2:19 are the *hayyah* in Hebrew, but none of them are suitable to be the *havvah*, as the man's new wife is eventually named in 3:20. Once again the text makes a play on words, quite lost to us in the English, both words deriving from the root word *haya* meaning 'to live'.

Now if we take this obviously figurative and literary passage, with all its linguistic plays on words, as referring to some early Near Eastern operation during which God both provides the anaesthetic and does the surgical manipulation of a male rib to generate a woman, then we will have missed the point of the text by reading it through modernist spectacles. No, if we go down that route then we are in real danger of abusing the text, which is about the foundations of marriage.

Marriage is an ordinance created by God and we mess about with it at our peril. It is one of the components of the relational life that God has planned for humankind, and this is highlighted at the start of the account with God's own analysis of the situation that 'It is not good for the man to be alone. I will make a helper (Hebrew: *ezer*) suitable for him' (verse 18, literally 'helper matching him'). The main use of the word *ezer* in the Old Testament is in describing God himself; in fact in 15 out of 21 cases it is God who is the *ezer* of man. In Deuteronomy 33:29 the people of Israel are called blessed because 'Who is like you, a people saved by the Lord? He is your shield and helper [*ezer*]'. The psalmist prays: 'We wait in hope for the Lord; he is our help [*ezer*] and our shield' (Psalm 33:20). So the woman is being called to work alongside the man, imaging the kind of way in which God helps us, in order to fulfil together the awesome responsibility of subduing the earth.

The language of being taken from the man's side, coupled with the man's exclamation on being brought together with the woman ('bone of my bones and flesh of my flesh'!), both serve to emphasise the intimate complementarity between the man and the woman. As has often been said: 'not from his head to rule over him, or from his feet, to be trodden on by him, but from his side, to be his equal'. The unstated implication here is

that the woman is one with the man in knowing God, in receiving his commands and 'walking with him' (cf. 3:8). What we
have here is vivid metaphorical language to express some profound theological truths that lie at the heart of the marriage
relationship in which both partners are believers. Jesus
referred to the passage in these terms, highlighting not the
man and the woman as individuals with names, but as representing male and female: "'Haven't you read," Jesus replied,
"that at the beginning the Creator 'made them male and
female,' and said, 'For this reason a man will leave his father
and mother and be united to his wife, and the two will become
one flesh'"? (Matthew 19:4–5). To end up discussing rib operations rather than the ordinance of marriage at the end of
Genesis 2, is to miss the point entirely.

Unlike 'the *adam*', who receives no specific naming, the
woman is named *havva* (Eve, 'life') in Genesis 3:20 'because
she would become the mother of all the living'[125]. The precise
meaning of this verse has been much discussed by commentators. The naming of *hawwa* may be introduced here to bring
some further life and hope into the rather dark picture of the
Fall (to be discussed in the next chapter), which involves so
much anguish and alienation. The phrase 'she would become
mother of all living', added retrospectively by the narrator,
might refer to Eve's role as the mother of all those who were
eventually to experience new life by knowing God, fulfilling
the promise by faith of verse 15.

Adam and Eve in the rest of Scripture

We do not have to read much further in the Genesis text to find
the clear implication that 'the man' and 'the woman' were not
the only people around at that time. When Cain was cursed by
God following his murder of his brother Abel, he complains to
God: 'Today you are driving me from the land, and I will be
hidden from your presence; I will be a restless wanderer on the
earth, and whoever finds me will kill me' (4:14). It is not wild
animals that Cain is scared of here, but other people, as verse
15 makes clear. Two verses later we find Cain 'building a city'.
This does not sound like a non-populated world.

The passages that follow may therefore be best interpreted

as describing the 'godly line' of Adam and Eve who, though fallen, had been entrusted with the great responsibility of godly stewardship of the earth, contrasted with those people described who were not in this godly line. The birth of Seth to Adam in 4:25 was seen by Adam as a replacement for the murdered Abel, and it is perhaps not coincidental that the growth of Seth's family is associated with the comment: 'At that time men began to call on the name of the Lord', a phrase used elsewhere in Genesis of the patriarchs (as in 12:8, 13:4 etc), implying perhaps the institution of divine worship.

In the toledoth found at the start of Genesis 5, introducing the 'account of Adam's line', we find that just as Adam was created in God's image, so Adam 'had a son in his own likeness, in his own image; and he named him Seth', and it is Seth's onward genealogy that is then described in the rest of this chapter. This might help us in interpreting the otherwise rather difficult Genesis 6:2: 'the sons of God saw that the daughters of men were beautiful, and they married any of them they chose' (and compare verse 4). In the context of this narrative the 'sons of God' might refer to those in the godly line leading back to Adam, as in the genealogy reproduced in Luke 3:38: '...the son of Enosh, the son of Seth, the son of Adam, the son of God'. If that interpretation is correct, and I present it very tentatively as this is a notoriously difficult passage to interpret, then the passage may be referring to the perils of marrying outside the godly community. Then, as now, don't marry unbelievers! Whatever the correct interpretation might be, it is clear that judgement follows, as described in 6:5ff with the account of the flood.

The godly line leading from Seth culminates with Noah and his family in 5:32, but the family history and likeness is picked up again in the toledoth of Noah who 'was a righteous man, blameless among the people of his time, and he walked with God' (6:9). Noah did what Adam and Eve failed to do immediately after the Fall, continue to 'walk with God' (3:8). This is what being part of the godly line really means – godly practice. After God had brought Noah and his family safely through the waters of the flood, the covenant is renewed and the godly community continues: 'This is the sign of the covenant I am making between me and you and every living creature with you, a covenant for all generations to come: I have set my rainbow in the clouds, and it will be the sign of the covenant between me and the earth' (Genesis 9:12–13).

Adam is mentioned in the New Testament just nine times, mostly in the context of the Fall and its significance as the backcloth for the subsequent saving work of Christ, so we shall postpone discussion of those citations until the following chapters. Eve is mentioned only four times in the whole Bible, of which two mentions are in Genesis 3 and 4, and two in the New Testament. In the book of Acts the NIV translation has Paul proclaim in Athens 'From one man he made every nation of men, that they should inhabit the whole earth...' (Acts 17:26). However, the NIV has added the word 'man' which is in none of the original Greek manuscripts, which simply say: 'From one he made every nation of men...', so Paul here is most likely highlighting the more general point of the common humanity of his hearers, a major theme in this particular sermon.

Human evolution – the genetics

Before seeing whether there is any connection at all between the biblical teaching about Adam and Eve, and the evolutionary theory of human origins, it is important to understand the present state of play with regard to human evolution. This will be a brief thumbnail sketch, and references will be provided for those who wish to read further[126].

First it should be emphasised that our shared inheritance with the apes is one of the most certain conclusions of contemporary biology. The reason for being so sure is because of the kind of comparative genomics that we introduced in Chapter Three. The record of our evolutionary past is indelibly inscribed within the DNA of every cell of our bodies. We are all walking genetic fossil museums! I find it ironic that people who deny our shared inheritance with the apes are carrying around in their own bodies about 10 million million (10^{13}) copies (the DNA content of each cell) of their evolutionary history. One copy would be enough to make the point, but in fact we have 10^{13} copies.

By using the term 'shared inheritance with the apes', we do not mean that anatomically modern humans (us) have directly descended from the apes: all this means is that we once shared a common ancestor with the apes. In fact our last common ancestor is estimated to have lived about 6 million years ago, followed by extensive diversification of our lineages through multiple stages. Since we now know not only our own complete DNA sequence, but that of other primates, such as the chimpanzee and rhesus macaque, together with partial sequence information from the genomes of many other primates, we are in a much stronger position than even a few years ago to track the evolutionary histories of different genes and sequences.

Before looking at this in more detail, a few definitions might be useful. *Homo sapiens* (us) is one of about 200 examples of living primates, which collectively comprise the order Primate, which in turn is one of the 22 living orders of the class of Mammals[127]. Primates in this context refer not to archbishops in the Church of England, but to a collection of animals that began to become more common about 50 million years ago following the extinction of the dinosaurs and that share certain features in common. The 200 primate species alive today represent the remains of an adaptive radiation that probably gave rise to about 6,000 species altogether. Primates are characterised by particular anatomy of the hand and feet, overall style of locomotion, visual abilities, intelligence, aspects of reproductive anatomy, life-history and dental architecture. Living primates today vary hugely in size from the mouse lemur which weighs in at 80 grams to the mountain gorilla which is 2,000 times bigger. They can be categorised into four broad groups:

- The prosimians, which include lemurs, tarsiers and bush-babies. Lemurs are found particularly in South America.
- The New World monkeys, such as howler monkeys, spider monkeys and marmosets. Again these are restricted to Central and South America (hence the name).

- The Old World monkeys, such as macaques and baboons, found in Africa and East Asia.
- The hominids, which comprise apes and humans, the apes likewise being found in Africa and East Asia, and the humans – just about everywhere we look! The apes include animals such as chimpanzees, gorillas, orang-utans and gibbons. Remember that there is no such species as 'an ape', only different types of ape, such as chimpanzee etc. So if you want to tell your child 'stop behaving like an ape!', it might be good to refine the exhortation a little more precisely ('Stop behaving like a gibbon!').

Modern genetics has led to more sophisticated classification systems than those shown here, but the terms used above remain in common use. Another common term is 'hominin' which refers to the various species in the 'human family', all those approximately 20 new species that have been described in the fossil record since 1940, now no longer alive, which track human evolution from our last common ancestor with the apes. So *Homo sapiens*, anatomically modern humans, who began to emerge 200,000 years ago, is the only species of hominin left alive. Therefore do not be confused when the term 'human' is used in the biological literature; it is common to use it as an adjective to describe hominin fossil species, but there is no judgement of value here, the word is being used in a biological sense in the context of comparative anatomy, not to talk about humans 'made in the image of God'.

With some definitions now in place, we shall look at a few examples of the ways in which modern genetics has established our common inheritance with the apes beyond any reasonable doubt.

Pseudogenes

Think about your first cousin, real or imagined. Let's say she is the daughter of your mother's sister. She has a dimple. You have a dimple. Dimples are inherited. So you dig out some old pictures of your grandmother, your mother's mother, when she was a girl, and sure enough, there is the dimple! In this scenario your grandmother is your last common ancestor on your mother's side of the family. You could of course repeat the process for all kinds of inherited traits. For example, try clasping your hands together. Now look at your thumbs. Which thumb is over which? It may well be different from your unrelated friend, but your sibs or children are more likely to have your left-over-right thumb than the other way round.

These kinds of inherited traits are actually due to multiple genes, so dimples won't keep going for ever down the family tree, because the dimple-encoding genes will start getting diluted out by other face-building genes. But now let's imagine that there is some totalitarian regime that comes into power (perish the thought) and they tattoo upon everyone's arm a unique 30-digit number with the instruction that the children of each person must be tattooed with the same number, and when that child has children the unique number has to be tattooed on their children's arm, and so on for generations. Let's also imagine that it is the female's number that dominates in every marriage, and that all females in the world at the start-point of the totalitarian regime coming to power are tattooed with different randomised 30-digit numbers.

What would happen a few hundred generations later? Clearly some numbers would die out because individuals might not have children for whatever reason. So gradually some numbers would begin to disappear, but other numbers would become 'successful' and proliferate. Hundreds of generations and thousands of years later each person would be able to find very easily distant relatives all round the world bearing the unique number tattooed on their arms. Furthermore, it would be a simple matter to identify the original common ancestor who 'started off' that unique number in the first place.

If we go on to imagine these unique numbers scattered round our genomes, specified as nucleotide base sequences, rather than as numbers stamped on our arms, we begin to grasp the power of genetics for working out common ancestry. In fact a 30-digit number is very small in comparison with the specificity built into the sequences of the four different types of nucleotide base letters of the genetic alphabet when they are built up into sequences of DNA hundreds or thousands of letters long. Gone are the days when those in the physical and chemical sciences could accuse biologists of not being sufficiently precise in their data – the exquisite specificity of long stretches of DNA is as exact as anything we can find in science. This is why the sequence of sections of human DNA that tend to vary a lot between individuals is used to generate a 'genetic fingerprint' in forensic analysis, because the chances of another person displaying the same set of sequences is so very small. Such genetic data are now frequently used in court to secure convictions.

In the same way, the finding of unique DNA sequences in common provides powerful evidence of common ancestry, because the chances become so remotely small that a particular specified sequence would have arisen twice by chance. This is the case not for the protein-encoding genes that are usually under strong selection pressure because their protein products are critical for the health, survival and reproductive success of the organism, but for that 50% of our genomes that are composed of non-functional, parasitic DNA, like transposons, and for the pseudogenes that have lost their function. Even if the very occasional transposon eventually gains some useful function and becomes a functional DNA sequence, it is still vastly outnumbered by the transposons that have no function and that continue to enter the genomes of both animals and humans.

We have already introduced pseudogenes in Chapter Three: genes that were functional in our distant ancestors, and that retain their function in living representatives of those lineages, but which have been switched off in our own genomes, lying there like derelict machinery as a vivid reminder of our evolutionary history. Pseudogenes attain their non-functionality by accumulating a small number of mutations that mean that they can no longer be transcribed properly into mRNA, or a truncated version of the gene is transcribed, or a dysfunctional protein is produced. Sometimes a premature 'stop codon' is introduced right in the middle of the gene, like a mutant full-stop appearing in the middle of a sentence, disabling the gene. Genes need 'promoter regions' in the DNA that allow them to be switched on properly, and so mutations in these regions can also generate pseudogenes. Remember that a single mutation can put the sequence of DNA letters 'out of frame', so that a genetic sentence that made perfect sense before is now rendered gibberish. Whereas many pseudogenes are easily recognisable, some have accumulated so much damage that sophisticated computer programs are necessary to identify them[128].

It turns out that the human genome contains at least 19,000 pseudogenes, and more continue to be identified, so it seems likely that these derelict genetic fossils in our genomes out-number protein-encoding genes, an astonishing and very recent finding. A great practical advantage is that we can now do detective work on the fossils and trace very precisely where they come from in our own evolutionary histories. Each mutated pseudogene is unique, and therefore arises from an unrepeatable unique event, hence the use of pseudogenes in historical investigation.

We have already highlighted the fact that all mammalian genomes studied so far contain about 1,000 genes involved in smell; the so-called olfactory genes, of which no less than 63% are switched off in humans, in other words they are pseudo-genes. This means that about 300 human olfactory receptor pseudogenes are still functional genes in the genomes of rats and mice. This difference is not surprising when we consider how dependent rodents are on their sense of smell for survival and reproductive success. In many primates such as ourselves, in which smell is not so critical, some of our olfactory 'fine-tuning' can be lost without danger to life or limb. So mutant olfactory genes are not weeded out by the winnowing process of natural selection, but contribute to our great pseudogene collection in the musty cabinets of our genetic fossil museums.

One of the olfactory genes well illustrates how genes are converted to pseudogenes. To understand what follows all you need to know is that there are four different kinds of nucleotide base in the DNA alphabet (abbreviated A, C, G, T) organised into three-base triplets called codons, which encode an amino acid building block in a protein sequence, or 'stop' signals indicating the end of a gene (like the full-stop marking the end of a sentence). In addition you need to know that there are 20 different amino acids and that their sequence in a protein is precisely defined by the sequence of A, C, G and T letters in the DNA, arranged in the triplet codons, each triplet encoding one amino acid. Each amino acid is in turn also represented by a different letter of the alphabet, but it is not necessary for what follows to know which letter applies to which amino acid.

The olfactory gene in question is fully active in chimpanzees, orangutans and gibbons, but has been passed on to humans with a G to T mutation[129]. This mutation has transformed the eleventh triplet of bases GAA (encoding the amino acid known as glutamic acid, 'E') to TAA (an inactivating stop signal, '*'). So the amino acid sequence of the relevant section of the olfactory protein generated now looks like this:

human	MANENYTKVT*FIFTGLNYN...
chimpanzee	MANENYTKVTEFIFTGLNYN...
gorilla	MANENYTKVTEFIFTGLNYN...
orangutan	MANENYTKVTEFIFTGLNYN...
gibbon	MANENYTKVTEFIFTGLNYN...

What this means is that since our last shared ancestor with the apes about 6 million or more years ago, on a particular day of the week in a germ cell of a particular hominin, a mutation occurred changing the 'G' to a 'T', and the whole human population has now inherited that mutation, resulting in the production of a non-functional truncated protein due to the mutant 'stop' signal. These kinds of sequences are like the unique numbers tattooed on the arm in our analogy introduced above. Our genomes are tattooed with their evolutionary past. The chances of that particular olfactory gene, with its hundreds of amino acids, non-functional and bearing the critical mutation, appearing 'out of nowhere' into our genomes, is vanishingly small. The only coherent interpretation is that we have inherited the now dysfunctional gene from our animal past.

As a further example, think of why sailors in previous centuries used to suffer from scurvy on long voyages. The reason is that their stocks of fruit ran out after a few weeks at sea, depriving them of the vitamin C needed to prevent scurvy. So why can't we make vitamin C ourselves, given that most other mammals make it? Mammals such as rats and mice have a gene called *gulo* which encodes an enzyme called *L-gulono-γ-lactone oxidase* (GLO – hence the name of the gene) which is needed to synthesise vitamin C. But a mutation entered into the primate lineage more than 40 million years ago, so we all now have only the non-functional pseudogene version of *gulo* and have to keep eating all those oranges to stay healthy. Here is the reason why[130]:

	80	90	100
Rat	GAGGTGCGCT	TCACCCGAGG	CGATGACA
Human	G*G*GGT*A*CGCT	TCACC*T*G_G*A*	CGATGACA
Chimpanzee	G*G*G*C*T*A*CGCT	TCACC*T*G_G*A*	CGATGACA
Orangutan	G*G*GGTGCGCT	TCACCC*A*_G*A*	CGATGACA
Macaque	G*G*GGTGCGCT	TCACCC*A*_*A*G	CGATGACA

This shows the nucleotide sequence (nucleotide numbers 80–107) in the part of the gene that has been mutated. The rat sequence makes a functional GLO enzyme, so rats don't need to eat oranges to stay healthy. As you can see from the Table, the primate gene sequences are nearly identical to the rat's, but they lack an 'A' at nucleotide 97. That this random, highly unlikely mutation is present in all the primate species examined indicates that it occurred only once in an ancestor of the great apes and macaques. The chances of the same mutation happening more than once in exactly the same genetic letter in a gene thousands of letters long is, again, vanishingly small.

You do not relish the thought of sharing common ancestry with the rat, do I hear you say? At least our common ancestry with the rest of the living world should help to keep us humble! Since we have more than 19,000 pseudogenes in our genomes, there are hundreds of other examples of this type of detective work going on to delineate our ancestry, much of it still being published[131]. All of these examples point to the indelible stamp of our evolutionary past upon our genomes.

Transposable elements

We have previously introduced in Chapter Three the idea of the transposable elements or jumping genes that comprise nearly half our genomes. These are those 'copy-and-paste' sequences of DNA that have no function, but which provide further valuable genetic fossils for tracking our own evolutionary history. If one of these sequences has been inserted at a particular specific location in the genomes of different species, then this demonstrates unequivocally that these species must all have descended from the same common ancestor. We share nearly all (99%) of these fossilised inserts into our genomes in common with chimpanzees, most with macaques, and many with distantly related mammals. The most common type of inserts number 3 million in all and many are up to 6,000 nucleotide base pairs long, in other words sequences that could not possibly have ended up in our own genomes by a random process independent of our ancestry.

To give an idea of how powerful such observations are for understanding our ancestry, consider the following example illustrated in Figure 11:

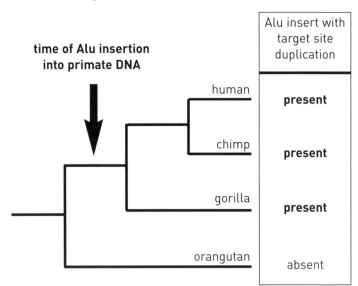

In this example the 'jumping gene' is known as an 'Alu insert'. It is hundreds of nucleotide base-pairs long. It has inserted into a non-protein coding region of the genome of the common ancestor of human, chimp and gorilla, but is not present in the DNA of the orangutan. This tells us immediately that the insertional event must have taken place after our lineage split off from the orangutan about 12–15 million years ago. Just to demonstrate how easy it is to identify the exact Alu insert involved, Figure 12 shows the precise insertion site in the genomes of the species involved:

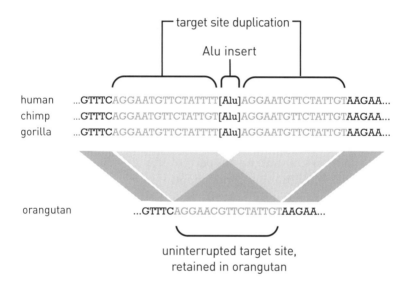

Anybody can read the evidence! Looking along the DNA letters (nucleotide bases) in the chromosomes of human, chimp and gorilla we can pick out immediately that the 'Alu insertion' sequence has located in exactly the same place in each genome, with only tiny mutational changes between the sequences around the insertion site: but the insertion is completely missing from the orangutan at precisely the same spot where the uninterrupted sequence is shown. For those who enjoy playing detective, it is worth spending a few minutes on

Figures 11 and 12. Genomes are great places for sleuthing and working out what happened.

Multiply this type of observation thousands of times, and you get an idea how powerful are these genetic fossils in revealing our evolutionary past.

Retroviral insertions

More genetic sleuthing is made possible by the 8% of our DNA that originally came from retroviruses, inserted in sequences from 8,000 to 11,000 nucleotide bases long, therefore not difficult to miss! When someone is infected with a retrovirus like HIV, the DNA from the virus is incorporated into their cells. In the case of HIV the main cells to be targeted in this way are the body's T cells which are involved in defence against viral attack, which is why HIV is such a deadly disease because it knocks out the body's own defence system. But in many cases retroviruses incorporate their DNA message into genomes without any harm to the individual, and in some cases this infection occurs in germ line cells, meaning that the inserted DNA becomes a permanent part of the genome of all the descendants of that single individual.

So once again our cells are like little history books, faithfully reproducing for our interest evolutionary histories that go back millions of years. A single example will serve to make the point:

human	CTCTGGAATTC[HERV]GAATTCTATGT
chimpanzee	CTCTGGAATTC[HERV]GAATTCTATGT
bonobo	CTCTGGAATTC[HERV]GAATTCTATGT

This shows the insertion site of a retrovirus known as K105, thousands of nucleotide base pairs long and indicated here as [HERV], which is located at precisely the same site in our own genomes and those of our ancestors[132]. Again by tracking back in the primate record far enough in evolutionary time it is possible to find where K105 no longer appears in the genome. In other words on a particular day of a particular week in a particular year, millions of years ago, that particular retroviral DNA sequence was inserted into a particular germ cell of one of our ancestors, and it has been there ever since; we all continue to make millions of copies of it, very precisely, every day of our lives. That is an amazing thought.

Chromosome fusions

We humans have 23 pairs of chromosomes whereas the great apes have 24 pairs. The story of our 'missing pair' provides another great piece of historical sleuthing that reveals our shared ancestry with the apes. To understand the story we need to know what a chromosome pair looks like, as Figure 13 illustrates. The ends of the chromosomes are called telomeres and the place in the middle where the two chromosomes join is called the centromere. What happened during evolution is that two separate ape chromosomes (known as 2p and 2q) fused to form our human chromosome 2, the second largest of our chromosomes. This happened by 'head-to-head' fusion, that is the telomeres of two smaller ape chromosomes fused at

centromere

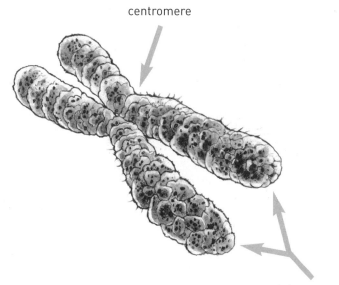

telomeres

Figure 13. A pair of human chromosomes joined at the position known as the centromere. Each chromosome consists of a single DNA molecule packed tightly with proteins.

their telomeres to form one much larger chromosome, like this (Figure 14)[133]:

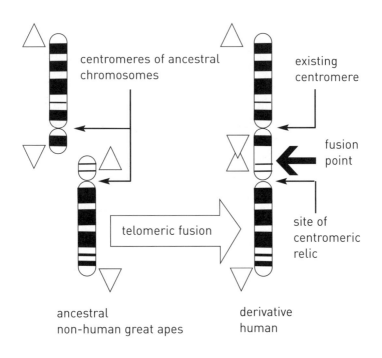

centromeres of ancestral chromosomes

existing centromere

fusion point

telomeric fusion

site of centromeric relic

ancestral non-human great apes

derivative human

In this diagram the triangles represent the telomeres, and so the double triangle on the right represents the place where the fusion took place to generate the human chromosome. The DNA sequences in the human chromosome are exactly as expected from this scenario. Telomeres consist of many repeats of the nucleotide sequence TTAGGG, and at the fusion point of the human chromosome, where the two telomeres fused, this sequence is found 'head to head'. The functional centromere in chromosome 2 lines up with with the chimpanzee chromosome 2p chromosomal centromere. The remains of the redundant centromere from one of the ancestral ape chromosomes can also be found as shown. The DNA sequence of the rest of human chromosome 2 matches very precisely the sequences of the two separate chimpanzee chromosomes 2p and 2q that were involved in the fusion. Taken together these data make it overwhelmingly likely that human chromosome 2 was derived by the fusion of two ancestral ape chromosomes, providing further compelling evidence for our shared ancestry with the apes.

Is God a deceiver?

We have mentioned here only a few of the hundreds of examples that could be provided of unique signatures that identify our common ancestry with the apes. To use the tattooed 30-digit number on the arm analogy, it is as if our own arms were covered with hundreds of unique numbers that we can trace directly back to the apes.

Of course a person who refuses to believe this overwhelmingly convincing body of data can always say something like 'Could not God have created humans separately from the apes and just implanted in the human genome these millions of different unique sequences to make it look as if we share a common ancestry with the apes, even though this is not really the case?' The suggestion that God has planted misleading 'molecular fossils' in our bodies is parallel to the suggestion that God planted misleading physical fossils in the rocks to test the faith of the believer. The obvious and profound theological problem with such a suggestion, as we considered in Chapter Six, is that it makes God into a deceiver on a grand scale. It would mean believing in a God who deliberately confuses people, making it look certain that we had shared common ancestry with the apes, when really this was not the case.

Such a deceiving God is not the God of the Bible who 'is right and true; he is faithful in all he does' (Psalm 33:4). If God were such a deceiver then how could we be sure about his great covenant promises? Indeed, how could we be sure about his great promise to us of eternal salvation? No, we cannot go down that road, for in so doing we distort the scriptural revelation of God in Christ, who is 'the faithful and true witness, the ruler of God's creation' (Revelation 3:14). Telling the truth about God's creation is a profound responsibility and is part of our worship.

Chapter 10:

Who were Adam and Eve? Genesis and Science in Conversation

Human evolution – the big picture

So far we have considered only the genetic data that demonstrate our biological unity with the rest of living things, but these are not the only kind of data that tell us about our own evolutionary story. For the specifics we have to go to the fossil record, which provides a fascinating jigsaw puzzle with the main sections of the picture now clear, but with many more pieces yet to be discovered to fill in the details. Human evolution looks like a classic 'evolutionary bush', of the kind that is familiar in the emergence of any new species, with our own kind as one of the twigs, albeit a very important twig!

Unlike today, 25 million years ago the carbon dioxide level in the atmosphere was falling and the earth was cooling, leading to the retreat of tropical forests in several parts of the world. Primates no longer enjoyed such a wide range of habitats, but Africa was an exception. There the apes emerged as a distinct primate lineage, eventually spreading out to the Middle East and Asia. The gibbons split off as a separate lineage about 18 million years ago, the other lineage of apes continuing to grow in size, hence the term 'the great apes', eventually giving rise to the, the only representative left today of this evolutionary twig, just surviving in its Indonesian habitat. Other great apes in Asia went extinct, such as the huge *Gigantopithecus* that is estimated to have been 10 feet high and weighed in at more than 500 kg, not something to mess with on a dark night.

The next big branching point in our own evolutionary history may have taken place as long as 8–11 million years ago when our lineage emerged from the ancestors of the gorillas[134], later branching off again from our closest living relatives, the chimpanzees and bonobos[135]. Genetic data suggest that the last common ancestor of humans, chimpanzees and bonobos lived 5–7 million years ago. Remember that we are not descended from chimpanzees, but our line and their line have been evolving independently since that time. Neither we nor they existed 7 million years ago, it's just that we share a common ancestor.

Figure 15 now illustrates the general picture of what happened next. The earliest identifiable hominins on our lineage date from around 6 million years ago and consist of a cluster of species, such as *Sahelanthropus* with a skull that looks quite chimpanzee-like from the back, but with teeth that are characteristic of more recent hominins. Palaeontologists can tell a lot from the minute study of teeth, often the best preserved part of such ancient fossils. *Ardpithecus ramidus* is a fossil species discovered in 1994 dating from 4.4 million years ago, which also combines ape-like as well as more recent features. Although Figure 15 gives the impression that these very early hominins are on the same lineage leading to modern humans, this is not really yet known, and it is possible that several hominin lineages branched off from the apes, only one of which led to modern humans.

Things become much clearer with the next major group of hominin species to emerge, the *Australopithecus* who lived during the period 2–4 million years ago. Many of the fossil finds of these and other early hominins have been made in the Great Rift Valley in Ethiopia. There in 1973 the dramatic discovery was made of the first *Australopithecus*, a 3.2 million year old female skeleton, 40% intact, nicknamed Lucy because the Beatles song 'Lucy in the Sky With Diamonds' was playing in the anthropologists' campsite at the time. Other fossils of the same species were found soon afterwards and were called *Australopithecus afarensis*, displaying a fascinating mixture of the anatomical features of apes and modern humans[136]. Lucy was small, just a few feet high and weighed somewhat over 30 kg. In the males of the species the brain

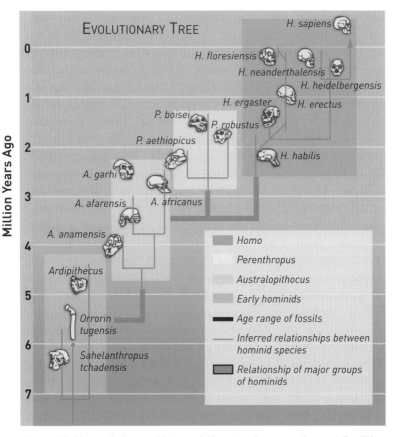

Figure 15. The evolutionary history of *Homo sapiens* over the past 7 million years. The boxes show the four main groups of hominid species recognised by most scientists working in the field. The thick branches connecting the boxes indicate the general consensus about how the groups are related. [From Zimmer, C. (2006) *Where Did We Come From?*, Hove: Apple Press, p. 41.]

size reached 450 cc (as measured from fossil skulls), only about a third of the size of modern humans. Lucy had an upright, bipedal anatomy (that is she had the anatomy to walk on two feet, like us). It was probably hominins like Lucy who left behind the bipedal footprints found in the volcanic ash at Laetoli in Tanzania, dating from 3.5 million years ago. At the same time Lucy retained several chimpanzee-like features, such as long arms, hooked fingers, and a chest shape more characteristic of chimps than humans.

Yet it is unlikely that Lucy and her kind were the first to

prefer walking on two legs. The bones of a 6-million-year-old hominin called *Orrorin tugensis*, discovered in Kenya in 2002, suggest bipedal locomotion, and although *Sahelanthropus* from the same period is known only from fossilised parts of the skull, these alone are sufficient to indicate an upright posture. The hole at the base of the *Sahelanthropus* skull, known as the foramen magnum, through which the brain is attached to the spinal nerve, is under the centre of the skull as in humans, and not at the back, as in the apes. Despite these very early signs of bipedality, the brain size of hominins did not start surpassing that of chimpanzees until millions of years later, around 2 million years ago. Furthermore, the first stone tools do not start appearing until 2.6 million years ago. So bipedality in itself was insufficient to drive the 'cultural revolution' that was associated with the increase in brain size that occurred over the past 2 million years. The construction and use of more sophisticated tools, together with increasingly complex social structures, are both thought to have played critical roles in expanding brain size[137].

Our own genus *Homo* emerged in Africa over the period 2–3 million years ago. The precise lineage leading to *Homo* is still much discussed. One possibility is that the immediate precursor was Lucy's species *Australopithecus afarensis*, but there are other possibilities. Several species of *Homo* were thriving at the same time. *Homo habilis* was alive in Africa up to about 1.6 million years ago and had a brain somewhat larger than that of *Australopithecus*, up to 680 cubic centimetres, nearly half the size of the human brain. With long arms and short legs, *Homo habilis* retained some ape-like characteristics, and may even have still spent some time in trees. This was unlikely to have been the case with *Homo ergaster*, which begins to appear in the fossil record about 1.8 million years ago, which in many ways looked a lot more like us than it did like *Homo habilis*, growing as tall as six feet with long legs, narrow hips and a barrel-shaped ribcage in place of the funnel-shape that characterised both Lucy and the chimpanzees. The skull also began to look much more like our own and the brain size was also increased to about two-thirds that of today's humans. One possibility is that *Homo ergaster* emerged as a rather successful long-distance runner, natural selection operating to favour that repertoire of characteristics that would give reproductive success to groups of hunters on the African savannah.

A closely related species to *Homo ergaster* is *Homo erectus*, indeed so close that some anthropologists lump them all together as variants of the same species. One possibility is that *H. ergaster* arose in Africa about 2 million years ago and then emigrated to Asia where it evolved into *H. erectus*. Whatever the exact sequence of events, it is clear that *H. erectus* was the first hominin species to migrate extensively out of Africa from about 1.8 million years ago, leaving its fossil remains in Asia, as far east as Indonesia and in parts of Europe, dating from 1.8 million years to as recently as 30,000 years ago. The appearance of *H. erectus* was associated with the development of more sophisticated tools. Instead of simply chipping rocks to make a sharp edge, tools were now cut into predetermined and more versatile shapes, the so-called Acheulean technology after the town of St Acheul in France where such tools were first discovered. This more advanced technology was again associated with increased brain size, now in the range 850–1,100 cubic centimetres.

Until recently it was thought that *H. habilis* evolved into *H. ergaster/erectus*. However, recent fossil discoveries have shown that *H. habilis* was co-existing 1.44 million years ago with *H. erectus* near Lake Turkana in Kenya, so it now seems more likely that both species share a common ancestor and represent different twigs on the evolutionary bush. In some ways the problem with tracking the evolutionary line leading to *H. sapiens* from our last common ancestor with the apes is not the lack of fossil specimens, but their abundance, leading to alternative scenarios as to how the pieces of the jigsaw might fit together. As more and more hominin fossil remains are discovered, so the details of the jigsaw will begin to look clearer.

Surprises are indeed often just round the corner in this field. Anthropologists digging in a cave on the Indonesian island of Flores made an announcement of their amazing discovery in 2004: they had found the fossil remains of several tiny hominins about three feet high with brains only a third the size of our own, about the size of a chimpanzee's[138]. Most

surprising of all was the very recent date of these fossils, ranging from 95,000 to only 18,000 years ago. Nicknamed the hobbit by those working on the specimens, the fossils have
stimulated a huge debate in the scientific community, with
some suggesting that they represent a new species, named *H.
floresiensis*, and others arguing that they were really examples
of our own species suffering from microcephaly in which a
genetic defect leads to stunted growth. At the time of writing,
the jury is still out, but several observations suggest that they
might indeed represent a new species, sharing several anatomical similarities with *H. erectus*. One fascinating possibility is
that *H. floresiensis* represents a population of *H. erectus* that
settled in the island of Flores, over time shrinking in size, a
common evolutionary phenomenon in species that adopt
island habitats. The issue will likely eventually be settled by
DNA studies, as the recent date of the latest 'hobbit' specimens
should allow the isolation of DNA samples for analysis.

Eventually *H. erectus* became extinct at different times in its
very varied geographical locations, to be replaced in some
areas by a fresh wave of African *Homo* emigrants. These were
the *Homo heidelbergensis*, sometimes known as archaic *Homo
sapiens*, who appeared in Africa about 600,000 years ago with
anatomical features distinct from *H. erectus*, not least a further
increase in brain size to 1,200 cubic centimetres, only 200 cc
short of the average size of modern humans. Archaic *Homo
sapiens* spread from Africa all over Europe and right across
Asia to China. They were great hunters and their communal
hunting practices are thought to have been a driver in select-
ing for agility, endurance, and both neuronal and cultural
development. Their wooden hunting spears dating from
400,000 years ago have been found in the remains of an
ancient lake in Germany, with the bones of butchered horses
nearby. Already by 300,000 years ago they were making a new
type of stone tool, known as Levallois tools, in which large
flakes of rock were shaped for use as knives. This type of tool
use was the first significant change in technology to take place
in a million years; it was as if *H. erectus* technology had simply got stuck, and it required some important changes in the
brain of archaic *Homo sapiens* to allow the creativity and fore-

thought that led to such advances. Yet there is no evidence that they buried their dead, nor any sign of art.

The Neanderthals

About 300,000 years ago a further twig on the evolutionary bush appeared in Europe: the Neanderthals, most likely descended from *H. heidelbergensis*, and well adapted to the harsh climatic conditions they would have experienced as the northern ice cap advanced and then retreated across Europe in a succession of ice ages. Neanderthals were powerfully built with long skulls, brains as big as humans, huge noses, large ridges over their brows and barrel-shaped chests, weighing about 30% more than modern humans of the same height. Neanderthals are our first cousins, albeit rather scary ones. They were skilled hunters, focusing on particular game, such as deer and bison. Examination of their fossils has revealed arthritis, stab wounds and broken bones. Neanderthals lived in small groups in caves rather than in constructed dwellings. They buried their dead, although without any artefacts suggesting belief in an after-life, nor is there any convincing evidence for Neanderthal religion, nor art. Whether the Neanderthals had any kind of language is still hotly disputed and the simple answer is that we don't really know.

Following an extensive European ice age, Neanderthals migrated to the Levant from 80,000 years ago, retreating back into Europe 50,000 years ago, before finally going extinct about 30,000 years ago. Their total range was extensive, stretching from the Iberian peninsula (now Spain) in the west, to Uzbekistan in the east. Yet their effective population size was probably never very large, around 3,000 ranging up to 12,000 individuals based on genetic studies[139]. The reasons for their extinction are not known, but since modern humans co-existed with the Neanderthals in Europe for at least 10,000 years, even successively sharing the same caves, it is possible that it was competition by humans for the same food resources under harsh climatic conditions that finally took the Neanderthals to extinction. But disease and climate change also provide equally good explanations, and all three of these factors may have been involved. It has been possible to extract

DNA from Neanderthal bone specimens and analysis of mito-chondrial DNA sequences is consistent with the idea that mod-ern humans and Neanderthals last shared a common ancestor about 500,000 years ago, and that there has been no significant interbreeding between the two species. A more ambitious proj-ect is underway to generate a complete sequence of the Neanderthal genome; once completed, the sequence will shed further light on this question.

Homo sapiens

The emergence of *Homo sapiens*, anatomically modern humans, from 200,000 years ago, follows a pattern very simi-lar to that set by *H. erectus* and *H. heidelbergensis*, with initial evolution taking place in Africa, followed by migration to the rest of the world. *H. sapiens* most likely evolved from an archaic *H. sapiens* species such as *H. heidelbergensis*, although the details remain unknown. The oldest well-characterised fos-sils of anatomically modern humans come from the Kibish formation in S. Ethiopia and their estimated date is 195,000 +/– 5,000 years old[140]. Other well-established fossil skulls of our species have been found in the village of Herto in Ethiopia and date from 160,000 years ago as established by argon isotope dating[141]. Some limited expansion of our species had already taken place as far as the Levant by 115,000 years ago, as estab-lished by partial skeletons of unequivocal *H. sapiens* found at Skhul and Qafzeh in Israel. But significant emigration out of Africa does not seem to have taken place until around 70,000 years ago onwards, with modern humans reaching right across Asia and on to Australia by 50,000 years ago, then back-track-ing into Europe by 40,000 years ago, where they are known as the Cro-Magnon people. By 15,000 years ago they were trick-ling down into N. America across the Bering Strait[142].

Genetics has been of enormous help in tracking the evolu-tion and migration of *H. sapiens*, whereas apart from Neanderthal studies, the remains of other hominin species are simply too old for the extraction of DNA samples. Mitochondrial DNA, with its 16,569 nucleotide base pairs and 37 genes, has been particularly useful in this respect for two distinct reasons. First, its mutation rate is about ten times faster than for nuclear DNA due to inefficient DNA repair, generating a 'genetic clock' in which the accumulation of mutations can be roughly calibrated with time, at the same time providing a measure of relatedness which depends on how different or similar are the variant versions of mitochondrial DNA sequences. Second, like Jewishness, mitochondrial DNA is inherited only from the mother, since the mitochondria coming from the sperm are lost from the zygote shortly after fertilisation, leaving the mother's mitochondria as the source of all the mitochondria that eventually end up in all the cells of our bodies. So unlike nuclear DNA, which is constantly being mixed by the process of sexual reproduction, mitochondrial DNA provides a more straightforward reading of the mutational changes that accumulate over generations and that characterise differences between different human populations.

Simply by drawing family trees on the back of an envelope we can easily show that the mitochondrial DNA of all the people alive in the world today must have originated from a single woman, the so-called 'Mitochondrial Eve' (Figure 16). It will be remembered that mitochondria are the cell's tiny power-stations, located outside the nucleus, and containing their own small portion of DNA. In some ways the term 'Mitochondrial Eve', much used in the popular press when the concept was first introduced in the 1980s, is a misleading one. It does not at all mean that this woman was the only female human alive at the time; it just means that female transmission with a large enough number of generations will eventually lead back to only one woman, by definition, who can be the origin of all mitochondria. Think of the 'tattooed number on the arm' illustration that we used above. As we work through many thousands of generations, eventually all numbers except one will fail to be transmitted, leaving a single number on the arms of a complete population. It is the first woman to bear that number on her arm that then becomes the 'Mitochondrial Eve' in this illustration. But remember that the same mode of transmission does not apply in the case of the bulk of our DNA, the nuclear DNA, which undergoes extensive reshuffling in each generation as mutated versions of DNA from both parents are combined.

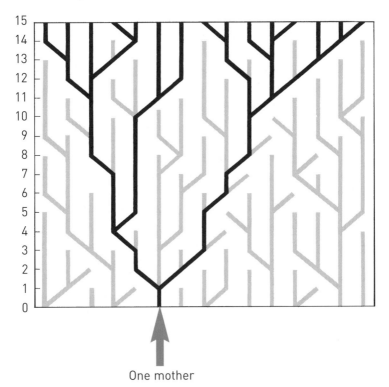

One mother

Figure 16. The way in which our mitochondrial DNA is inherited from a single woman, the so-called 'Mitochondrial Eve'. Only 15 generations are shown for the sake of simplicity. Note that there were many other women alive at the time of 'Mitochondrial Eve', but their lineages eventually died out.

Extensive investigations of mitochondrial DNA sequences from human populations around the world have revealed two fascinating insights into human evolution. The first is that the 'genetic clock' data point to the existence of a 'Mitochondrial Eve' in Africa approximately 150,000 years ago, consistent with the fossil data for the emergence of *H. sapiens* described above. This finding provided strong support for the 'Out of Africa' model for human evolution that currently holds sway[143]. Had there, for example, been extensive interbreeding between the *H. sapiens* populations and the more ancient *H. erectus* populations that overlapped extensively in time with *H. sapiens*, then much older dates for the putative Mitochondrial Eve would have been expected. The second important insight arising from human mitochondrial DNA sequence studies is that all non-African mitochondrial DNA from anywhere in the world is remarkably similar, whereas there are greater mutational differences between the mitochondrial DNA of different African populations. This is consistent with the idea that different human populations lived in different parts of Africa over the period 200,000–100,000 years ago, and that the waves of emigration from Africa that occurred after 75,000 years ago did so in the form of relatively small numbers of people, perhaps a few thousand or less, who then spread out to transmit their mitochondrial DNA to what is now the whole non-African population of the world. We are so used to large human populations today, that we forget that for a significant portion of our early history the human population was really small, the genetic data suggesting that at times the total population during the time when we were all Africans was only a few thousand individuals. From a scientific perspective this is important because evolution can occur more rapidly in small populations due to the rapid spread of beneficial genes. From a theological perspective, we could so easily have gone extinct like the Neanderthals, and it is a sign of God's loving sovereign plan and purposes for humankind that we were preserved.

Other genetic methods besides the study of mitochondrial DNA continue to be useful in the investigation of human evolution. For example, because only males contain the Y chromosome and pass this on to other males, DNA sequences from this chromosome can be analysed as a kind of male equivalent of mitochondrial DNA analysis. Although estimates vary, genetic analysis of Y chromosomes from male samples collected from populations around the world suggest that the male individual from whom all present Y chromosomes in the world are derived lived in Africa around 100,000–150,000 years ago[144]. Again remember that this does not mean that this was the only male alive at the time, only that the male descendents of the other males then alive led to lineages that eventually lacked further descendents, in much the same way that Figure 16 illustrates for female mitochondrial DNA transmission. Also the male from whom all our (males') Y chromosomes are inherited does not necessarily mark the precise time when our species emerged, only the time when the particular male happened to be alive from whom all current male Y chromosomes originated.

Other portions of human DNA are being actively used to explore human evolution, a huge research field that we cannot survey in detail here. For example, 'microsatellites' are short stretches of DNA containing repeated segments of short nucleotide sequences between two and five base-pairs long, that accumulate mutations rapidly and are therefore useful in forensic DNA analysis to provide individual 'genetic fingerprints'. Studies on such sequences from people in widely different geographical locations suggest that all the microsatellite sequences originate from an individual who lived 156,000 years ago. What is striking about these and other genetic approaches is that their results are all consistent with our relatively recent emergence as a separate species in Africa during the past 200,000 years.

The cultural development of Homo sapiens

Our knowledge of the cultural and social life of the first 100,000 years of human existence is sparse. We were hunter-gatherers. We made a few innovations in tool use, but not much. The people at Herto started making blades out of obsidian. By 164,000 years ago at Pinnacle Point on the coast of South Africa there were humans who left behind 57 pieces of ochre (haematite), almost certainly used for colouring, together with miniature stone tools and evidence for the use of shellfish as food[145]. By 125,000 years ago humans had settled at various places on the coast of Africa where they engaged in fishing, collecting oysters and seal-hunting. Trading of tools was probably taking place over many hundreds of miles. This is inferred from the fact that obsidian blades dating from 100,000–130,000 years ago have been found in a cave in Tanzania, and the nearest obsidian deposits are about 200 miles away, suggesting that trading of materials and/or tools was taking place at this early date, since today's hunter-gatherers do not normally forage for food and materials more than 50 miles away from home base. By 70,000 years ago different groups of *H. sapiens* were making different types of tools in different parts of Africa. Systematically engraved red ochre from a cave in Blombos, South Africa, dates from around the same period, as does the oldest known ornament, 39 snail shells with holes drilled through them, presumably for hanging round the neck.

Yet it is not until the so-called Upper Palaeolithic Revolution that began around 50,000 years ago that one begins to find really significant human cultural innovations. These include the introduction of a whole range of more sophisticated tools made of bone, stone and wood. Then from 30,000 years ago comes a flowering of artistic expression, particularly marked in Europe, where more than 150 examples of wonderful cave art date from the period 31,000–12,000 years ago, mostly found in France and Spain, the oldest in the Chauvet Cave in the Ardeche Valley in France dating from 31,000 years ago. All of this art is associated with the Magdalenian peoples, the late Cro-Magnons who succeeded the Neanderthal populations in these areas. From the same period come brooches, carved animals and numerous figurines, the 'Michelin-tyre' ladies, generally made from ivory or stone, whom some have suggested represent tribal goddesses, but whose real purpose may have been merely decorative.

Soon after comes the first clear evidence for deliberate burials, the earliest from two sites in which the skeletons of Cro-Magnon people have been discovered at two locations now in the Czech Republic, dating from around 25,000 years ago. The famous Sungir site in Russia dating to about 22,000 years ago contains several burials, including the skeletons of two children placed head to head. One was covered in around 5,000 beads, which strongly suggests that they were part of the clothing in which the child had been buried. In addition some 250 perforated Arctic fox teeth encircled its waist as if they had once been attached to, or formed, a belt. An ivory pin lay near the child's throat. Sungir is one of the oldest known cases in which ornaments are actually found on human skeletons. The presence of other valuable decorative items in these and other sites are certainly consistent with the belief in an after-life at the time in these human communities, though they do not prove it. It is of course quite possible to take care in burying people without necessarily believing in an after-life (elephants also bury their dead). Conversely some religions today believe that physical death is not the ultimate end of life, and yet do not bury bodies but rather cremate them as in Hinduism.

The development of language

When exactly language developed in the human lineage remains a hotly discussed topic and there are currently no clear answers. Three main factors impinge on the resolution of this question. The first is anatomical: at what point did hominins develop the type of anatomy that would allow speech? One relevant piece of anatomy that can be measured in fossil skulls is the size of the hypoglossal canal, which is the hole at the bottom of the skull through which the nerve passes between the brain and the tongue. A huge amount of information needs to flow from the brain to the muscles controlling the tongue, jaw and lips in order to regulate speech, and more information flow means a bigger nerve. Indeed, the human hypoglossal canal is significantly larger than that found in the *Australopithecines* and the great apes, and is similar to that found in the skulls of archaic *H. sapiens*, suggesting that this neuronal equipment was up to the task from around half a million years ago onwards. But it is only fair to add that some studies have shown quite a bit of overlap in the measurements from these different species, so measuring hypoglossal canal sizes does not provide a straightforward answer. Perhaps more relevant are the important anatomical changes in modern humans that allow the breathing control that is necessary for speech. The position of the larynx is also important, with a larynx positioned low in the neck necessary for adult speech, a human feature apparently shared at least by archaic *H. sapiens*.

Having the right kind of mental apparatus is also a key factor in the development of language, not just the neuronal circuits essential for language itself, but also a 'theory of mind'[146]. This is the ability of our own minds to realise that there are other minds that think like ours and that have intentions and purposes that may be similar or even quite different to ours. We take this 'mind-reading' completely for granted but it is in fact a crucial aspect of our identity as humans. To engage in communal religious beliefs, for example, several different orders of intentionality are required, in fact four and perhaps as many as five. In an example given by Robin Dunbar, with each level of intentionality numbered: 'I suppose [1] that you think [2] that I believe [3] that there is a God who intends [4] to influence our futures because He understands our desires [5]'. In general humans seem to be limited to five orders of intentionality, and only a minority can cope with six orders. It also appears that there is an approximately linear relationship between brain size and the number of orders of intentionality in the hominin lineage, as Figure 17 illustrates. Dunbar speculates that fourth order intentionality would not have appeared until about 500,000 years ago, about the time of the emergence of archaic *H. sapiens*, with fifth order intentionality appearing with anatomically modern humans, perhaps along with language.

A third very active area of research that seeks to elucidate the development of language is genetic. Great interest was aroused when a research team working at Oxford announced in 2001 that there were mutations in the FOXP2 gene in a Pakistani family whose members displayed certain characteristic linguistic defects. This has led to intensive investigation of this gene, showing that it has undergone rapid evolution (viz. become more diverse in its sequence) since our lineage branched off from the apes. But of course there is no single 'language gene' that by itself has facilitated the emergence of language. Instead it is likely that hundreds of different genes have required mutational changes in order to build the right kind of neuronal apparatus for language. The 'finishing genetic touches' may well have taken place since the emergence of modern humans. The fact that anthropologists vary in their estimates as to when language developed, from 500,000 years ago to 50,000 years ago, in itself illustrates how little we really know; but all investigators seem agreed that human language was in place by 50,000 years ago. One possibility is that the development of language acted as the trigger, or was itself stimulated by, the human cultural flowering that began at around that period.

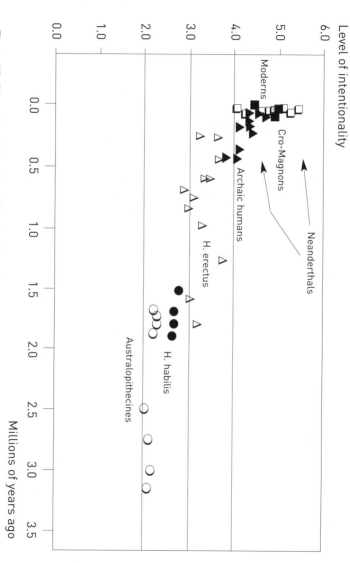

Figure 17. The estimated levels of intentionality that may relate to the hominid ancestors of *Homo sapiens* based on the size of the frontal lobes of fossil hominids as measured from cranial volumes. The achievable levels of intentionality are based on data obtained from monkeys, apes and modern humans. Each point represents the mean value for one population of fossil hominids. [Figure is from Dunbar, R. *The Human Story*, London: Faber & Faber, 2004, Figure 6, p. 191.]

The Neolithic era

Certainly language was firmly in place by the time that humans began to give up their hunter-gatherer lifestyles and engage in settled farming from around 10,000 BC onwards during the Neolithic era. This transition was gradual and occurred in somewhat different ways in different parts of the world. For example archaeology has shown that hunter-gatherers lived in the village of Abu Hureyra on the banks of the Euphrates (now flooded because of the creation of the Tabaka Dam), using it as their base from 12,300 BC. The village was then abandoned, but subsequently re-occupied by settled farmers by 9,000 BC, with the villagers growing wheat and barley on the alluvial plain[147]. In Palestine farmers lived in the village, then city, of Jericho from 9,600 BC onwards and it has been continuously occupied to the present day. Archaeological evidence suggests that Jericho originally had around 500 inhabitants; as Steven Mithen comments, 'perhaps the very first time in human history that a completely viable population was living in the same place at the same time'[148].

A whole string of Neolithic settlements have now been discovered, stretching all the way up to Turkey, and down through what is now south Jordan, many of these sites still being actively excavated. The sites have revealed thriving Neolithic cultures, with farming, art and evidence for ritualistic practices, the precise meaning of which are difficult to decipher. In fact the site of Gobekli Tepe in south-east Turkey shows clear evidence of being a ritual centre, with no dwellings around it, containing circular rooms, with benches set back against the walls, and supported by massive limestone pillars decorated with wild animals and other symbols. The religious themes seem linked to the fear and danger of the wild.

All the various Neolithic centres of the area, right down through the Jordan Valley, were linked by active trade routes. We know this because, for example, the fine obsidian (jet-black, shiny volcanic glass) used in all the settlements of the area came from a single source of obsidian located in southern Turkey. By about 8,000 BC the people of the Neolithic village of Cayonu in southern Turkey were taking copper ore from deposits 20 km away and beating them into beads, hooks and metal sheets.

In the earliest settlements people were clothed with animal hides or fur, or occasionally knotted fibres, but by the time the town of Beidha near Petra in Jordan was established around 8,000 BC, the people were wearing the earliest form of linen, dyed green and made into tunics and skirts. The domestication of sheep, goats and dogs was all involved in the transition to the settled life of the earliest town and village farmers, with domesticated horses and donkeys appearing a few thousand years later.

In China, rice was cultivated from 9,500 BC onwards, and is associated in domesticated form with Neolithic sites such as Bashidang, a town which thrived from 7,000–5,000 BC, displaying highly developed technologies with wooden implements such as ploughs and shovels, reed mats, cane ropes and bamboo baskets. In Japan the transition from hunter-gatherer to more settled life took place over the same period, and Japanese pottery is the most ancient in the world. The oldest known lacquered object in the world also originates from Japan, a red-lacquered comb placed with a burial site dating from 7,000 BC. In many other parts of the world the hunter-gatherer lifestyle remained dominant, notably in Australia, where the 250,000 or more Aborigines were all hunter-gatherers when the first European settlement was established there in 1788.

The point of this brief outline of the Neolithic period is to highlight two facts. The first is that there were plenty of people all round the world in Neolithic times, engaging in economic, religious and cultural activities easily recognisable as typically human, even though not all made the transition to settled domesticated farming practices at the same time. Second, Mesopotamia, that area between the Tigris and Euphrates rivers now known as Iraq, is the cradle of civilisation in the sense that one finds here the earliest development of urbanisation, civic life, extensive trade, industrial production and centralised authority. Already by 6,000 BC, Mesopotamia had flourishing agricultural communities and extensive urban life. By 3,500 BC larger Mesopotamian cities began to appear, together with the invention of writing. In addition there were now major urban centres in places such as Tell Brak in north-eastern Syria, where urban growth took place about 4,000 BC and where there is good evidence for violent confrontations[149]. It is against this cultural and historical background that one needs to consider the early chapters of Genesis.

Are humans still evolving?

One of the concerns that Christians often express concerning human evolution is whether that process is continuing today and, if so, will humans themselves eventually develop into another species, given enough time? And if that is the case, what then of God's purposes for humankind made in his image?

There are strong reasons for thinking that such a concern is unfounded. Certainly in the strict sense of the term 'evolution', human genomes are evolving all the time as humans face new adaptive challenges, particularly the challenge of warding off new pathogens. The adaptive responses of populations to different environments are there for all to see. The skins of humans became whiter as they moved from the tropics to cooler environments. Humans such as Inuits and Lapps who have lived for thousands of years in arctic conditions have developed stocky bodies that lose much less heat than the tall Africans of the tropics. Specifically they have shorter shins relative to their thighs, an adaptation to the cold that also evolved in the Neanderthals as they coped with the ice ages of Europe.

The HapMap project introduced in Chapter Three is also uncovering a fascinating selection of genes that remain under active natural selection in human populations. For example, variants of two genes linked to infection with the Lassa virus are favoured in West Africans[150]. It is not surprising to find genes involved in disease protection under natural selection as medical care remains inadequate in many parts of the world, and in any case is insufficient to cure every disease under the best of conditions. The number of duplicates of individual genes may also be under continued natural selection in human populations. For example a starch digestion gene has been found to be duplicated in people who traditionally have starch rich diets.

Yet all such interesting evolutionary changes are of course a very long way from the emergence of a new species, and there are three very good reasons why such a new speciation event is very unlikely to happen.

The first is directly due to the command of Jesus to love our neighbours as ourselves. As the benefits of Western hygiene and medical care have spread around the world, much of this spread as a direct result of medical missionary work that gathered pace from the nineteenth century onwards, so the chances of people reaching reproductive age, even though afflicted by different diseases or other disabilities, has vastly increased. In other words it is as we obey the command of Jesus to care for the physically weak and handicapped that we stop further significant human evolution dead in its tracks, for the simple reason that modern medical care, as it gradually spreads around the world, is a great 'genetic leveller', giving to all people a greater opportunity to achieve reproductive success.

Second, as most human populations increase in prosperity, so they start having fewer children on average, for social reasons; so the criterion of 'differential reproductive success' becomes less significant because couples tend to have only two children anyway (or whatever the precise small number might be in different countries) irrespective of their particular genetic or economic status.

Third, speciation occurs in isolated populations, but in the global village in which we currently live, the existence of such an isolated population is highly unlikely, especially given that speciation in mammalian populations most likely takes tens of thousands of years.

The only possible speciation events that might arise from human populations both arise from sci-fi scenarios. The first is the colonisation of distant planets by a human population that remains isolated from planet earth for tens of thousands of years; a most unlikely scenario. The second is the deliberate changing of the genomes of certain individuals, but not others, by genetic engineering, to create a new race of beings that could reproduce only amongst themselves. Apart from the fact that such genetic manipulation is currently scientifically impossible, and illegal, such developments would be likely to occur only if some mad dictator decided to enforce such an enterprise, and we hope and pray that such a horrendous initiative never materialises!

Adam, Eve and evolution

We have now briefly surveyed the Bible's teaching about Adam and Eve, and given a highly compressed account of our current understanding of human evolution. We are therefore ready to address the question 'What relationship, if any, might there be between these two accounts?'

At the outset we must confess, we really don't know the precise answer. There are simply too many unknowns in both the evolutionary account, and in our own interpretation of Scripture, to be dogmatic on this issue. Certainly we can present various models describing what the relationship might be, as we will do below, but at the end of the day we cannot be certain which, if any, of our models is the correct one. Therefore it is pointless to present this issue as if it were cut and dried with no room for justifiable differences of opinion. Least of all is it an issue that should become a bone of contention amongst Christians, as if it were some central point of doctrine on a par with the death and resurrection of Jesus for our sin. It is fine to have our convictions on the matter, but let us also remember that this is a secondary issue which is not essential for salvation. When at that 'great and terrible Day' we are called to give account of our lives, our precise beliefs about Adam and Eve will not, I suspect, be a major feature of the questions asked.

Further, all the various views involve interpretation of the biblical text and invoking possible scenarios that go well beyond the text itself. The whole point of models as used in science is to put together different facts, ideas and speculations to generate an account that makes sense of something. No one can say that their particular model is the 'obvious one' that is simply read off from the Genesis text without invoking other possible factors. All models involve the incorporation of ideas and speculations that are not found within the biblical narratives.

In addition, there is no solid evidence that any apes or hominins besides *H. sapiens* have ever held religious beliefs.

Therefore, to the best of our knowledge, we are unique in that respect. Furthermore, there is absolutely no evidence that beings prior to *H. sapiens* were spiritually alive, in the sense of having a saving personal knowledge of God. So at some point in our history it must be the case that humans experienced spiritual life, a personal knowledge of God that they had not had before. Therefore we cannot escape the historical question as to when that might have happened, even though we might not have sufficient data to be able to give a firm answer.

We will now consider different models that have been proposed to relate the theological teaching of the early chapters of Genesis concerning Adam and Eve with evolutionary biology. I will present each model as positively and as sympathetically as possible, since I believe that this generates the best kind of discussion, although my own favoured model will become apparent as we proceed, not least by the space it receives compared to the others. The models are labelled A–E to facilitate identification during the discussion, and each model will be reconsidered in the context of the doctrine of the Fall in the following chapter, for our understanding of the Fall is inevitably closely linked to our understanding of Adam and Eve. Models A–C are consistent with the current scientific account of human evolution, whereas models D and E are not.

Model A

Model A is an ahistorical view that basically kicks the whole issue into touch by suggesting that there is no connection at all between the theological and biological narratives. The purpose of the early chapters of Genesis, from this perspective, is to provide a theological account of the role and importance of humankind in God's purposes, cast in the mould of a narrative of Adam and Eve which is a myth in the technical sense of being a story or parable having the main purpose of teaching eternal truths without the constraints of historical particularity. This model therefore treats the question of the coming into being of the first spiritually alive humans as essentially unanswerable, and focuses instead on the relevance of the Genesis accounts for our current understanding of humankind made in God's image.

Model B

Model B is a gradualist protohistorical view, meaning that it is not historical in the usual sense of that word, but does refer to events that took place in particular times and locations. Model B suggests that as anatomically modern humans evolved in Africa from 200,000 years ago, or during some period of linguistic and cultural evolution since then, there was a gradual growing awareness of God's presence and calling upon their lives to which they responded in obedience and worship[151]. Therefore the earliest spiritual stirrings of the human spirit were in the context of monotheism, and it was natural at the beginning for humans to turn to their Creator, in the same way that children today seem readily to believe in God almost as soon as they can speak. In model B, the early chapters of Genesis then represent a retelling of this early episode, or series of episodes, in our evolutionary history in a form that could be understood within the Middle Eastern culture of the Jewish people of that time. Therefore, as with model A, the Genesis account of Adam and Eve is a myth in the technical sense of that word, albeit one that refers to real putative events that took place over a prolonged period of time during the early history of humanity in Africa.

Model C

Model C is also a protohistorical view in the sense that it lies beyond history as normally understood, but like model B looks for events located in history that might correspond to the theological account provided by the Genesis narrative. Unlike model B, this model locates these events within the culture and geography that the Genesis text provides. The aim here is not to start imposing scientific meanings on a theological text, but to ask what kind of events might lie 'behind the text' that would be consistent with the theological account provided. According to model C, God in his grace chose a couple of Neolithic farmers in the Near East, or maybe a community of farmers, to whom he chose to reveal himself in a special way, calling them into fellowship with himself – so that they might know him as a personal God. It is not that there were no settled farmers beforehand, but from now on here would be a community who would know that they were called to a holy enterprise, called to be stewards of God's creation, called to know God personally. It is for this reason that this first couple, or community, have been termed *Homo divinus*, the divine humans, those who know the one true God, the Adam and Eve of the Genesis account[152]. Being an anatomically modern human was necessary but not sufficient for being spiritually alive; as remains the case today. *Homo divinus* were the first humans who were truly spiritually alive in fellowship with God, providing the spiritual roots of the Jewish faith. Certainly religious beliefs existed before this time, as people sought after God or gods in different parts of the world, offering their own explanations for the meaning of their lives, but *Homo divinus* marked the time at which God chose to reveal himself and his purposes for humankind for the first time.

Model C also draws attention to the representative nature of 'the Adam', 'the man', as suggested by the use of the definite article in the Genesis text as discussed above. 'The man' is therefore viewed as the federal head of the whole of humanity alive at that time. This was the moment at which God decided to start his new spiritual family on earth, consisting of all those who put their trust in God by faith, expressed in obedience to his will. Adam and Eve, in this view, were real people, living in a particular historical era and geographical location, chosen by God to be the representatives of his new humanity on earth, not by virtue of anything that they had done, but simply by God's grace. When Adam recognised Eve as 'bone of my bones and flesh of my flesh', he was not just recognising a fellow *Homo sapiens* – there were plenty of those around – but a fellow believer, one like him who had been called to share in the very life of God in obedience to his commands. The world population in Neolithic times is estimated to lie in the range 1–10 million, genetically just like Adam and Eve, but in model C it was these two farmers out of all those millions to whom God chose to reveal himself.

Just as I can go out on the streets of Cambridge today and have no idea just by looking at people, all of them members of the species *Homo sapiens*, which ones are spiritually alive, so in model C there was no physical way of distinguishing between Adam and Eve and their contemporaries. It is a model about spiritual life and revealed commands and responsibilities, not about genetics.

The text of Genesis 1 makes clear that the whole of humankind without any exception is made in God's image, including certainly all the other millions of people alive in the world in Neolithic times and since. Model C suggests that it was through God's revelation to Adam and Eve that the understanding of what that image actually meant, in practice, was made apparent to them. It meant a personal relationship with God, obedience to his commands, the start of God's new family on earth consisting of all those who would come to know him personally. Paul says that 'I kneel before the Father, from whom his whole family in heaven and on earth derives its name' (Ephesians 3:14–15). Families have to start somewhere, and God chose to start his new family on earth with two very ordinary individuals, saved by grace like we are, and sustained by the 'tree of life' (upon which see more below). It is in that sense that model C proposes their federal headship in relation to the rest of humanity, an idea that becomes of particular relevance in our later discussion of the Fall.

Imagine that the United Nations decides to organise a huge international competition in order to fund the founding of a top university in a low-income country that will then be made accessible to anybody from any country of the world, rich or poor. The rich countries of the world agree to put billions of pounds into the prize fund. All the participating country has to do is to choose one male and one female academic from their country who will compete in an international quiz against all the other countries. If they win, not only will they obtain the prize money for their country to fund the new university, but part of the deal is that they themselves will automatically become its new founders and mentors, and the international fund is so large that all students will have free places. So the two academics exercise federal headship with respect to all those who subsequently participate in their new academic community in the years to come, enjoying their studies in the knowledge that their financial support is already secured.

The analogy is not perfect, and illustrates only the salient points under discussion (so please do not start speculating on what happens to first year students who fail their exams!), but serves to convey the basic idea of federal headship.

Note that the students with free places are not descended genetically from the two founders, but enter into the blessings of the new institution by choosing to participate. A new way has been opened up to a high quality educational community that was not there before. So with model C, the idea is that following on from God's initiative in the lives of Adam and Eve, the way is opened up for any person anywhere in the world to enter God's family by faith and obedience, so establishing God's new international family on earth. By calling Adam and Eve into relationship with himself and with each other, God revealed himself right at the beginning as the relational God, a pattern that continues right through the rest of the Bible.

Model D

Model D represents the various views that we can cluster together under the heading 'old-earth creationism' or 'episodic creationism'. Although this model encompasses a variety of variant versions, in general it suggests that the earth is very old, as the scientific data indicate, but that God has intervened in a miraculous way at various points in evolutionary history, particularly in the creation of the genetic code, the first cells, the main 'kinds' of animal and in the creation of humankind. This model therefore perceives a striking discontinuity between all living things and Adam and Eve, who were created directly by God out 'of the dust of earth', and not as a result of an evolutionary process.

Model E

Model E is represented by young-earth creationism, which maintains that our planet was created by God around 10,000 years ago, that all living things were created within six literal 24-hour days by a series of miracles, and that in particular Adam and Eve were created miraculously out of the ground on the sixth day.

Comparing the models

Model A has the disadvantage that it loses contact with any kind of historical narrative, even though the one fact in this context that all Christians agree upon is that at one stage in human history, humans began to know the one true God in a personal way, so it is difficult to avoid protohistorical questions altogether. Model A also has the inevitable consequence of evacuating the Fall of any historical content, as we shall consider in the following chapter.

Model B has many attractions, and is plausible as a possible scenario, but has the disadvantage of suggesting that behind the theological narrative of the early chapters of Genesis are events that happened not in the Near East at all, but rather in the Africa of (presumably) more than 100,000 years ago. Such a retelling of earlier events in theological terms is by no means impossible, but does empty that retelling of any Near Eastern context and detaches the account from its Jewish roots.

Models A–C are all perfectly consistent with evolutionary biology, in the sense that they all agree that evolution per se really has nothing to do with the Adam and Eve account described in Genesis. Having the human attributes that emerged during the evolutionary process are necessary for fellowship with God – consciousness, free will, language, relational social structures, capacity for prayer – but these in and of themselves are insufficient to bring about fellowship with God; they are necessary but not sufficient, then as now.

By contrast, models D and E are incompatible with the current scientific understanding of human evolution, since they deny any continuity between the animal world and humanity. One problem amongst many with both models is that the scientific evidence for our shared ancestry with the apes is so overwhelming, as summarised above, that it is difficult to avoid the theologically problematic conclusion that God is some kind of deceiver – making it look as if our genomes are in developmental continuity with the animal world, when really they are not. As it happens, there are no biblical reasons for holding to either model D or E, providing we do not start trying to read the biblical text as a scientific textbook, rather than as the theological text that it is intended to be, and providing miracles are not invoked for events that the Genesis text itself does not describe as miraculous.

This leaves model C, *Homo divinus*, which is worth pursuing a little further. Let us reiterate: of course the point with this model, as with the others, is not that the model itself is found within the Genesis text – it is not. The idea is to generate a working model that will explore the possible 'narrative behind the narrative', the events in human history that might at least be 'consistent with' the Genesis theological account.

The cultural context of the Genesis account does look very like that of Neolithic farmers. Precious metals and other materials are mentioned such as gold and onyx (Genesis 2:11–12), and bronze and iron (Genesis 4:22): items that would have been of little interest to hunter-gatherers. 'The Lord God took the man and put him in the Garden of Eden to work it and take care of it' (Genesis 2:15), is strongly suggestive of settled farming, consistent with God's words to Cain in Genesis 4:12: 'When you work the ground, it will no longer yield its crops for you'. Mention of musical instruments (Genesis 4:21) is likewise characteristic of settled communities. The cultural context of Adam and Eve as real individuals, farmers in a community of the Near East, perhaps around 6,000–8,000 years ago, is consistent with the Genesis text. Within the frame of the Genesis account, there were other humans around in addition to the godly line of Adam and Eve, since Cain expressed fear of being killed during his time as 'a restless wanderer on the earth' (Genesis 4:12). As a bonus the model therefore explains the hoary old chestnut as to where Cain got his wife from!

Genealogical data are also consistent with Adam and Eve being real historical figures who lived around 6,000–8,000 years ago. Although the seventeenth century Archbishop Ussher famously generated a date for Adam and Eve based on biblical genealogical information that placed their creation at 4004 BC, in fact even in Ussher's time there was a range of estimates. The reason for this is that biblical genealogies can use 'son of' in the sense of 'descended from', thereby summarising many generations in a single brief phrase. Genealogies are also sometimes presented in the Bible in a formalised way to make theological points, rather than for historical completeness, as for Matthew's genealogy of Jesus, which is arranged in three groups of 14 generations in Matthew 1, although this involves omitting several of the generations mentioned in the relevant Old Testament lists. As it happens, the precise designation of date makes little difference to the main idea underlying model C.

Luke's genealogy (Luke 3:23–38) certainly appears to highlight both the identity of Adam as a real historical figure, as well as his designation as the 'son of God', one who was part of God's new family on earth: '...the son of Enosh, the son of Seth, the son of Adam, the son of God' (Luke 3:38). The general stance of Scripture is to view Adam as a historical figure, and we will consider some of the relevant New Testament passages further, in the context of the Fall, in the following chapter.

The flood is a further issue that requires addressing in connection with the proposed *Homo divinus* of model C. There is no reason not to accept the Genesis account of the flood as a historical event in which the godly Noah and his family were saved. But model C would interpret the flood account as referring to the saving of those who 'walked with God' (Genesis 6:9), together with the livestock that were essential for their welfare, through a local, albeit devastating, flood that affected the area of the Euphrates valley and its surrounds. In fact there is no geological evidence for a global flood, and the language of Genesis that refers to 'every living thing on the face of the earth' being 'wiped out', may very well simply refer to that 'world' with which Noah and his family were familiar. It was the people of God who were were saved in the Ark, just as today baptism continues to symbolise salvation for every believer (1 Peter 3:20–21). And those who were saved and eventually emerged onto dry ground to experience a renewing of their covenant with God (Genesis 9:11–17) were not the genetic progenitors of the world's population, but the spiritual progenitors of all those who since that time have experienced God's saving grace. Once again, seeking to impose a scientific (in this case genetic) account upon an ancient, theological text, is simply barking up the wrong tree. Apart from anything else, there are certainly no genetic data suggesting that all humankind originated from one family in the Near East about 6,000–8,000 years ago.

Model C will not answer all the theological questions that one might like to ask. For example, what was the eternal destiny of all those who lived before Adam and Eve? The answer really is that we have no idea. But we can be assured with Abraham: 'Will not the Judge of all the earth do right?' (Genesis 18:25). Thankfully we are not called to judge the earth, and we can leave that safely in the hands of the one who 'judges justly' (1 Peter 2:23). The question asked about those who lived prior to Adam and Eve is not dissimilar to other questions that we could ask. For example, what was the eternal destiny of those who lived in Australia at the time that the law was being given to Moses on Mt Sinai? Again, we really don't know and, again: 'Will not the Judge of all the earth do right?' Christians who spend time speculating about such things can appear as if they are the judges of the world's destiny, forgetting that that prerogative belongs only to God.

I do not know if model C is correct. But for myself I am happy to use it as a working model, and if a better model comes along I will readily discard C and adopt the new one. At the least I think it is important for Christians to see how different levels of discourse, theological and scientific, can integrate to form a coherent narrative, at least in principle. This is one area amongst many where there is no need to pit science and faith against each other.

Model C also fits with the way that Scripture focuses on the calling of individuals to fulfil God's will. Later in the biblical text, God was to call Abraham to leave his home country and set out for the promised land, to call Moses to help set his people free from their bondage to slavery, to call Mary to bring the Saviour into the world, and to call a host of other prophets and leaders to fulfil specific tasks in his sovereign plan. So the calling of two Neolithic farmers to be the recipients of God's specific commands, in order that they might walk with him, setting the pattern for all those subsequently who likewise walk with God, seems not at all out of keeping with the general tenor of the biblical revelation.

Chapter 11

Evolution and the Biblical Understanding of Death

A significant problem that some Christians have with the notion of Darwinian evolution is that it involves billions of years of death in which countless numbers of animals and plants, not to speak of bacteria, come and go in what seems like a mind-numbingly huge escalator of life, passing on inevitably towards death. Not only does evolution involve the death of individual animals, but it also involves extinctions of whole species on a massive scale, as we have already described in Chapter Five, so that more than 99% of all the species that have ever lived are no longer alive today.

How could a good and loving God, so the objection goes, create humankind by such a painful and wasteful process, one which involves an element of competition in which genomic differences confer reproductive advantages on some animals rather than others? And how could a loving God create through a process that involves genetic diversity which not only generates new species, but which also generates genetic diseases and scourges upon our well-being and happiness such as cancer? In addition, some Christians believe that no kind of death existed before the Fall, so rendering the whole notion of evolution impossible before one even leaves the starting block.

Without doubt the scale of death on this planet is indeed huge. There are an estimated 5×10^{30} bacteria in the world, more than 92% living underground and weighing roughly equivalent to all the plants in the world. That is certainly a lot more than the 10^{22} stars in the universe and it involves a huge amount of daily death. If the death of bacteria seems a matter of little concern, we might consider the roughly 155,000 human deaths every day or nearly 108 every minute. If we stacked the number of human bodies that die every day on top of each other then the pile would stretch nearly 30 miles into the sky. That's every day.

Clearly to address such a huge topic adequately would require a book in itself, but in this brief chapter we can at least make a start. And the best place to start, as always, is with Scripture.

What does the Bible say about death?

The Bible knows of three types of death: physical death; spiritual death here and now; and eternal spiritual death. We will consider these in turn.

Physical death

As we work through all the passages about death in the Old Testament, the first thing that strikes us is how earthy and matter of fact are the narratives about death. We have our allotted span on earth and then we depart to *sheol*, that shadowy world of the departed which is the destiny of all following death (Job 30:23)[153]. Although there are hints of the possibility of resurrection in the later books of the Old Testament, there is no developed resurrection teaching within the old covenant, and neither is *sheol* the same as the New Testament doctrine of hell, but rather a more neutral resting place which represents all the disadvantages of loss of life, yet without any particular advantages either. *Sheol* is an ever-present backcloth to death in the Old Testament, where it is mentioned 476 times, generally translated as 'the grave', but with far more content in the Hebrew than that word conveys in English. *Sheol* is a place of no return. Death itself is envisaged as the 'journey of no return' (Job 16:22). It is its final inevitability which casts a gloomy shadow over the term in its Old Testament usage: 'For *sheol* cannot praise you, death cannot sing your praise; those who go down to the pit cannot hope for your faithfulness' (Isaiah 38:18).

The Old Testament ideal is a long and useful life obeying God's will, followed by death. Genesis 25:8 provides a typical summary of the death of a great leader: 'Then Abraham breathed his last and died at a good old age, an old man and full of years; and he was gathered to his people'. Living to a ripe old age was seen as a blessing from God. King David 'died at a good old age, having enjoyed long life, wealth and honour (1 Chronicles 29:28). Good kings 'rested with their fathers' when they died (e.g. Solomon in 1 Kings 11:43; Jeroboam in 1 Kings 14:20). Psalm 90:5 speaks of the 'sleep of death'. 'Devout men are taken away, and no one understands that the righteous are taken away to be spared from evil. Those who walk uprightly enter into peace; they find rest as they lie in death' (Isaiah 57:1–2).

The death of both humans and animals is seen as being entirely under God's sovereign control. When Hannah gave thanks to God at Shiloh for her newborn, she prayed 'The Lord brings death and makes alive; he brings down to the grave (*sheol*) and raises up' (1 Samuel 2:6). As Job expressed the matter: 'In his hand is the life of every creature and the breath of all mankind' (Job 12:10). God is often seen as the direct agent of death. Genesis 38:7 states bluntly that 'Er, Judah's firstborn, was wicked in the Lord's sight; so the Lord put him to death'. The king of Israel reveals quite clearly the current understanding of God's role in life and death when he objects to the letter sent to him with the request to cure Naaman of his leprosy: 'Am I God? Can I kill and bring back to life?' (2 Kings 5:7).

Yet when the Old Testament speaks in rather blunt language for our refined ears about God 'killing people', it does not necessarily imply some miraculous intervention. In 1 Chronicles 10:4 King Saul was wounded in battle and then committed suicide by falling on his sword, but that does not prevent the narrator from commenting a few verses later that the reason he died 'was because he was unfaithful to the Lord; he...even consulted a medium for guidance' (verse 13), concluding 'So the Lord put him to death' (verse 14). The Old Testament does not always distinguish between primary and secondary causes, so an account of Saul killing himself is not seen at all as a rival explanation for being killed by God. Today we might call these 'complementary accounts' of the same event, viewing the same reality from different perspectives.

Nowhere in the Old Testament is there the slightest

uggestion that the physical death of either animals or humans, after a reasonable span of years, is anything other than the normal pattern ordained by God for this earth. As already noted when discussing the immanence of God in creation, he is seen as the direct agent in the death of animals in Psalm 104:29 when he 'takes away their breath' so that 'they die and return to the dust'. The same psalm reminds us that 'the lions roar seeking their food from God' (verse 21). When the Lord speaks to Job out of the storm, he points out to Job that it is he, not Job, who satisfies the hunger of the lions and provides food for the ravens, carnivorous animals and birds (Job 38:39–41). Those two chapters of Job in particular (Job 38–39) reveal a God who revels in the richness and diversity of his created order, complete with all its wildness and food-chains: the battle-horse who 'paws fiercely, rejoicing in his strength, and charges into the fray' (39:21), the eagle whose 'young ones feast on blood, and where the slain are, there is he' (39:30).

This does not at all mean that animals are without value, far from it, the Levitical law made clear that if anyone took the life of an animal they should pay restitution, although it is also clear that this was referring to a domesticated animal that was owned by someone (Leviticus 24:18). But as far as 'wild untamed nature' is concerned, there is no doubt that the God revealed to us in the pages of the Old Testament not only sustains it but is also the one worthy of praise by 'everything that has breath' without any exceptions (Psalm 150:6). 'Praise the Lord from the earth, sea monsters and all deeps!' (Psalm 148:7).

After the flood, specific permission was given to humankind to eat animals, providing that there was no consumption of blood (Genesis 9:3–4), for 'it is the blood that makes atonement for one's life' (Leviticus 17:11). Later on the detailed laws were given about what animals could or could not be eaten, making clear in the process that the hunting and eating of meat was normal practice for God's people (Leviticus 11). Eating lots of meat was seen as one of God's blessings: 'When the Lord your God has enlarged your territory as he promised you, and you crave meat and say, "I would like some meat," then you may eat as much of it as you want' (Deuteronomy 12:20).

A striking aspect of the Old Testament texts is the sheer scale of animal death involved in the sacrificial system, either killed in atonement for sin or as thanksgiving offerings. On the second day of thanksgiving for the completion of the building of the temple under the leadership of King David 'they made sacrifices to the Lord and presented burnt offerings to him: a thousand bulls, a thousand rams and a thousand male lambs, together with their drink offerings, and other sacrifices in abundance for all Israel' (1 Chronicles 29:21).

In Western urbanised societies we tend to be sheltered from the sight of animal death, but this is not the case for most people of the world for whom the killing of animals is a normal aspect of everyday life. During the first week that we moved to live in Ankara, Turkey, it happened to be the Kurban Bayram ('Sacrifice Holiday'), the time when Muslims remember the willingness of Abraham to sacrifice his son Isaac (whom Muslims think was Ishmael). Each family is expected to sacrifice a sheep or a goat by cutting its neck and then eating the meat and offering it to others in the neighbourhood, especially the poor. In the days leading up to the Bayram the streets of Ankara were crowded with sheep and lambs 'led like lambs to the slaughter'. Personally I hate seeing an animal being killed, but on the Bayram day a whole family, including tiny children who could barely walk, would gather round the sheep in the street as the herder cut its throat, watching impassively as the blood flowed into the gutter. The whole city smelt like an abattoir. This gives just a small idea of what it was like to live in Old Testament times when the ritual slaughter of animals played such a central role in the everyday life of God's people.

The kind of death in the Old Testament that was seen as abnormal was an unusually early death, or death due to punishment by God. King Hezekiah clearly did not think his number of years was ripe enough when he fell ill and was on the point of death (2 Kings 20:1), but God graciously answered his prayer and added 15 years to his lifespan. The psalmist often cries out to God to be delivered from *sheol*, or gives thanks for such deliverance (e.g. Psalm 18:4–5; 30:3; 71:20; 86:13). Early death can certainly be caused by sin: 'As heat and drought snatch away the melted snow, so the grave snatches away those who have sinned' (Job 24:19). A link between sin and physical death is likewise seen in 2 Samuel 12 when King David repented of his sin of adultery and Nathan tells David that 'The Lord has taken away your sin. You are not going to die'; although it then turned out that David's son was still destined to die prematurely as punishment (12:13–14).

It is clear from these contexts that it is not death per se which is caused by sin, but rather premature death which is seen as specific punishment for specific sins. And of course irrespective of whether death is expected (Genesis 23:1–2) or tragic (2 Samuel 18:33), the sense of grief, loss and mourning is always there at the parting of a loved one.

When we move from the Old to the New Testament it is the difference between walking in a wood by moonlight and then the same wood the next day in bright sunlight: the contrasts now look much more stark. With the preaching and practices of the kingdom of God, physical death looks more like an enemy to be overcome. Jesus raises the dead. Jesus weeps at the tomb of Lazarus. 'The last enemy to be destroyed is death', writes Paul (in 1 Corinthians 15:26). With the proclamation through Jesus of the good news of the kingdom, it is as if a door has been opened up from the future into the present, with a bright light shining through, making physical death look much darker than it was before. Physical death has no place in the fulfilled kingdom of God, the new heavens and the new earth. 'He will wipe every tear from their eyes. There will be no more death or mourning or crying or pain, for the old order of things has passed away' (Revelation 21:4).

Following the death and resurrection of the Lord Jesus to save us from sin, resurrection of the believer to eternal life now becomes the dominant message of the New Testament: so physical death for the believer in the New Testament is never something to be feared. Jesus has come to 'free those who all their lives were held in slavery by their fear of death' (Hebrews 2:15), for Jesus 'has destroyed death and has brought life and immortality to light through the gospel' (2 Timothy 1:10).

The New Testament often speaks of believers who die as 'falling asleep'. When Jesus raised Jairus' daughter from the dead, he told the wailing mourners that 'She is not dead but asleep' (Luke 8:52). After Lazarus had died, Jesus told his disciples: 'Our friend Lazarus has fallen asleep; but I am going there to wake him up' (John 11:11). His disciples misunderstood and thought that Jesus was talking about physical sleep, but 'Jesus had been speaking of his death' (verse 13).

When Paul was preaching the gospel in Pisidian Antioch, he remarks that 'when David had served God's purpose in his own generation, he fell asleep; he was buried with his fathers and his body decayed' (Acts 13:36). Paul did not want the believers 'to be ignorant about those who fall asleep, or to grieve like the rest of men, who have no hope' (1 Thessalonians 4:13) for Jesus 'died for us so that, whether we are awake or asleep, we may live together with him' (1 Thessalonians 5:10).

In fact we learn in the New Testament the very reason for physical death itself, for 'flesh and blood cannot inherit the kingdom of God, nor does the perishable inherit the imperishable' (1 Corinthians 15:50). Unless we first die physically, we cannot obtain our resurrection bodies by which means we inherit God's fulfilled kingdom. The only exception to that would be if Jesus comes again while we are still alive, but that has not been the case for all believers up to the moment that I write these words (though who knows what might be the case tomorrow – we need to be ready!).

The New Testament takes the world of Old Testament death, in which physical death is accepted as the normal lot of humankind, and transforms it into something that has no place in the future kingdom of God, at the same time subverting the sting of death by the power of the resurrection. The shadowy world of *sheol* crystallises out into the stark black and white contrast of hell and of heaven.

Spiritual death

The phrase 'spiritual death' is not found within the biblical text itself, but provides a handy way of describing alienation from God caused by sin. The idea appears in the Old Testament in embryo but is rampant in the New Testament. The picture painted for us of the casting of Adam and Eve out of the Garden of Eden in Genesis 3 provides for us one of the most vivid pictures of spiritual death anywhere in the Bible, as we shall consider in more detail in a moment. It is as seen from the theological perspective of the New Testament that it seems most appropriate to understand this chapter in Genesis as referring to spiritual death.

In other places also in the Old Testament, the idea of spiritual death is found in embryonic and clearly poetic form. 'Stolen water is sweet; food eaten in secret is delicious!' cries the tempting woman of Proverbs 9, but, comments the writer, using the present tense 'little do they know that the dead are there, that her guests are in the depths of *sheol*'. 'I will ascend above the tops of the clouds; I will make myself like the Most High' declare the Babylonians in Isaiah 14. Oh no, you won't, says the prophet, you are already 'brought down to *sheol*, to the depths of the pit' (verse 15). You're as good as dead.

The notion of spiritual death is so intrinsic to the New Testament that it is often only by the context that it's possible to distinguish it from physical death, and sometimes the two types of death are thoroughly intertwined.

John's Gospel in particular highlights the fact that eternal life begins now as we are released from bondage to spiritual death through faith in Christ: 'I tell you the truth' says Jesus, 'whoever hears my word and believes him who sent me has eternal life and will not be condemned; he has crossed over from death to life' (John 5:24). When Jesus says 'I tell you the truth, if anyone keeps my word, he will never see death', his listeners are furious at his claims, but for our present purposes it is Jesus' highlighting of the contrast between spiritual life and spiritual death that is most striking. Of course those who trusted in him would die physically, but in another sense, says Jesus, they would 'never die' because they were released from the power and penalty of sin.

In his great letter to the Romans Paul expounds the way in which the law reveals our sinful nature and our need for salvation through Christ alone:

'I found that the very commandment that was intended to bring life actually brought death. For sin, seizing the opportunity afforded by the commandment, deceived me, and through the commandment put me to death' (7:10–11), but 'through

Christ Jesus the law of the Spirit of life set me free from the law of sin and death' (8:2). When Paul was 'put to death' as the law revealed the power of sin in his life, he was not referring to physical death, but to spiritual death, at least in the first instance. Believers are those who have 'died to sin' (6:2), 'who have been brought from death to life' (6:13).

The theme of the law bringing spiritual death is repeated again and again through the epistles of Paul, but the blackness of spiritual death is always contrasted with the possibility of repentance and faith leading to life in Christ. Referring to the Mosaic law, Paul writes about 'the ministry that brought death, which was engraved in letters on stone...' (2 Corinthians 3:7). 'You were dead in your transgressions and sins...' said Paul, writing to the church in Ephesus (Ephesians 2:1), 'but God, who is rich in mercy, made us alive with Christ even when we were dead in transgressions – it is by grace you have been saved' (2:4–5). 'When you were dead in your sins and in the uncircumcision of your sinful nature, God made you alive with Christ' (Colossians 2:13). As spiritual death is replaced by spiritual life, so the fruits of love show evidence of new life, for: 'We know that we have passed from death to life, because we love our brothers. Anyone who does not love remains in death' (1 John 3:14).

No one who reads the New Testament can fail to be impressed by the stark reality of spiritual death painted there for us, but equally the hope of resurrection life in Christ is highlighted in the same breath to give us hope and encouragement.

The 'second death'

There is a third type of death introduced to us in the New Testament, and that is the spiritual death that continues on after this life, the permanent death that is sometimes called the 'second death'. Jesus speaks of it in Mathew 10:28: 'Do not be afraid of those who kill the body but cannot kill the soul. Rather, be afraid of the One who can destroy both soul and body in hell'. The actual phrase 'second death' appears only in the book of Revelation, where it occurs four times. The early suffering churches in Asia Minor are reassured by the words of Jesus: 'He who has an ear, let him hear what the Spirit says to the churches. He who overcomes will not be hurt at all by the second death' (Revelation 2:11). Then finally (in Revelation 20:14) we learn that death itself is 'thrown into the lake of fire. The lake of fire is the second death'. The Grim Reaper itself is ushered out of the drama even as the new heavens and the new earth are ushered in.

What is striking about the notion of the 'second death' is that it is this kind of death, and this alone, of which we should really be afraid according to Jesus. Physical death is essential if we are going to move on in the purposes of God to inherit the kingdom with our new resurrection bodies in place. Spiritual death is bad, but it can be put right by putting our faith in the finished atoning work of Christ upon the cross for our sin. But the second death is truly scary, for from that there is no going back. It represents eternal death, permanent separation from God.

With this background survey on the Bible's understanding of death complete, we are now in a better position to address the biblical teaching about the Fall. What is the connection between death and the Fall?

Chapter 12:
Evolution and the Fall

The doctrine of the Fall has attracted a huge amount of exposition and commentary over the centuries. Our aim here will be to consider the doctrine within the particular context of the evolutionary history of humankind already outlined. The main approaches will be discussed according to the models A–E introduced in Chapter Ten for the various understandings of Adam and Eve. As already emphasised, our understanding of the Adam and Eve narrative will set the stage for what we believe happened at the Fall. Once we have briefly outlined the models in this context, we will then take a closer look at the Genesis text itself, together with some interpretative passages in other parts of Scripture, in order to compare the various models.

Model A
Remembering that this model perceives the Genesis narratives as purely theological texts without any historical content, the understanding of the Fall in model A therefore follows naturally from this starting point. The Fall in this view is the eternal story of Everyman. It is a theological narrative that describes the common human experience of alienation from God through disobedience to God's commands. Every person repeats the story in their own experience as they fall short of what God expects of them. It is a story that highlights the fact of spiritual death that characterises humankind. In this ahistorical view, therefore, talk of human evolutionary biology is irrelevant, and the physical death of both animals and humans is seen as happening throughout evolutionary history.

Model B

Model B is the protohistorical view which suggests that following the evolution of anatomically modern humans, there was a gradual growing awareness of God's presence and calling upon their lives. The Fall then becomes the conscious rejection of this awareness in favour of choosing their own way rather than God's way. In model B, therefore, the Fall is a historical process happening over a long period of time, leading to spiritual death. The Genesis account of the Fall then becomes a dramatised retelling of this ancient process through the personalised Adam and Eve narrative placed within a Near Eastern cultural context. As with model A, the physical death of both animals and humans is seen as happening throughout evolutionary history.

Model C

Model C, it will be remembered, proposes that Adam and Eve were real historical people, dubbed *Homo divinus*, the progenitors of God's new family on earth, comprising all those who would enter into a personal relationship with God by faith. So the Fall in model C becomes the disobedience of Adam and Eve to the expressed revealed will of God, bringing spiritual death in its wake, a broken relationship between humankind and God. In an extension of this model, just as Adam is the federal head of humankind, so as Adam falls, equally humankind falls with him. Federal headship works both ways. Just as a hydrogen bomb explodes with ferocious force, scattering radiation around the world, so sin entered the world with the first deliberate disobedience to God's commands, spreading the spiritual contamination of sin around the world. And as with model A, the physical death of both animals and humans is seen as happening throughout evolutionary history. Model C is about spiritual death.

Model D

In the old-earth creationism of model D, Adam and Eve were created directly from the 'dust of the ground', without evolutionary antecedents, and lived in the literal Garden of Eden, followed by their fall from grace upon disobeying God's commands[154]. The variants of this model generally envisage the physical death of plants and animals as occurring before the Fall, but see the Fall as bringing about both the physical and spiritual death of Adam and Eve. In other words, Adam and Eve would have been immortal (had they not sinned) either on the earth, or by transfer to heaven without the intervention of physical death (opinions differ on this point).

Model E

The young-earth creationism of model E differs quite markedly from Model D in the context of the Fall, because apart from believing in an earth created only about 10,000 years ago, and an Adam and Eve formed directly 'out of the dust', this model also suggests that there was no death at all before the Fall, at least of animals containing blood. In addition, at the Fall there were marked changes in the laws of science so that, for example, the second law of thermodynamics now began to apply, whereas it had not applied before, leading to death and degradation in the biological world. Like model D, this model envisages that Adam and Eve would never have died physically or spiritually had they not sinned.

The Fall in the Genesis text

I sometimes wonder whether Christians do not take more of their doctrine of the Fall from the pages of Milton's *Paradise Lost* than they do from the pages of sacred Scripture. Indeed, the language of 'Fall' is not at all scriptural, and the term is not used within the Genesis text or elsewhere. 'How sin began' might be a more suitable title, but we will stick with the language of 'Fall' as shorthand. There is always a danger in taking a biblical doctrine and building upon it great castles in the air, castles which are not really justified by the text itself. When we come to the text of Scripture, we find a very brief account, sparing in detail, but bringing out clearly the key points so that we don't miss them. In some ways the narrative is more striking by what it leaves out than by what it puts in, without the slightest sign of interest in answering all the questions that our curiosity might pose, but what is left in provides some key theology which is essential for understanding the rest of the biblical message.

In what follows we shall continue to interpret the first few chapters of Genesis as a text expressed in figurative language written for the purpose of conveying theological truths accessible to all people in whatever era or culture. As already emphasised, the figurative interpretation of Genesis 2 is not in response to evolution, but an expository tradition with deep roots in church history.

The Garden of Eden (Genesis 2:8) represents the abundant and fertile environment in which Adam and Eve enjoyed fulfilling their responsibilities to care for the earth. Models C–E all agree that these responsibilities were fulfilled by Adam and Eve as settled Neolithic farmers caring for their crops. The writer speaks of planting a garden in Eden 'in the east', presumably east in relation to Israel, so the oases of the Mesopotamian plain, the heartland of human civilisation, may be the kind of environment envisaged. Whenever Eden is mentioned in the Old Testament, it is pictured as a well-watered oasis, a place of abundance in contrast to arid desolation (e.g. Isaiah 51:3; Ezekiel 31:9; 36:35). Gordon Wenham points out that it is in the east that the sun rises and 'light is a favourite biblical metaphor for divine revelation' (Isaiah 2:2–4; Psalm 36:10), concluding that 'it seems likely that [Eden] is symbolic of a place where God dwells. Indeed there are many features of the garden that suggest it is seen as an archetypical sanctuary, prefiguring the later tabernacle and temples'[155].

Attempts to assign a specific geographical location to the Garden of Eden have always failed since the Genesis text incorporates many ideas of richness and geographical location that, taken together, do not fit any particular place[156]. For example, the river flowing out of Eden and dividing into four branches (or 'heads' 2:10) may be a way of highlighting the fertility of the garden. In real geography, of course, tributaries come together to join to form the main river, but here we have the reverse, the river *from* Eden separating into the headwaters of the Pishon, Cush, Tigris and Euphrates rivers (2:10–14). The inspired text intends, perhaps, to underline God's presence as the ultimate source of all the physical blessings and resources that were so essential for human welfare at that time. The Tigris and Euphrates are well-known features of Mesopotamia, but no rivers called Pishon or Cush have ever been identified. Furthermore, Pishon 'winds through the entire land of Havilah, where there is gold' (2:11). Other passages in the Old Testament that mention Havilah suggest that it represents the area of Saudi Arabia, which was certainly a source of gold in ancient times (e.g. Genesis 25:18; 1 Samuel 15:7). So what the writer may be wishing to do here is to link up many ideas of richness and abundance that came from widely dispersed areas in order to generate a composite picture of the wonders and richness of the world that God had brought into being for Adam and Eve to cultivate and to enjoy. Such an interpretation fits with the presence of the precious stones listed in 2:12. Furthermore, rivers in the rest of the Bible are frequently used to symbolise God's presence: 'There is a river whose streams make glad the city of God, the holy place where the Most High dwells' (Psalm 46:4). In the final chapter of the book of Revelation, which in so many ways parallels the description of the Garden of Eden in its symbolic description of the fulfilled kingdom of God, we find 'the river of the water of life, as clear as crystal, flowing from the throne of God and of the Lamb, (Revelation 22:1). Here the river of abundance flows out of the presence of God, just as it does in Genesis 2:10. Nowhere in the rest of Scripture do we find people looking for the Garden of Eden as a specific geographical entity, or referring to it as a specific place, surprising indeed if we take the language non-figuratively, as it should then be well lit at night (Genesis 3:24)!

At the centre of the garden in the Genesis 2 narrative are two trees, the 'tree of life and the tree of the knowledge of good and evil' (2:9). Adam is told that he can eat from any trees in the garden, but 'you must not eat from the tree of the knowl-edge of good and evil, for when (literally on the day, *yom*) you eat of it you will surely die' (2:16–17). A huge amount of ink has been spilt on what exactly these trees represent, and there is no room for dogmatism on a topic that has engaged exposi-tors for so long without any universal agreement. Nevertheless the main points seem clear. The tree of life symbolises the life with God that was so apparent in the garden and there is no reason to think that Adam and Eve are not pictured as having free access to this tree – it was not forbidden to them. The

Bible often uses a tree to symbolise the life and presence of God, hardly surprisingly in desert lands in which the sight of a green tree in an oasis still continues to bring healing to the tired and dusty traveller. The one who meditates on God's law 'is like a tree planted by streams of water, which yields its fruit in season and whose leaf does not wither' (Psalm 1:3 cf. Jeremiah 17:8). The golden candlestick kept in the tabernacle may well have been a stylised tree of life, shedding light on the twelve loaves that symbolised God's life that sustained the twelve tribes of Israel (Exodus 25:31–35; Leviticus 24:1–9). Wisdom 'is a tree of life to those who embrace her' (Proverbs 3:18). The fruit of God's presence in the life of the believer is likened to a tree of life: 'The fruit of the righteous is a tree of life...' (Proverbs 11:30) and 'The tongue that brings healing is a tree of life' (Proverbs 15:4). Once again the parallel is found in the symbolism of Revelation 22 where 'On each side of the river' of the new Jerusalem 'stood the tree of life, bearing twelve crops of fruit, yielding its fruit every month. And the leaves of the tree are for the healing of the nations' (verse 2). The Bible could not be more clear that the 'tree of life' represents God's presence, with godly fruits resulting in the context of human lives.

The forbidden 'tree of the knowledge of good and evil' is found only within this Genesis narrative, which means that we cannot rely on light shed from other scriptural references to interpret what it means. Satan in the form of a serpent is telling either a half-truth or an outright lie when he tells Eve that if she eats of this fruit 'your eyes will be opened, and you will be like God, knowing good and evil' (Genesis 3:5); for although the eyes of both Adam and Eve were indeed opened after eating the forbidden fruit, the narrator comments ironically, that far from becoming God-like, all they noticed was their nakedness! So it is difficult to interpret the forbidden tree as meaning that they had no actual knowledge of right and wrong prior to the Fall, given that such an interpretation depends on the serpent's dodgy suggestions. A more likely interpretation comes from the observation that the term 'good and evil' in Hebrew is used in legal literature of the period to describe legal responsibility. The tree of the knowledge of good and evil then becomes a potent symbol of moral autonomy, the eating of which expresses the human desire to go his or her own way rather than God's way. The Hebrew word for 'knowledge' has a wide range of meanings which include 'experience'. By eating the fruit, Adam and Eve exercise and experience their own moral judgement, separating it from God's. That really is evil, and it is the evil consequences of disobeying God's commands that we see in the world ever since. It is obedience to God's law which gives the real 'light to the eyes' (Psalm 19:8), not disobedience.

The serpent is not identified within the narrative, but elsewhere in Scripture is taken to symbolise Satan (Revelation 12:9; 20:2), 'a liar and the father of lies' (John 8:44) who has been 'sinning from the beginning' (1 John 3:8). The connection of the eating of plant food, a snake and the loss of life occur also in the Gilgamesh Epic, in which Gilgamesh finds a plant that provides the secret of life, but a snake swallows the plant, depriving him of immortality. Here in Genesis 3 life proceeds not from the plant but from God. Wisdom, life, come from obeying God ('the fear of the Lord'), and life is lost through disobedience. What kind of life? After Adam and Eve succumb to the serpent's crafty suggestions which cast doubt on the veracity of God's word, far from dropping dead as the warning of Genesis 2:17 might indicate, their eyes are opened to see their own nakedness, which they proceed to cover, and then hide from God. All the consequences of the spiritual death that results from sin are here portrayed vividly for us –

- **shame** in verse 7: 'Then the eyes of both of them were opened, and they realised they were naked.'
- **fear** in verse 10: The man answered, 'I heard you in the garden, and I was afraid because I was naked; so I hid.'
- **blame** in verse 12: The man said, 'The woman you put here with me – she gave me some fruit from the tree, and I ate it.'
- **alienation** in relationships in verse 16: 'and he will *rule* over you.'
- **alienation** from that which gives satisfaction and identity to men and women – work, childbirth (verses 16–19).

As previously highlighted, Genesis 3 provides for us one of the most powerful descriptions of spiritual death in the whole of Scripture. Just as Genesis 2:4 makes it very difficult to interpret *yom* as necessarily meaning a day of 24 hours in the Genesis context, so equally the failure of Adam and Eve to physically drop dead on the *yom* that they disobeyed God highlights once again the need to interpret the meanings of words by their context. Here in Genesis 3 the passage is quite clear that Adam and Eve died as a result of their sin, just as God had warned, but they died spiritually. Along with the potent consequences of sin just surveyed, they were cast from the Garden of Eden with its tree of life so that they would not eat from it and 'live forever' (verse 22). The wording seems chosen to underline the dismal reality of their exclusion from God's presence and close off any suggestion that Adam and Eve could recover their fellowship with God through their own efforts, incidentally highlighting the figurative nature of the language, God 'placed on the east side of the Garden of Eden cherubim and a flaming sword flashing back and forth to guard the way to the tree of life' (verse 24).

The fruits of disobedience were indeed bitter. But under the new covenant the way back to the tree of life is opened up through the atoning work of Christ on the cross: 'Blessed are those who wash their robes, that they may have the right to the tree of life and may go through the gates into the city' (Revelation 22:14).

As a result of Adam and Eve's disobedience, God curses not them, but the serpent (3:14) and, through Adam, the ground (3:17). The figurative nature of the language is underlined by the curse upon the serpent – 'you will eat dust all the days of your life' (verse 14). Clearly snakes do not eat dust. The vivid language, to cite Wenham, implies 'abject humiliation, especially of enemies' (see also Psalm 72:9; Isaiah 49:23; Micah 7:17). But there is also a ray of hope: 'he will crush your head and you will strike his heel' (verse 15). Despite the life-long enmity between humankind and the forces of evil and death, God will ultimately have the victory through Christ. Although in the context the full implications of the messianic hope contained in this prediction are embryonic, New Testament language follows up on this passage to describe this ultimate victory of Christ over Satan (Romans 16:20; Hebrews 2:14; Revelation 12).

The curses in Genesis 3 represent a complete disruption of human lives. To the woman God said 'I will greatly increase your pains in childbearing; with pain you will give birth to children'. The implication here is that women certainly knew all about the pain of childbearing prior to that time (otherwise why use the Hebrew term *rabah* meaning 'increase' or 'multiply'?), but the impact of sin caused a sense of alienation from this role that was so central to the idea of God's blessing in the life of a woman in that cultural context.

God's curse upon the ground through Adam in 3:17 is expressed very precisely: 'Cursed is the ground *because of you...*' Farming would henceforth be associated with 'painful toil' and it would be a real sweat; the earth would produce 'thorns and thistles' (verse 18), weeds that grew up and contaminated the crop when the farmer wasn't caring for his fields properly. Elsewhere in Scripture, the presence of 'thorns and thistles' is seen as a sign of God's judgement (e.g. Hosea 10:8; Hebrews 6:8)[157]. No longer would the man's work be pure joy, but rather spoilt by sin, so that Adam would no longer be a really effective earth-keeper, looking after the *adamah* as he should. The reminder to the man that he will return 'to the dust' (verse 19) seems not to be a consequence of his disobedience, but rather a reminder that sweating away to extract crops from the earth is actually quite appropriate when we recall that Adam is destined to return to the earth anyway.

Nowhere in this tightly narrated theological text is there any suggestion that the earth itself was cursed in isolation from Adam, or that anything physically changed in either the earth or the heavens as a consequence of the Fall. Such dramatic apocalyptic language is frequently used elsewhere to denote God's judgement (e.g. Isaiah 13:10; 24:19–20) but is completely absent from the austere language of Genesis 3. Amazing suggestions are sometimes put forward about how the 'laws of nature' changed at the Fall, but there is no evidence for such speculations from the biblical text, nor indeed from science. Those really are 'castles in the air': not only that, but they seem to directly contradict Scriptures indicating that it is God who gives the young lions their prey and the ravens their carrion, and that it is this present earth that he created – not some earth so amazingly different that it hardly resembles it.

The Fall in the rest of Scripture

The Fall narrative is notable by its absence from the rest of the Old Testament in the sense that allusions to it as a specific narrative are rare. On the other hand one could say that virtually every page displays the reality of the Fall in that the ravages of sin are so apparent in page after page.

When the Garden of Eden or the Fall narrative is mentioned, it tends to be interpreted as a figurative account in the way that we have been suggesting. A striking example is found in Ezekiel 28, where God says to the king of Tyre: 'In the pride of your heart you say, "I am a god; I sit on the throne of a god in the heart of the seas." But you are a man and not a god, though you think you are as wise as a god' (verse 2). There is a clear resonance here with the serpent's claim in Genesis 3 that when Adam and Eve ate the forbidden fruit, they would be 'like God'. Then Ezekiel takes up the lament in vv 12–13: 'You were the model of perfection, full of wisdom and perfect in beauty. You were in Eden, the garden of God...' going on to picture the fall of the king of Tyre as his exclusion from Eden. Truly, pride comes before a fall.

The tough message of judgement that Jeremiah is called by God to convey to the people of God leads to a book that portrays virtually a reversal of the creation narrative of the early chapters of Genesis. Jeremiah 4 gives a graphic account of this reversal: 'I looked at the earth, and it was formless and empty; and at the heavens, and their light was gone' (verse 23 and following verses). The phrase 'formless and empty' is the same *tohu vebohu* phrase found in the Hebrew of Genesis 1:2. In Jeremiah it is as if the disobedience of God's people is unravelling the beauty of the created order that God has brought into being. 'I looked, and there were no people; every bird in the sky had flown away...' (4:25) – talk about playing the Genesis text backwards, a Fall and more!

But it is in the New Testament that we find Pauline passages expounding the Fall of Adam more explicitly and we need to look at these with care.

The Fall in Romans

In the first few chapters of the letter to the Romans, Paul establishes that all have sinned and fallen short of the glory of God (3:23) and so all are in the same position of requiring justification by faith (3:22). The Gentiles have fallen short of the dictates of their conscience for 'when Gentiles, who do not have the law, do by nature things required by the law, they are a law for themselves, even though they do not have the law, since they show that the requirements of the law are written on their hearts, their consciences also bearing witness, and their thoughts now accusing, now even defending them' (2:14–15). The Jews, by contrast, have the advantage that they have received the revelation of the law given by Moses, but they have fallen short of that standard also, so that 'All who sin apart from the law will also perish apart from the law, and all who sin under the law will be judged by the law' (2:12). Everyone is in the same boat, the only hope is God's grace and salvation as God's gift, 'For God does not show favouritism' (2:11).

The idea of the Gentiles falling short of the dictates of conscience could be taken as support of model B; here is a situation where people lack any specific revelation of God's law, albeit still having the witness of the wonder of creation itself (1:18–20). Might this provide a description of those emerging modern humans in Africa who, according to model B, gradually gain spiritual awareness of God's claim upon their lives, yet reject it? Taken in isolation the passage might indeed provide such a possible interpretation. Yet it has to be taken in the context of the teaching of Romans as a whole.

The heart of Romans 5 is in verse 8: 'God demonstrates his own love for us in this: while we were still sinners, Christ died for us'. What have we been saved from? We were enemies of God, but have now been reconciled through the death of his Son (verse 10). What went wrong to make us 'enemies of God'? '...sin entered the world through one man, and death through sin, and in this way death came to all men, because all sinned' (verse 12), with verse 14 making clear that the 'one man' to whom Paul refers is Adam: '...death reigned from the time of Adam to the time of Moses, even over those who did not sin by breaking a command, as did Adam, who was a pattern of the one to come'. Paul is here reiterating his earlier point that it is sin that brings spiritual death, not the law per se, because sin existed before the law came on the scene.

The idea of spiritual death because of sin and spiritual life obtained through Christ is further developed in Romans 5:17: 'For if, by the trespass of the one man, death reigned through that one man, how much more will those who receive God's abundant provision of grace and of the gift of righteousness reign in life through the one man, Jesus Christ?' Spiritual life starts now, as we repent of our sin and put our faith in Christ, resulting in the new birth that Jesus explained to Nicodemus involved a spiritual, not a physical, re-birth (John 3:4–5). In the rest of Romans 5, Paul draws out this powerful parallel between the first Adam who brought sin and death, and the second Adam who brings eternal life. When Paul says in verse 18 that 'just as the result of one trespass was condemnation for all men, so also the result of one act of righteousness was justification that brings life for all men', he is not of course implying an automatic universal salvation, but rather that the saving benefits of Christ's death are potentially available to all who put their trust in him, as the rest of his epistle makes clear. And this salvation brings eternal life (5:21), spiritual life that begins now and will continue throughout eternity as we inherit our resurrection bodies, shielding us from the 'second death'.

The identification of Adam as a historical figure, just as Jesus is a historical figure (e.g. verses 14 and 17) is intrinsic to Romans 5, thereby providing support for model C in this respect. There seems no reason to suppose that Paul doubted that the Adam of whom we spoke was a real person – the 'one man' (Adam) is compared with the 'one man' Jesus. The language is also consistent with the idea of federal headship (e.g. verses 12 and 17), another feature of model C, although verse 12 makes it clear that spiritual death came to all men by them actually sinning. Each person is responsible for his or her own sin.

Paul develops the idea of spiritual life and death further in Romans 6 where now we the believers are 'buried with him through baptism into death' (6:4), meaning death to the 'old man' as we identify with the death of Christ, definitely not physical death – fortunately! In fact 'if Christ is in you, your body is dead because of sin, yet your spirit is alive because of righteousness' (8:10). Yet with respect to our life without Christ: 'What benefit did you reap at that time from the things you are now ashamed of? Those things result in death!' (6:21). Again these passages refer to spiritual death and make sense only within that understanding. They do not support the idea that Adam's sin brought physical death into the world.

The Fall in 1 Corinthians 15

This is a closely parallel passage to Romans 5, but in this chapter the discussion is about the bodily resurrection of Jesus, leading on to Paul's concern in verse 12 that there were some in Corinth denying altogether that the dead could be raised. If that is the case, says Paul, then those who 'have fallen asleep in Christ are lost' (verse 18), but then goes on to emphasise that because as a matter of fact Christ has risen, he is like the 'first-fruits of those who have fallen asleep' (verse 20). Our future resurrection hinges completely on the past fact of Christ's resurrection. And then come the key verses 21 and 22: 'For since death came through a man, the resurrection of the dead comes also through a man. For as in Adam all die, so in Christ all will be made alive'. Once again we have the parallel between the spiritual death that has engulfed, like a noxious cloud, the whole of humankind, and the spiritual life without which we will not inherit our resurrection bodies, and which is accessed by faith. Salvation, to put it crudely, is a package deal. Eternal life begins now. If we are in Christ now, then that new life will continue for eternity in our resurrection bodies. The 'natural body' comes first (verse 44), just as Adam had a natural body at the beginning (verse 45), but the 'last Adam', Jesus himself, 'is a life-giving spirit' (verse 45), bringing out the contrast between our present physical bodies which are destined to physical decay, and the resurrection life that Christ gives, which is eternal. After Christ comes again 'the last enemy to be destroyed is death' (verse 26), clearly referring in this context to physical death. There is no doubt that in the New Testament physical death is an enemy to be destroyed, because it has no place in the fulfilled kingdom of God.

This passage is important because it highlights once again the points alluded to in Romans 5, the idea of a real historical Adam who stands in contrast to the second Adam: Christ. We are all either 'in Adam' or 'in Christ'. The passage also brings out once more the idea of federal headship (verses 21 and 22), but it extends the emphasis to highlight the contrast between the earthy first Adam on the one hand, with his natural body destined to physically die, and the resurrection life of Christ that represents eternal life for all those who are 'in Christ'. I would like to suggest that whereas this passage does not exclude other models, it does look quite consistent with model C.

There is a further key point in this section that we have already alluded to previously, namely that 'flesh and blood cannot inherit the kingdom of God, nor does the perishable inherit the imperishable' (verse 50). To achieve immortality in the form of a resurrection body we first need to shed our old physical bodies (verse 53). Truly we can cry triumphantly with the apostle: 'Where, O death, is your victory? Where, O death, is your sting?' (verse 55), but in joining in that victory song, we need to realise its implication. Physical death is intrinsic to the purposes of God for human life on this earth, and we cannot inherit the kingdom without going through its portal.

We could work that out also on the back of an envelope, starting with God's command in Genesis to humankind to 'Be fruitful and increase in number; fill the earth...' (Genesis 1:28). If people didn't die, let alone other living things, and carried on multiplying with, let's say one new generation every 30 years then the earth would be packed solid with people after a few thousand years with standing room only, a bit like the Piccadilly Line at rush hour[158], not most people's idea of paradise! Thankfully God has intended the world to be more like the transit lounge at London Heathrow Airport where we have our stay, important as that is, but then move on.

Romans 8:18–27

The final passage we need to look at is one that has often been used to construct ideas about what happened at the Fall. Picking up from where we left off in the epistle to the Romans, Paul in Romans 8 is contrasting our new life in the Spirit with our old sinful natures. A Christian is a 'Christ-in person', says Paul – if you do not have the Spirit of Christ then you are not a Christian (verse 9). So here is the stark choice set before us: if we live according to our old sinful nature we will die, referring to spiritual death, but if we live by the Spirit we will live (verse 13). It is the people who live by the Spirit who are children of God (verse 14), demonstrated also by the close relationship they enjoy with their heavenly Father in his family (verses 15–16). As family members they are also heirs, destined to inherit the new heavens and new earth that God has in store for us; but as co-heirs with Christ 'we share in his sufferings in order that we may also share in his glory' (verse 17). The way of glory in Scripture always passes through the pathway of suffering, but 'our present sufferings are not worth comparing with the glory that will be revealed in us' (verse 18).

This leads Paul on to think of the consequences of our salvation, and of our new role as 'sons of God', for the whole created order: 'The creation waits in eager expectation for the sons of God to be revealed' (verse 19). It is at this juncture that we enter a passage that has kept commentators and theology PhD students happily busy for many centuries! For the fact of the matter is that we cannot be too dogmatic about the interpretation of what follows because Paul's language is ambiguous in places. But we can try to achieve a coherent reading of the text. Paul looks to the day when the creation itself will be brought into the kind of freedom in the Spirit that the children of God experience and which he has just spent the first part of the chapter explaining (verses 19–20). The creation was subjected to frustration not of its own choice (Paul does not believe in Mother Earth!) but 'by the will of the one who subjected it' (verse 20). Who might that be? Presumably God, because only God has power over the created order. But it has been subjected 'in hope that the creation itself will be liberated from its bondage to decay and brought into the glorious freedom of the children of God'. Just as we 'groan inwardly as we wait eagerly for our adoption as sons, the redemption of our bodies' (verse 23), so says Paul, 'the whole creation has been groaning as in the pains of childbirth right up to the present time' (verse 22).

It is possible that Paul has in mind the consequences of the Fall in this section, although that allusion is not that obvious and there is no direct citation. In this interpretation Paul has in mind God's curse upon the earth through Adam in Genesis: 'Cursed is the ground because of you; through painful toil you will eat of it all the days of your life...' (Genesis 3:17). The disruption to the created order that came about through Adam's sin then becomes the 'frustration' to which the earth has been subjected because it is not being looked after properly by humankind as God had intended. Its 'groaning' arises from this failure of good stewardship, and from the waiting involved. Just as the expectant mother has to wait for the joyful occasion of the birth, painful as that is, and just as we personally experience suffering as we wait for the redemption of our bodies in future resurrection, so the creation waits and groans until it is once again looked after properly by redeemed humanity, the 'children of God'.

Such an interpretation is reflected in the comment of Francis Bacon back in the seventeenth century: 'For man by the Fall fell at the same time from his state of innocency and from his dominion over creation. Both of these losses however can even in this life be in some part repaired; the former by religion and faith, the latter by arts and sciences'.[159] In referring to 'the glorious freedom of the children of God', Paul might also have in mind here the future hope of the earth, that it will be transformed into a new earth, just as our mortal bodies will be transformed into resurrection bodies.

Although a link to the Fall in Paul's mind is not impossible, after all he has spent chapter 5 expounding Adam's sin, the more obvious Old Testament resonances of this passage are found in Isaiah 24–27[160]. The punishment of the earth in these chapters is followed by a wider cosmic judgement upon heavenly powers, followed by the Lord's glorious reign upon Mount Zion. The righteous wait expectantly for the Lord's coming, their suffering as they wait like the birth pangs of a woman in labour (Isaiah 26:17), but the dead will live and 'shout for joy' (26:18). So as Jonathan Moo points out, here in these chapters we have a number of thematic parallels with Romans 8, including 'the suffering of the earth due to the Lord's punishment of human sin, the personification of creation's response to judgement, the promise that God's glory will be revealed, the present waiting of the righteous in expectant hope, the use of birth-pang imagery, the defeat of death and the possibility of life before death'.

Such reflections do not exclude the possibility of Genesis 3 being in Paul's mind as he wrote Romans 8, but do make it more likely that the book of Isaiah was the key source for his train of thought. If that is the case, then Romans 8 becomes a description of how the destiny of the earth is closely linked to the future of humankind through what Isaiah 24:5 calls an 'eternal covenant'.

What is clear from this discussion is that there is no scope from Romans 8:9–22 for building a castle in the air in which dramatic physical changes occur in the earth at the Fall, affecting the measurement of time and the laws of nature. But the passage does highlight the role played by redeemed humanity in the purposes of God for the earth both now and in the future.

Pain and death before the Fall?

In the evangelical circles in which I was raised it was common to believe that there was no pain, disease or suffering of any kind before the Fall, but that all these came into being following Adam and Eve's disobedience. From the perspective of Christian apologetics this seemed on the face of it to be convenient, because it meant that all the bad things in the world could be blamed on human sin and so were not God's responsibility.

Actually, however, it does not really solve the moral problem of suffering at all, because if the suffering of animals really started with the human Fall, then God would remain morally responsible for linking the two things. Why, for example, should deep sea fish begin to suffer as a result of a human sin far away and on land? In a sense it would be less of a problem if animal suffering were linked to a whole system of creation designed to eventually lead to a new principle of morality, than if animal suffering were arbitrarily linked in this way to human action.

As I grew in the Christian faith, the position I had unthinkingly adopted seemed increasingly untenable. I started studying biology and learning incontrovertible evidence, which we have already surveyed in this book, that death has been present on the earth since the beginning of life, and that indeed the two go together, we cannot have one without the other. I also learnt about fossils and visited the Natural History Museum to see the thousands of fossil specimens of blood-containing animals that had died millions of years ago. I discovered that dinosaurs were suffering from osteomyelitis more than 65 million years before the Fall, that viruses and bacteria have been endemic for billions of years (remember the stromatolite beds?), and that genetic variation in DNA meant that ageing, death and disease had always been present in living things.

So I went back to the Bible and was quite surprised to find that in any case there was no evidence at all for the kind of Milton's *Paradise Lost* type imagery of the pre-Fall state upon which I had been raised.

If one takes the Genesis story within its context, then God mandates the eating of plants by animals and humans, so biological death is implicit in this passage (Genesis 1:29–30). It is unlikely that this text refers to vegetarianism, more likely that it is highlighting the theological point that animal sacrifice was necessary only for those who had sinned. The use of animals for food and for sacrifice is closely linked as the Genesis text progresses. It was God who provided Adam and Eve with garments made from animal skin after the Fall (3:21), Abel kept and sacrificed sheep (4:2–4) and Noah distinguished clean and unclean animals (7:2). The first thing Noah does when he finally leaves the Ark is to sacrifice some of the rescued clean animals and birds (8:20), and this is followed by the renewal of God's covenant to Noah in which he expressly mandates the eating of all animals, except for their blood (9:3–4).

But in all these accounts, and indeed in the rest of Scripture, there is never any indication that there was no physical death or eating of meat before the Fall.

Likewise neither does the Bible teach that there was no pain before the Fall. We have already noted Eve's increased pain in childbirth as a consequence of the Fall. And though we may not like the idea, pain is actually essential to our health and well-being[161]. Pain is an essential property of biological life, especially as nervous systems become more developed. All organisms, even single-celled organisms like bacteria and yeast, have mechanisms for sensing their environment.

With higher organisms the awareness of pain becomes greater as sentience increases. Feeling pain is an inevitable consequence of sentience. Therefore brain complexity, awareness of the environment and experience of pain appear to increase in parallel. Possessors of consciousness are uniquely aware of the joys of sex, good food, a beautiful sunset and an enjoyable evening at the theatre, but by the same token can be acutely aware of pain when it happens. Pain for us, as for all living organisms, is essential for survival.

This is illustrated very vividly by those rare medical conditions in which sensory experience in general, or pain in particular, is much reduced or even lacking altogether, such as hereditary, sensory and autonomic neuropathies[162]. Individuals have been described coming from three different Pakistani families with a complete inability to feel pain due to mutations in a particular sodium channel[163]. The patient who initially drew medical attention was a child who performed 'street theatre'. He placed knives through his arms and walked on burning coals but experienced no pain, dying before his 14th birthday by jumping off a house roof. All this because of a single point mutation in the gene encoding one of his ten different types of sodium channel. We really do need pain to stay alive!

But do we really need so *much* pain to ensure our survival? The biological answer is almost certainly 'yes'. Our nervous system has been shaped by millions of years of evolution to generate precisely the types of pain which will be most likely to ensure our survival. The mammals whose nervous systems worked inefficiently and failed to pass urgent 'action' messages back to the brain are presumably amongst the species which became extinct and failed to pass their genes on to us. The pain levels that we experience, however much we might dislike the idea, have played a critical role in our evolutionary past and continue to be essential for ensuring our survival in the present. Without pain we would be walking around on broken legs, happily going to school with meningitis, merrily ignoring fatal tumours and munching on broken glass with rotting teeth. In short, our lives would be considerably briefer than they are at present.

So pain is a practical good, which of course does not mean that we should not try to alleviate the suffering it brings, both in humans and in animals. We have duties toward the whole created order, and we should do to others what we would wish that they do to us. Since we would prefer the relief of pain, we should wish the same to others.

Jesus himself was active in curing people who suffered 'severe pain' (Matthew 4:24), out of compassion, and because pain does not belong to the fulfilled kingdom of God (Revelation 21:4). The ministry of Jesus was always aimed at bringing the blessings of the future kingdom into the present; as he taught us to pray: 'Your will be done on earth as it is in heaven' (Matthew 6:10).

We engage in the healing ministry of Jesus not because we are looking backwards to some supposed pre-Fall state when there was no pain, but because we are looking forward to the new heavens and the new earth in which there will be no more pain. Therapeutic attempts now, to reduce pain in people and animals, act as signposts to the kingdom.

The Fall and models A–E

Where does this leave us with models A–E? Hopefully not too confused! It will be apparent by now that I do not think that holding to either models D or E is a realistic option in the light of either Scripture or science. Both animal and human pain and physical death have been with us from the beginning, otherwise we wouldn't be here to discuss it. Those who deny the reality of physical pain, disease and death before the Fall are like ostriches with their heads in the sand. The reality will not go away.

That leaves us with models A–C. In fact either model B or C will readily incorporate model A as far as the Fall is concerned. Christians believe that we repeat the Fall in our own lives by our own sinful actions, a reality described for us by Paul so graphically as he faced the high expectations of God's commands: 'Sin revived and I died' (Romans 7:10). But a problem with models A and B is that they tend to lead people (albeit not necessarily) into a doctrine of the Fall which is, I think, not found in Scripture.

If the Genesis Fall account is either purely ahistorical and figurative (model A), or the story of the gradual alienation from God that occurred during some unspecified early era in the emergence of *H. sapiens* (model B), then the interpretation of the Fall can readily start to centre around human anti-social behaviour, or the emergence of conflict, or even just human behaviours required for basic survival. But, important as these things are, I would suggest that they do not bring us to the heart of the biblical doctrine of the Fall, which is not about sociobiology, but about a relationship with God that was then broken due to human pride, rebellion and sin against God – with profound consequences for the spiritual status of humankind, and for human care for the earth. The Fall is about moral responsibility and sin, not about misbehaviour, and sin involves alienation from God. A relationship cannot be broken by sin unless the relationship exists in the first place.

When we write the discussion sections of our scientific papers, it is commonplace to say that our data are 'consistent with' the particular model that we are proposing to explain our results. I will not say more than that I think that model C is reasonably 'consistent with' both the biblical and scientific data. It may be wrong and I would not wish to hold to it more than tentatively. But it provides, I believe, a reasonable working model for proposing an anthropological history lying behind the inspired, figurative, theological essay that Genesis

1–3 provides, and I for one am happy to hold to this model until a better one comes along.

Model C will not answer every question that we might like to know, for the simple reason that we are not told. For example, if something like model C is correct, what does the Fall imply in practice for the local aboriginal population of Australia whose ancestors had been living there for tens of thousands of years prior to the lives of Adam and Eve in the Near East? The short answer, of course, is that we don't know. Thankfully, as already emphasised, God is the just judge of the world, not us, a fact which personally makes me very relieved. But model C does suggest that if we were looking down on planet earth from the moon with our 'spiritual life detection glasses' on, thousands of years ago, then suddenly we would have noticed a bright light appear in the Near East, shedding its light round the world, only to be dimmed, but not extinguished, as sin and spiritual death entered the world. Something happened there with eternal consequences for the spiritual status of all humankind.

Part of the problem when discussing the Fall with Christians, is the common tendency to imagine Adam and Eve as superhuman, living in an environment that sounds a bit like heaven on earth. It is an image readily nurtured by secular Enlightenment thinking in which man becomes the measure of all things, so that the pre-Fall world becomes the world of the perfect welfare state in which we are cushioned against every care and concern. As we experience new life in Christ, the emphasis is then on restoration to this envisaged paradise. But these scenarios go way beyond anything that we find in the biblical text, in which Adam and Eve are encountered as ordinary people, made from the dust like us, destined to return to the dust like us, but given the amazing delegated responsibility to care for God's earth, a responsibility that can be fulfilled properly only by living in close fellowship with God. The emphasis in the rest of Scripture is then on looking forward to the new heavens and the new earth, rather than always looking back to Eden.

Still, whether we are looking forward, or looking back, or both, we are all faced with the theological challenge as to how our faith in a God of love can co-exist with the reality of a world of suffering, some of it the direct result of the evolutionary process itself, and it is to that topic that we now turn.

Chapter 13:
Evolution, Natural Evil and the Theodicy Question

The question before us is how a good God could choose to bring about all of biological diversity, including us, by such a long and wasteful process that involves so much death and suffering. Whole books are written on such topics, and all I can do here is reflect on a few of the issues involved, focusing not on the moral evil that arises from human free will, but from the so-called 'natural evils' that are implicit in the evolutionary process[164].

Arguments addressing this problem are encompassed within the overall enterprise of theodicy, a term referring to all those attempts to explain how a good and all-powerful God could create a world with suffering and evil in it, so attempting to 'justify the ways of God to men'. The term theodicy derives from the famous book of that name written by the great philosopher and mathematician Gottfried Leibniz (1646–1716) and published in 1710.

I should start by saying that there is a great danger in tackling this kind of topic that the discussion might seem demeaning to someone personally going through a period of suffering. I remember hearing a highly articulate academic at the top of his field, facing some pressing medical challenges, telling a group how he feels demeaned when present in a general discussion on the topic of suffering, as if any kind of rational reflections would ever be sufficient to meet his actual experience of suffering, or indeed do pastoral justice to it – and clearly they would not. I am sensitive to such issues, so the section that follows comes with a 'health warning': these are not the kind of reflections that are likely to be of much help to someone actually passing through a period of suffering (although they might be), but I think they do have pastoral significance in preparing us for times when we will experience suffering in the future, as of course we all will.

Nor should our discussion of biological death in a slightly arid, scientific kind of way, ever diminish the horrible reality of the loss of a loved one. Because of the actions of tectonic plates there are mountains on the earth. Because there are mountains there are people who enjoy climbing them, but some of whom by the same token occasionally die in the attempt. Here are the words of Nicholas Wolterstorff, professor of philosophical theology at Yale University, reflecting on the death of his son in a climbing accident: 'But please: don't say it's not really so bad. Because it is. Death is awful, demonic. If you think your task as comforter is to tell me that really, all things considered, it's not so bad, you do not sit with me in my grief but place yourself off in the distance away from me. Over there, you are of no help. What I need to hear from you is that you recognize how painful it is. I need to hear from you that you are with me in my desperation. To comfort me, you have to come close. Come sit beside me on my mourning bench'.[165]

I would also want to echo the words of Paul Fiddes, another father who has lost a son under tragic circumstances, when he writes 'that no argument finally convinces. We cannot rationalise God, or fully explain suffering and evil'.[166]

I am also reminded of John Hick's wise words in the preface to the book which has become something of a classic in this field: *Evil and the God of Love*. Hick writes: 'In seeking to justify the ways of God to man, one is inevitably tempted to extend faith's dim sense of a hidden divine purpose and sovereignty into an open map of providence such as could be available only to the Creator Himself'. Yet having made such important qualifications, there is no need to remain silent; there is plenty that can be said, and in many ways the biology gives us a lot of help on the matter. The source of the problem turns out also to present some solutions.

Already in the nineteenth century we find Asa Gray writing to Darwin from Harvard and arguing that animal and human pain are not features of nature to be deplored, but rather necessary concomitants of the creative process. We are now in a far better position than Gray ever was to see just how true that is. Biology is a package deal. Once we have carbon, phosphorus, oxygen, nitrogen and the other key elements for life, synthesised in the dying moments of exploding stars, then this is the package we're likely to get given this planetary environment. This means that virtually any plus that we care to mention – something that we as humans see as positive for our life and well-being – is going to have an inevitable minus, something that is deleterious to our well-being. We can construct a vast table, of which the examples shown here are just a tiny sample, of all the examples that could be given[167]:

Biology is a 'package deal'

PLUS	MINUS
Life	Death
Survival	Pain
Mutations are essential for our existence and our diversity	Mutations cause cancer and genetic diseases
Apoptosis is essential for development and prevents cancer	Apoptotic dysfunction can cause cancer
Bacteria are essential for a healthy life	Bacteria can kill us
Eating	Increases Reactive Oxygen Species → DNA damage → ageing

As noted in previous chapters, life, at least carbon-based life of the kind with which we are familiar, is impossible without death. No multicellular animal can live by deriving all its energy needs from chemical elements; all are completely dependent on the food chain whereby organic molecules synthesised in other organisms are passed on to them. We are living in an incredibly dynamic world in which there is a huge amount of daily coming and going. The dead of all kinds are constantly making room for the living. All of life is interdependent.

We have also seen how mutations are essential for our evolutionary history and for our diversity. Without mutations we wouldn't be here because there would have been no diversity upon which natural selection could have acted. And without genetic variation between us all, we would all be clonal, looking identical. But it is that same genetic variation which affects our susceptibility to certain diseases, and which causes genetic diseases or cancers – necessary costs of living in a carbon-based life world.

The first large-scale study aimed at discovering cancerous mutations in a specific collection of genes that encode a class of enzymes called kinases revealed that out of 518 kinase-encoding genes analysed from 210 different cancers, 1,000 mutations were identified, of which 158 were identified as actual drivers of carcinogenesis[168]. Recently 50 research teams used 500,000 genetic markers from each of 17,000 individuals to identify 24 genetic risk factors for 7 common human diseases[169]. This gives some idea of the scale of what is being referred to here. And a further fascinating observation is that variant versions of some genes found in monkeys that don't cause diseases for them, do cause diseases when present in humans[170].

In anthropic accounts of the fine-tuning of the physical constants of the universe, the example is given of Fred Hoyle's discovery of the precise resonances in carbon that facilitate its synthesis from helium via beryllium. Without this particular resonance no carbon would have been made in the stars and we would not be here. But arguably not only carbon-based life, but also carbon-based pain, suffering, disease and death are written into that same anthropic script. Biology really is a package deal.

The question of waste
The objection that evolution is a very 'wasteful' process is, I think, not a very weighty objection from a theological perspective. The staggering size of the universe with its 10^{11}

galaxies each containing about 10^{11} stars provides a useful background for thinking about the subject. It has sometimes been suggested that the Creator is wasteful since he has made a universe which is so vast and so old. But the fact is that the universe needs to be this vast and this old in order for elements such as carbon and oxygen to be synthesised, and so for life to be able to emerge. The present size of the universe is related to its present age multiplied by the speed of light. If the universe were the size of our solar system, then it would last for only about one hour, clearly insufficient time for a fruitful earth! The universe has to be this big in order for us to exist.

The time factor is also vital in the emergence of all the biological diversity that we see on our planet today. As we have seen, speciation is a relatively slow process, the Cambrian explosion happened only relatively recently in earth's history. Why then and not earlier? Further research may well clarify why this should be the case. The gradual increase in the oxygen level in the earth's atmosphere, once photosynthesis got going, is important in the diversification of life on earth, but many factors are involved. As our scientific knowledge increases, it might well be possible to start describing more generalised 'principles of emergence' which describe and predict the pace of evolution. The discovery of life on other planets would help in this process considerably. It is much more difficult to make generalisations when we only have one example, the life that exists on planet earth.

Theologically it is difficult to know what 'waste' might mean for God. Waste compared to what? Christians worship the God who says that 'every animal of the forest is mine, and the cattle on a thousand hills. I know every bird in the mountains, and the creatures of the field are mine' (Psalm 50:10–11). The God who flings 10^{22} stars into space and 'calls them all by name' (Isaiah 40:26), is also the great naturalist who enjoys all the richness and diversity of the natural world that he has brought into being, including its impressive carnivores like lions. It is therefore not surprising that being made in God's image involves the delegation to some extent of the tasks of the heavenly naturalist (Genesis 2:19–20).

In Proverbs 8 we find a vivid description of the role that

Wisdom plays in the appreciation and enjoyment of the created order: 'I was there when he set the heavens in place, when he marked out the horizon on the face of the deep... Then I was the craftsman at his side. I was filled with delight day after day, rejoicing always in his presence, rejoicing in his whole world and delighting in mankind' (verses 27, 30–31).

In highlighting the unique value of humankind as being made in the image of God, there is no need to downgrade the value of the rest of the biological world. It should all be valued by us, just as it is by God. Humans were not around to appreciate the beauty and wonder of the planet and its biological diversity for more than 99% of its history, but God was: and if God chooses to create by a long process that seems very slow to us, then so what? 'With the Lord a day is like a thousand years, and a thousand years are like a day' (2 Peter 3:8). Just as some Christians want instant sanctification without all the tough challenges of being gradually transformed into the likeness of Christ, so they want a God who is more like a magician, waving the magic wand to bring things into being instantaneously. But all we know of God tells us that is not how he has chosen to create, either in our own lives, or the life of the church, or the people of Israel.

All analogies of God's creative work are inadequate, but God can perhaps be likened to the great artist in the studio, with energy, creativity and paint flying in all directions, out of which process emerges the richness and diversity of the created order. This is a very different picture from the manager of an industrial enterprise doing everything possible to reduce wastage. Appropriate as that might be for such commercial contexts, we should beware of trying to make God in our own image when it comes to the question of waste.

The question of cruelty
The notion of cruelty implies forethought and the conscious decision to act in a cruel way, qualities of thought that are usually uniquely assigned to humans. Whilst cruel rats and malevolent weasels might exercise such wicked designs in the pages of children's books, to the best of our knowledge the real animal world is amoral and has no ethics.

Whether there is genuine animal intentionality rather than 'merely' animal behaviour remains a hotly debated issue, but irrespective of the answer to this question there is general agreement that animals are not morally responsible for their actions in any way resembling human responsibilities. A lion may be shot for mauling someone who enters its enclosure, but this is to prevent further mauling, not because the lion needs punishment.

The revelation of God's moral law given in the Bible provides a pattern which, if obeyed, highlights the immense contrast between human and animal behaviour. Because we have free will, we can exercise moral responsibility and choose not to be dictated to by our animal passions, a task made considerably easier if we are willing to allow the Holy Spirit to fill our lives (Romans 7:14–25).

Some people find it problematic that cats play with mice before they kill them, not even bothering to eat them half the time because they've just consumed a tin of cat food; or that sharks sometimes use seals like a basketball, tossing them around in the air before finally eating them for breakfast. The point is that if we did that, then we could rightly be accused of cruelty, because we can choose not to do it, but for the cat or the shark, it is just part of their cat-ness or of their shark-ness. Often such behaviour, as with the cat, is all part of their hunting instincts, and is necessary for honing the skills necessary to keep them alive. If your whole body is designed to run after something that moves, then subdue it, then kill and eat it, it's not surprising if your body swings into action at the slightest movement, even though it might be a ball of string and you're not that hungry anyway. That's not cruelty, that's just being catty.

The question of theodicy

The way that theologians and philosophers tackle the theodicy question tends to emerge from their understanding of God and of his interactions with the world. Many commentators insist on God's omnipotence but suggest that he has deliberately chosen to restrict his power in order to allow the created order to be itself and in a sense express its own 'freedom'. The theologian

Jack Haught, for example, focuses particularly on the theological notion of 'kenosis', of God letting the creation be itself out of love, 'willing to risk the disorder and deviation that actually occur in the evolution of cosmic beauty'. W.H. Vanstone speaks of God's activity in creation, 'in which each step is a precarious step into the unknown'. The perceived advantage for constructing a coherent theodicy is that God is no longer directly responsible for the ills of the created order, but instead its 'disorder and deviation' to use Jack Haught's phrase are consequences of giving creation its freedom to develop.

My own view reflects a somewhat more robust expression of God's omnipotence that highlights God's faithfulness in both creating and sustaining the properties of matter, properties which as a matter of fact do perfectly fulfil his intentions and purposes. The idea here is not of the divine puppet-master, but of the God who actively endows the universe with all those properties and potentialities that bring about his will.

There is therefore no room in this view for 'kenosis' in the context of God's creative work, because God is in no sense denying his own nature in the creative process. As John Hick writes: '...the actual universe, with all its good and evil, exists on the basis of God's will, and receives its meaning from His purpose'. Similar views are expressed by reformed theologians such as Henri Blocher in his fine book *Evil and the Cross*.

A strong view of God's omnipotence and sovereignty over the created order fits better, I would suggest, with the biblical doctrine of creation that we summarised in Chapter Two. Furthermore, I think the science is becoming more consistent with such a view than might have seemed the case only a decade or so ago. As we will briefly review in the following chapter, the possibility of making predictions in biological systems is now beginning to look much more feasible, at least in principle. If with our very limited human knowledge we are already beginning to talk about the possibility of prediction in the evolutionary process, something that would have been deemed unrealistic until very recently, then it doesn't seem to me to make much sense to talk about a creator God who didn't and doesn't really know what is going to happen in his creation.

The biblical understanding of God is of one who knows the

end from the beginning. As God says through the prophet Isaiah: 'I make known the end from the beginning, from ancient times, what is still to come. I say: My purpose will stand, and I will do all that I please' (Isaiah 46:10). There is nothing accidental in the overall direction of the created order, any more than there is in the fulfilment of God's plan in bringing salvation to lost humanity through Christ. This is the gospel which represents 'God's secret wisdom, a wisdom that has been hidden and that God destined for our glory before time began' (1 Corinthians 2:7). Such passages generate a 'strongly intentional' view of God in relation to his creation in general and his people in particular. The heavenly author writes the script and bestows upon the universe properties continually sustained by him that will instantiate the script according to his perfect plan.

The author J.K. Rowling recounts that before she set out to write her seven Harry Potter novels, the general plan of the whole series was in her mind, and then the broad outline written out on a sea of paper notes surrounding her on the living-room floor. The details of the books were worked out as each novel was written, and many of those details could have been otherwise without changing the overall structure of the drama; but the ultimate fate of Harry Potter and Voldemort were written into the script from the beginning. This is the 'strong intentionality' of the author.

What we can call, by contrast, a 'weakly intentional' view of God's interaction with the world, in which the creation departs from his will, tends to promote a particular perspective on the evolutionary process itself generating what have been termed 'evolutionary casualties'. In a created order with precarious deviations from the Creator's will, there will surely be casualties: but these are dealt with differently by different thinkers in the field. Holmes Rolston speaks of a cruciform creation ('a creation formed through the cross') like a passion play involving 'the slaughter of the innocents', referring to the victims of the evolutionary process. Rolston suggests that the suffering experienced by countless creatures in the evolutionary process is redeemed by the chance of life that it offers to other living things in the ecosystem.

For the theologian Christopher Southgate this does not go far enough[171]. Southgate has no problem with pain and the death of organisms that have flourished in the evolutionary process, but identifies evolutionary casualties as being those individual animal lives that never had the opportunity to flourish, perhaps by early predation. Southgate writes: 'These tortured or frustrated lives surely call for redemption by the God who gave rise to the evolutionary order', envisaging some kind of end-time fulfilment for such casualties.

I have to admit that I feel uneasy about such human attempts to engage in the art of divine bookkeeping. All living things give their lives in some sense for others. We are all part of that long food chain without which the biosphere cannot function. Our own bodies almost certainly contain molecules derived from the bodies of people long since dead, and much of our bodies comprise recycled molecules from dead animals and plants. Personally I can see no need to invest the world of biological diversity with the dramatic language of passion plays, evolutionary casualties and the need for the redemption of animals that led 'unfilled lives'. By contrast the biblical text is characterised by an earthy realism when describing the created order.

On the one hand we have a clear duty to care for the whole created order, including a proper stewardship of the animal kingdom, but on the other hand I think we should beware of over-sentimentalising the animal kingdom. This is a particular characteristic of the British, brought up as we are on Winnie the Pooh, Piglet and Tigger, together with Flopsy, Cottontail and Peter, not to speak of all their many descendants in the countless children's books in this genre. Don't get me wrong, I love this genre, but I remember also that real tigers can kill, bears can maul, and even wild pigs can be extremely rough. Part of the problem in even discussing this question is that people so often live in big cities, quite divorced from the world of animals in the wild, thereby exacerbating the tendency to sentimentalise.

Indeed Isaiah envisages the messianic kingdom as being where the 'wolf and the lamb will feed together, and the lion will eat straw like the ox, but dust will be the serpent's food'

(Isaiah 65:25), but this is a 'highly symbolic and poetic description of the complete harmony and peace which is to prevail with the coming of the messianic age'[172]. Such passages are not intended to provide us with the natural history of the fulfilled kingdom of God. Isaiah sees no contradiction in saying of the messianic kingdom that 'no lion will be there' in another passage (Isaiah 35:9), meaning simply that people will be able to dwell in peace. Apart from the hints that we receive in passages such as Romans 8, Scripture is quite silent about the redeemed future of animals and plants. There is plenty of scope here for speculation, but the real answer is that we will not find out until we get there.

I suggest a different theological approach to living organisms as far as the present is concerned.

First, they have intrinsic value that is bound up with their own being. The value of bacteria is in their intrinsic nature. The value of a bear is in its unique characteristics; each organism operating within its own ecological niche and expressing its own specific nature. They are not merely of instrumental value, useful only because they serve our own purposes in some way; they have their own value defined by their own being.

Second, each organism is of value to God as part of his created order. As we have already noted, page after page of the Old Testament remind us of God's delight in all the creatures of his creation. For nearly all of our planet's history, only God was around to enjoy their presence on the earth.

Third, each creature plays its part in the overall evolutionary narrative – we, living-kind, are all part of the great repository of genomic information. We are all connected, we all share the same genetic code, and very similar flesh and blood. We all share in life and death.

Austin Farrer vividly puts the question: 'Poor, limping world, why does not your kind Creator pull the thorn out of your paw? But what sort of a thorn is this? And if it were pulled out, how much of the paw would remain? How much, indeed, of the creation? What would a physical universe be like from which all mutual interference of systems was removed? It would be no physical universe at all'. The living world is a package deal.

So what does theodicy look like with a God who has set intentions and purposes for the world that are being, and will be, fulfilled through the created order? This brings us to John Hick's idea of the present world as a 'vale of soul-making'. In this account, when God created the heavens and the earth as Genesis 1:1 declares, he did not create heaven – instead he created the present universe as a preparation for the new heavens and the new earth. It was a good world, just as Genesis tells us, a world perfectly fit for purpose. So God created a tough world, a world which had, and has, to be subdued by humans made in his image. It is a world in which there is pain and death and plenty of challenges to our comfort and well-being. It is a world in which moral and spiritual growth is made possible – more like a Boot Camp than a Holiday Camp. No pain, no gain. It is certainly not a world in which anyone can afford to feel comfortable or complacent. It is a world in which dependency upon God's grace is the only safe option. But God is preparing a new heavens and a new earth where there will be no more pain or suffering, and ultimately the whole of the created order will be redeemed and its best aspects will be brought into the fulfilled kingdom of God, although the details of exactly what that involves are not given to us.

It is, I think, this tension of the present evil age with the age which is to come – the fulfilled kingdom of God – that brings out most clearly the characteristics of 'natural evil', arising not as a consequence of moral evil, brought about by the actions of people with free will, but rather in its contrast to the fulfilled kingdom of God in which Jesus will finally be Lord. John 9:1: 'As Jesus went along, he saw a man blind from birth. His disciples asked him, "Rabbi, who sinned, this man or his parents, that he was born blind?" "Neither this man nor his parents sinned," said Jesus, "but this happened so that the work of God might be displayed in his life... Having said this, he spat on the ground, made some mud with the saliva, and put it on the man's eyes. "Go," he told him, "wash in the Pool of Siloam" (this word means Sent). So the man went and washed, and came home seeing'. Jesus sees illness in the Gospel accounts as evil, not because of sin, but because of eschatological incompleteness. Perhaps the man's blindness was congenital, caused by genetic variation, but irrespective of the cause, it does not belong in the age which is to come. Instead it provides an opportunity for works of compassion in the present evil age in which we find ourselves.

As a pragmatic observation, there is no doubt that human pain and suffering can be used to bring people to a saving faith or, if we are Christians, as a means through which God can work in our lives. C.S. Lewis famously wrote that 'God...shouts in our pain. It is His megaphone'. Most Christians who have been around a bit on life's pilgrimage will remember times when experiences of pain or suffering of some kind have awoken them from spiritual sloth or been used by God to point to areas of disobedience in their lives that require attention. I know that has been my experience. Of course the fact that God in his sovereignty can use such things for a positive outcome is not at all a reason for neglecting to combat pain and suffering medically and in other ways, just a recognition that they can provide special opportunities for spiritual growth in this vale of soul-making.

I have been constantly surprised to encounter Christians time and again who have come to faith through suffering. Some years ago I was giving a research seminar in a university in Japan. After the seminar was over, my host took me for a meal in a local restaurant. As I got into his car I noticed a Bible on the back seat, and that soon led to a conversation in which I discovered that he was a Christian. As we later sat cross-legged eating our *tampara*, the full story of his spiritual journey and that of his family emerged. I was glad for the darkness of the restaurant, lit only by small lanterns, as he spoke, so that the tears trickling down my face as I listened were less visible. Both he and his wife had been from Buddhist backgrounds. Soon after they were married their first child was born dead. As a result of the trauma, his wife had undergone a severe mental breakdown. This led to prolonged treatment from a psychiatrist, who turned out to be a Christian. This eventually led to them both putting their trust in Christ, finding no healing for their pain except at the cross. Their families on both sides were very opposed to their new faith.

Much later her mother, who lived alone in Kobe, was there

when much of the city was destroyed by an earthquake. Fearing the worst my host had driven into the city some days later, but could not find her flattened house – the whole neighbourhood had been destroyed. But eventually he found her still alive in a refugee shelter, albeit with only the clothes she stood up in – all else was lost. He brought her to live with them in their home near Tokyo and through living in the warmth of a Christian family she eventually found Christ.

Meanwhile his own mother had developed cancer, and came from a town far away to be hospitalised near my host. They visited her in hospital regularly, and she too put her faith in the Lord Jesus before she died. So the Lord in his sovereignty had used different types of suffering to bring a whole extended family into newness of life.

The really big theological puzzle for us right now is why the cost in terms of suffering, disease and death needs to be *that* high in order to bring God's new redeemed family, by freely willed response, into the new heavens and the new earth. Why can't God just create the new heavens and the new earth, without death, pain or suffering, and then place perfect humans within it? After all, that is the future hope of all those who have put their trust in Christ. Why can't we have the future now? For some reason, God's future redeemed family can be established only through the cross, through suffering, and living through this vale of soul-making. There is a greater good that can only be achieved this way.

'In bringing many sons to glory', writes the author of the letter to the Hebrews, 'it was fitting that God, for whom and through whom everything exists, should make the author of their salvation perfect through suffering' (Hebrews 2:10). Just as our Lord Jesus has been made 'perfect' or 'complete' through suffering, so we have been called to follow in his steps. 'Therefore we do not lose heart. Though outwardly we are wasting away, yet inwardly we are being renewed day by day. For our light and momentary troubles are achieving for us an eternal glory that far outweighs them all' (2 Corinthians 4:16–17). The path to the new heavens and the new earth passes through the cross, where Christ took upon himself all the sin, evil and suffering of the world, so that we might be freed from the bondage of sin, leading also in turn to the redemption of the earth itself, ushering in the 'age which is to come'.

Of course we don't have all the pieces of the jig-saw puzzle assembled in our hands to understand fully all the reasons for the divine methods used to achieve God's purposes – how could we? But one day when we 'see Him face to face' (1 Corinthians 13:12), perhaps then some of the remaining pieces will fall into place.

Sometimes even one extra piece of data can make sense to an otherwise puzzling situation. A couple of weeks before writing this my wife and I were walking on holiday in the mountains of south-west Turkey using our trusted guide-book. As all hikers know, the challenge on a new walk in another country is always that of finding the correct start of the walk, Once that is achieved, everything else tends to follow. In this case the guidebook told us to find the mosque in a certain village, fork past it to the right, go past the cemetery and then find the track to the left. Finding the mosque was easy enough, but nothing else matched the rest of the description. We stopped for a chat with the Imam (leader) of the mosque. He was as puzzled as we were but for different reasons. Why did we want to walk along the valley when we had a car and there was a perfectly good road? Hiking in that part of Turkey is not yet a common pastime. After some confusing discussion and further fruitless exploratory investigations, we suddenly wondered whether there might be a second mosque in the village, further up the hillside and so invisible? There was. Once we started from the correct mosque, then the guidebook made perfect sense and we ended up having the most wonderful walk. It turned out that the first more visible 'incorrect' mosque had been built since the guidebook was published. One piece of mutant data, providing apparently the correct interpretation, was sufficient to make the whole story incoherent. One piece of correct data put it all back together again.

For a somewhat more scientific illustration of the same point, the role of quantum theory in current physics provides an analogy. From a utilitarian perspective it works perfectly as a theory – all experiments fulfil its predictions as expected: but we can't at present incorporate quantum theory within normal human logic and experience, although we might be able to do that one day.

So could it be that the biological package deal we have, or something very like it, really *is* the only way in which truly free humans can be formed and fashioned in such a way that they can respond freely to God's love and know him forever? We will never know the answer to that question, not in this life anyway. But even the possibility of an affirmative answer provides a very powerful theodicy. Just as we can't really make sense of quantum theory in our current state of knowledge, maybe if we had a few more missing pieces of the jigsaw the problem of natural evil might look very different. For the moment we have to wait in patience for answers that we have not yet been given.

And while we wait, let us never forget that Christ has fully taken the pain and agony of both physical and spiritual death upon himself in order that we might know real life now and have so much yet to look forward to: for 'We see Jesus, who was made a little lower than the angels, now crowned with glory and honour because he suffered death, so that by the grace of God he might taste death for everyone' (Hebrews 2:9).

For those who, as I do, hold to a strong view of God's authorship and sovereignty in the created order, this reflection from Diogenes Allen from Princeton Theological Seminary might represent an appropriate reflection with which to complete this chapter:

> Through Christ it is possible to understand how the Father's love is present in all things, even in suffering. Suffering can be regarded as a mark of our distance from God because we are subject to the cosmos simply by being creatures. Yet, depending on a person's response to suffering, a person can be in contact with God *through* their suffering and *in* suffering. To be in touch with the reality God has made, even when it is a painful touch, is to have indirect contact with him who is above it and who is above all else, love. Insofar as it is contact, it is good; insofar as it is painful, it is not. But what a difference when the *same* pain results from the grip of a friend, and not the mindless grip of nature.

Chapter 14:
Intelligent Design and Creation's Order

I have deliberately left a consideration of the Intelligent Design (ID) movement to last, partly because it raises a somewhat different set of questions from those we have been considering so far, but also because the backcloth of biblical creation doctrine within which this book is framed provides the basis for a critique.

Intelligent Design is an anti-Darwinian movement that seeks to identify highly specified examples of design in living organisms, putting these examples forward as evidence for a designer. The movement emerged into public consciousness during the early 1990s, launched with a series of books written by a law professor from the University of California called Phillip Johnson. Whilst on a visit to London, Johnson encountered Richard Dawkins' book *The Blind Watchmaker*, and it was partly goaded by Dawkins' anti-religious rhetoric that Johnson wrote his book *Darwin on Trial* in which he critiques evolutionary theory. It was Dawkins' assumption of the philosophy of naturalism, the idea that everything can be explained by science, without recourse to God or any supernatural entity, that most disturbed Johnson.

A significant development in the ID movement occurred in 1996 when a Catholic biochemist from Lehigh University in the US, Michael Behe, wrote a book called *Darwin's Black Box: the Biochemical Challenge to Evolution* (1996), recently updated in Behe's *The Edge of Evolution* (2007). A more mathematical perspective has been contributed by another US leader in the ID movement, William Dembski, in books such as *The Design Inference: Eliminating Chance Through Small Probabilities*

(1998) and *The Design Revolution* (2004). During the 1990s these and other ID proponents became associated with 'The Center for the Renewal of Science and Culture' based at The Discovery Institute in Seattle, now the centre of operations for ID activities. In the late 1990s they launched their 'Wedge Strategy' stating that the aim of the Center was 'nothing less than the overthrow of materialism and its cultural legacies'. 'Design theory promises to reverse the stifling influence of the materialistic worldview, and to replace it with a science consonant with Christian and theistic convictions'.[173]

The political profile of ID, largely a US movement although with influence elsewhere, was increased during the 1990s by a series of court cases in which local school boards in the USA sought to promote the teaching of ID in the classroom as an alternative to evolution. Unlike the national curriculum that characterises the educational system in the UK and other European countries, in the USA the curriculum is to a significant degree controlled by local school boards, elected by popular vote. The situation is complicated by the strict separation in the US between religion and the state, which means that there is no religious instruction in schools. When a school board was elected in a school in Dover, Pennsylvania, sympathetic to ID, they instructed teachers to teach ID alongside Darwinian evolution. This led to protests from parents, which in turn led to a highly publicised court case presided over in 2005 by Judge Jones, a practising Lutheran and Republican appointed by President Bush. The judge ruled that ID could no longer be taught in the classroom because it was 'not science' and failed to 'meet the essential ground rules that limit science to testable, natural explanations'.

My purpose in this chapter is not to consider further in any detail the history and politics of the ID movement[174], but rather to review the core ideas that are being expressed by ID proponents. For it is indeed a movement with a distinctive set of suggestions. Although during export of the ideas from the US they are sometimes presented by European interpreters as simply another way of expressing the traditional argument from design, I think this claim is unfair to the ID proponents themselves, who are explicit in saying that this is not the case[175]. I am a great believer in reading carefully the writings of any movement to understand what claims are being made by its chief proponents, so that we do not ascribe to people what we hope they might be claiming, when in reality they are not.

ID is not the same as young-earth creationism, although the UK media frequently confuses ID with creationism. Having said that, I think it would be fair to say that in some respects ID is a 'first cousin' of creationism, particularly in its strong opposition to Darwinian evolution. In fact, as we shall see, technically ID is a form of 'episodic creationism'.

As in any movement of ideas, there is considerable diversity of opinion amongst ID writers. Phillip Johnson's writings contain many of the traditional arguments against evolution found in creationist writings, some of which we have already considered in this book. Similarly John Lennox, an ID proponent in the UK, reiterates many of the standard creationist arguments against what he terms 'macroevolution' and 'common descent', and seems unaware of the recent advances in genetic and fossil data that we have reviewed in Chapters Three to Five[176]. William Dembski maintains that whereas 'organisms have undergone some change in the course of natural history', 'this change has occurred within strict limits and human beings were specially created'[177], although elsewhere he states that 'Intelligent Design is perfectly compatible with common descent'[178]. On the other hand Michael Behe holds firmly to belief in an old earth, our shared ancestry with the apes, and for a significant role for natural selection in the evolutionary process, writing that: 'It's hard to imagine how there could be stronger evidence for common ancestry of chimps and humans'.[179] Therefore one has to be cautious in assessing the views of ID proponents because they do represent a diverse range.

Writers on ID also represent a heterogeneous group from the point of view of religious beliefs and theology. Many of the original drivers of the movement were evangelical Christians such as Phillip Johnson, whose books were published mainly by evangelical publishers such as Inter-Varsity Press; yet Michael Behe is a Catholic; William Dembski turned to Eastern Orthodoxy in the 1990s[180], although he is now employed by a Baptist university; and another Fellow of the Discovery Institute, Jonathan Wells, was trained as a minister in the Unification Church founded by Sun Myung Moon.

ID proponents also include agnostics, and are explicit in claiming that ID is a strictly scientific idea without any necessary implications for belief in the God of Christian faith, although they mostly do see their arguments as inferring the necessity of design, and therefore an (unspecified) designer. So they do not start with Scripture in expounding their ideas, and the ID literature tends to be completely devoid of biblical references.

The reluctance within the movement to identify what the 'designer' might represent is well illustrated in the following exchange published in *The Guardian* in 2005, in which John Sutherland interviewed Michael Behe[181]:

- **Sutherland:** It's no secret that you are a Catholic. But, as I understand it, your scientific theory does not predicate God in any form whatsoever. You've suggested that the designer could even be some kind of evil alien. Is that right?

- **Behe:** That's exactly correct. All that the evidence from biochemistry points to is some very intelligent agent. Although I find it congenial to think that it's God, others might prefer to think it's an alien – or who knows? An angel, or some satanic force, some new age power. Something we don't know anything about yet.

In 1996, Phillip Johnson declared with regard to ID that 'This isn't really, and never has been, a debate about science. It's about religion and philosophy.' But since more recent ID proponents claim that their ideas are strictly scientific, we shall consider them here from the point of view of science, though even more from the perspective of biblical creation theology, because in the final analysis ID represents a revival of a certain type of natural theology, and should therefore be viewed in that light. My suggestion is that Phillip Johnson's 1996 statement is exactly right.

Irreducible complexity

Michael Behe proposes that there are in biological systems some entities so complex that they could not have evolved 'by chance' (by Darwinian processes). Behe provides a number of examples, such as the biochemical mechanisms involved in blood clotting, the immune system, other biochemical pathways and, most famously of all, the bacterial flagellum. Behe suggests that since such systems could only function properly if all the components are in place at the same time, and since it is impossible that something as complex as the flagellum could spring into being fully formed by an evolutionary mechanism, therefore evolution is unable, in principle, to provide an explanation for such entities. Such entities are thus called 'irreducibly complex'. An irreducibly complex structure is defined by Behe as '...a single system composed of several well-matched, interacting parts that contribute to the basic function, wherein the removal of any one of the parts causes the system to effectively cease functioning.'[182]

Dembski goes on to infer that when such 'irreducibly complex' systems are identified a 'design inference' can be made, meaning that the mathematical probability of such an entity coming into being by chance all at once is so tiny that the system in question must have come into being 'by design'. There is no way that it could have evolved by the 'numerous, slight successive modifications' that Darwin had envisaged for the stages of the evolutionary process.

The bacterial flagellum

There are several problems with these claims, and the first is scientific.

We can start with that icon of the ID movement, the bacterial flagellum[183]. This is indeed a wonderful piece of kit that enables bacteria to swim around, like a flexible oar with an outboard motor. The motor is powered by the transmission of ions and is embedded in the bacterial cell membrane, with the 'oar' sticking out (see Figure 18). There is quite a bit of diversity amongst bacteria in the precise structures of their flagella, but generally the ensemble consists of a basal body that

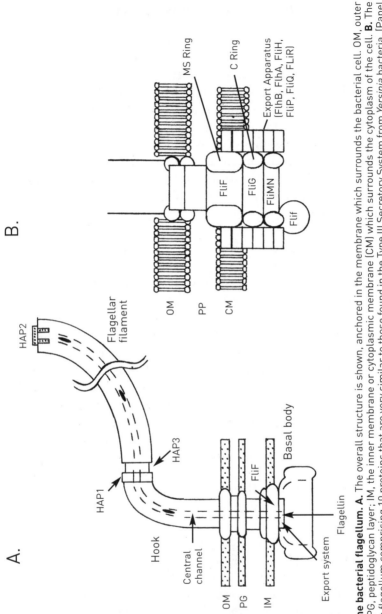

Figure 18. The bacterial flagellum. A. The overall structure is shown, anchored in the membrane which surrounds the bacterial cell. OM, outer membrane; PG, peptidoglycan layer; IM, the inner membrane or cytoplasmic membrane [CM] which surrounds the cytoplasm of the cell. **B.** The portion of the flagellum comprising 10 proteins that are very similar to those found in the Type III Secretory System from *Yersinia* bacteria. [Panel A: reproduced from Yonekura, K., et al. *Science* 290: 2148-2152, 2000; Panel B: reproduced by permission from K.R. Miller, Brown University, USA.]

anchors the apparatus in the bacterial cell membrane, a motor driven by ions, a switch, a hook, a filament, and then in addition an export system of other proteins is needed to get the flagellum to the bacterial cell surface[184]. Typically 40–50 genes are involved in generating the apparatus, and the flagellum itself comprises around 30 proteins.

If the idea of 'irreducible complexity' is correct, then none of the components or modules within the flagellum should have other independent functions, because in that case the flagellum would no longer be 'irreducible' – it would then be possible to break the system down to other components, upon which Darwinian natural selection could operate quite independently of the flagellum itself. As it happens the flagellum does have many components and modules which are used independently in other bacterial contexts[185]. For example, bacteria know how to attack and defend themselves, like every other living organism on the earth.

One of the ways they attack is by the use of the Type 3 Secretory System (TTSS) which injects poisons directly into other cells, like the 'virulence factor' injected by the *Yersinia* bacteria that cause bubonic plague (the 'black death' that ravaged European populations in medieval times). The interesting point about the TTSS, in the present context, is that it consists of around ten proteins that are all very similar to the basal body of the flagellum (see Figure 18). So here is a module that is integral to the function of the flagellum, but which also has a function quite independent of the flagellum in different bacteria: therefore the flagellum is not 'irreducibly complex' after all.

Indeed most of the components of the flagellum have roles and functions that are already known and are widely spread through living organisms. One portion of the flagellum operates as an ion exchange channel of the kind found functioning independently in the membranes of all bacteria. The ion-driven rotatory motor of the flagellum is likewise not at all unique: quite the opposite. The ATP synthase[186] which is central to this motor uses the movement of ions to produce ATP, the energy storage and transfer molecule of all living cells. This ATP synthase functions in all other bacterial membranes to use the energy exchange to produce rotatory motions. Similarly we find that the individual proteins of the flagellum are widely spread through living things with multiple uses. The flagellins found in the filament portion are similar to proteins known as pilins found on the cell surface of bacteria. In fact out of the 42 'standard flagellum proteins' required in bacteria such as *E. coli* (including some required for flagellar assembly), 27 have already been identified as having closely similar proteins in other bacteria.

These insights into the molecular structure of flagella make it easier to see how individual components of the system could have evolved separately by bestowing advantages on their host bugs quite independently of any role that they might have in flagella. Working out detailed evolutionary pathways in bacteria is made challenging by the phenomenon of lateral gene transfer whereby genetic information is swapped laterally between bacteria from different strains. It is for this reason, for example, that it is difficult to be sure whether the TTSS evolved from the flagellum or vice versa. However, by considering the 24 'core' proteins considered to be ancestral for all bacteria with flagella, a detailed suggestion describing the evolutionary history of the flagellum has been published[187]. This is definitely not the last word on the matter, and represents work in progress: but there is no reason not to think that the detailed evolutionary pathway of bacterial flagella will eventually be worked out to everyone's satisfaction.

Blood clotting

Similar scientific points apply to the blood clotting system that Behe described in *Darwin's Black Box* as representing an 'irreducibly complex system'. But science moves very fast, and already many of the steps in the evolution of this system have been elucidated. Once again it turns out that numerous components of the system have several different functions, so can simply be co-opted into the blood clotting system as required.

The mechanisms for blood clotting in most vertebrates like us are quite similar. They require the presence of a fibrous, soluble protein (fibrinogen) to circulate in our blood. Fibrinogen has a sticky centre, but this region is normally kept well covered by the rest of the molecule. To form a clot, a protease enzyme (thrombin) cuts off the outside of the fibrinogen so that the sticky portions, now called fibrins, can adhere to start clot formation. Proteases are enzymes (proteins that act as catalysts) that clip bits off other proteins.

So why does thrombin suddenly start clipping bits off fibrinogen? The answer is that thrombin itself is activated by another protease called Factor X. And then in turn Factor X requires two more proteases, Factor VII and Factor IX, to switch on Factor X, and they in turn need other factors, including Factor VIII, defective in haemophiliacs who therefore suffer from faulty blood clotting.

Altogether there are more than 20 components in the 'reaction cascade' that results in clot formation. Why so many? The answer is that the cascade of steps whereby one protease activates another provides an amplification system in which an initial trigger can produce a very rapid response at the bottom of the cascade. So if a single active factor (protease) can activate 20 molecules of the next factor in the chain, and then that one activates 20 more, then a millionfold amplification of the initial signal can readily be achieved by such a system. And the trigger that makes the 'clotting gun' fire is pulled by various factors released by damaged tissues, so activating the first factor in the chain. Clotting would still occur without the amplification system, but it would just happen a lot more slowly.

Could an evolutionary mechanism explain how this system came into being? As it happens, quite easily. It turns out that genes encoding proteases comprise as much as 3% of the whole human genome, so our bodies contain hundreds of different proteases. It is clear that many of them have arisen during our evolutionary history by gene duplication. The proteases that comprise the cascade of factors involved in blood clotting are all related to each other – they are all members of the same protein 'family'.

The next part of the scientific explanation for the evolution of blood clotting requires that we should be able to find a gene encoding for fibrinogen in a simpler organism than vertebrates where it does a different job. We should also be able to find simpler blood clotting systems in the animals from which vertebrates evolved. Both of these requirements have been ful-filled. In 1990 a gene encoding a protein similar to fibrinogen was found in the sea cucumber, an echinoderm[188]. As far as simpler blood clotting systems are concerned, it is intriguing to look at the systems that invertebrates use to prevent blood loss. Invertebrates such as starfish and worms don't bleed to death when they get a cut for two reasons. First, unlike ours their circulatory systems are under relatively low pressure. Second, and of more relevance to the present argument, they have various forms of sticky white blood cells that are good at plugging leaks. So if a blood vessel is broken then white blood cells are swept into the hole where they become sticky, bind to other proteins like collagen, and block any further escape of blood. As a system it's not nearly as good as ours, but it is quite adequate for animals that don't have hearts pumping their blood around at high pressures.

It is therefore quite easy to envisage how the vertebrate clot-ting system may have evolved. Since fibrinogen-like molecules were already present, most likely in the blood plasma and ini-tially for other functions such as maintaining the correct osmotic pressure, all that was then necessary was for a pro-tease such as thrombin to be mis-targeted to the blood as a result of a mutation, a not unlikely scenario. Together with thrombin activation by a further protease this would then give a simple three-component system sufficient to cause blood clotting. This simple mechanism alone would have given the first vertebrates using it an immense selective advantage, and the system would have therefore been passed on to many prog-eny. Other steps in the cascade may have been added later as incremental components, most likely because of gene duplica-tion as discussed above, gradually building up to the multi-component speedy system that is used in our bodies today.

So, far from being a 'black box', blood clotting mechanisms actually provide rather striking illustrations of the way in which multi-component systems can assemble by Darwinian mechanisms. The key point to remember is that such systems do not assemble all at once in a single organism (which really would be remarkable), but rather that each component is already present in order to carry out a different task altogether.

There are many examples in biology of 'moonlighting proteins' – proteins that carry out quite different tasks depending on whether they are inside the cell or outside, on the particular tissue in which they are located, or even on which specific location they occupy inside a cell[189].

For example, there is one enzyme called phosphoglucose isomerase which plays a key role in energy metabolism, but it also has at least four other quite different additional functions. This enzyme has probably been around in evolution for more than a billion years, because it is present in all the three major branches of life – the eukaryotes (like us), eubacteria (bugs) and archaea. So it has had plenty of time to be used for other functions. By bringing two or three proteins together that already exist for other functions, a simple system can be formed to do a specific job like blood clotting that gives the individual organism expressing that particular set of genes a big selective advantage. Later on in evolution, further components can be added to the system incrementally to make it more sophisticated.

Once a really efficient system is established in evolution, then organisms are naturally loathe to let it go. The vertebrate blood clotting system has remained very stable now for the last 400 million years of evolution that separate us from the puffer fish[190]. If there's a good system on board, why change it? Our own bodies are littered with molecules that go way back in evolutionary time, but are now used for quite different functions. For example, acetylcholine is a key neurotransmitter that we need for our nerves to talk to our muscles, but we can find acetylcholine also in plants and bacteria – which clearly have no muscles!

Receptors and ligands

Other examples are gradually being uncovered, showing the ways in which complex systems evolve. One of the conundrums that Behe sometimes highlights is the relationship between a receptor and its activating trigger. Receptors are the proteins embedded in cell membranes that transmit signals into the cell from the outside. To do this, another molecule, known as a 'ligand', has to bind very tightly to the receptor and trigger the signal. The chemical messengers circulating in our bloodstream known as hormones are typical ligands for different receptors. Since both the receptor and its ligand are necessary to be useful, how do they evolve together? It seems a typical chicken-and-egg situation. The answer in at least some cases seems to be the co-option of proteins already there followed by the loss of other competing ligands. For example, aldosterone is a hormone in our own bodies that binds to the mineralocorticoid receptor (MR), providing an important system for the regulation of electrolyte balance. The MR is very similar to the glucocorticoid receptor (GR) which in most vertebrates binds the stress hormone cortisol. Genetic tree analysis indicates that the gene duplication event leading to the GR and the MR took place more than 450 million years ago after the divergence of the jawless fishes. The GR binds cortisol really well, but a closely related hormone can also bind MR somewhat, so it can have some useful function even if aldosterone is not around. Indeed evolution of the ability to synthesise aldosterone is a relatively recent event, and this ability is found only in the tetrapods (animals that live on land). It has now been shown that the specificity of aldosterone for the MR rather than the GR is due to changes in just two amino acids[191]. By a process of 'ancestral gene resurrection' it has also been shown that these two tiny changes bestow upon GR the property of tight binding to aldosterone. So, long before aldosterone itself evolved, the mineralocorticoid receptor's ability to bind aldosterone was present as a structural by-product of its partnership with chemically similar, more ancient ligands. The authors of the paper describing this work suggest the term 'molecular exploitation' for this process of co-opting genes already present in the genome for new tasks.

Designer-of-the-gaps?

Though each supposedly 'irreducibly complex' system is proposed by ID proponents as being, in principle, inexplicable by normal evolutionary mechanisms, all we need to do is wait for a decade or so, often less, and a coherent evolutionary account begins to emerge. As Dembski admits 'If for every instance of biological complexity some mechanism could readily be produced that accounts for it, Intelligent Design would drop out of scientific discussion'.[192] This is a frank admission that the 'argument from ignorance' is a dangerous hostage to fortune. Remember that the 'design inference', and therefore the existence of a 'designer', is pinned in the central ID argument to the supposed inability of evolutionary mechanisms to be able, in principle, to explain the entity in question. As soon as more data come along, the argument for the designer then rapidly vaporises. In any case, once we agree (as several leading ID proponents do) that natural selection can explain some biological systems, but not others, then we have already agreed that complex systems can develop through Darwinian processes, so the argument from irreducible complexity then looks very weak.

It is not for nothing, therefore, that this central plank of the ID position has been accused of being a 'designer-of-the-gaps' argument, analogous to the much discredited 'god-of-the-gaps' argument in which 'god' is used as an explanation for some mystery that science cannot yet explain. Of course as science continues to advance, the supposed mystery then disappears, and the notion of 'god' gradually shrinks. The only difference here is that ID proposes an ill-defined 'designer' in the gap of our present ignorance. Of course many of ID's proponents do as a matter of fact believe that the creator God of the Bible has brought everything into being and sustains it, but they also believe that only through the gaps in our present knowledge do we have incontrovertible evidence that God is at work in design. Anyone holding to the robust biblical theism that we have been promoting throughout this book should find such an argument unnecessary.

If God is the author of the whole created order, as the Bible teaches, bringing about its origins and daily sustaining creation in all its myriad details, then all we scientists can do is to describe what God does, to the best of our ability. The point was well put by Augustine back in the early fifth century in the context of his discussion of miracles in a passage that we have cited in part already, when he wrote that 'When such a thing happens, it appears to us as an event contrary to nature. But with God it is not so; for him 'nature' is what he does'.[193]

The history of science is full of examples where people thought they had encountered a completely insoluble mystery, or thought that science could not advance any further, only for that mystery to be resolved, if not that decade, then maybe a century or so later. As Lord Kelvin pontificated in a speech to the British Association for the Advancement of Science around 1900, a few years before Einstein made his great discoveries: 'There is nothing new to be discovered in physics now. All that remains is more and more precise measurement'.

Darwin himself referred to the origin of species as 'the mystery of mysteries', but we have already seen in this book how the origin of species is actually now not all that mysterious, although of course that does not mean that our knowledge is complete, far from it. In Darwin's day the mechanism of inheritance was completely opaque and no one at that stage could possibly have imagined that the units of inheritance were strings of nucleotide bases contained within the molecule we now call DNA. In science we learn the wisdom of saying 'never say never'. Surprises are always round the corner, so making theological investments based on our present scientific ignorance is never a smart move.

Some Christians become nervous at this very rapid advance in the sciences, because they feel that this will somehow crowd out other types of explanation. But remember that there are many different types of explanation for this complex reality that we call life, and these levels are complementary, not rivals to each other. There are aesthetic, moral, legal, relational, sociological, political, historical and many other types of valid understandings of life in addition to the scientific and theological levels of understanding, and we need them all. For the Christian it is the theological 'upper level' explanations that encompass all the others and give them ultimate meaning in the overall scope of God's purposes for creation in general and for us in particular.

The idea of 'irreducible complexity', with its associated idea of a 'design inference', is actually very sterile for science and indeed, as we shall discuss further below, forms no part of scientific thought. Imagine that I have a PhD student in my laboratory, to whom I have given the task of working out a complex biochemical signalling pathway in the white blood cells that defend our bodies against viruses, but after a couple of years of hard work the student comes into my office saying 'I'm terribly sorry, I've worked on this project really hard for two years, but the signalling pathway just has too many components to analyse properly, so I think it's irreducibly complex and must be designed'. I will leave the subsequent conversation to your imagination, but the outcome would certainly include the student's being sent back to the laboratory to try a bit harder! Calling something 'designed' would not help to generate a set of experiments to test the hypothesis. How would my PhD student test the idea in the laboratory that the biochemical signalling pathway in question is designed? How could such an idea be falsified? Unless ideas in the biological sciences field are testable, leading on to a fruitful research programme, then they are sterile and in fact form no part of the scientific enterprise.

Ironically, as noted above, there is a core idea in ID, falsified in certain specific cases and inherent in 'irreducible complexity', that the individual components of the system do not have separate, independent functions. The case of the bacterial flagellum demonstrates that this core idea has been falsified, because there are modules within the flagellum that do have independent functions. The philosopher Karl Popper famously delineated potential falsification as one of the demarcation lines distinguishing science from non-science. If there are no data that could, in principle, falsify a theory, claimed Popper, then it has no place in science.

But before ID proponents jump on this as support for the idea that ID is a scientific theory after all, on the grounds that 'irreducible complexity' has been falsified in the case of the flagellum (and other cases besides), it is worth remembering that 'one swallow does not make a spring'. The potential to be falsified is a necessary but not sufficient ground for something to count as a scientific theory. For example, the theory that the planets exert baleful effects on human destinies is, in principle, falsifiable, but that does not in itself make the theory scientific (in the twenty-first century). Theories are accepted by scientists as being scientific when they have the potential to count as better explanations than other theories (a potential open to further experimental testing). This is why a theory which may have been counted as scientific in the seventeenth century may no longer be counted as a valid theory today – it was long ago tested, found wanting, and then discarded.

Has ID generated a research programme?

I read Behe's book *Darwin's Black Box* soon after it was published in 1996. There I read that the discovery that intelligent design had been at work in generating complex biochemical mechanisms 'must be ranked as one of the greatest achievements in the history of science': 'the discovery rivals those of Newton and Einstein, Lavoisier and Schroedinger, Pasteur and Darwin'[194]. Bold claims indeed, to put it mildly. Such a purported scientific breakthrough must surely lead to a fruitful research programme generating thousands of publications in the scientific literature?

To find out I went to PubMed, one of the most comprehensive of the scientific literature databases. It takes only a few seconds to scan all the millions of scientific papers in PubMed. I put in the phrases 'irreducible complexity' or 'irreducibly complex' and was able to find just seven examples where these appear in either the title or the abstract of peer-reviewed scientific papers[195]. In none of these cases were the phrases used in the sense that ID proponents give to them. In fact one was about nursing interventions in hospitals that apparently generate situations of 'irreducible complexity' – a somewhat alarming thought!

Surely, I reasoned, Behe himself would be generating a fruitful research programme centred around his idea of 'irreducible complexity'? I therefore searched in PubMed for publications from his laboratory, but could find only four peer-reviewed papers (which are the only ones that count in science); and none of these mention the concept in either the title or the abstract, nor indeed was the concept the topic of the paper[196]. So in more than a decade of scientific endeavour, the notion of 'irreducible complexity' does not appear to have generated a fruitful scientific research programme. Simply pointing out presumed difficulties in Darwinian explanations does not in itself count as scientific theory construction – a 'design inference' is not necessary to carry out such a critique and in itself it adds nothing to the discussion. All biologists know that there is much more work to do on evolutionary theory – and are thankful that this is the case, otherwise some would be out of a job!

ID proponents are quick to suggest that there is a conspiracy amongst editors of journals to prevent the publication of such material. But as I mentioned in the context of the same complaint from creationists, anyone who made well-substantiated discoveries significantly undermining the theory of evolution as currently understood, be they creationist or an ID proponent, would not only be able to publish those findings in the top journals, but would find themselves justly famous.

In reality, however, the 'design inference' forms no part of the practice of science for the two basic reasons surveyed. First, simply saying that something is 'designed' in biology leads to no increase in our understanding of the relationships between the various material components that make up living matter. Second, labelling a biological entity as 'designed' leads to no experimental programme that could be utilised to test the hypothesis.

In response to such criticisms, ID proponents normally cite methods of investigation such as archaeology, cryptography and forensic science, or the SETI programme that looks for evidence for intelligent life elsewhere in the universe. Dembski often refers to the film *Contact* in which the heroine (Jodie Foster) detects a pattern of signals from outer space that could only be interpreted as a sign of intelligence. Surely, so the argument goes, such scientific investigations show that looking for signs of intelligence is part of science? Well, sure, in a relevant context. But these are all examples where we already know that purposive human behaviours, or purposeful actions by potential little green men, are involved, so we are not surprised at finding evidence for such behaviour, at least when it comes to items such as archaeology and forensic science. Likewise we need the background knowledge that scientists would tend to send each other sequences of prime numbers in communicating from outer space. But these kinds of analogies are, I would suggest, simply irrelevant for understanding biological entities. For analogies to work there must be at least some connection between the two entities being compared. It is not all obvious to me, however, why the SETI programme should have anything to do with understanding the origins of the flagellum, and nor is a sequence of prime numbers as a potential intergalactic signal anything like DNA sequences. This is comparing apples and oranges. Each branch of scientific enquiry needs to be pursued using the methods and tools that are relevant for that particular discipline.

Coming back to earth to reflect on biological complexity, many people are understandably impressed when they read in the ID literature of the huge improbabilities involved in biochemical systems coming into being 'by chance'. But what the reader might easily miss is that the calculations are based on the whole system self-assembling all in one go. If we calculate the chances of a module comprising 30 components, for example, self-assembling by chance, then obviously this is an event with an infinitesimally small probability. But this is tilting at windmills. No scientist believes that this is the way that evolution works. Instead evolution works incrementally, each co-opted component or sub-module, as we have seen in the case of the flagellum, being added in stages, each stage giving some selective advantage to the organism in question.

So what we have in ID is the 'fallacy of large numbers': mathematicians assigning improbability numbers to things because they don't really understand the underlying biology. In fact I could very easily argue that all biological systems without exception are, in one sense, 'irreducibly complex' – that is just another definition for life. Thousands of gene products are needed to generate a cell. There is no such thing as a 'simple cell' or a 'simple biochemical pathway'. All are multicomponent systems that function properly only if all the components are present together. For sure, some are more complex than others, but any one system can be defined as 'irreducibly complex' by Behe's definition, so the notion becomes redundant because in reality it fails to distinguish one biological entity from another.

The scientific claims of the ID movement give further cause for concern in that the science presented can itself sometimes be wrong, let alone its interpretation. For example, Behe discusses at some length in his book *The Edge of Evolution* the evolution of resistance to the drug chloroquine that occurs in the malarial parasite *Plasmodium*. It does indeed provide a good example of evolution in action. Behe notes from the literature that two different mutations have to occur in the same gene in order to generate chloroquine resistance. Based on a report that such resistance occurs spontaneously in 1 out of 10^{20} parasites, Behe then applies this to human evolution, claiming that 'for humans to achieve a mutation like this by chance, we would need to wait a hundred million times ten million years'. But the calculation is based on fallacious premises. What Behe has done is to calculate the chances that these two exact mutations occur in the same gene in the same germ cell of a specific individual, certainly a very unlikely scenario. But even in his chosen example of *Plasmodium*, there is good evidence that chloroquine resistance occurs by sequential, not simultaneous mutations[197]. There can be a number of different mutational routes to drug resistance, just as there can to functional genetic variation more generally. Calculations of probability look very different when changes occur sequentially and incrementally.

Overall I'm afraid that this chapter has been rather negative, but sometimes it is necessary to clear the decks of unhelpful ideas, as I believe ID to be, in order to focus on something more useful. The more we look at Darwinian evolution taken as a whole, the more it seems to display precisely the signs of intelligence that ID proponents believe are located in those hidden non-Darwinian gaps. When we visit an art gallery, we often need to stand well back from a big canvas to appreciate the painting as a whole. This is now what we will do with evolution, and it is remarkable what patterns then begin to emerge.

Chapter 15

Evolution – Intelligent and Designed?

Given that the core tenets of Intelligent Design do not appear to be part of contemporary science, does ID fare any better as philosophy or theology? So far we have been using the word 'design' as if its meaning were unambiguous, but this is far from being the case. Like the multifaceted word 'chance', the word 'design' comes in many flavours and needs careful definition if we are to have a useful conversation.

It is understandable that most Christians feel instinctively positive when they hear the term 'intelligent design' used. After all, we believe in a creator God who is supremely intelligent and most Christians are familiar with the classic 'arguments from design' whereby the wonder, beauty and order of the universe are, quite rightly, cited as evidence for God's handiwork. 'The heavens declare the glory of God; the skies proclaim the work of his hands' (Psalm 19:1). Ironically the earliest place where I have found the phrase 'intelligent design' used in the literature (there may well be earlier instances) is in a lecture by James McCosh, president of the future Princeton University, and already quoted back in Chapter Seven, where McCosh uses the phrase to refer to God's creative actions in the process of Darwinian natural selection. So the term seems to have been undergoing its own evolution of meaning during the intervening years!

The meanings of design

Words are defined by their usage and the word 'design' is generally used with three rather distinct meanings in mind:

- Meaning A: **An arrangement of form and appearance, with overtones of purpose.** Look at some bacteria (under the microscope), or birds, or cats. They seem to know what they're doing – feeding, multiplying, building their nests, being a nuisance always on the wrong side of the door, and so forth, so we can readily say that they're biologically 'designed' for that purpose. But when we look at some rocks, they don't seem to be doing much, so we wouldn't usually think about using the word 'designed' for rocks. So in biological systems 'design' with meaning A is used to refer to the relationships between properties, form and function.
- Meaning B is **Specific detailed plan**. This is the language of the engineer, architect or clothes designer. There is clearly a mind here that specifies a plan rather precisely. The engineer has to get the specification just right, otherwise the bridge or building will fall down.
- Meaning C is **To have intentions and purposes**. It is the language of agency and of intentionality, the language of authorship. It is what J.K. Rowling has in mind when she writes out the notes for seven Harry Potter novels yet to be written – the details may change as she goes along, but the ending was always clear from the beginning: the wicked Voldemort would always get his comeuppance.

Where does ID belong in this range of meanings? It is a specialised subset of meaning B. Dembski perceives his 'design inference' as identifying those 'irreducibly complex' entities in biology that display 'specified complexity', which, it is suggested, could not have arisen by the kind of incremental steps that are involved in the evolutionary process. The 'design inference' then forms the basis for arguing for the existence of a 'designer' that plays the role envisaged in meaning B. There are, however, three problems with this approach, the first two philosophical, and the third theological.

The first problem – argument from ignorance

There is a much-used form of argument in the ID literature that goes like this. Here is a complex biological phenomenon like the flagellum or blood clotting. Does it display law-like behaviour, for example like the lipid membrane at the surface of cells spontaneously assembling due to the intrinsic proper- ties of lipids (an example of Behe's)? No? Then can its assem- bly be explained by a 'chance evolutionary process'? No? Then we are left with the only third alternative possible, and that is 'design'. This argument is put forward as 'an empirical method for detecting intelligence in nature'.

Apart from the obvious fact that, taken as a whole, evolution is not a 'chance process' as we have already emphasised, the rest of the argument is quite fallacious because it is based on an 'argument from ignorance'. The ID proponents are saying that because we don't know exactly how a complex entity evolved, therefore it didn't evolve, therefore it was 'designed'. But that is a non sequitur. We could equally well say, perhaps with more honesty, that if we cannot currently explain the exis- tence of some biological entity by law-like properties or evolu- tion, then we are just ignorant as to how it came into being and should do more experimental work to find out. Use of the word 'design' in this context is not an explanation for anything, just another word for ignorance.

The second problem – category error

The second significant philosophical problem that arises from the ID use of the word 'design' is that it reflects a 'category error' in the use of language. One invariably ends up in a mud- dle if metaphysical language and scientific descriptions are mingled.

Science began to make real progress from the seventeenth century onwards because the natural philosophers, like those in the early Royal Society, decided to focus on understanding the properties of the physical world without recourse to the type of teleological explanations that were so familiar in Greek philosophy – explanations that sought final goals and pur- poses, rather than the actual properties of things. As we have noted, this was not at all because the new natural philosophers denied that everything in God's world has an ultimate goal, far from it, just that to get the scientific job done it was necessary to focus on physical explanations for things. There is no doubt that this approach has been hugely successful.

To now assign the word 'design' to some biological entity is an attempt to introduce the language of Aristotelian teleology back into science, and many centuries of endeavour suggest that the attempt will be sterile. In scientific terms it simply doesn't count as an explanation for anything for, as already noted, it makes no predictions and leads to no experiments.

That 'the Emperor has no clothes' at this point is readily shown by asking ID proponents about how and when this supposed design was injected by the presumed designer into the biological process and at what stage. The type of answers given sound very like miraculous interventions, although ID writers are careful to say that they do not invoke the miraculous in their explanations.

Others speak of the designer 'front-loading' all the design information needed into the universe at the beginning, information which then 'materialises' at precisely the right point during biological development. But no explanation is given as to how such information can be preserved during the billions of years of the universe's history. This is what the scientific community calls 'arm waving'.

The third problem – the nature and identity of the designer

The third main problem with the ID notion of design is theological. ID proponents such as Dembski are explicit in denying that the detection of 'design' in biological phenomena necessarily points to the existence of the God of the Bible. As Dembski remarks, friends of ID include 'Buddhists, Hindus, New Age thinkers, Jungians, parapsychologists, vitalists, Platonists and honest agnostics, to name but a few', and ID 'doesn't even require that there be a God'[198]. 'In particular', writes Dembski, 'ID does not depend on the biblical account of creation'[199]. Therefore in inferring a 'designer' from the ID notion of 'design', without the benefit of biblical revelation, it is difficult to avoid the idea of a designer-God like a heavenly engineer who occasionally tinkers around with the creation that he has brought into being. But this is really nothing like the biblical revelation of God as Creator, the author of everything that exists, who is sovereign over every aspect of the created order. Indeed, the idea of God as 'designer' in this engineering sense is not found in the Bible, and the word 'design' is barely used. In the English of the NIV translation of the Bible, the words 'design', 'designs' or 'designed' are used 11 times in all, in every case with meaning B, referring to the design of the temple, or for 'machines designed by skilful men for use on the towers and on the corner defences to shoot arrows and hurl large stones' (2 Chronicles 26:15). This tells us that the idea of design with meaning B was around at the time, which makes it even more interesting that the idea was never applied as a metaphor for God's creative work. Personally, and this is certainly not intended as a slur on engineers, I am very relieved that I do not worship a heavenly engineer who occasionally tinkers around with the created order, but rather the God and Father of our Lord Jesus Christ who is the author of creation.

I think it is fair to conclude that ID is a form of reconstructed natural theology, indeed a very strong form, because at least in the hands of people like Dembski, the aim is to empirically demonstrate the existence of design, and so the designer, from science.

Natural theology is the attempt to demonstrate the existence of God, or in its strong form even some characteristics of God, based on the properties of the universe in general and our world in particular. The biblical basis for at least some form of natural theology is found in Paul's comment: 'Since the creation of the world God's invisible qualities – his eternal power and divine nature – have been clearly seen, being understood from what has been made, so that men are without excuse' (Romans 1:20). The whole point of the content of this passage is that everyone without exception could see the wonders of God's creation ('since what may be known about God is plain to them' verse 19), and should be able to draw the obvious conclusion that there was a divine power and nature behind this amazing and beautiful world, otherwise the punchline 'that men are without excuse' wouldn't be reasonable. Yet no one needs a PhD in biochemistry to conclude from the wonders of creation that there is a God. Phillip Johnson remarks that 'theists who believe that God is real should not assume that he never played a detectable role in biological creation', referring to the ID notion of 'design' in this context. 'Detectable'! Anybody anywhere in the world, from tribes living in the jungle (easier there) to city dwellers (maybe harder) can open their eyes to see what God has done, they don't need to study any formal biology.

But equally Paul makes it clear that the knowledge gained by this route of what we now call 'natural theology' is limited – which is why we need the rest of Romans (and the Bible!) to explain what kind of God this is and what he has done for us in Christ. So natural theology can take us as far as believing that there's a great divine power out there of some kind, but we then need the biblical revelation to take us on to know God as the personal God who loves us and saves us, the God who can be known only by faith.

So I find it worrying from a Christian perspective that ID proponents are so insistent that they do not look to Scripture for their core beliefs, but instead to a form of natural theology in which the God of the book of Romans is replaced by a vague 'designer'. One reason for this stance is the desire to present ID as a 'strictly scientific' idea in order to get it into US school classrooms. But the kind of design/designer argument being presented, which involves knowledge of the complex structures of biochemical systems, is entirely alien to the biblical concept of natural theology, in which the evidence for the existence of God's eternal power and divine nature is accessible to all.

ID and naturalism

Without reading far in the ID literature we find it is 'philosophical naturalism' which is the main target. No problem there: Christianity is inimical to philosophical naturalism. The problem begins, however, with Phillip Johnson's bad habit of using the words 'natural', 'naturalistic' and 'naturalism' quite differently from how those words are normally employed in philosophical discourse (in the arts the words are used with different meanings again, just to confuse matters).

We have already defined 'naturalism' in its philosophical sense in Chapter Eight as that 'view of the world that excludes the supernatural or spiritual'. Yet Phillip Johnson offers comments such as the following:

> It is conceivable that God for some reason did all the creating by apparently *naturalistic* processes, perhaps the better to test our faith, but surely this is not the only possibility. My writings, and those of colleagues like Michael Behe, argue that design is detectably present in biology, that *naturalistic* substitutes like the blind watchmaker mechanism are inadequate and contrary to the evidence...[200]

In the same book chapter Johnson also comments that 'theistic evolution can more accurately be described as theistic *naturalism*'[201]. But according to the dictionary understanding of 'naturalism', a term like 'theistic naturalism' is an oxymoron, that is, a contradiction in terms, like calling someone a 'fascist communist'. Christian theism, the kind of theism to which Johnson is referring in this passage, refers to the belief in a creator God who is the origin and sustainer of all that exists. So God cannot possibly create by 'apparently naturalistic processes' for the simple reason that if there is a God who creates, then there are no 'naturalistic processes' because naturalism is false. Except for the really postmodern (or the very confused) there can be no simultaneous belief in both God and naturalism.

In these and many other passages in his books Johnson draws a contrast between what he perceives to be the 'designed aspects' which can be recognised and detected against a backcloth of 'naturalistic explanations'. This contrast is made even more starkly in the writings of Behe, who writes:

> The laws of nature can organize matter – for example, water flow can build up silt sufficiently to dam a portion of a river, forcing it to change course. The most relevant laws are those

of biological reproduction, mutation, and natural selection. If a biological structure can be explained in terms of those natural laws, then we cannot conclude that it was designed[202].

This seems to be a very clear statement expressing the belief that there is a 'two-tier universe', one tier involving 'natural laws' and the other tier involving 'design'. Lest we be in any doubt about the interpretation of this statement, Behe gives the example of a cell as an illustration of what he means: 'Some features of the cell appear to be the result of simple natural processes, others probably so. Still other features were almost certainly designed. And with some features, we can be as confident that they were designed as that anything was'[203]. Once again Behe is drawing here a distinction between 'natural processes' which reflect 'natural laws', and entities that are 'designed'.

Showing that ID proponents are consistent in their claims on this point, Dembski comments that the '...design theorist is not committed to every biological structure being designed. Naturalistic mechanisms like mutation and selection do operate in natural history to adapt organisms to their environments'[204]. Again: 'If specified complexity is exhibited in actual biological systems, we are justified in attributing such systems to design. That's not to say that every aspect of such systems is designed. (Some aspects may be due to purely natural forces)'[205].

Here, as in the rest of his book, we see clearly that Dembski envisages a biological world largely explained by 'naturalistic mechanisms' and 'natural forces', and against this backcloth 'designed systems' may be detected. Indeed, without such a backcloth, the rest of his argument would make little sense, since if the identification of designed entities is to be possible, then a non-designed 'naturalistic' backcloth is essential to facilitate the detection of the 'designed' components.

Does all this matter, or is this beginning to sound like hair-splitting? Actually I think it matters a lot, because the ID literature gives the impression that there is something inherently 'naturalistic' about certain aspects of the created order and not about other aspects, and such thinking appears to stem from a very inadequate doctrine of creation. As we have been at pains to emphasise, in biblical creation theology, the natural order is seen as a seamless web of God's creative activity. All scientists can do is to describe God's creative activity to the best of their ability. Often their theories will be wrong and will need to be modified or discarded. But within this framework of a robust biblical theism, there is nothing in the created order without exception that is not created and sustained by God. Science is definitely not a naturalistic enterprise for the Christian who is a scientist. How could exploring God's world be a naturalistic endeavour!

Philosophical naturalism, like any philosophy, resides inside the heads of some people but not others, profoundly influencing their daily lives and work. It will do so irrespective of whether they are scientists, lawyers, factory workers, poets, car mechanics or whatever. One of the puzzling features of Johnson's writings is why he targets science as the evil empire which acts as the headquarters for philosophical naturalism – whereas I had always thought that 'honour' belonged to lawyers! The fact of the matter is that there are many Christians within the scientific community, far more than in the humanities, and the influence of Christian theology on the emergence of modern science has always given a first-cousinly feel to the relationship between the two enterprises. Thankfully people like Richard Dawkins form quite a rare species within the biological research community and even most of my secular colleagues deem him to be an extremist. Speaking personally I have never experienced any particular antagonism towards my Christian faith during nearly four decades within the biological research community. Science is a holy enterprise because it involves uncovering the wonders of God's creation. Let's keep it that way.

Is evolution designed?

I have been quite critical of trying to impose 'meaning B' of design on to biology: it didn't get Aristotle very far and it won't help us. But asking whether the evolutionary process is consistent with the 'meaning C' of design is a different question. Is evolution consistent with a God who has intentions and purposes for his creation? Scientists habitually use that little phrase 'consistent with' in the discussion sections of our scientific papers. We don't 'prove things' in biology, but we do gather data that can count for or against a theory. In a scientific paper we will argue (of course!) that the body of data presented is 'consistent with' our current favourite model.

There are of course some secular scientists who argue that evolution is not consistent with the idea of direction and purpose. According to the late palaeontologist Stephen Jay Gould, we are a 'momentary cosmic accident,' albeit a 'glorious accident.' Summing up his view, Gould writes: 'Wind back the tape of life to the early days of the Burgess Shale; let it play again from an identical starting point, and the chance becomes vanishingly small that anything like human intelligence would grace the replay'. This is a highly contingent view of evolution, suggesting that its consequences could have been completely otherwise, had it not been for a few critical chance events.

The philosopher Daniel Dennett agrees – asking whether the complexity of biological diversity can 'really be the outcome of nothing but a cascade of algorithmic processes feeding on chance? And if so, who designed that cascade?' Dennett answers his own rhetorical question by saying: 'Nobody. It is itself the product of a blind, algorithmic process'. 'Evolution is not a process that was designed to produce us'.

So Gould, Dennett and quite a collection of other popular commentators would like to insist that a proper understanding of the evolutionary process excludes any possibility of understanding it as displaying any evidence of plan or purpose. Are they right?

Well of course a Christian, as we have seen in this book, will find it perfectly possible to give a providentialist account of the evolutionary process by which God fulfils his perfect plan and purposes through biological history. The atheist, by contrast, has no basis for thinking that there might be an ultimate purpose in such an account. But the question I'd like to ask here is somewhat different. Does the evolutionary account display properties that are more consistent with a theistic or with an atheistic account of the world? I would like to suggest that recent biological discoveries clearly point to the theistic account as providing a more reasonable explanation for the existence of the overall story of evolution on planet earth, and I will give just a few examples of what I mean.

Intelligent evolution

In Chapters Three–Five, we showed that, taken as a whole, evolution is far from being a chance process. It is tightly organised and highly constrained.

For many years biologists incorporated the language of 'progress' into their scientific discourse. But after the development of the neo-Darwinian synthesis, the fusion of natural selection and genetics with the help of maths that took place in the 1920s and 1930s, evolutionary theory became a more rigorous science and the language of progress began to appear less frequently in the evolutionary literature, although biologists such as Julian Huxley still wrote books for a popular audience extolling the idea of evolutionary progress on a grand scale.

I think biologists were, and are, right to exclude teleological notions (ideas of ultimate goals) from their professional discourse. What I want from my car mechanic is to mend my car, not to discuss the best route to Edinburgh. Biologists need to get on with the job in hand in their professional work, not pontificate about its ultimate meaning in their scientific papers.

But once we stand back and look at evolutionary history as a whole, then the idea of progress is inescapable. As Sean Carroll, a well-known evolutionary biologist from the University of Wisconson-Madison, remarks in a review in *Nature*: 'Life's contingent history could be viewed as an argument against any direction or pattern in the course of evolution or the shape of life. But it is obvious that larger and more complex life forms have evolved from simple unicellular ancestors and that various innovations were necessary for the evolution of new means of living'. Carroll chooses his words carefully, but if pressed every biologist has to admit that multicellular organisms *are* more complex than bacteria, that mammals *are* in some sense more advanced than yeast, and that the human brain has more capacities than that of a shrew. So it is perverse to deny some form of directionality to the arrow of biological time.

One interesting observation is that underlying biological complexity we discover networking principles that are turning out to be fewer and simpler than they might have been. Given that in every cell complex networks of interactions occur between thousands of metabolites, proteins and DNA, this is quite surprising.

As Uri Alon from the Weizmann Institute comments:

> ...Biological networks seem to be built, to a good approximation, from only a few types of patterns called network motifs...The same small set of network motifs, discovered in bacteria, have been found in gene-regulation networks across diverse organisms, including plants and animals. Evolution seems to have 'rediscovered' the same motifs again and again in different systems...[206]

In this respect it is interesting to see, in the recent scientific literature, challenges to Gould's idea of an extreme contingency operating in the evolutionary process. In reality it doesn't look like that: the mechanisms of life look highly constrained, far more than we ever realised even a decade or so ago.

Take proteins, for example, recalling that there are 20 different amino acids in a protein which can easily be several hundred amino acids long. In principle this could generate an astronomically huge number of different protein structures. With more than 300 genome sequences now available from different organisms, and with the 3-D structures of thousands of proteins now solved, it is a striking fact that if we examine all the known proteins in the world, and their structural motifs, based on all the genomes that have been sequenced so far, we find that the great majority can be assigned to only 1,400 protein domain families. About 200 of these domains are common to all kingdoms of life. In other words, all living things are united, not only by having the same genetic code, but also by possessing an elegant and highly restricted set of protein structures. Only this particular set, presumably, will carry out all the various functions that are required for proteins to organise the biochemical processes of life.

Those looking at the evolution of specific proteins have also been impressed by the highly constrained way in which their structures have been achieved. A research group from Harvard published a paper in 2006 entitled 'Darwinian evolution can follow only very few mutational paths to fitter proteins'[207]. It is intriguing to read the final sentence of their abstract: 'We conclude that much protein evolution will be similarly constrained. This implies that the protein tape of life may be largely reproducible and even predictable'. Until recently, to talk about evolution as being in any sense 'predictable' would have been deemed heretical in the scientific literature, so it is interesting to see the language creep back in, forced simply by what scientists are observing by looking at the mechanisms of life.

Here is a further example of that trend. So-called 'fitness landscapes' play an important role in evolutionary discourse. These traditionally represent topographical pictures of the adaptation of different populations to local ecological niches, visualised in the same way that three-dimensional models can be used to give a good idea of mountainous areas like the Alps. The peaks represent those areas of 'optimal fitness' at which a population is well adapted to its particular environment.

The concept of 'fitness landscapes' can also be applied to enzyme structure and function, as Figure 19 illustrates. Enzymes are the proteins that catalyse the processes of life. Again it turns out that the evolutionary pathways to arrive at a particular function of a particular enzyme are remarkably constrained. In other words, there are only a few ways to arrive at a particular protein function because only some mutations will get you there and not others. It is as if an evolutionary path is laid out in front of the gene encoding the enzyme, and the genetic dice keeps being thrown until the enzyme structure is generated that optimises fitness for its particular function. This is no random process, each step along the way being preserved by benefits to the organism that uses the enzyme. As the authors conclude in a recent paper in *Nature*: 'That only a few paths are favored also implies that evolution might be more reproducible than is commonly perceived, or even be predictable'[208].

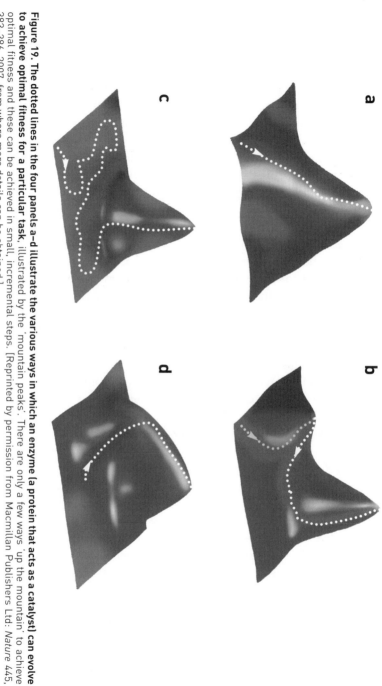

Figure 19. The dotted lines in the four panels a–d illustrate the various ways in which an enzyme (a protein that acts as a catalyst) can evolve to achieve optimal fitness for a particular task, illustrated by the 'mountain peaks'. There are only a few ways 'up the mountain' to achieve optimal fitness and these can be achieved in small, incremental steps. [Reprinted by permission from Macmillan Publishers Ltd: *Nature* 445, 383–386, 2007, from where more details can be obtained.]

The 'evolution of evolvability' is one of the trendy areas of current biological research. In other words: what kind of molecular systems have to develop in order to give rise to all the biological diversity that we see today? How can there be such diversity between different mammals, like humans, chimpanzees and mice, despite the fact that we all possess a mere 20,000–25,000 genes? The answer is that the emergence of new species only rarely seems to involve much in the way of radical changes in proteins, but has a lot to do with how different 'systems modules' are connected together[209]. Existing regulatory circuits are employed in new ways in the evolution of feathers, insect wings, butterfly eye-spots and much else besides[210]. This involves the use of adaptor and docking proteins that are used to join up signalling pathways inside cells. If you have ever played with a Lego kit, then you will have a good feel for how cellular signalling pathways operate, with the outside of the cell being connected to the inside by means of 'receptors'. The evolvability of biological systems is helped along by the key 'connecting pieces' that enable the 'Lego modules' to link together to form many different complexes displaying different functions.

The phenomenon of 'convergence' in evolution also highlights the way in which the process taken as a whole displays evidence of order and constraint. Convergence refers to the repeated evolution in independent lineages of the same biochemical pathway, or organ or structure. It has been recognised for a long time in evolutionary biology, and recently dramatically highlighted by Simon Conway Morris, professor of palaeobiology at Cambridge University, by gathering together hundreds of examples of convergence in his book *Life's Solution – Inevitable Humans in a Lonely Universe*[211].

As Conway Morris remarks: 'Convergence offers a metaphor as to how evolution navigates the combinatorial immensities of biological "hyperspace"'[212]. For example, the convergence of mimicry of insects and spiders to an ant morphology has evolved at least 70 times independently. The technique of retaining the egg in the mother prior to a live birth is thought to have evolved separately about 100 times amongst lizards and snakes alone. Compound and camera eyes taken together have evolved more than 20 different times during the course of evolution. If you live in a planet of light and darkness, then you need eyes – so that's what you're going to get!

One of the most remarkable, and readily visible, examples of convergence is illustrated by the similarities between the marsupials that have evolved separately in Australia and South America, many of which look very similar to their equivalent placental counterparts in other parts of the world. It was only a few million years ago that the Isthmus of Panama joined together North and South America, whereas Australia started separating from Antarctica about 100 million years ago.

Marsupials are animals like kangaroos and wombats that give rise to less developed young and suckle them in an external pouch, whereas placentals are animals that nourish their young to a later developmental stage in the uterus before birth. Many Australian marsupials find their placental counterparts in Africa, each species looking quite similar because it has evolved to fill up similar ecological niches. Other marsupials are found in South America and likewise have their counterparts elsewhere. Figure 20 illustrates the striking similarities between the dagger-like teeth of the placental sabre-tooth cat (lower) and the marsupial equivalent found in South America (upper, known as thylacosmilids), yet the sabre-tooth in both cases has evolved quite independently. If a big cat is to be an efficient hunter in a particular environment, then these are the teeth it might well get.

In a commentary on Gould's idea of ultimate randomness in evolutionary history, Conway Morris writes that it is '...now widely thought that the history of life is little more than a contingent muddle punctuated by disastrous mass extinctions that in spelling the doom of one group so open the doors of opportunity to some other mob of lucky-chancers. ...Rerun the tape of the history of life... and the end result will be an utterly different biosphere. Most notably there will be nothing remotely like a human...Yet, what we know of evolution suggests the exact reverse: convergence is ubiquitous and the constraints of life make the emergence of the various biological properties [e.g. intelligence] very probable, if not inevitable'[213].

So the rolling of the genetic dice in evolution is a wonderful

Figure 20. Evolutionary convergence in the sabre tooth between the marsupial species (upper panel) and the placental cat (lower panel). Copyright Marlene Hill Donnelly [the Field Museum, Chicago], with permission, reproduced from Figure 10 of Marshall, L.G. 'The Great American Interchange – an invasion induced crisis for South American Mammals, pp. 133–229, in *Biotic crises in ecological and evolutionary Time*, edited by M.H. Nitecki [Academic Press, Orlando, Florida].

TIME

= Non-productive genomes

= Genomes that work

Figure 21. The World of Genomic 'Design Space'.

way of generating both novelty and diversity, but at the same time it appears to be restrained by necessity to a relatively limited number of living entities. If we live in a universe with this kind of physics and chemistry, and on a planet with these particular properties, then what we see is what we are likely to get. If we imagine design space in the evolutionary process as a matrix of billions of little grey boxes, as Figure 21 illustrates, each box representing a possible genome, then the number of black boxes that can be filled successfully appears to be really small. In other words, only a relatively tiny number of genomes will generate organisms that can flourish in the different ecological niches on planet earth, and the evolutionary process keeps 'finding' these again and again. The black boxes indicate the evolutionary lineages leading to the various animals and plants that we see around us on the planet today.

So we are living in an ordered universe, not at all a random universe, but an anthropically fruitful one in which there is a biological narrative culminating in us as its observers. We cannot really say, on a purely scientific basis, that the biological diversity we observe is 'inevitable' – for our experience of life's existence is based on exactly one example – but since the universe is likely to have a uniform biochemistry, the data so far would suggest that life anywhere in the universe might look rather similar.

Evolutionary history on this planet displays overall increased complexity, genomic constraint and convergence. This seems to be more consistent with a providentialist account for the overall meaning of biological diversity, including ourselves, in which God has intentions and purposes for the created order, and render less plausible the claims made by Gould, Dennett and others that evolutionary history is a totally random walk that might have ended up quite differently.

In fact it is intriguing to note that just as Christians have often utilised the disastrous god-of-the-gaps type arguments, as already discussed, seeking to place their argument for God in the present gaps in our scientific knowledge, so it is possible that here we have an 'atheism-of-the-gaps' type of argument in which atheists seek to support their disbelief in God based on interpretations of scientific data which appear initially plausible due to lack of knowledge about the data, but appear less believable as our understanding of the process – in this case the evolutionary process – becomes more complete.

To my mind the most recent findings from evolutionary biology are more consistent with the plan-like theistic account that the Bible reveals to us, than with an atheistic account in which the existence of such an ordered, constrained, directional history of life must always remain anomalous. There seems to be a biological anthropic principle that is parallel to the anthropic principle in physics pointing to the fine-tuning of the physical constants of the universe that are just right for life to exist. In biology it is beginning to look as if the whole system is set up in such a highly organised way that the emergence of intelligent life was inevitable. The ID proponents would be much better off in spending their time expounding the 'intelligence' of those aspects of the created order that we do understand from a scientific perspective, rather than focusing on the bits that we don't.

Chapter 16
The Origin of Life

When I read the *Boys' Own* stories of my youth, there was always a 'last redoubt' (usually in a cave halfway up a cliff or other likely spot) where the heroes would hole up to make a last-ditch stand against the invading hordes. The origin of life and of the biological information needed to make living things function, seems to play this kind of role in the creationist and ID literature. Even if Darwinian natural selection succeeds in explaining the evolutionary history of all living organisms that contain DNA: 'Well tell me where does the DNA come from – tell me that!' is a commonly heard retort.

Now at present we have very little idea as to where the DNA does come from, although that doesn't mean that we have no idea at all, and we shall look at some of the ideas and the research in a moment. In any case does the outcome matter theologically?

I would like to suggest that theologically it doesn't matter two hoots whether we ever manage to understand the origin of life scientifically or not. The simple reason is that God's work in creation is not dependent upon whether we understand it or not. Imagine that you were living in the time of Darwin when no one had a clue about the genetic mechanisms involving DNA, the whole process of inheritance was a big 'black box', and a further century was to go by before the situation became clearer with the elucidation of the structure of DNA in the early 1950s. As Christians, in what period might we have been more amazed at God's creation: in 1855 when nothing was known about the mechanisms of inheritance, or in 1955 when the discovery of DNA's properties had led to remarkable breakthroughs in such understanding? 1955 gets my vote! Thank God people in earlier generations didn't simply throw up their arms when faced with the deep mystery of inheritance and say 'it's designed!', but instead got down to the hard work of finding out how God did it.

Yet one still reads, in the ID literature, of the impossibility that life could emerge out of chemicals by sinister sounding 'blind, materialistic, naturalistic forces'. But wait a minute, these are God's chemicals, God's materials, that are being talked about here. A mystery bigger than the origin of life is why Christians should ascribe pagan-sounding characteristics to God's world. Is this God's world or isn't it? Imagine going into an artist's studio, seeing the tubes of paint arranged in neat rows on one side, and then telling the artist 'you've chosen the wrong type of paints, they're really hopeless!' I think we would all agree that would be insulting. But to confidently proclaim that the precious materials God has so carefully brought into being in the dying moments of exploding stars do not have the potentiality to bring about life, seems to me equally insulting. Christianity, in a sense, is a very materialistic religion. We believe that all the materials of the universe without exception are God's materials. 'Who are you, oh man', to tell God what potentialities are or are not built into his materials? (echoing Romans 9:20, albeit in a rather different context). All we'll ever come up with anyway, if ever, is a detailed step-by-step description as to how God did it.

In fact scientific study of the origin of life has only really taken off in the past half a century. One reason for this slow start is that biochemistry is a relatively recent discipline and the scientific tools and concepts to even begin to address the problem only developed from the 1950s onwards. Space exploration and astrobiology, the identification of organic materials and the search for life on other planets, have also given a huge boost to the field.

A more philosophical problem, known as vitalism, also retarded the research field in earlier years. This was the idea, with very deep historical roots, that the *élan vital*, to use the expression of Henri Bergson (in 1907), infused all living things, distinguishing them from brute matter. This idea became quite popular in the first half of the twentieth century (and remains popular in New Age circles), inhibiting interest in further research. In some ways vitalism acted like ID, retarding further scientific investigation, because if there is a mysterious force that 'explains' living matter, then what experiments would there be to test that?

The ID fascination with generating highly improbable numbers is as unhelpful as the notion of vitalism. John Lennox, for example, is well aware of the dangers of the 'god-of-the-gaps' arguments, and yet still believes that the origin of life and of biological complexity represents a 'gap' in principle and not in practice, that can never be filled except by invoking the notion of a designer, a notion that effectively labels this view as a form of episodic creationism[214]. The reason Lennox is so convinced about this point is that if we calculate the chances of complex things coming into being by random processes then it is very improbable that this will happen. Of course. We all agree on that. If the usual set of monkeys are set to work randomly typing on keyboards, then little progress is made.

All this does is provide the challenging parameters within which scientists engaged in origin of life research have to work. No one in the field believes that life started with complex molecules like proteins or DNA, as Lennox seems to think, so all the calculations about huge improbabilities are a waste of time. If something is highly improbable, then most likely it didn't happen that way (although it may have done), and it leaves the challenge to researchers in the field to get on with the hard work of finding out how it did happen. Why do creationists and ID folk spend so much time tilting at windmills?

Origin of life research

This is a big enough topic to fill a book on its own, so all I will attempt here is to flag up some of the ways in which origin of life research is being carried out, showing that the problem is not insoluble in principle[215]. Whether it will eventually prove to be soluble in practice is a moot point and it is best to keep an open mind on the question.

Even if scientists manage to come up with a convincing

sequence of chemical and biochemical steps leading from basic organic chemicals to a living system, we would still be left wondering whether that was the way it actually happened back at the beginning. As already emphasised, we certainly don't have as yet a convincing set of steps of that kind: this is a real gap in our current scientific knowledge, make no mistake about it.

Also remember that origin of life studies are not really part of evolutionary biology, which focuses on the transmission of heritable traits by means of DNA, but belong more to the research area of chemists, biophysicists, geophysicists and biochemists. One of the fun aspects of this field of investigation is that it brings together so many different disciplines. Personally, however, I'm glad that it's not my field, believing in the late immunologist Peter Medawar's dictum that science is about 'the art of the soluble'. Since life is short, I prefer to tackle scientific problems which have some possibility of success in my lifetime, but on the other hand I admire scientists who 'boldly go' into areas where the chances of success are not that high. Funding in this area, we may not be surprised to hear, is more abundant in the USA and is often linked to NASA and its space exploration programme. My own guess is that it will take at least another century before we have a reasonable idea of the detailed sequence of events whereby life began, but I may be completely wrong, and predicting the pace of scientific advance is notoriously difficult. A few major discoveries could easily transform the picture.

What would help a lot, as already indicated, is if we found fossil life, or even extant life, on other planets. This is by no means impossible, and there have already been such claims, albeit not substantiated, based on meteorite material arriving on earth from Mars. With other examples of life available, we could then begin to compare and contrast with our own. Perhaps the most useful scenario would be discovery of incipient life at a stage earlier than DNA, proteins and cells. This is the stage that we will never see on planet earth (unless it's lurking somewhere deep underground), not only because it would be impossible to detect in fossil form (unlike cells), but because it would quickly have been devoured by cells once they emerged.

A basic problem with the research field, and equally the problem with trying to approach the question from the stance of mathematical probability, is that no one can actually agree what life is! It might seem obvious that life consists of entities that grow and multiply independently, like bacterial cells, but cells are very complex and undoubtedly there were a whole series of stages of emerging complexity, perhaps hundreds, between the basic organic building blocks of life and cells. Everyone is agreed that life is an 'emergent' phenomenon, meaning that at some stage a collection of chemicals and molecules began to display properties that were quite distinct from simply the sum of their parts, and could not have been predicted by looking at the individual components[216]. But there must have been many different stages at which such emergence occurred, each of them critical in its way, and it would be impossible to make a sharp demarcation between 'life' and 'non-life' at any one of those stages.

For the first half billion years or more of the earth's existence, it faced such an onslaught of meteorites that the emergence of life during that time would have been highly unlikely. One estimate puts the number at 17,000–22,000 impacts during this period, of which several were massive, of the kind that would wipe out life as we know it should they happen today.

Look at the moon on a clear night and note all the craters – many of those were made at the same time that the earth was being bombarded, and the only reason that the craters are not more visible on earth is because of erosion and the fact that the earth's crust is constantly being renewed by plate tectonics. Not until 4 billion years ago did the meteorite bombardment ease up sufficiently for the conditions to become more conducive to life. The earliest (indirect) evidence for life is from 3.8 billion years ago, but by 3.5–3 billion years ago the evidence for fossil cells becomes unequivocal. So on the geological scale of time, at least, cellular life emerged on earth remarkably quickly.

Carbon and the building blocks of life

Life as we know it depends on the remarkable chemical combining power of carbon. Carbon is like one of those Lego bricks with knobbly bits on four of its sides that can be used to stick together to other bits to make almost anything. Indeed the Lego kit taken as a whole provides a nice analogy for the chemical building blocks of life. The different pieces of Lego are designed in such a way that they can fit together in many different ways, but the possibilities are constrained by their particular size, shape, presence of knobbly bits on which side of the piece, and so forth. Likewise the chemicals of the periodic table (the summary chart of all the chemical elements) are designed to combine together in only some ways, and not others, to form all the matter of the world. There is a huge amount of incipient information wrapped up in these chemical properties: just as lots of different things can be made with those Lego pieces, but their design will be constrained by the available pieces in the kit, so the design of life is built into the periodic table.

Watch a small child starting to play with Lego pieces for the very first time. Apart from gnawing pieces (and occasionally trying to swallow them), the more creative phase starts with sticking pieces together in groups of two or three. This is the easy part. Similarly we find the basic building blocks of life being formed anywhere we look in the universe, up or down. The so-called 'dense molecular clouds' of outer space are rich in chemicals that can be detected and identified by their characteristic absorption and emission of light. Don't be fooled by the term 'dense' – these clouds are anything but dense by earthly standards, but more than 140 different compounds have been identified in such clouds, many of them quite large molecules containing a dozen atoms or more[217]. These include the polycyclic aromatic hydrocarbons (PAHs) of the kind which form the essential components of living things. Because space is huge, the actual amounts of these organic compounds in space are likewise huge, so that the mass of PAHs detectable in space has been estimated to be much higher than the total biomass (mass of biological material) here on earth.

Many of these carbon-based compounds, including some not yet detected in molecular clouds, have been found in the meteorites that continue to arrive on earth, albeit thankfully with less intensity than 4 billion years ago. Meteorites are fragments of asteroids that are about the same age as the solar system. The so-called 'carbonaceous meteorites', ones that contain carbon-based compounds, have been intensively studied, and after carefully excluding the possibility of contamination, have been shown to contain simple amino acids, and compounds related to both sugars and lipids. There is no evidence (yet) that any of these compounds in turn resulted from life on other planets, but given that they survive their landing on earth and that meteorites vigorously showered the earth during the period prior to the emergence of life, the contribution of such building blocks for life cannot be ignored.

Nor can the possibility that life was transferred from Mars to earth. Conditions on planet Mars were much more conducive to life at the time when the earth was still too hot to handle. It was then wetter, perhaps even with oceans, in sharp contrast to its present inhospitality for life. More than 20 Martian meteorites have so far been discovered on earth, typically spending a million years in space before they get here, with more no doubt yet to be discovered. Though not (yet) providing evidence for life on Mars, several are richly carbonaceous, containing significant amounts of amino acids, the building blocks of proteins. It is not impossible that a large meteorite carrying Martian microbes arrived here on earth 4 billion years ago, so that we are all Martians after all, but I wouldn't bet my life on it. Experiments have shown that microbes could survive such a long journey through space followed by the massive impact of landing on earth. The origin of life on Mars of course just pushes the investigation to a more distant time and location; there is no particular reason to prejudge the issue one way or the other, as usual it is best to keep an open mind.

One fascinating observation arises from the fact that many of the key building blocks of life exist in mirror-image forms. The two forms are like hands; one is a mirror reflection of the other. Amino acids are all 'left-handed' whereas the sugars that make up RNA and DNA are all 'right-handed'. Scientists who synthesise these chemicals in the laboratory find that they are made as a mixture of left- and right-handed molecules. So why is it that all the amino acids in living things are left-handed?

Study of a pristine meteorite found in the icy wastes of Antarctica, a particularly good environment for protection from contamination, revealed that extraterrestrial amino acids are biased in a left-handed direction[218]. In addition, the precursors from which they are derived also display the same bias. So there seem to be processes going on in the universe that display a tendency towards generating left-handedness in amino acids, and every protein in our bodies reflects that tendency.

Several different types of location on earth have been shown to be feasible sites for the synthesis of the basic building blocks of life. The essential ingredients are an energy source, such as heat or lightning, together with simple carbon compounds and, for some putative locations, an atmosphere simulating that of the early earth. Although the precise early atmosphere remains a topic of active discussion, it is thought to have been composed mainly of carbon dioxide, carbon monoxide, nitrogen and water vapour, with traces or small quantities of methane and ammonia.

One possible location where such an atmosphere is less relevant is provided by the hydrothermal vents, abundant on the ocean ridges that are found in both the Pacific and the Atlantic, where hot volcanic gases escape, allowing a rich and exotic biosystem to flourish. The fact that microbial fossils have been recovered from 3.5-billion-year-old hydrothermal deposits has highlighted these high pressure aquatic environments as possible sites for emerging life. One advantage of such environments is their protection from the damaging effects of the sun's UV light that would tend to break up unprotected complex carbon compounds. Reproduction of the high pressure, hot environment of such vents in the laboratory can lead to the generation of ammonia and amino acids. The addition of various minerals acting as catalysts leads to the generation of different repertoires of carbon-rich molecules[219].

Other locations for the synthesis of quite complex organic molecules include deep under the earth, a happy hunting ground also for microbiologists searching for unusual bugs. There is evidence that the earliest bacteria were 'extremophiles', organisms that live under extreme conditions of heat, cold or pressure.

Cellular life, once formed, can be amazingly robust. Bacteria can survive for hundreds of thousands of years deep down in the Antarctic ice. But no one knows whether extremophiles were the only organisms amongst many to survive the harsh conditions of the early earth's surface, or whether they really do represent the first type of microbes to evolve. Irrespective of the answer, reproduction in the laboratory of the hot, pressured conditions of deep earth provides interesting possibilities for the synthesis of the molecules of life.

Some proposals for the synthesis of the key building blocks of life have been worked out in considerable detail. For example, the German chemist Gunter Wachtershauser has put forward a detailed theory based on the properties of iron and nickel sulphides such as pyrite, minerals found in abundance at hydrothermal vents. In this system simple molecules like carbon monoxide and hydrogen react on sulphide surfaces to produce larger molecules. By a long and complex process a chemical cycle is formed that can copy itself, displaying at least one of life's important aspects. In Wachtershauser's view the steps to such a system are inevitable and fast, taking 'maybe two weeks'![220]

Not surprisingly such bold claims have been met by some scepticism, but the approach has launched a research programme for further work, which is what science is all about. This is a field where it very easy to snipe from the sidelines, not so easy to come up with creative alternatives that can be tested.

Making the macromolecules

In any event, making the 'small carbon molecules' of life is not that problematic. But making the bigger molecules – the so-called 'macromolecules' required for life – not to speak of assembling them into a self-replicating system, is a different matter altogether. Nevertheless, some modest progress has been made in this arena.

Once the macromolecules of life are generated, they have the remarkable property of self-assembly, folding up correctly to form specific functions. The properties of matter, arranged in the correct way, are far more amazing than most people realise. Our bodies contain thousands of proteins that, once synthesised in the correct sequence, fold up spontaneously to form precisely the right structure to carry out their duties. Occasionally they need the helping hand of other proteins called chaperones to fold properly, but most proteins do it all themselves without any help.

We can put a human gene, for example, into bacteria so that it makes the encoded protein, which then folds itself correctly in the test tube. It does this by containing a mixture of water-loving ('hydrophilic') and water-hating ('hydrophobic') amino acids. The hydrophobic amino acids arrange themselves in the interior and the hydrophilic ones outside, and it is this plus a few other chemical tricks that drives the protein to adopt the correct conformation in a matter of seconds, highlighting at the same time the critical role that water plays in the processes of life. This is going on in our own bodies automatically millions of time every day and we don't praise God for it. We should.

Even more remarkably, different proteins can self-assemble, often without any outside help, to form complex ensembles like 'biological microchips' that carry out the functions of life. My own research involves studying the functions of such microchips. It's as if we were watching a bunch of Lego pieces floating in the bath and they suddenly self-assembled to form a little boat. That is how the iconic flagellum self-assembles and anyone can watch a film of this happening on the web[221].

Of course correct self-assembly requires exactly the right sequence of amino acids being present in each protein, a big gap from having the amino acid Lego pieces jumbled randomly on the floor: but this is not the case with lipids. We have already noted that lipid-like molecules are found in meteorites and can be synthesised from simple starting materials under conditions mimicking those of the early earth. A certain type of lipid called a phospholipid has a hydrophilic 'head' and a long carbon-rich hydrophobic 'tail'. Put lipids into water and they self-assemble to form the famous 'lipid bilayer', driven by the same kind of forces found in protein self-assembly, with two layers back-to-back with each other like Custer's last stand, hydrophilic heads facing out, hydrophobic tails inside facing each other. Such lipid bilayers are the structures that make up the membranes of every cell in our bodies.

Back in the 1960s at my own research centre, The Babraham Institute, a biochemist called Alec Bangham found that a simple manipulation of such lipids could trigger the spontaneous generation of tiny closed vesicles called liposomes in which the lipid bilayers close up to form self-contained units. At the time this was seen as an interesting but somewhat esoteric observation without practical application, but since that time liposomes have found many different uses in drug delivery, gene therapy and the cosmetic industry, to name but a few (yet another example of basic research delivering products of great commercial value that could never have been predicted).

Since that time the Swiss biochemist Pier Luigi Luisi has made significant advances in understanding the remarkable self-assembly properties of lipids. Luisi has shown that liposomes are not static entities, but can grow, absorbing new lipid materials from their environment. Liposomes are also autocatalytic, acting as templates for the formation of more vesicles. Under the right circumstances they can even divide, a primitive form of replication. One possibility is that during the emergence of life, structures like liposomes were formed that captured collections of macromolecules. Given that lipid bilayers are impermeable to water (otherwise we would dissolve in the bath), and that today's cell membranes contain hundreds of proteins that allow communication across the lipid bilayer, one big challenge will be to work out how that kind of system emerged, although the permeability problem is already being addressed experimentally[222].

To show that such work is not at all remote from the materials available on the early earth, consider this experiment carried out by David Deamer who once took a sabbatical with Alec Bangham at Babraham back in 1975, getting enthused by the origins of life research field in the process. Deamer obtained a 90 gram chunk from the famous Murchison meteorite that originated in Mars and was found in a field near Melbourne in Australia. Following chemical extraction, he was surprised to find that more than 0.1% of the material was organic, containing a collection of carbon-based compounds. After isolating the lipid fraction, the researchers suspended them in water where they spontaneously formed the type of tiny lipid vesicles that Bangham had first observed. Organisation is indeed built into the very fabric of the universe.

Synthesis of non-lipid complex macromolecules could not have taken place in the very dilute solutions of the earth's early oceans, and there is a host of ideas as to how this occurred, some more convincing than others, but some of the ideas at least are backed up with experimental support. Complex emergent systems require a sufficient concentration of interacting reagents in the same location. Where might that happen?

Clay surfaces provide an interesting matrix for chemical reactions with enormous surfaces if the particles are small. A cubic centimetre of clay can contain particles with a surface area equivalent to nine tennis courts[223], certainly enough to be getting on with. Clay minerals consisting of strongly bonded silicon and aluminium atoms also display regular compositional differences that might impart particular orders to the sequences of molecules. Amino acids can be allowed to concentrate on to clays, polymerising to form small protein-like molecules several dozen amino acids long, a scenario that could be reproduced in small drying, clay-lined pools of water[224].

Clays can also be used as scaffolds for the synthesis of RNA, the molecules that are essential for the synthesis of proteins in the cells we know today. As long as the nucleotides are introduced to the clay surface, RNA molecules 10 nucleotides long can be formed within a few hours, and lengths of 50 nucleotides or more after two weeks. The Harvard geneticist Jack Szostak has carried out experiments in which clays, RNA nucleotides and lipids were mixed together in the same experiments, resulting in RNA-containing vesicles[225]. Certainly these are a long way from life, but they give some idea as to how compartmentalisation of the molecules of life might have started in the early earth.

Weathered mineral surfaces display countless cracks and pores that could provide other types of matrices for chemical synthesis. Feldspar can contain millions of such little pockets, approximately the size of living cells, able to provide protective zones for molecular self-organisation. Another mineral group known as double-layer hydroxides comes in many variants containing different metals; they have been used for the synthesis of sugars with a phosphate attached to them, a highly significant step because these form the backbone of every molecule of RNA or DNA.

The metabolic powerhouse of life

Small, closed environments for early-life chemical reactions to occur are important because it seems likely that protected self-replicating systems came into being very early in the emergence of life. During my first term at Oxford (1964) to read biochemistry we had lectures by the then professor of biochemistry, Sir Hans Krebs, Nobel Prize winner and already famous for his discovery of the Krebs Cycle (or citric acid cycle), a key metabolic pathway that is universal to all living cells. Prof. Krebs chose to give us a term's lectures on how, step by step, he had discovered the citric acid cycle back in the 1930s. Biochemistry then still being a relatively new subject (at least for Oxford) there were only 16 of us in the whole year, and I am sorry to say that by the end of term the numbers attending Krebs' lectures had dwindled to only two or three. I also have to confess that his presentation style was less than scintillating, and bright-eyed, bushy-tailed first years want to hear the latest stuff, not how someone had discovered something 30 years previously. *Now* I'd be fascinated to hear those historic lectures over again, because indeed the Krebs Cycle is central to life as we know it.

The cycle consists of 11 chemical components each made of carbon, oxygen and hydrogen and starts with the 6-carbon citric acid which is then shaved down to form successively smaller molecules containing five, four, and then three carbons, each molecule made being the starting point for the synthesis of a whole range of other key molecules that are essential for cellular life as we now know it.

A fascinating discovery that Krebs did not know at the start, is that certain primitive microbes can run his cycle in reverse. So we now start with the 2-carbon molecule acetate and then keep adding carbon dioxide molecules to form, successively, the 3-carbon pyruvate, 4-carbon oxaloacetate, until we get round the cycle to the 6-carbon citric acid, which then splits into one molecule of acetate and one of oxaloacetate, enough starting materials now for two cycles. So the reverse citric acid cycle is a self-duplicating engine that doubles on every turn. The reverse cycle illustrates how carbon dioxide could be 'fixed' (incorporated) into more complex carbon molecules long before the much more complicated process of photosynthesis came along.

Today each step of the cycle is catalysed with its own enzyme (remember that enzymes are specialised proteins), so how did it get going before there were any enzymes? One possibility, proposed by Wachtershauser, is that sulphides such as pyrite were the original catalysts. Interestingly enough, many 'modern' metabolic enzymes have at their core a small cluster of iron or nickel and sulphur atoms, reminiscent of tiny portions of sulphide minerals. Could these 'original catalysts' have been incorporated into the more efficient enzymes that came later? Time will tell, but there is an interesting research programme here that looks fruitful.

The RNA world

One key macromolecule that we have not discussed much so far is RNA. Origin of life discussions often revolve around the chicken-and-egg question as to whether catalysts came first, followed by information-containing molecules that could pass instructions on to the next generation, or vice versa. It was therefore with great excitement that it was discovered in the early 1980s that RNA molecules can act not only as repositories of genetic information, but also act as catalysts like enzymes. RNA molecules containing such catalytic activity are known as ribozymes, all singing and dancing molecules that provide a possible route round the chicken-and-egg dilemma. This has led to the 'RNA world' hypothesis, the idea that RNA was the key information molecule that emerged prior to DNA, enabling the transmission of genetic information upon replication. RNA has a structure very similar to DNA, differing in just one of the nucleotide bases, so can perform similar genetic functions.

The range of reactions that can be catalysed by ribozymes is quite impressive, and these catalytic functions are found in cells from all the main branches of life, suggesting that they could be ancient mechanisms that have been retained since life began. For example, ribozymes can catalyse the cleavage (dividing into smaller pieces) and joining together of other RNA molecules. They can also catalyse all three of the main stages of protein synthesis, the process in cells whereby amino acids are placed into just the right sequence to make a functioning protein. They can even control gene expression[226] and strands of RNA can also replicate themselves. True, ribozymes have a limited range of abilities as catalysts compared to enzymes, but if they predate proteins in the history of life, as seems likely, then they were top of the class in their day. What is more important, they have what it takes to help life get off the ground.

Artificial selection in the laboratory of ribozymes that become more and more efficient in carrying out tasks like RNA replication, provides important clues about the way that the initial ribozymes may have been selected over much longer periods of time[227]. Just as Darwin learnt a lot about natural selection by studying the breeding of pigeons, so biochemists today can learn a lot about how natural selection might operate on the molecules of life 'in the wild' by artificially speeding up the process in the laboratory.

The innate instability of RNA is also being addressed by studies on ribozyme stabilisation and catalysis under cold conditions. The fact that very small ribozymes can act as catalysts under cold conditions, joining together other RNA strands to generate bigger molecules, may also provide an important clue as to the location of early life forms – these might have emerged very slowly under ice rather than faster in warmer environments where RNA becomes less stable[228].

Alain Monnard, a chemist at Harvard, has also suggested that ice crystals might be used as a matrix for the polymerisation of the nucleotide bases that make up the RNA. Ice crystals could have concentrated nucleotides by up to 500 times, into microscopic veins of liquid. In fact Hauke Trinks at Hamburg has grown RNA polymers in artificial sea ice by incubating at temperatures in the range −7°C to −24°C over a period of a year, generating RNA chains up to 400 nucleotides long[229]. In lipid-rich environments RNA-like polymers can also be synthesised from their basic nucleotide components, by the simple procedure of inducing hydrous (watery) followed by anhydrous (no water) conditions, thereby mimicking conditions of the prebiotic earth[230]. In the final hydration step the RNA polymer is found spontaneously enclosed within lipid vesicles.

RNA and the origins of the genetic code

In today's cells various types of RNA play many different roles, and their function as ribozymes is not the most important one in our contemporary protein-rich environment. One vital role of RNA in the synthesis of proteins is as so-called 'transfer RNAs' or tRNAs for short. Every amino acid has a specific tRNA to which it binds.

Imagine the amino acid as a brand of car and each tRNA as a chauffeur that drives only that particular brand. We have previously introduced the triplet codon in DNA that specifies a particular amino acid, and the way in which the mRNA conveys a mirror-image copy of the DNA information out to the cytoplasm of the cell, where it attaches to an assembly line supported by ribosomes. The mRNA contains a series of 'anti-codons' for each amino acid derived from the DNA nucleotide triplet codons.

Each tRNA chauffeur in turn contains the codon specific to its make of amino acid to which it selectively attaches. Since the tRNA codon is again the 'mirror-image' of the mRNA anti-codon, we can see that we're back to the codon again; each tRNA contains the exact triplet codon for its amino acid that you find in the DNA itself. So now what happens is that the tRNA grabs its amino acid partner at one end and uses its triplet codon to plug into the precise anti-codon in the mRNA. Once the different amino acids become lined up in the specified order on the mRNA/ribosome assembly line, then an enzyme comes along to clip them together with peptide bonds, and hey presto you soon have a complete protein.

If all that makes the head swim a bit, we must be thankful that it is all on automatic and we don't have to think about it consciously, because that process is happening many millions of times in the cells of every person who reads this page. But, I'm mentioning that process for a specific reason, which is to ask: where did the DNA triplet code come from? There's a huge scientific literature that attempts to answer that question, but I want to flag up one particular theory, because it illustrates how the generation of information in biology can mean something very different from other fields, such as computing.

With a triplet code and four different nucleotides there are 64 possible codons for 20 amino acids, but in practice some of the codons are used as 'start' and 'stop' signals for protein synthesis, and the code is degenerate in that many amino acids are encoded by more than one codon. Remarkably it seems that this particular set of triplet codons really are optimised to a very high degree to carry out their functions efficiently.

This question has been worked on extensively by Freeland and co-workers who estimate that the number of genetic codes, comprising various numbers of nucleotides per code that might be functional, is around 270 million, yet the 64 triplet codons that are in fact used are far more efficient than the millions that might have been used, concluding that 'nature's choice [on earth] might indeed be the best possible code'[231]. How come?

This is where the 'Escaped Triplet Theory' comes into play[232]. The basic idea is actually quite simple. It is that the amino acids themselves originally 'chose' the optimal triplet codons. Remember that amino acids are present in meteorites and many of them can be synthesised under prebiotic conditions. It turns out that if we take randomised RNA sequences with a length roughly equivalent to tRNAs, and we see which ones interact preferentially with a certain amino acid, then we are far more likely than mere chance would allow to pick out precisely those RNA molecules that contain the triplet codon that we know specifies that particular amino acid. In other words, the 3D structure of the RNA molecule is influenced to a considerable degree by the presence or absence of a particular sequence of three nucleotide bases. This amino acid tends to bind to those RNA molecules that have certain triplet bases and not others.

So perhaps it is not so surprising that the triplet codon system that we've inherited is so optimally suited for its task. Maybe it was actually selected for the task by the amino acids that are now encoded for by our DNA rather than by our RNA (remember that RNA code can be converted back into DNA). The triplets have 'escaped' from their original role of helping to optimise the structure of RNA molecules so that they interact better with some amino acids rather than others, and the 'escapee triplet codons' have ended up playing a central role as the genetic code which is universal in all cells on earth today. My own hunch is that if we find life on other planets, then it will use DNA also and the triplet code might look remarkably similar to our own because the chemistry of the universe looks very similar everywhere we look.

The Personal Identification Numbers (PINs) that we all now use to get money out of cash machines, or open secure doors at work, all start life as randomised 4-digit numbers. They don't mean anything. But once they get chosen to do a specific task (be *our* PIN), then they become really important, not to be forgotten. This is analogous to the way information creeps into biological systems – by chemicals having properties, by those properties then leading to larger ensembles of components, which in turn become dependent on each other and are selected for their success in some functional output. Biological complexity emerges by small degrees, until wonderful new properties become apparent in the fullness of time.

All we have done here is to flag up a few possible pieces of the jigsaw puzzle of the origin of life. The gaps are still far bigger than the space occupied by the putative pieces. I started this chapter by saying that it could be another century before we have a reasonable handle on how life may have started. Reading through the literature again, maybe I'll revise that to half a century – the advances being made really are very significant, but there's a long way to go.

In none of this account have we been talking about 'blind, natural forces' doing things, because for the Christian such language is inappropriate. We are living in God's world. These are God's chemicals and God's molecules that we are talking about, God's liposomes and God's RNA world. As I've already highlighted, why Christians would want to ascribe pagan notions like 'blind natural forces' to God's holy materials, beats me. God must love materials because he's made so many of them. Fortunately he loves us even more, but that doesn't mean we should down grade his non-biological materials in any way. God says that they are 'good'; so should we.

We started with Genesis in this book, so it is appropriate that we should finish with biogenesis. In the beginning 'the earth was formless and empty, darkness was over the surface of the deep, and the Spirit of God was hovering over the waters' (Genesis 1:2). All we have done in this book in general, and this chapter in particular, is to explore some of the amazing ways in which the Spirit of God began to bring living order into a formless and empty world. We should praise God for the little we do know and understand, not make any theological or apologetic investments based upon our present scientific ignorance.

Postscript

Hopefully my own answer to the question posed by the title of this book will by now be apparent. If it is not, then I must be a very poor communicator! Personal saving faith through Christ in the God who has brought all things into being and continues to sustain them by his powerful Word, is entirely compatible with the Darwinian theory of evolution which, as a matter of fact, provides the paradigm within which all current biological research is carried out. There is nothing intrinsically materialistic, anti-religious or religious about evolution – all these categories are imposed upon the theory from outside. Evolutionary history is perfectly consistent with the creator God revealed in the Bible who has intentions and purposes for the world, including us. Holding to evolution as a biological theory should not affect one whit the Christian's belief in the uniqueness of humankind made in God's image, the Fall, the reality of sin and our need for redemption through the atoning work of Christ on the cross for our sins. We should let scientific theories do the job that they are intended for in the context of scientific practice, and not seek to transform them for ideological purposes. Atheists are as guilty of those kinds of transformations as are some Christians.

Christians should let the scientists get on with their work, without thinking that they are engaged in some sinister conspiracy to promote materialism and naturalism. All scientists can do is investigate and seek to understand the works of God. What's wrong with that? Of course their descriptions of God's works are incomplete, but that is what keeps scientists busy every day – actually we're paid to study God's world, an amazing privilege!

Christians who make it their mission to attack evolution, in the mistaken assumption that it is anti-God, are embarrassing and bring the gospel into disrepute. I cannot put the point better than Augustine did back in the early fifth century when he was commenting on the attitudes displayed by some Christians towards the science of his day:

> Now, it is a disgraceful and dangerous thing for an infidel to hear a Christian, presumably giving the meaning of holy scripture, talking nonsense on these topics; and we should take all means to prevent such an embarrassing situation...the shame is not so much that an ignorant individual is derided, but that people outside the household of faith think our sacred writers held such opinions, and, to the great loss of those for whose salvation we toil, the writers of our Scriptures are criticized and rejected as unlearned men[233].

The sad fact is that not all Christians have heeded Augustine's warning. The public promotion of creationism and ID continues to create intellectual barriers for scientists, significantly diminishing the likelihood of their taking the gospel seriously. Some very high-profile scientists, now atheists or agnostics, were Christians in their teenage years but gave up the faith because some well-meaning member of their local church told them that they couldn't be a real Christian and believe in evolution at the same time. Promoting such a false dichotomy is not only theologically false (read the book of Galatians!) but also very damaging to the spread of God's kingdom. Launching attacks on evolution is divisive and splits the Christian community, putting up unnecessary barriers for those who wish to know more about the core beliefs of the Christian faith. My own experience within the scientific community is that the word 'Christian' is now often equated with the ideas of creationism or ID, making it that much harder to share the good news about Christ.

Christian campaigns against evolution represent a giant 'red herring', distracting believers from far more important pursuits. We are faced with the huge challenge of reaching a lost world with the message of the gospel. Why not take all that money, energy and human gifting and abilities, and use them for evangelism? What about the medical and economic needs of the world? Instead of putting millions of pounds and dollars into publishing glossy magazines attacking evolution, why not put that money into helping the poor, or tackling HIV, or funding orphanages?

Ironically those Christians who are most enthusiastic at talking about creation are not always the same people who are most involved in creation care. We are currently facing the crisis of global warming, not to speak of environmental degradation and biodiversity loss on a massive scale. Instead of spending energy on creationist campaigns, why not put that energy in doing what God told us to do in Genesis, to care for his creation, to be good stewards of all that he has delegated to us? One day we will be called to give account of what we have done with our lives. The ones who buried their talent in the ground will not be treated sympathetically (Matthew 25:14–30). The real challenge for us is not giving the 'correct' answer to the title posed by this book, but whether we are looking after creation here and now as we prepare for the new heavens and the new earth, and whether we are truly investing our lives in a way that will extend God's kingdom.

Notes

1. All Biblical citations are from the New International Version (NIV).
2. D.J. Jordan, 'An Offering of Wine', PhD Thesis, Dept. of Semitic Studies, University of Sydney, 2002, p. 115. I am indebted to Dr Peter Williams, Warden of Tyndale House, Cambridge, for drawing my attention to this example. The fact that the word is similar in Akkadian does not settle the matter, but tips the balance of probability.
3. Ali Şimşek, personal communication
4. Lucas, E. 'Science and the Bible: Are They Incompatible?' *Science and Christian Belief* 17: 137–154, 2005.
5. e.g. see Mark 12:36; Acts 1:16; Acts 4:25; Hebrews 3:7; 2 Peter 1:21.
6. J.K. Rowling, *Harry Potter and the Half-Blood Prince*, p. 178.
7. *The Times*, 3 Jan 2007, p. 13
8. H. Blocher, *In the Beginning*, Leicester: Inter-Varsity Press, 1984, pp. 37–38.
9. This section is an expanded and amended version of some passages that originally appeared in D.R. Alexander, *Rebuilding the Matrix – Science and Faith in the 21st Century*, Oxford: Lion, 2001.
10. P. Harrison, *The Fall of Man and the Foundations of Science*, Cambridge: Cambridge University Press, 2007.
11. R. Dawkins, *The God Delusion*, Bantam Press, 2007.
12. Although the Hebrew has no word for 'creation' as such, the concept is certainly there in the Old Testament, and is present in several words used in the Greek.
13. Augustine, *De Genesi ad literam (The Literal Meaning of Genesis)*.
14. Hebrew only has perfect (completed action) and imperfect (incomplete action) tenses. Although it is legitimate from the context to translate this text as future, this is an interpretive decision, and the decision is compounded by the fact that the Hebrew uses a participle in any case, which of course has no tense.
15. e.g. *terata* in Acts 2:19 cf. *mopheth* used in Deuteronomy 29:3.
16. Cited by C. Brown, *Miracles and the Critical Mind*, Grand Rapids: W.B.Eerdmans, 1984, p. 217.
17. e.g. as in 2 Corinthians 12:12; Hebrews 2:4; Acts 8:13, etc.

18. See D.R. Alexander (ed.), *Can We Be Sure About Anything? Science, Faith and Postmodernity*, Leicester: Apollos, 2004.

19. W. Shakespeare, *Antony and Cleopatra* Act 2, scene 2, 191–194.

20. e.g. in J.H. Brooke, *Science and Religion – Some Historical Perspectives*, Cambridge University Press, 1991; D.R. Alexander, *Rebuilding the Matrix – Science and Faith in the 21st Century*, Oxford: Lion, 2001.

21. Augustine, *De Genesi ad literam (The Literal Meaning of Genesis)*, ii, 9, AD 405.

22. Calvin, *Commentary on Genesis*, 1.15.

23. Calvin, *Commentary on the Psalms* 136.7.

24. J. Wilkins, *Discourse Concerning a New Planet*, 1640.

25. Kepler, *Gesammelte Werke* 3.31.

26. For an account of the reception of Darwinian evolution in the nineteenth century, see D.R. Alexander, *Rebuilding the Matrix – Science and Faith in the 21st Century*, Oxford: Lion, 2001.

27. This section provides a brief summary of the points made more fully in White, R.S. *The Age of the Earth*, Faraday Paper No 8, 2007 (free download from www.faraday-institute.org).

28. L. A. Hinnov, 'Earth's orbital parameters and cycle stratigraphy', In F. Gradstein, J. Ogg, and A. Smith, (eds) *A Geologic Time Scale 2004*, Cambridge University Press, 2004, pp. 55–62.

29. EPICA Community Members 'Eight glacial cycles from an Antarctic ice core', *Nature* 429: 623–628, 2004.

30. DNA stands for Deoxyribonucleic Acid

31. Pearson, H. 'What is a Gene?' *Nature* 441: 399–401, 2006.

32. There are two further rare amino acids known as selenocysteine and pyrrolysine that are used only in special contexts.

33. RNA stands for ribonucleic acid.

34. Check, E. 'Hitting the on switch', *Nature* 448: 855–858, 2007.

35. Church, G.M. 'Genomes for all', *Scientific American*, Jan 2006, pp. 33–39.

36. Ledford, H. 'All about Craig: the first "full" genome sequence', *Nature* 449: 6–7, 2007.

37. See also: 'The personal side of genomics', *Nature* 449: 627–632, 2007.

38. Francis Collins, *The Language of God*, New York: Free Press, 2006

39. Pearson, A. 'Genomics: junking the junk DNA', *New Scientist* 11 July 2007.

40. Check, E. 'Genome project turns up evolutionary surprises', *Nature* 447: 760–761, 2007.

41. Pearson, A. 'Genomics: junking the junk DNA', *New Scientist* 11 July 2007.

42. Sterck, L. et al., 'How many genes are there in plants (…and why are they there)?' *Current Opinion in Plant Biology* 10: 199–203, 2007.

43. Cordaux, R., Hedges, D.J., Herke, S.W. and Batzer, M.A. 'Estimating the retrotransposition rate of human *Alu* elements.' *Gene* 373, 134, 2006.

44. Callinan, P.A. and Batzer, M.A. 'Retrotransposable elements and human disease.' *Genome Dynamics* 1, 104, 2006.

45. One micron is one millionth of a metre or approximately 1/25,000 of an inch, so 10 microns comes to 1/100th of a millimetre. If a pinhead is

about 1 millimetre across, then this means that you could comfortably line up 100 cells across the top of a pinhead.

46. This rough estimate comes from Prof. S. Jones. Don't take the comparison too seriously – it just means a very long way indeed. Basically you can do the calculation yourself on the back of an envelope by multiplying 6 feet x 10^{13} and then converting to miles or kilometres and seeing what happens.

47. Baylin, S.B. and Schuebel, K.E. 'The Epigenomic Era Opens', *Nature* 448: 548–549, 2007.

48. My research group has recently been working on the regulation of protein function by the 'deamidation' of certain amino acids which occurs after the DNA of a cell is damaged. Disruption of this process can cause cancer. Those afficionados interested in the nitty-gritty of such matters can read more in Zhao, R., Yang, F.-T., and Alexander, D.R. 'An oncogenic tyrosine kinase inhibits DNA repair and DNA damage-induced Bcl-x_L deamidation in T cell transformation' *Cancer Cell*, 5: 37–49, 2004, and in Zhao,, R., Oxley, D., Smith, T.S., Follows, G.A., Green, A.R. and Alexander, D.R. 'DNA Damage-induced Bcl-xL Deamidation is Mediated by NHE-1 Antiport Regulated Intracellular pH', *PLoS Biology*, doi:10.1371/journal.pbio.0050001, 2007 (this is an on-line journal freely available to all).

49. Redon, R. et al. *Nature* 444: 444–454, 2006; Strange, B.E., et al., *Science* 315: 848–853, 2007.

50. Holmes, B. 'Genomics: We are all numbers', *New Scientist*, 8 April 2006.

51. www.hapmap.org. See 'The International HapMap Project' *Nature* 426: 789–796, 2003. The '1000 Genomes Project' was also launched in early 2008 – the plan to sequence the complete genomes of 1,000 people; see *Nature* 451: 378–379, 2008.

52. An excellent account of the ways in which genes build bodies is given in much greater detail in S.B. Carroll, *Endless Forms Most Beautiful*, London: Weidenfeld & Nicolson, 2005.

53. *PLoS One* 2: e694, 2007.

54. For an entertaining read on how the different parts of our bodies end up as they are, see N. Shubin, *Your Inner Fish: a Journey into the 3.5-Billion-Year History of the Human Body*, Allen Lane/Pantheon, 2008.

55. Fortna A. et al., 'Lineage-Specific Gene Duplication and Loss in Human and Great Ape Evolution', *PLoS Biol.* 2004 July; 2(7): e207. Published online 2004 July 13. doi: 10.1371/journal.pbio.0020207. A pioneering book in this field was S. Ohno, *Evolution by Gene Duplication* London: George Allen and Unwin; 1970.

56. Louis, E.J. 'Making the most of redundancy', *Nature* 449: 673–674, 2007.

57. P. Skelton (ed.), *Evolution*, Addison-Wesley, 1993, p. 99.

58. Ibid p. 105.

59. Definition slightly adapted from F. Ayala, *Darwin's Gift to Science and Religion*, Washington: Joseph Henry Press, 2007, p. 51.

60. This is a real example. If you change the amino acid cysteine to a serine at position 817 in my favourite molecule, CD45, by genetically engineering a mouse line, then CD45 loses its function completely and the mice become severely immunosuppressed (unable to fend off viruses and bacteria normally). In fact the mice don't mind because they're kept in a near-sterile environment where there are no nasty bugs around. But it matters a lot in children – if they (very rarely) lack CD45 then they become very ill due to severe immunosuppression. See: McNeill, L. Salmond, R.J. Cooper, J.C., Carret, C.K., Cassady-Cain, R.L., Roche-Molina, M., Tandon, P., Holmes, N. and Alexander, D.R., 'The differential regulation of Lck kinase phosphorylation sites by CD45 is critical for T cell receptor signalling responses', *Immunity* 27: 425–437, 2007.

61. De Roode, J. 'The moths of war', *New Scientist* 8 December, 46–49, 2007.

62. 'Be fruitful and increase in number...'

63. Carroll, S. 'Chance and necessity: the evolution of morphological complexity and diversity', *Nature* 409: 1102–1109, 2001.

64. I have taken the lists that follow from F. Ayala, *Darwin's Gift to Science and Religion*, Washington: Joseph Henry Press, 2007, p. 72.

65. Most living mammals are placental: 1,135 out of 1,229 genera.

66. F. Ayala, op. cit. p. 74.

67. M. Ridley, *Evolution*, Oxford: Blackwell 3rd edn, 2004, p. 406.

68. Ayala, F.J. and Coluzzi, M. 'Chromosome speciation: Humans, Drosophila, and mosquitoes', *Proceedings of the National Academy of Sciences USA*, 102: 6535–6542, 2005. For a review on speciation in plants, see Hegarty, M.J. and Hiscock, S.J. 'Hybrid speciation in plants: new insights from molecular studies', *New Phytologist* 165: 411–423, 2005.

69. M. Ridley, op. cit., p. 53.

70. Hughes, C. and Eastwood, R. 'Island radiation on a continental scale: exceptional rates of plant diversification after uplift of the Andes', *Proceedings of the National Academy of Sciences USA*, 103: 10334–10339, 2006.

71. Ayala, F.J. and Coluzzi, M. op. cit.

72. D. Schluter, *The Ecology of Adaptive Radiation*, Oxford University Press, 2000.

73. Verheyen, E. et al. 'Origin of the superflock of Cichlid fishes from Lake Victoria, East Africa', *Science*, 300: 325–329, 2003.

74. Irwin, D.E. et al., 'Speciation in a ring', *Nature* 409: 333–337, 2001.

75. Rudyard Kipling, 'The Ballad of East and West' in *A Victorian Anthology*, 1837–1895.

76. For further details of a story which of course in real life is more complex than the brief summary provided here, see M. Ridley, *Evolution*, Oxford: Blackwell 3rd edn, 2004, pp. 50–52.

77. E.A. Ostrander, U. Giger and K. Lindblad-Toh, *The Dog and its Genome*, Cold Spring Harbor Laboratory Press, 2005.

78. Blaxter, M. 'Two worms are better than one', *Nature* 426: 395–396, 2003.

79. McKenna, P. 'Hidden species may be surprisingly common', *New Scientist* 19 July 2007.

80. Stork, N.E. 'World of insects', *Nature* 448: 657–658, 2007.

81. www.barcoding.si.edu

82. Cretaceous comes from *creta*, the Latin for chalk, the German for chalk is *kreide*, hence K/T not C/T, because 'C' in English already stands for another era, the Carboniferous.

83. It is likely that the asteroid came from the so-called Baptistina asteroid family – a huge collection of asteroids that was generated when two much larger asteroids collided about 160 million years ago, sending this collection of smaller asteroids off into their new orbits in space. See *Nature* 449: 30–31, 2007. For a general discussion on asteroid impacts and extinction, see Reilly, M. 'The Armageddon Factor', *New Scientist*, 8 December, 42–45, 2007.

84. Cifelli, R.L. and Gordon, C.L. 'Re-crowning mammals', *Nature* 447: 918–919, 2007.

85. Wible, J.R. et al., 'Cretaceous eutherians and Laurasian origin for placental mammals near the K/T boundary', *Nature* 447: 1003–1006, 2007.

86. For summaries of this fascinating discussion, see Lane, N.: 'Reading the book of death', *Nature* 448: 122–125, 2007; Ward, P. 'Mass extinctions: The microbes strike back' *New Scientist* 9 Feb 2008.

87. For example, see Ciccarelli, F.D. et al., 'Toward automatic reconstruction of a highly resolved tree of life', *Science* 311: 1283–1287, 2006. Note the word 'Toward' in the title. This is work in progress and such 'trees' or 'bushes' (my preferred word) will get increasingly accurate as time goes on and more genomes are sequenced. The 'tree' in this particular paper was based on 31 universal protein families and covered the genome sequences from 191 different species.

88. Dennis, C. 'Coral reveals ancient origins of human genes', *Nature* 426: 744, 2003.

89. King, N. and Carroll, S.B. 'A receptor tyrosine kinase from chaonoflagellates: molecular insights into early animal evolution', *Proceedings of the National Academy of Sciences USA*, 98: 15032–15037, 2001.

90. S.B. Carroll, op. cit., p. 139.

91. D. Noble, *The Music of Life*, Oxford University Press, 2006, pp. 30–31.

92. Hooper, R. *New Scientist*, 12 August 2006.

93. Hamilton, G. 'The Gene Weavers', *Nature* 441: 683–685, 2006.

94. For an interesting discussion of the way in which information from the study of genetic fossils and 'real' fossils is integrated together, see Raff, R.A. 'Written in stone: fossils, genes and evo-devo', *Nature Reviews Genetics* 8: 911–920, 2007.

95. Useful general introductions to fossils are given in M. Ridley, *Evolution*, Oxford: Blackwell 3rd edn, 2004, p. 524ff, and in P. Skelton (ed.), *Evolution*, Addison-Wesley, 1993, pp. 446ff.

96. O'Donoghue, J. 'A forest is born', *New Scientist*, 24 November, 38–41, 2007.

97. Awramik, S.M. 'Respect for stromatolites', *Nature* 441: 700–701, 2006; Allwood, A.C. et al., 'Stromatolite reef from the early Archaean era of Australia', *Nature* 441: 714–718, 2006.

98. Biologists organise living things into related groups that are given different names depending on the level. Starting from the 'bottom' and working up we have first of all a species – organisms that breed only within their own kind. Species are grouped into genera, genera into families, several families combine to make up an order, several orders to make a class (like Mammals), classes to make a phylum (like the Chordates, all animals that possess a neural chord) and phyla to make a Kingdom (like Animals).

99. Bottjer, D.J. 'The early evolution of animals', *Scientific American*, August 2005, pp. 30–35.

100. I am indebted to Richard Dawkins, arguably Britain's most enthusiastic atheist, for this nice metaphor! See R. Dawkins, *The Ancestor's Tale*, Phoenix, 2004. In case you are put off reading Dawkins by his anti-religious rants, you might be surprised to know that this book is, in my view, a rather good and very readable introduction to evolutionary history. I didn't keep a strict count when I read it, but I think Dawkins managed only a couple of anti-religious comments in a book of 685 pages, surely worthy of *The Guinness Book of Records*!

101. Pursuing all these fascinating connections would take us too far from the main theme. On the connection see: M. Ridley op. cit., pp. 538–539.

102. Those interested in further details on such examples can find them in: D.R. Falk, *Coming to Peace With Science*, Downers Grove: InterVarsity Press, 2004; F. Ayala, *Darwin's Gift to Science and Religion*, Washington: Joseph Henry Press, 2007. The evolution of the whale is well described in: Sutera, R. 'The origin of whales and the power of independent evidence' from www.indiana.edu/~ensiweb/lessons/wh.or.11.pdf. For a more technical account try: Thewissen, J.G.M. and Bajpai, S., 'Whale origins as a poster child for macroevolution', *BioScience* 51: 1037–1049, 2001, available for free download with lots of other great materials on the evolution of whales and other species from the Thewissen laboratory at: http://www.neoucom.edu/DEPTS/ANAT/Thewissen/.

103. For more information on *Ichthyostega* see Carroll, R.L. 'Between water and land', *Nature* 437: 38–39, 2005.

104. Cook, G. *Boston Globe*, 6th April, 2006.

105. Ahlberg, P.E. and Clack, J.A. 'A firm step from water to land', *Nature* 440: 747–749, 2006; Daeschler E.B. et al, 'A Devonian tetrapod-like fish and the evolution of the tetrapod body plan', *Nature* 440: 757–763, 2006.

106. This quotation and the other information about Gosse is taken from the splendid biography by A. Thwaite, *Glimpses of the Wonderful – the Life of Philip Henry Gosse 1810–1888*, London: Faber & Faber, 2003.

107. M. Ridley, op. cit., pp 261–262.

108. I have been dependent on a number of books written by conservative evangelical biblical scholars for the sections that follow, so rather than

foot-noting them frequently through the Chapter, I am grouping them all together here and greatly value all of their helpful contributions: D. Kidner, *Tyndale Commentary on Genesis*, London: The Tyndale Press, 1967; G.J. Wenham, *Word Biblical Commentary* Vol 1 Genesis 1–15, Waco, TX: Word Books, 1987; E. Lucas, *Can We Believe Genesis Today?*, Leicester: Inter-Varsity Press, 2nd edn, 2001; H. Blocher, *In the Beginning*, Leicester: Inter-Varsity Press, 1984; T. Longman III, *How To Read Genesis*, Paternoster Press, 2005; W.R. Godfrey, *God's Pattern for Creation*, P & R Publishing, 2003; P. Marston, *Understanding the Biblical Creation Passages*, Lifesway, 2007; Lucas, E. 'Science and the Bible: Are They Incompatible?' *Science and Christian Belief* 17: 137–154, 2005.

109. Alexander, T.D. 'Genealogies, Seed and the Compositional Unity of Genesis', *Tyndale Bulletin* 44.2, 1993.

110. See *Numbers and Genesis 1* p. 169.

111. Origen *First Principles*, Butterworth, G. (trans.), London: SPCK, 1936, Bk. 4, ch. 3.

112. The written record of the proceedings of the British parliament that records speeches verbatim.

113. Seely, P.H. 'The Meaning of *Min*, "Kind"', *Science and Christian Belief* 9: 47–56, 1997.

114. H. Morris, *A Biblical Basis for Modern Science*, Baker, 1984, p. 47.

115. The examples given here are just a few of the many examples provided in P. Marston, *Understanding the Biblical Creation Passages*, Lifesway, 2007, pp. 24–28, where the original citations to the writings of Henry Morris can be found.

116. I have covered the responses to Darwin in greater detail in Chapter 7 of D.R. Alexander, *Rebuilding the Matrix – Science and Faith in the 21st Century*, Oxford: Lion, 2001.

117. Erwin Baur, quoted in Max Wienreich, *Hitler's Professors: The Part of Scholarship in Germany's Crimes Against the Jewish People*, New Haven: Yale University Press, 1999 rpt., p. 31. Italics in the original.

118. R. Dawkins, *The Blind Watchmaker*, 1986, p. 6.

119. Lamarckism here refers to the idea that acquired characteristics can be inherited e.g. a giraffe stretches its neck to reach food on a high branch and then passes its longer neck to its progeny. This idea does not form part of current evolutionary theory, although examples of Lamarckian inheritance are still proposed occasionally.

120. R. Dawkins, 'A Survival Machine' In *The Third Culture*, edited by John Brockman, New York: Simon & Schuster, 1996, pp. 75–95.

121. Lewis Carroll, *Alice in Wonderland*.

122. J.H. Brooke, *Science and Religion, Some Historical Perspectives*, Cambridge: Cambridge University Press, 1991, p. 162

123. Hess, R.S. 'Genesis 1–2 and recent studies of ancient texts', *Science and Christian Belief* 7: 141–149, 1995.

124. This is well illustrated by the way in which different translations introduce 'Adam' as a personal name into the text: the Septuagint (Greek

translation of the Old Testament) at 2:16; AV at 2:19; RV and RSV at 3:17; TEV at 3:20 and NEB at 3:21).

125. The NIV translation here is certainly possible, but the key phrase could equally well be translated as 'because she was the mother...' or 'because she became the mother...'

126. An accessible overview is given by C. Zimmer, *Where Did We Come From?* Hove: Apple Press, 2006. For the detail see R. Lewin and R.A. Foley, *Principles of Human Evolution*, Oxford: Blackwell, 2nd edn, 2004.

127. R. Lewin and R.A. Foley, *op. cit.*, pp. 127ff.

128. The pseudogene field has been pioneered by Mark Gerstein's laboratory at Yale University which runs a useful web-site at www.pseudogene.org for those who are interested in reading more. For an accessible review see: Gerstein, M and Zheng, D. *Scientific American* 295: 48–55, 2006.

129. Rouquier, S., Friedman, C., Delettre, C. et al. 'A gene recently inactivated in human defines a new olfactory receptor family in mammals', *Hum Mol Genet* 7, 1337, 1998.

130. Ohta, Y. and Nishikimi, M. 'Random nucleotide substitutions in primate non-functional gene for L-gulono-γ-lactone oxidase, the missing enzyme in L-ascorbic acid biosynthesis', *Biochim Biophys Acta* 1472, 408, 1999.

131. The pseudogene examples shown here are taken from an excellent review on the topic by Finlay, G. '*Homo divinus*: The ape that bears God's image', *Science and Christian Belief* 15: 17–40, 2003. This review contains many other examples.

132. The example is from Finlay, G. (2005) op. cit.

133. The Figure is reproduced from Finlay, G. (2005) op. cit.

134. 'Oldest gorilla ages our joint ancestor', *Nature* 448: 884, 2007.

135. Sequencing of the chimpanzee and human genomes has enabled a precise comparison cf. *Nature* 437: 69–87, 2005. There are about 35 million single-nucleotide changes which separate us from our nearest living relatives, representing about 1% of the genome. In addition there are around 5 million deletional or insertional differences which means that 3% of each genome is different from the other based on this criterion. So the deletions and insertions win over the point mutations in terms of generating a different genome. The proteins encoded by genes are extremely conserved, with 29% being identical and the rest differing by only two amino acids on average. Fifty-three known or predicted human genes are missing or disabled in the chimpanzee genome.

136. Wood, B. 'A precious little bundle', *Nature* 443: 278–279, 2006.

137. See R. Dunbar, *The Human Story* London: Faber, 2004.

138. Wong, K. 'The Littlest Human', *Scientific American*, February, 41–49, 2005; Powledge, T.M. 'What is the hobbit?' *PLoS Biology* 4: 2186–2189, 2006.

139. Foley, R.A. and Mirazon Lahr, M. 'The base nature of Neanderthals', *Heredity* 98: 187–188, 2007.

140. McDougall, I. et al. *Nature* 433: 733–736 2005.

141. White, T.D. et al. *Nature* 423: 742–747, 2003; Clark, J.D. et al. *Nature* 423: 747–752, 2003.

142. A useful account of the spread of humanity out of Africa can be found in: Jones, D. 'Going Global', *New Scientist*, 27 Oct, 36–41, 2007.

143. The mitochondrial data are consistent with an African origin, but by themselves are not conclusive. See Rosenberg, N.A. and Nordborg, M. 'Genealogical trees, coalescent theory and the analysis of genetic polymorphisms', *Nature Reviews Genetics* 3: 380–390, 2002. However, further strong support for the 'Out of Africa' model of human origins has come from detailed study of human skull dimensions, see: Manica, A. et al., *Nature* 448: 346–348, 2007. For those interested in the way that computational methods are used to construct lineages based on genetic variation in populations, see: Marjoram, P. and Tavare, S. 'Modern computational approaches for analysing molecular genetic variation data', *Nature Reviews Genetics* 7:759–770, 2006.

144. Dates as recent as 50,000 years ago have also been suggested, but are disputed. See the discussion in Bertranpetit, J. 'Genome, diversity, and origins: The Y chromosome as a storyteller' *Proceedings of the National Academy of Sciences USA* 97: 6927–6929, 2000.

145. McBearty, S. and Stringer, C. 'The coast in colour', *Nature* 449: 793–794, 2007.

146. R. Dunbar, op. cit. has a helpful discussion on the relation between brain size and a 'theory of mind'. See also S. Mithen, *The Prehistory of the Mind*, London: Thames & Hudson, 1996.

147. S. Mithen, *After the Ice: a Global Human History 20,000–5,000 BC*, London: Weidenfeld & Nicolson, 2003.

148. Ibid., pp. 58–59. Other descriptions here of Neolithic settlements are based on the same source.

149. Ur, J.A. et al. 'Early Urban Development in the Near East', *Science* 317: 1188, 2007; Lawler, A. 'Murder in Mesopotamia?', *Science* 317: 1164–1165, 2007.

150. Hayden, E.C. 'Similar, yet so different', *Nature* 449: 762–763, 2007.

151. Model B has been well presented by Day, A.J. 'Adam, anthropology and the Genesis record – taking Genesis seriously in the light of contemporary science'. *Science & Christian Belief*, 10: 115–43, 1998.

152. To the best of my knowledge the term *Homo divinus* was first used by John Stott in this way in the *Church of England Newspaper* 17 June, 1968, then in J.R.W. Stott, *Understanding the Bible*, London: Scripture Union, 1972 p. 63. The idea has also been helpfully discussed in several publications by R.J. Berry who provides a good discussion of issues raised in this section in Berry, R.J. and Jeeves, M. 'The nature of human nature', *Science & Christian Belief* 20: 3–47, 2008. See also Berry, R.J. *Creation and Evolution, not Creation or Evolution*, Faraday Paper No 12, 2007 (free download from www.faraday-institute.org).

153. P.S. Johnston, *Shades of Sheol – Death and Afterlife in the Old Testament*, Leicester: Apollos, 2002.

154. The model is well described by M.S. Whorton, *Perils in Paradise*, Milton Keynes: Authentic, 2005.

155. G. Wenham, op. cit., p. 61.

156. See the discussion in G. Wenham, op. cit., pp. 64–67.

157. Hilary Marlow also points out that 'the theme of thorns and briers symbolising what is wrong in society is especially strong in Isaiah 1–39, where it is used in antithesis to vineyards which denote literal and metaphorical fertility and flourishing'.

158. The Piccadilly Line is one of the branches of the London Underground (subway system).

159. F. Bacon, *Novum Organum* II, §52

160. Moo, J. 'Romans 8:9–22 and Isaiah's Cosmic Covenant', *New Testament Studies* 54: In Press, 2008.

161. P. Brand, *Pain: the Gift Nobody Wants*, Diane Publishing, 1999.

162. Nash, T.P. 'What use is pain?', *British Journal of Anaesthesia* 94: 146–149, 2005.

163. Cox, J.J. et al. 'An SCN9A channelopathy causes congenital inability to experience pain', *Nature* 444: 894–898, 2006; Waxman, S.G. 'A channel sets the gain on pain', *Nature* 444:831–832, 2006.

164. I have found the following books helpful in the writing of this Chapter: J. Hick, *Evil and the God of Love*, London: MacMillan, 1985 edn; W.B. Drees (ed.) *Is Nature Ever Evil?*, New York: Routledge, 2003; M.M. Adams and R.M. Adams, *The Problem of Evil*, Oxford University Press, 1990; M.M. Adams, *Horrendous Evils and the Goodness of God*, New York: Cornell University Press, 1999; J.V. Taylor, *The Christlike God*, London: SCM Press, 1992; M.S. Whorton, *Peril in Paradise*, Milton Keynes: Authentic, 2005; A. Elphinstone, *Freedom, Suffering and Love*, London: SCM Press, 1992; A. Farrer, *Love Almighty and Ills Unlimited*, London: Collins, 1962; R. Swinburne, *Providence and the Problem of Evil*, Oxford University Press, 1998; H. Blocher, *Evil and the Cross*, Grand Rapids: Kregel, 1994; B. Hebblethwaite, *Evil, Suffering and Religion*, London: SPCK, 2000; M. Larrimore, (ed.) *The Problem of Evil – a Reader*, Oxford: Blackwell, 2001.

165. N. Wolterstorff. *Lament For a Son*, London: Eerdman, 1987.

166. P. Fiddes, *Past Event and Present Salvation*, London: Darton, Longman & Todd, 1989, p. 207.

167. The term 'apoptosis' in this table refers to the ability of cells to commit 'suicide' once they detect that DNA damage is present. If the cells do not die as they should, then there is a danger that they will accumulate yet more DNA damage, eventually turning into cancer cells. Apoptosis also plays a key role in the normal development of organs such as the brain. The term 'reactive oxygen species' refers to a potentially dangerous form of oxygen that can cause DNA damage in our cells – but we make such 'dangerous oxygen' in our cells every time we eat.

168. Greenman, C. et al. *Nature* 446: 153–158, 2007

169. Bowcock, A.M. 'Guilt by association', *Nature* 447: 645–646, 2007.

170. Check, E. 'Make way for monkeys', *Nature* 446: 840, 2007.

171. C. Southgate in G. Bennett and T. Peters (eds.) *Evil, Evolution and Genocide* In Press, 2008. I am indebted to Christopher Southgate for a pre-print of his chapter in this volume.

172. *The Broadman Bible Commentary*, Nashville, Tennessee: Broadman Press1971, p. 232.

173. *The Wedge Strategy*, The Center for the Renewal of Science and Culture, The Discovery Institute, Seattle, Washington, USA, circa 1998.

174. A task carried out by R. Numbers in *The Creationists*, Boston: Harvard University Press, 2nd edn 2006.

175. e.g. W.A. Dembski, *The Design Revolution*, Downers Grove: InterVarsity Press, 2004, see chapter 7.

176. J. Lennox, *God's Undertaker – Has Science Buried God?* Oxford: Lion, 2007. Although the author defends ID in the latter chapters of this book, chapter 6 reads more like a standard creationist text.

177. Dembski, W.A. 'What every theologian should know about creation, evolution and design'. *Transactions* 3: 1–8.

178. W.A. Dembski and M. Ruse, *Debating Design – From Darwin to DNA*, Cambridge: Cambridge University Press, 2004.

179. M.J. Behe, *The Edge of Evolution – the Search for the Limits of Darwinism*, New York: Free Press, 2007.

180. Numbers op. cit., p. 384.

181. *The Guardian*, 12 September, 2005.

182. M. Behe, *Darwin's Black Box*, New York: The Free Press, 1996, p. 39.

183. Apel, D. and Surette, M.G. 'Bringing order to a complex molecular machine: the assembly of the bacterial flagella', *Biochimica et Biophysica Acta Biomembranes*, In press, 2007.

184. Pallen, M.J. and Matzke, N.J. 'From the origin of species to the origin of bacterial flagella', *Nature Reviews Microbiology* 4: 784–790, 2006.

185. K.R. Miller, 'The Flagellum Unspun' in W.A. Dembski and M. Ruse, *Debating Design – From Darwin to DNA*, Cambridge: Cambridge University Press, 2004, chapter 5.

186. ATP stands for Adenosine Triphosphate, the main energy containing molecule of the cell which is used to transfer energy from one place to another.

187. Liu, R. and Ochman, H. 'Stepwise formation of the bacterial flagellar system', *Proceedings of the National Academy of Sciences USA* 104: 7116–7121, 2007. See also some critical comment in Doolittle, W.F. and Zhaxybayeva, O. 'Evolution: reducible complexity – the case for bacterial flagella', *Current Biology* 17: R510–R512, 2007.

188. Xu, X. and Doolittle R.F. 'Presence of a vertebrate fibrinogen-like sequence in an echinoderm', *Proceedings of the National Academy of Science, USA* 87, 2097–2101, 1990.

189. Jeffery, C.J. 'Moonlighting Proteins', *Trends in Biochemical Sciences* 24, 8–11, 1999; Aharoni, A. et al., 'The evolvability of promiscuous protein functions', *Nature Genetics* 37: 73–76, 2005.

190. Jiang, Y. and Doolittle, R.F. 'The evolution of vertebrate blood coagulation as viewed from a comparison of puffer fish and sea squirt genome, *Proceedings of the National Academy of Science, USA*, 100, 7527–7532, 2003.

191. Bridgham, J.T. et al., 'Evolution of hormone-receptor complexity by molecular exploitation', *Science* 312: 97–101, 2006.

192. W.A Dembski and M. Ruse, op. cit. p. 323.

193. Augustine, *De Genesi ad literam (The Literal Meaning of Genesis.*

194. M. Behe, op. cit., pp. 232–233.

195. In scientific publishing the only papers that count for anything academically are those published in peer-reviewed journals. 'Peer review' means that submitted papers are sent out for review to other experts in the field before the editor of the journal decides to accept or reject the paper. In the most prestigious journals the rejection rate can be 90% or more.

196. These PubMed searches were carried out on 24 November 2007. I checked with Michael Behe that these statistics are correct and he kindly confirmed them by e-mail, also pointing out that he has two further publications in more philosophical journals that are not listed in PubMed. These are: Behe, M.J. 'Self-organization and irreducibly complex systems: A reply to Shanks and Joplin' *Philosophy of Science* 67: 155–162, 2000; Behe, M.J. 'Reply to my critics: A response to reviews of Darwin's Black Box: the biochemical challenge to evolution', *Biology and Philosophy* 16: 685–709, 2001.

197. More details may be found in a review by Miller, K. 'Falling over the edge' *Nature* 447: 1055–1056, 2007.

198. W.A. Dembski, *The Design Revolution*, p. 25.

199. Ibid., p. 41.

200. P.E. Johnson, in P.E. Johnson and D.O. Lamoureux (eds.) *Darwinism Defeated? The Johnson-Lamoureux Debate on Biological Origins*, Vancouver: Regent College Publishing, 1999, p. 52, my italics.

201. Ibid., p. 50, my italics.

202. M.J. Behe, *Darwin's Black Box*, p. 203.

203. Ibid., p. 208.

204. W.A. Dembski, *The Design Revolution*, p. 63.

205. Ibid., p. 141.

206. Alon, U. 'Simplicity in biology', *Nature* 446: 497, 2007.

207. Weinreich, D.M. et al. *Science* 7 April, 111–114, 2006.

208. Poelwijk, F.J. et al., 'Empirical fitness landscapes reveal accessible evolutionary paths' *Nature*: 445: 25 Jan 2007.

209. Bhattacharyya, R.P. et al. 'Domains, Motifs, and Scaffolds: the Role of Modular Interactions in the Evolution and Wiring of Cell Signaling Circuits, *Annual Reviews of Biochemistry* 75: 655–680, 2006; Wagner, G.P. et al., 'The road to modularity', *Nature Reviews Genetics* 8: 921–931, 2007.

210. Muller, G.B. 'Evo-Devo: extending the evolutionary synthesis', *Nature Reviews Genetics* 8: 943–949, 2007; Canestro, C. et al., 'Evolutionary

developmental biology and genomics', *Nature Reviews Genetics* 8: 932–942, 2007.

211. S. Conway Morris, *Life's Solution – Inevitable Humans in a Lonely Universe*, Cambridge: Cambridge University Press, 2003.

212. op. cit., p. 127.

213. op. cit., pp. 283–284.

214. J. Lennox, op cit. chapters 9–11.

215. I have found two books in particular useful in preparing this chapter: S. Conway Morris, op. cit. and R.M. Hazen, *Genesis – the Scientific Quest for Life's Origin*, Washington: Joseph Henry Press, 2005.

216. For a more technical take on this point, see Hazen, R.M. et al., 'Functional information and the emergence of biocomplexity', *Proceedings of the National Academy of Sciences USA*, 104: 8574–8581, 2007.

217. Carbon-based compounds in such clouds range in complexity from having only two or three atoms (e.g. CO, HCN, CO_2, H_2O etc) to having as many as 13 atoms (e.g. cyano-penta-acetylene [$H(C_2)_5CN$]). See also: Kwok, S. 'The synthesis of organic and inorganic compounds in evolved stars', *Nature* 430: 985–991, 2004.

218. Pizzarello, S., Huang, Y. and Alexandre, M.R. 'Molecular asymmetry in extraterrestrial chemistry: Insights from a pristine meteorite', *Proceedings of the National Academy of Sciences USA*, 29 Feb 2008, 10.1073/pnas.0709909105.

219. R.M. Hazen, *Genesis – the Scientific Quest for Life's Origin*, Washington: Joseph Henry Press, 2005, chapter 8.

220. In response to a question in a recent seminar. Ibid., p. 113.

221. See: http://stock.cabm.rutgers.edu/blast/ and http://www.nanonet.go.jp/english/mailmag/2004/011a.html.

222. Monnard, P.A. et al., 'Models of primitive cellular life: polymerases and templates in liposomes', *Philosophical Transactions of the Royal Society of London B Biological Sciences* 362: 1741–1750, 2007.

223. S. Conway Morris, op. cit., p. 53.

224. Deamer, D. et al. 'Self-assembly processes in the prebiotic environment', *Philosophical Transactions of the Royal Society of London B Biological Sciences* 361: 1809–1818, 2006.

225. Deamer, D. 'A giant step towards artificial life?' *Trends in Biotechnology* 23: 335–338, 2005.

226. Winkler, W.C. et al. 'Control of gene expression by a natural metabolite-responsive ribozyme', *Nature* 428: 281–286, 2004.

227. Chen, X. et al., 'Ribozyme catalysis of metabolism in the RNA world', *Chemical Biodiversity* 4: 633–655, 2007; Voytek, S.B. and Joyce, G.F. 'Emergence of a fast-reacting ribozyme that is capable of undergoing continuous evolution', *Proceedings of the National Academy of Sciences USA*, 104: 15,288–15,293, 2007.

228. Vlassov, A.V. et al., The RNA world on ice: a new scenario for the emergence of RNA information', *Journal of Molecular Evolution* 61: 264–273, 2005.

229. Fox, D. *New Scientist*, 12 August, 35–38, 2006.

230. Rajamani, S. et al., 'Lipid-assisted synthesis of RNA-like polymers from mononucleotides', *Origin of Life and Evolution of Biosphere*, 16 Nov 2007.

231. Freeland, S. and Hurst, L. *Trends in Biochemical Sciences*, 25: 44–45, 2000.

232. Yarus, M. et al., 'Origins of the genetic code: the escaped triplet theory', *Annual Reviews of Biochemistry* 74: 179–198, 2005.

233. Augustine, *On the Literal Meaning of Genesis*, trans. J. H. Taylor, New York: Newman Press, 1982, p. 42.

Index

Acts of the Apostles, 28, 31, 37, 187, 200, 250, 354n5,n15,n17

Adam, 158, 164, 166
anthropological basis, 191, 200, 234–35, 243
as 'living soul', 195
created in God's image, 192, 235
earthy character, 163–66, 194, 262
in Garden, 164
generations of Adam, 152–53, 199
given dominion, 192,
gives name, 103, 165
historical or not, 16, 235–39, 241–242, 265
navel, 140–141
in New Testament, 200
sent out from Garden, 250–51.
See also adam

adam (Adam), meanings, 191–98
male and female, 192
male, 193.
See also Adam and Eve

Adam and Eve, 13, 131, 163, 167, 191, 199, 200, 214, 240, 243, 250–251, 254–263, 270, 272, 275

adaptive radiation, 90–91, 106–7, 201, 357n72

Africa, 84, 91, 96–98, 102, 127, 202, 226, 327
human origins, 214–225, 236, 240, 264

Agassiz, Louis, 174

age of earth. *See* earth

Akkadian, 17, 354n2

Allen, Diogenes, 292

Alon, Uri, 323

amino acids
building blocks of proteins, 338
coded for by nucleotides, 75–76, 109, 205
hydrophilic, 341
hydrophobic, 341
'left-handed', 338–39
in meteorites, 338
mRNA 'anti-codons' for, 347
mutations and, 112
number used in proteins, 55, 355n32

phosphorylation, 67
position in protein, 81
in primate genomes, 61n135
sequence, 55, 57, 134, 205, 346
tRNA binding, 347
Amos, 25
amphibians, 62, 124, 125
anaemia, sickle cell, 83–84
anteaters, 82–83, 91
antibiotic resistance, 84
apocalyptic, 20, 262
Apostles' Creed, 15
Aramaic, 193
architecture
dental architecture, 201
in Intelligent Design, 313
via regulatory genes, 70.
See also Hox genes
Aristotelianism
and Bible, 46
and Copernicanism, 46
teleology, 315, 320
'asah (make), 24–26
Assyrian, 17, 193
astronomy,
and Bible, 44–46
and past history of universe, 138
corroborates dating methods, 53
atheism
Collins and atheism, 58
Darwin's position, 170
Dawkins, 42, 47, 132, 179, 181–82
denies purpose in nature, 321
Dennett, 179

evolution and atheism, 47, 174, 180, 182, 352
and naturalism, 186
overcome by natural theology, 62
Athens, 28, 187, 200
atoms
in clay minerals, 343
God's control, 189
in metabolic enzymes, 345
in organic compounds, 337, 366n217
radioactive atoms, 50, 133
atonement, 247–48
Augustine
deplores scientific ignorance, 352
on God and nature, 33, 305
on interpreting Bible, 44, 155–56, 354n13, 355n21, 365n193, 367n233
Australia, 231, 327, 342
arrival of first humans, 221
Ediacaran fossils, 88, 122
marsupial fauna, 91, 327

Babylonian literature
sheds light on Bible, 17, 160, 162–63, 182, 193
Bacon, Francis, 269
bacteria, 48, 67, 75, 80, 115, 177, 118, 120, 244, 271, 272, 279
ancestors of mitochondria, 115–116
asexual reproduction, 79
fossilized as stromatolites, 121
mutation rates, 78

number of genes, 90
resistance to antibiotics, 84
used to make human proteins, 110
value in God's eyes, 287
bacterial flagellum, 307, 310, 314, 341
described, 297–99 (*figure, 298*)
icon of Intelligent Design, 297
independent components, 299, 307
irreducible complexity, 297, 299
possible precursors, 299–300
Bangham, Alec, 342–343
bara' (create), 24–26, 29, 35, 162
bases, nucleotide, 211, 306, 346, 348
differ slightly in RNA, 345
differences among dog breeds, 101
like letters of 'alphabet', 203, 205, 209
point mutations, 75–76, 78
sequences, 203
triplets (codons), 205–206, 348.
See also codons
base-pair(s) of DNA, 55, 57, 60, 80, 208–9, 210, 225
in human mitochondrial DNA, 221–22
Baur, Erwin, 178
Behe, Michael, 293, 295–97, 300, 303, 308, 310–11, 314, 318–19

Bergson, Henri, 333
Berner, Robert, 107
Besant, Annie, 176
Bible
authority, 46, 151, 181
biblical chronology, 156, 158–59, 164–65, 194
Calvin on Bible, 45
conservative reading, 41, 152, 359n108
figurative reading, 21, 154–57, 160, 166–67, 191, 197, 257–58, 261–265, 274
historicity, 153, 156, 159
inspired, 11, 19, 23–24, 155, 257, 274
interpreted in Near Eastern context, 152, 154, 160–2, 192, 197
liberal reading, 41
literalist reading, 20–23, 34, 140, 156, 158, 166–67, 197, 239, 255
translation, 16–18, 23, 64–65, 194–95, 200, 316, 360n124, 361n125
biology
Christians as often ignorant, 48
birds, 62, 82, 87, 88, 100, 103, 125, 147, 313
in Bible, 30, 155, 164, 192, 247, 271
Blocher, Henri, 284, 354n8
blood clotting, 297, 300–303, 314
blue-green algae. *See* cyanobacteria
bombardier beetle, 149

Boyle, Robert, 32
brain, 65, 68, 77, 86, 114–15,
    146, 363n127
    and consciousness, 272–73
    of human ancestors, 215,
    217–19, 228
Burgess Shale, 122, 321

Calvinist, 45, 172, 173
Cambrian era, 52, 122–23, 143
Cambrian explosion, 87–90,
    113–14, 124–25, 187, 281
carbon
    basic element of life, 135,
    279–81, 336–345, 366n 217
carbon dioxide level, 125, 214
Carnegie, Andrew, 175–76
Carroll, Sean, 322
catastrophes, 104, 106–108
catastrophism, 124
Catholic Church. *See* Galileo
cells
    earliest, 88, 336
    nucleus, 55, 57, 62,
    number, 48, 78
    replication, 55, 61, 63, 76, 84
    size, 63
cell types
    gamete, 79–80, 117
    germ, 62, 77–79, 134, 206
    somatic, 62–63
chance
    biblical teaching, 133
    evolution and chance, 32–35,
    310
    three definitions, 133–34
chaos, in Bible, 154, 162
chlorophyll, 139, 143
chloroplast, 115–17

choanoflagellates, 111, 358n89
Christian beliefs
    central vs. peripheral doc-
    trines, 12
    on evolution, 11–12
chromosomes, 62–65 (*figure*
    64)
    doubling, 113
    fusion, 211–213
    human No. 2, 211–13
    human X and Y, 63, 224–25
    in primate evolution, 209,
    211–13
    in sexual reproduction, 117
1 Chronicles, 246, 248
2 Chronicles, 316
Church Fathers, 44
co-option of proteins, 146–47,
    304
codons
    'anti'-, 347
    possible number, 348
    stop, 76, 204
    start, 76
    triplet, 75, 109, 205–6, 47–49
Colossians, 30, 252
Collins, Francis, 58–59
comparative anatomy, 137,
    201–202, 215–16
common descent, 108, 125,
    137, 295
complexity, 85, 119, 310, 343,
    349
    increases over time, 86, 90,
    125
    irreducible, 297–300,
    304–309
    of cells, 88
    of genome, 58

of molecules, 334, 336, 339, 341, 343

of organs and systems, 66, 72, 142

of organisms, 59–60, 65, 70, 113

Conway Morris, Simon, 132, 326–27

Copernicanism, 43, 46

conservative Christian interpretation. See Bible

convergence, 134, 326–27, figure 328, 330

creation

biblical understanding, 26, 27–46, 181, 284, 319–20

Christian theology, 172–73

continuous, 29–31, 172

deceptive, 139–42, 213, 240

no necessity, 28

creation stories, 160–63, 182, 193.

See also Genesis

creationism, 295, 309, 332, 352–53

as doctrine of all Christians, 15

as special view of some Christians, 15

'episodic', 239, 295, 334

evolutionary, 169–90

not same as Intelligent Design, 295

old earth, 15, 239, 255

young earth, 15, 149, 166, 180, 239, 256, 295

creativity

divine, 23–26, 29–31, 154, 282

human, 26, 219,

of evolution, 85, 86, 107

Cro-Magnon(s), 221, 226

cyanobacteria, 87, figure 89, 117, 122

cytoplasm, 57, 115–16, figure 298, 347

Dana, James, 173

Darwin, Charles, 124, 139, 170, 171, 175, 177, 188, 278, 306, 346

education, 169

religious beliefs, 169–70

separated science from religion, 169

Darwinism

religious supporters, 171–74

See also ideological use of evolution

dating methods, 50–55

ice layers, 54

genetic changes, 54–55

geomagnetic reversals, 53

Milankovitch cycles, 53

radioactive decay, 50–51, 54

tree rings, 54

Davenport, Charles, 178

Dawkins, Richard, 28, 42, 47, 132, 170, 179–82, 293, 320, 359n100

Dead Sea Scrolls, 17, 124

Deamer, David, 342

death, biblical understanding, 244–253

deceiver, God as deceiver. See creation, deceptive

Deism, 28, 31, 169–170, 189

Dembski, William, 293, 295, 297, 304, 309, 313, 315–16, 319

Dennett, Daniel, 179, 182, 321, 330

design, definitions, 312–13

'designer of the gaps', 304–5

determinism, genetic, 69

Deuteronomy, 37, 142, 161, 167, 197, 248, 354n15

development, evolutionary, 83, 93, 104
  as self-development, 171
  of complex systems, 305
  of the eye, 142–147
  of molecular systems, 326
  of nervous system, 272

development of organs and organisms, 55, 62, 65, 70–72 (*figure 71*), 79, 86, 91, 96, 101, 114–15, 118, 127, 363n167 *See also* Hox genes

dinosaurs, 87, 104, 106, 125, 201, 271

Discovery Institute, 294, 296

diversity, biological
  explained by Darwin, 48
  extinction and, 104–8
  from biblical 'kinds', 149–50
  increases over time, 86
  mammalian, 125
  sudden increases in, 87. *See also* Cambrian explosion
  tied to biological evils, 277–80

diversity, genetic, 60, 67
  gene flow, 80
  mutations and, 73–79
  of human individuals, 73

recombination and, 79–80

Divine Architect of Freemasons, 28

DNA (deoxyribonucleic acid), 55, *figure 56*, 57
  contains genetic code, 55, 57,
  human, 57
  mutations, 75–79
  packed into chromosomes, 62–63
  preserves record of evolution, 200
  regulates protein production, 57.
  See also diversity, genetic; chromosome

DNA barcoding, 103

Dover Intelligent Design trial, 294

Drummond, Henry, 172

duplication, gene, 76–77, 113–14
  accounts for expanded genomes, 61

earth
  created by God, 15, 25
  early condition, 339–343
  proposed age, 15, 49–51, 239, 256

Ecclesiastes, 46

Eden, Garden of, 16, 149 164, 193, 194, 251, 257, 258, 261, 263, 275,
  figurative for Origen, 156
  'old earth' interpretation, 255
  recalls Near Eastern prehistory, 241

Ediacaran fauna, 88, 122, 129, 131

Einstein, Albert, 137, 306, 308

embryos, 86, 96, 114

empirical methods
  stimulated by creation doctrine, 28
  crucial to modern science, 39
  in Intelligent Design theory, 314, 316

Engels, Friedrich, 176

engineering
  biological, 62
  genetic, 109–110, 114, 233, 357n60
  reverse, 114, 138

entropy, and evolution, 138–39

Enuma Elish, 162–63

enzymes, 67, 75, 111, 134, 301
  coded for by genes, 65
  defined, 324

Ephesians, 238, 252

Epicurean philosophers, 28, 187

eras, geological, *figures 52*, 89

eukaryotes, 87, *figure 89*, 303

Eve, 198, 200, 237, 259, 272
  anthropological basis for, 191, 200, 234–35, 243
  in New Testament, 200
  sent out from Garden, 250–51
  whether historical, 16, 235–39, 241–42.
  See also 'Mitochondrial Eve'

evolution
  accepted by biologists as fact, 130
  convergent. *See* convergence
  not a chance process, 132–35, 314, 322
  of elephants, 126
  of horses, 126
  of the eye, 134, 142–50 (*figure 145*)
  of turtles, 126
  of tetrapods, 126–28 (*figure 128*)
  of whales, 126, 359n102

evolutionary pathways
  constrained, 147, 324
  challenging, 300
  parallel, 146

evolution, ideological use, 174–80
  by atheism, 179–80
  by capitalism, 175–76
  by colonialism, 17–77
  by communism, 176
  by eugenics, 177–78
  by militarism, 177
  by Nazism, 179
  by socialism, 176

evolutionary creationism, 181–90
  historical background, 169–174

Exodus, 158, 259

experimental confirmation
  for evolution, 136–38
  for Intelligent Design, 307

extinction, 104, 125, 187, 201, 220
  mass extinction, 87, 104–8, *figure 105*, 244, 327, 358n3

Ezekiel, 21, 257, 263

Fall, the, 131, 149, 163, 193, 198–200, 351
and anthropological data, 254–76
historical aspect essential, 240
Farrer, Austin, 287
Fiddes, Paul, 278
1 Corinthians, 12, 249, 250, 266, 285, 291
1 John, 252, 260
1 Kings, 133, 246
1 Peter, 242, 243
1 Samuel, 246, 258
1 Thessalonians, 250
flood, biblical, 121, 199, 242, 247
fossils, 119–28, 215, 219–21, 271, 339
genetic, 108–112, 119, 141, 205, 208, 210
fruit fly, 60, 70, *figure 71*, 91, 92
Fundamentals, The, 174
fungi, 103, 110

Galatians, 11, 352
Galileo, 33, 44–45 *See also* Augustine and Catholic Church, 43–44
Galton, Francis, 177–78
genes, 55–72
alternative splicing, 66–67
defined, 55
human number, 57
'jumping'. *See* transposons
regulatory, 70, 78, 112, 147
'selfish', 66.
See also Hox genes

Genesis, 16, 26, 33–34, 85, 103, 151–68, 193–200, 241–43, 245–47, 249, 251, 257–63, 267, 269, 271, 281, 288, 350.
See also Bible; creation stories; Eden, Garden of; Fall
genetic code, 55, 57, 239, 287, 323, 347–49
genetic drift, 81, 113
genome, 57–62, 65–69, 72, 73–85, 101
defined, 57.
See also fossils; Hox genes
geographical distribution of species, 137
geological column, 123–24
Gilbert, William, 45
God
creator, 15
immanent, 28–33
not an engineer, 28, 315–16.
personal, 33–34
transcendent, 27–28
Trinitarian, 33–34.
See also Bible; creation; creativity; Fall; *Genesis*
'god of the gaps', 184–85, 305, 330, 334
Gondwana, 91
Gosse, Philip Henry, 139–41
Gould, Stephen Jay, 140, 321, 323, 327, 330
Gray, Asa, 172, 181, 188, 278–79

Haught, Jack (John), 284
heaven(s), 28, 31, 36, 38, 44–45

created by God, 15, 24, 26, 35, 282

not to be worshipped, 161

Hebrew (language). *See* Bible

Hebrews (Biblical book), 15, 19, 30, 35–36, 249, 262, 290, 292, 354n5,n17

Hick, John, 278, 284, 288

historical sciences, 136

evolutionary theory, 137

history, Bible as history. *See* Bible; Fall

Hitler, Adolf, 177–179

Holy Spirit, 33–34

hominids, 87, 202, *figures 216*, 229

Homo sapiens, 201–202, *figure 216*, 219, 221, 225, *figure 229*, 237

Hox genes, 70–72 (*figure 71*), 114–15

humans, 73

Huxley, Julian, 322

Huxley, Thomas Henry, 170, 173

hybrids, 94–96, 100

inbreeding, 80

incremental steps in evolution, 136, 142, 302, 303, 310–11, 313, *figure 325*

information

back-up system in chromosomes, 65

imparted to creation by God, 34

information in DNA, 55, 57, 59, 61, 65

in non-biological sciences, 112

insects, 90, 92, 107, 120, 125, 326

intelligent design in nature, 119, 172–73

as Christian notion, 312

Intelligent Design (ID) theory, 183, 293–311

on naturalism, 317–20

on origin of life, 332–333

as reconstructed natural theology, 316

as science, 293–311

as theology, 312–17, 352

irreducible complexity. *See* complexity

Isaiah, 24, 25, 26, 28, 35, 154, 245, 246, 251, 257, 261, 262, 269, 270, 281, 285, 286–87, 363n157

Jeremiah, 30, 154, 259, 263

Jesus

as agent of creation, 30, 34, 36, 316

interprets creation stories, 157, 198

and non-literal interpretation, 21–22

Job, 25, 29, 30, 33–34, 37–38, 245, 246, 247, 249

John, Gospel according to, 21, 22, 30, 34, 157, 250, 251, 260, 265, 288

Johnson, Phillip, 293, 295, 296, 317, 318, 320

journals, 39–40, 131, 309, 365n195

"junk" DNA, 59–60

Kellogg, Vernon, 177
Kelvin, Lord, 306
Kepler, Johannes, 46
Kettlewell, Bernard, 82
Kingsley, Charles, 141, 171
Krebs, Hans, 344

Lagrange, 184
Lamarckism, 180, 360n119
Laplace, 184
Leibniz, Gottfried, 184, 277
Lennox, John, 295, 334
'letters', chemical, 55, 57, 75,
    76, 203–209
Leviticus, 247, 259
Lewis, C.S., 289
liberal Christian interpretation.
    See Bible literalism. *See*
    Adam; Bible; creation sto-
    ries; Eve; Fall; Jesus
literature, biblical
    need to determine type, 18
    not scientific, 39–43
    types found in Bible, 20–21
Lucas, Ernest, 162
Luisi, Pier Luigi, 342
Luke, Gospel according to, 22,
    23, 34, 159,
    199, 242, 250
Lutherans, 46, 184, 294

machinery. *See* molecular
    machinery
macroevolution, 93, 101–103,
    295, 359n102
Majerus, Michael, 82
malaria, 83–84, 96–97, 311

mammals, 69, 87, 90, 92, 103,
    107, 109, 201
    chromosomes, 65
    diversity, 69, 72, 125, 326
    evolution, 87, 90, 106, 109,
        126, 233, 272, 322, *figure 328*
    fossils, 107, 126
    genomes, 69–70, 71, 73, 75,
        90, 114, 115, 118, 205, 207,
        208,
    marsupial, 91, 327, *figure
        328*
    placental, 91, 327, 357n65
Mark, Gospel according to, 34,
    157, 354n5
Marsden, George, 174
Marx, Karl, 176, 180
materialism
    Intelligent Design and mate-
        rialism, 294, 333
    positive biblical type, 163,
        333
    science and materialism, 351
matter, 337, 341
    in *Genesis*, 163
    properties sustained by God,
        29, 142, 188, 284
    scattered by entropy, 138
Matthew, Gospel according to,
    30, 35, 85, 159, 198, 242,
    273, 353
McCosh, James, 172, 181, 312
Medawar, Peter, 335
messenger RNA (mRNA), 57,
    66–67, 76, 204
meteorites, 338, 348
microevolution, 93, 101–102
Micah, 261
Milankovitch, Milutin, 53

miracles, 38, 305
  as including God's creative acts, 15, 36
  as distinct from God's creative acts, 189
  biblical words for, 36–37
  confused with secondary causes, 246
  defined, 39
  denied by some theologians, 41
  essential to creationism, 239
  invoked by Intelligent Design, 315
  invoked to explain solar system, 184
Mithen, Steven, 230
mitochondria, 116–17
  defined, 115
  DNA used in anthropology, 221–25
  evolutionary origin, 115
'Mitochondrial Eve', 222–23, figure 223
mitosis, 79
modernism, 46, 151, 157, 197
  defined, 40
  religion and modernism, 42
  shaping theology, 41
molecular machinery, 76, 117, 364n183
Monnard, Alain, 346
Moo, Jonathan, 270
Moore, Aubrey, 171–72
Moore, James, 170, 173, 174
morphology, 93, 146, 326
Morris, Henry, 149, 166–67
Mother Nature as pagan conception, 32

multicellular organisms, 78, 87, 88, figure 89, 90, 111, 115, 122, 279, 322
mutations, 73, 75, 78, 204, 279
  chromosomal, 77
  deletion, 76
  duplication, 76–77
  insertion, 76
  inversion, 77
  point mutations, 75
  rate, 78–79
  role of God, 187
  translocation, 77

natural philosophy, 32, 39, 44–46, 183–84, 314
natural selection, 73, 81–86, 113
  defined, 81
  ideological use, 175, 177–78
  in fish-to-tetrapod evolution, 127
  in human evolution, 217–18, 232
  known as 'survival of the fittest', 81
  theological response to, 172
natural theology, 62, 316
  contrasted with Christian, 171–72
  Intelligent Design a revival, 296
  influence on Darwin, 170
  supplemented by revelation 317
  tries to integrate Darwinism, 171
naturalism
  defined, 183

malleable notion, 183
'methodological', 183, 185
philosophical, 186
undesirable terminology, 185–186
nature
    after the Fall, 262, 270
    Boyle's view, 32
    concept not found in Bible, 31
    consistency, 29
    continuity, 29
    Deistic notion, 31
    distinguished from creation, 31
    Greek philosophical notion, 31
    regularity, 38
    sustained by God, 247, 284
    Victorian notion of laws, 170
Neanderthals, *figure 216*, 220–2
Nehemiah, 29, 38
Newton, Isaac, 184–85, 308
niche in ecology, 82–83, 90–91, 99, 106–107
nucleotides, 55, 57, 60, 67. *See also* bases, nucleotide; DNA; genes; genome; mutations
nucleus of cell, 110, 115, 122, 222
    defined, 55–57
Numbers, 142
Nurse, Paul, 111

order of creation, 24, 32, 34, 35, 38, 154
    contingent on God, 28

sustained by God's will and Word, 30
organic compounds
    in space clouds, 337, 366n217.
    See also carbon
Origen, 155–56
Origin of Species, 124, 139–40, 169–72, 175
Orr, James, 174

pathways. *See* evolutionary pathways
peppered moths, 82
Philo, 155, 156
photosynthesis, 125, 139, 143, 281, 345
plants, 61, 77, 78, 87, 90, 92, 94, 96
plasmids, 84
plate tectonics, 54, 336,
polyploidy, 94, *figure 95*
pre-adaptation, 146
proteins
    defined, 55
    evolution, 324
    synthesis, 57, 343, 346, 348. *See also* amino acids; DNA; enzymes
Proverbs, 17, 133, 251, 259, 281–82
Psalms, 29, 43
pseudogenes, 112, 118, 202, 204, 205, 207

radioactive decay. *See* dating methods
reproductive isolation. *See* speciation

reptiles, 87, 124–125, 147
retroviruses, 60–61, 109, 210
Revelation, 31, 36, 213, 249, 253, 258, 259, 260, 261, 262, 273
ring speciation. *See* speciation
Rockefeller, J.D., 176
Rolston, Holmes, 285
Romans, 18, 35, 251–52, 262, 264, 265, 266, 267, 268, 270, 274, 283, 316, 333
Royal Society, 32, 40, 45, 183, 314
Russell, Bertrand, 141

science
    based on observed regularities, 38
    mediaeval meaning, 39
    modern meaning, 39
    thrives in open societies, 130
scientific debate, 131
scientist, origin of word, 39
Scriptures. *See* Bible
2 Corinthians, 189, 252, 290, 354n17
2 Kings, 158, 246, 248
2 Peter, 36, 282, 354n5
2 Samuel, 21, 249
2 Timothy, 42, 249
Sedgwick, Adam, 123–24
selection pressure, 83, 113, 117, 118, 146, 204
Selous, F.C., 176
Shakespeare, William, 42
Shaw, George Bernard, 175
Smith, William, 123
Southgate, Christopher, 286
speciation

allopatric, 94, 97
    not clearly distinct from variation, 102
    reproductive isolation, 100–101
    ring, 99–101
    sympatric, 94
species
    defined, 93
    number, 103
Spencer, Herbert, 175, 177, 179
Stoic philosophers, 28, 187
stromatolites, 121–22, 271
symbiosis, 115
Szostak, Jack, 343

thermodynamics, second law. *See* entropy
transposons, 60–61, 204
Trinks, Hauke, 346

Vanstone, W.H., 284
variation, 93
    beneficial, 75, 81, 82, 98, 224
    injurious, 75, 81, 82
    neutral, 75, 81, 82
Venter, Craig, 58
viruses, 80, 117–18, 232

Wächtershäuser, Gunter, 340, 345
Wake, David, 101
Warfield, Benjamin, 174, 181
Wells, Jonathan, 296
Wenham, Gordon, 160, 257, 261
Whewell, William, 39
Wilkins, John, 45–46, 148
Winchell, Alexander, 173

Wolterstorff, Nicholas, 278
Wright, Edward, 45
Wright, George, 173–74

yatsar (form), 24–26, 194
yeast, 60, 109, 110–11, 272, 322
zygote, 222